PERFORMANCE ANALYSIS

for Public *and* Nonprofit Organizations

XIAOHU WANG, PHD

Department of Public Administration
University of Central Florida
Orlando, Florida

JONES AND BARTLETT PUBLISHERS

Sudbury, Massachusetts

BOSTON   TORONTO   LONDON   SINGAPORE

World Headquarters

Jones and Bartlett Publishers
40 Tall Pine Drive
Sudbury, MA 01776
978-443-5000
info@jbpub.com
www.jbpub.com

Jones and Bartlett Publishers
Canada
6339 Ormindale Way
Mississauga, Ontario L5V 1J2
Canada

Jones and Bartlett Publishers
International
Barb House, Barb Mews
London W6 7PA
United Kingdom

Jones and Bartlett's books and products are available through most bookstores and online booksellers. To contact Jones and Bartlett Publishers directly, call 800-832-0034, fax 978-443-8000, or visit our website www.jbpub.com.

This publication is designed to provide accurate and authoritative information in regard to the Subject Matter covered. It is sold with the understanding that the publisher is not engaged in rendering legal, accounting, or other professional service. If legal advice or other expert assistance is required, the service of a competent professional person should be sought.

Screen shots reprinted by permission from Microsoft Corporation.

Production Credits
Acquisitions Editor: Jeremy Spiegel
Editorial Assistant: Maro Asadoorian
Production Director: Amy Rose
Production Assistant: Julia Waugaman
Senior Marketing Manager: Barb Bartoszek
Associate Marketing Manager: Lisa Gordon
Manufacturing and Inventory Control Supervisor: Amy Bacus
Composition: SNP Best-set Typesetter Ltd., Hong Kong
Cover Design: Brian Moore/Kristin E. Parker
Cover Image: © gualtiero boffi/ShutterStock, Inc.
Printing and Binding: Malloy Incorporated
Cover Printing: Malloy Incorporated

Library of Congress Cataloging-in-Publication Data
Wang, XiaoHu, 1962–
 Performance analysis for public and nonprofit organizations / by XiaoHu Wang.
  p. cm.
 Includes bibliographical references and index.
 ISBN-13: 978-0-7637-5106-7
 ISBN-10: 0-7637-5106-5
 1. Nonprofit organizations—Management—Evaluation. 2. Non-governmental organizations—Management—Evaluation. 3. Public administration—Evaluation. 4. Evaluation research (Social action programs) I. Title.
 HD62.6.W36 2009
 658.5'62—dc22   2008036771

6048

Printed in the United States of America
13 12 11 10 09 10 9 8 7 6 5 4 3 2 1

Contents

Preface

This book is a step-by-step guide on how to use analytical tools to analyze and to improve performance in public and nonprofit organizations. It teaches how to present performance information effectively, discover underperformance, find out the causes of underperformance, and evaluate the effectiveness of performance improvement efforts.

The book focuses on the application of performance analysis tools. It uses factual examples and cases to illustrate the application of these tools in the real world. It illuminates the application by powerful and easy-to-use Microsoft Excel data analysis and graphical presentation procedures.

Aside from the fact that there is no book on the market about how to conduct performance analysis in public and nonprofit organizations, there are two basic reasons why I wrote this book.

First, I want to help public and nonprofit managers use performance information. Empirical studies have shown that a large number of governmental and nonprofit organizations have collected performance information. The challenge to them now is how to use the information to improve performance.

Second, I want to develop an effective learning tool for students in statistical and analytical technique courses in public administration, public management, and nonprofit management programs. I have taught statistics and quantitative techniques in a Master of Public Administration (MPA) program since 1997, using some of the most popular statistics books in public administration and policy. Nevertheless, many students told me that they were unlikely to use the statistics tools in the books because they were unsure when to use them in the real world. After all, the books arrange topics by statistics (i.e., descriptive statistics, inferential statistics, univariate analysis, bivariate analysis, multivariate analysis), while students face managerial issues in all shapes and forms. These books engage a conversation that is mainly statistical, without a context of managerial premises and conditions for the use of statistics. Students may learn very well about a statistical concept and calculation but still do not understand the managerial context to which the statistical tool applies. Consequently, they often fail to understand the managerial importance of statistical tools they learn, and worse, fail to recognize the correct tool to use when a managerial issue arises. This phenomenon, which I call "pseudo-learning," happens to many students, although it probably occurs more among preservice students whose service and managerial experiences are very limited.

This book intends to correct this problem by providing a managerial context that bridges statistical concepts and the managerial reality. The managerial context is performance management in which performance data are presented, monitored, and analyzed. It is in this performance management context that the usefulness and applicability of statistical tools are illuminated for the learner.

Once a performance issue is raised, management should follow a logical model of performance improvement by describing and monitoring the performance, detecting the cause of existing underperformance, and evaluating performance enhancement initiatives. The coverage of this book follows this model to present performance analysis tools in the following fashion.

Describing Current Performance Status → Monitoring Performance Trend → Understanding Causes of Underperformance → Evaluating Results of Performance Enhancement Initiatives

Consequently, topics are covered in 6 sections. The first section defines performance analysis (Chapter 1) and discusses organizational and technical capacities required to conduct performance analysis (Chapter 2). The second section focuses on how to describe performance information effectively (Chapters 3 and 4). The third section examines the tools to monitor performance and to detect signs of underperformance (Chapters 5, 6, and 7). Identifying causes of underperformance is the topic in the fourth section (Chapters 8, 9, and 10). The fifth section presents tools on how to evaluate the effectiveness of performance enhancement initiatives (Chapters 11, 12, and 13). The book is concluded with a chapter on how to write a performance analysis report (Chapter 14).

Several criteria are used in selecting topics to cover. First, a topic must be important in performance management in public and nonprofit sectors. Managers are frequently asked to present performance information to stakeholders, monitor performance activities and trends, detect causes of underperformance, and evaluate performance enhancement initiatives. These topics are included in the book. Second, the coverage of topics reflects the latest developments in the field of performance management. Covered are the tools proven useful and effective in performance management, such as tools in benchmarking, performance monitoring, and performance evaluation. Third, a topic is analytical in nature, which means that a technical solution is needed and data presentation and analysis are involved.

The book focuses on application. It is about using what is learned. During my decade-long teaching experience of analytical tools, I have learned that the most effective way to stimulate learning is the application of the materials. If readers know they can and will use what they learn, they are more interested in learning it. This book emphasizes the application of performance analysis tools in the real world. Its goal is to familiarize readers with the application of these tools so they can use these tools in their own organizations.

Several specific tactics are used in the book to facilitate the learning of application. First, the book uses a case study approach to illustrate the application of performance analysis concepts and tools. Each chapter starts with a discussion of tools and related concepts, with examples. It then presents a factual case study to demonstrate the use of the tools. The chapter ends with a list of practice questions. This presentation method is the result of my longtime experience teaching analytical techniques, which often required repetitive examples, cases, and exercises for student learning and application. This method stresses the importance of the case study. The case study allows students to understand the conditions under which a tool can be properly used. It also stimulates student interest and learning by relating the tools to a real-world scenario. Each case study presents a step-by-step guide to application. A case starts with a presentation of a performance management scenario in which proper tools can be applied, then demonstrates the application of the tools in solving the problem, step by step. The practice questions reinforce the reader's understanding of the tools and also allow the reader to experience possible variations of a tool.

In addition, Microsoft Excel spreadsheet software is used to assist performance data analysis. Compared with other popular statistical software on the market, Excel has apparent advantages in accessibility, cost, and graphical presentation. Its graphical presentation features are superior to many statistical software programs. More important, Excel functions in data analysis are sufficient enough for performance analysis in most public and nonprofit organizations. This book provides step-by-step Excel programming for performance data analysis.

This book targets two primary user groups. The first is managers in public and nonprofit organizations who want to learn how to analyze and improve their organization's performance and accountability. The second group includes students in public administration, public management, and nonprofit management programs. The book can be used in a course that teaches statistics or analytical techniques in the public or the nonprofit sector. It can also be used in a course that focuses on performance management, public management, or nonprofit management in these programs. Of course, it is written for anyone who is interested in performance analysis.

Because the calculations can be performed with Excel, the math requirement for the reader is minimal. A reader can readily understand the materials and exercises with a basic knowledge of high school algebra.

Acknowledgments

I am very grateful to many people for their support, their encouragement, and their suggestions. First, I want to thank the people I worked with at Jones and Bartlett Publishers: David Cella, Jeremy Spiegel, Maro Asadoorian, Lisa Gordon, Julia Waugaman, and many others.

I thank the following reviewers for their comments on a draft of this book.

Michael E. Day
Office of the Ohio Auditor of State

Steve Modlin
East Carolina University

Patrick Brobeck
Office of the Ohio Auditor of State

Eric Scorsone
Michigan State University

Lynne Weikart
Baruch College

Max Stephenson
Virginia Tech

Michael Card
University of South Dakota

Jack L. Dustin
Wright State University

I enjoy the support and encouragement from my previous and current colleagues at the University of Central Florida. I am particularly grateful to Professor Mary Ann Feldheim, the chair of Department of Public Administration, who is a source of constant support and encouragement for my writing. Many students in my analytical technique courses provided critiques to some materials in this book. Finally, special thanks to my wife, Yan, for her constant support and love. She accompanies me in many hours of working and writing. This book is a product of her sacrifice.

Section I

Foundations

CHAPTER 1

Introduction: What Is Performance Analysis?

I magine that you took an exam and did poorly. A few weeks later, you retook the test and did much better. If someone asked what you did to improve, what would you say? Maybe you studied harder this time, knew the materials better, prepared better, or your test-taking skill improved. Realize that you try to tell *why* your performance has improved. The ultimate goal of performance analysis is to find out why performance changes and what to do to improve it. But before doing that, you have to know what performance is.

Many people have written about performance. In this chapter, we use the literature to discuss what performance is and what may affect performance. We also define performance analysis and discuss the uniqueness of performance analysis in the public and nonprofit sectors.

What Is Performance in Public and Nonprofit Organizations?

If you score 98 on a 100-point test, you perform well academically. If you make more money, you perform better financially. If you win an election, you do well politically. Similarly, if a police department clears more cases, a fire department responds to emergencies faster, a hospital treats more patients, and a public health department processes more insurance claims, we say they perform better. In the public management literature, *performance* is often referred to as a state of actions, products, accomplishments, results, impacts, or achievements. Thus, *organizational performance* is an organization's actions, products, accomplishments, results, impacts, or achievements.

Keep a few things in mind when you talk about organizational performance. First, it is *organizational*, not individual. Although organizations consist of individual workers, it is incorrect to equate the aggregate of individuals' performances to organizational performance. Valiant soldiers do not necessarily transform to the winning of a war. Diligent individuals in intelligence agencies did not prevent the terrorist attacks on September 11, 2001. Individual workers surely affect organizational performance, but they have to work with many other things such as technology, infrastructure, and the decision-making structure. In fact, it is largely unknown how individual performances, working with other factors, transform to organizational performance. There are many cases where high individual performances do not add up to high performance organizations. The tool to define and to assess individual performances is often known as *performance appraisal*. This book does not deal with performance appraisal.

Organizational performance is not the performance of a network either. Imagine that you live in a metropolitan area with multiple service providers. When you make a 911 medical emergency call, the incoming medical unit does not have to come from your city. It may come from the station closest to you, regardless of the jurisdiction authority. Nowadays, many public services are provided by multiple providers in public, nonprofit, or private sectors. These providers constitute something known as *public service networks*. It is conceivable that some networks perform better than others, so it is possible to measure the performance of a network. However, network performance and organizational performance are different in the key stakeholders involved and the performance evaluation criteria used (Provan and Milward 2001). This book does not concern network performance.

What does *organizational* mean? The term is used broadly in the literature. It can be as large as a state or a large city, or as small as a local government's parks and recreation department of three employees. It can be a subunit in an organization such as a patrol division of a local police department, a fire station in a fire protection department, or an activity, a process, or a program in an organization.

Additionally, organizational performance has an output–outcome orientation. An organization's performance can be understood by its role in the process of providing products or services. This process, known as the *production process*, consists of four phases: the inputs, the process, the outputs, and the outcomes (shown in Figure 1–1).

Suppose that you study hard and get a good grade in a college course. The inputs in this process are the time, the energy, and the money you spend for the course. So the *inputs* of a production process are the resources consumed to produce certain activities or products. During the study process, you could learn the subject by attending lectures, by using the group or individual study method, by applying your computer skills, and by allocating time on different reading materials required for the course. By the end of this process, you would finish all readings, assignments, and exercises—you would complete the course. The completion of the course is an output of your study process. *Outputs* are the amount of the product produced, or the service provided in a production process.

The completion of the course does not necessarily mean success. It does not say anything about whether or not you have achieved your learning goal in this course. Having certain outputs does not mean that the outputs are desirable or valuable. *Outcomes* are the direct impact of a product or a service on the desirable goal of the production process. Two elements are essential to distinguish outcomes from outputs. First, an output amounts to be the product

Figure 1–1

An Organization's Production Process.

Inputs ⇒ Process ⇒ Outputs ⇒ Outcomes

produced or the service completed, while an outcome is the impact of the product or the service. Outcome is not the product or the service itself. Second, outcome is related to the goal established for the production process, while output often says little about the accomplishment of the goal. An outcome is the goal-related impact in a nutshell. In the literature, performance is either outputs or outcomes. Inputs are not considered performance. In this book, *performance* is defined as an organization's outputs or outcomes. Moreover, we largely look into outcomes because they reflect more on an organization's ultimate goals and missions than outputs do, though our discussion will also involve outputs in the cases where outputs and outcomes are closely related and difficult to distinguish.

A few other concepts are derived from outputs or outcomes. If you spend 3 hours to complete an assignment while your classmate spends 4 hours, you are more *efficient* than your classmate. In this example, the completion of the assignment is an output, and the amount of time spent is an input. *Efficiency* is the level of output for a given level of input (resource consumption). An organization is more efficient if it consumes less resource to produce the same outputs or it consumes the same resource to produce more outputs. So efficiency combines measures of outputs and inputs. Similarly, *effectiveness* is the level of outcomes for a given level of input. A student is an effective learner if he or she learns things quickly. In this case, learning is an outcome, and the time spent is the input. We will come back to these concepts in the next chapter when discussing measurement of performance.

What is quality? The simple answer is that quality is a specific outcome. If a local police department reduces crimes and improves response times, it is a high-performance organization. But can the department *consistently* perform at this high level? Can we predict that, at this time next year or in the following years, the police department is still there chasing criminals and improving response time? *Quality* refers to consistency, predictability, or reliability of a product or a service. An organization is high quality if it can perform well in a consistent, reliable, and predictable manner.

What Affects Performance?

Why do some students do better than others at school? It could be that they spend more time studying, they study more in a group with other students to share more information, or they happen to know the subject before. Also, it could be that they prefer the instructor's lecturing style, they are naturally born good test takers, they use a tutor, or they have a small class size that allows better chances to ask questions. Indeed, there are many possible reasons for a student's academic performance.

Similarly, why do some governments or nonprofits perform better than others? Because there are numerous possible factors that could influence organizational performance, scholars develop methods, formally known as *performance management models*, to classify these factors in group and then study how they may affect performance. For example, the factors that influence a student's academic performance could be classified as student related (e.g., studying harder, studying in group, studying the same materials, being a good test taker); instructor related (e.g., instruction methods, teaching styles); or study environment related (e.g., use of tutor, studying online).

Table 1–1

What Affects Performance? A Summary

Performance cause	Definition	Example
Environment	An organization's political, socioeconomic, and legal context.	A high income community provides plentiful financial resources for an organization to improve performance.
Client characteristics	The composition of income, age, gender, education level, and other individual attributes of the population served.	Younger clients in a job training program earn more after the training.
Primary work efforts, core work processes, technology	An organization's efforts of setting goals, developing objectives, carrying out activities and operations, as well as its method of converting resources to products or services.	Clearer goals help an organization assemble and concentrate resources to achieve better performance.
Administrative or organizational structure	How centralized (or decentralized) the power of decision making and service delivery is in an organization.	Educational institutions with more decision-making powers delegated from the higher authority are more productive in research and teaching.
Managerial roles, strategies, actions	Managerial behaviors and actions of an organization's management team.	Managers in high-performance organizations frequently and actively adopt managerial tools such as need assessment, strategic planning, and performance measurement.

These factors that influence performance are called *performance causes*. One popular performance management model, developed initially by Laurence Lynn, Carolyn Heinrich, and Carolyn Hill, classifies performance causes into categories of environment, client characteristics, primary work efforts–core work processes–technology, administrative or organizational structure, and managerial roles–strategies–actions (Lynn, Heinrich, and Hill 2000; Hill and Lynn 2004a). Of course, it is very likely that the above performance causes affect performance simultaneously and collectively. Now, we review the literature explaining how performance causes affect performance, with special attention to the limited empirical studies. A summary of this review is in Table 1–1.

The Environment

Just like you can blame your poor academic performance on a lousy study environment such as a slow computer, a noisy roommate, or an instructor's difficult teaching style, you can attribute an organization's performance to its political, socioeconomic, and legal contextual factors that include the political structure, performance of economy, funding constraints, legal institution or constraints, and other external environmental factors. A local police department with more financial resources could hire more officers to respond more quickly to residents' demands for services. A city administration with a more politically divided legislature may need extra effort to improve its performance in order to please diversified political interests. The literature shows that the adoption and implementation of performance measures, a prerequisite for performance improvement, are strongly affected by political stakeholders' willingness to support or engage in performance management activities (Ammons and Rivenbark 2008; Aristigueta and Van Dooren 2007; Julnes and Holzer 2001; Ho 2006; Yang and Hsieh 2007).

Resource availability is one of the key factors influencing organizational performance in a review of empirical evidence of organizational performance studies since 1970 (Boyne 2003). A similar result, shown in a study of 534 school systems in Texas, indicates that teachers' salaries are positively associated with school performance, defined as the percentage of students who passed standardized tests. In high-performance schools, instructional funds and state aid are also positively associated with school performance (Gill and Meier 2001). Funding sources may also affect organizational performance. A study of substance abuse treatment organizations indicates a higher proportion of revenues from Medicare or Medicaid instead of private insurance–patient fee is negatively associated with the participants' probability to work full time after treatment (Heinrich and Fournier 2004). Private funding sources may suggest a more strict requirement for performance improvement. The state of local economy also appears to affect organizational performance significantly. A study of welfare programs in Michigan county governments shows that a county with a larger proportion of manufacturing jobs has greater difficulty moving welfare recipients out of welfare assistance (Sandfort 2000). The same study suggests that an economy with a higher unemployment rate reduces the chance of a welfare recipient moving out of welfare.

Client Characteristics

Imagine you manage a city that has a large retiree population and an emerging population of young immigrants looking for jobs. Because the retirees and the immigrants may want different types of services (e.g., retirees for more health care and immigrants for more English education), it is conceivable that your resources would be stretched to meet these diversified demands, and your performance of service provision would be affected. Clearly, an organization's performance can be affected by the characteristics, attributes, and behaviors of the residents or clients it serves.

A study of the federal Job Training Partnership Act (JTPA) shows that young (22 to 29 year old) male clients with some post high school education achieved the highest postprogram earnings, an outcome performance of JTPA. Minorities, high school dropouts, and welfare recipients received less postprogram earnings (Heinrich and Lynn 2000). A study of school systems in Texas indicates that school performance is negatively associated with high percentages of students from low-income families and minority students (Gill and Meier 2001).

A study of substance abuse treatment organizations indicates that participants' ages and their previous drug treatment experiences may affect clinical outcomes of the organizations. Younger participants with previous drug treatment experiences are less likely to decrease the use of drugs after the program. The study also shows that gender, race, and education of participants may affect the program-level outcomes. A male participant with a high school diploma is most likely to continue or to begin work after the program (Heinrich and Fournier 2004).

Primary Work Efforts, Core Work Processes, and Technology

Organizational performance is affected by how clear an organizational goal is, as well as how its employees work toward the goal and how hard they work. First, it matters to performance if an organization has a clear mission and service objectives and if it has a process of daily operations that relates each individual employee's activities to the mission and objectives. A survey of federal employees indicates that clearer goals help organizations assemble and concentrate resources to achieve desirable organizational performance (Chun and Rainey 2005).

Second, as stated above, it is conceivable that organizational performance is affected by how individual employees work and how hard they work. An employee survey indicates that employee perceived organizational performance is positively associated with employees' level of job satisfaction, motivation to serve the public, affective commitment to organizations, and organizational citizenship behaviors (Kim 2004). Similarly, a study of 22 human service organizations providing early care and education services shows that teacher satisfaction about job and salary is positively associated with school readiness assessed by participants' parents (Selden and Sowa 2004).

A study of Texas school districts shows that schools with more female teachers in classrooms have higher student attendance, lower teacher turnover, and higher student test scores (Meier, Mastracci, and Wilson 2006). The authors attribute this performance difference to intensified personal interactions among teachers and between teachers and students, which facilitates the effective and smooth operations of an organization.

Third, the technology may also affect an organization's performance. Here, the term *technology* is used broadly to include all methods that convert resources to products or services in an organization. For example, the technology in a job training program for the unemployed could be the types of training provided such as job search training, job skill training, and problem-solving training.

A study of welfare programs in Michigan county governments suggests that workshops stressing job-seeking skills, such as interview techniques, resume preparation, or cover letter preparation, may increase program participants' chances of better financial earnings (Sandfort 2000). A study of state welfare reforms indicates that the states having more restrictive requirements for participants to receive financial assistance experienced the greater reduction in the number of people on welfare (Jennings and Ewalt 2000). The same study finds that states developing systematic practices to serve welfare clients report greater reduction in the number of people on welfare.

In a study of school systems, small class size and teachers' certification are found to be positively associated with school performance (Gill and Meier 2001). The study of JTPA shows that on-the-job training activities may significantly increase participants' postprogram earnings than classroom training or less-intensive training activities such as job search and counseling (Heinrich and Lynn 2000).

Administrative or Organizational Structure

A manager trying to hire workers could find that he or she does not have the hiring authority. An employee who comes up with innovative ideas could realize that there are no incentives or rewards to do so. Clearly, an organization's performance can also be affected by its decision-making or service delivery structure, which is further reflected in the organizational type, the level of integration–coordination of the decision making, administrative rules–incentives, budgetary allocations methods, contractual arrangements, and the institutional culture–value on how things should be done. An argument has been made that organizations with a higher level of managerial autonomy may be more productive because autonomy frees up ideas for effective communications and actions (Rainey and Steinbauer 1999).

Comprehensive reviews of the empirical literature suggest that the change of formal organizational structure in program designs, administrative decision-making processes, and organizational service delivery processes has significant impact on organizational performance (Hill and Lynn 2004b; Forbes and Lynn 2005). A survey of federal employees shows that employees given more flexibility to complete their work believe that their organizations perform at a higher level (Brewer and Selden 2000).

A study of the public higher education governing structure in the United States indicates that research productivity and financial resources are higher at universities with a statewide board of a more decentralized system that allows more freedom for individual institutions in research, teaching, and other academic activities. The authors explain that decentralized public institutions, which may rely less on states for funding, have to push their administrators to a business model in exploring more external funding opportunities and in increasing research publications (Knott and Payne 2004).

A study of public welfare programs reveals that the number of service providers may have a negative impact on organizational performance measured as the proportions of welfare caseload in employment (Sandfort 2000). The same study also indicates that an organization's systematic provision of client assistance on child care and transportation could increase the probability of welfare recipients moving off of welfare rolls.

The service delivery structure may also affect organizational performance. Nowadays, the private sector is involved in many public service deliveries as contractors or administrators. The JTPA study indicates that, when the private sector representatives assume more authority as administrative entities, the participants' postprogram earnings increase. The study argues that this improvement happens because of the private sector's more outcome-oriented managerial approach, its strong emphasis on performance requirement, and its greater centralization of program resources and service delivery processes. On the other hand, studies also show that, when the private sector representatives are given larger roles in program administration, fewer services were provided directly by the administrative entity, and for-profit organizations were getting more contracts (Heinrich and Lynn 2000; Heinrich 2002). A study of substance abuse treatment organizations shows that participants in private treatment organizations are more likely to continue or to begin to work full time after the treatment program (Heinrich and Lynn 2000).

A study of nonprofits providing early care and education services shows that the extent of interagency collaborative and networking relationships may have a positive impact on staff turnover and school readiness perceived by the parents of the program participants (Selden, Sowa, and Sandfort 2006). It is argued that a strong network improves an organization's ability to increase resources and to deal with external changes and uncertainties (O'Toole and Meier 1999).

Managerial Roles, Strategies, and Actions

A great leader can make a great organization. High performance of an organization may be the result of a manager's leadership practices in goal setting, worker motivation–support, problem-solving skills, and delegating ability. Improved performance may also be the result of good staff–management relations and communication, professionalism of managers, or practices in managerial monitoring, control, and evaluation.

How much do public management and public managers contribute to organizational performance? Several reviews of empirical evidence in about 1000 U.S. and international studies show a significant role of public management in governance (Boyne 2003; Hill and Lynn 2004b; Forbes and Lynn 2005). One review of 65 statistical analyses places executive leadership, managerial practices, organizational culture, and organizational strategies as the most important factors in influencing organizational performance among other factors of organizational environment, design, and structure (Boyne 2003).

How does public management affect organizational performance? Attempts have been made to model the impact of public management on organizational outcomes. A model developed by Ingraham and Donahue (2000) on the role of public management in organizational outcomes depicts public management as a process that converts resource inputs to policy outcomes. The management process consists of subsystems in financial management, human resource management, capital management, and information technology management, integrated by managerial practice in leadership, information use, and resource allocations, and cultivated by the system of performance management that facilitates a trend of performance improvement for results.

Another model advocated by Hill and Lynn (2004b) indicates that the management impact on performance stems from (1) the development of performance targets and strategic priorities; (2) the design of a proper administrative structure in decision making and service delivery to facilitate performance improvement; (3) the use of managerial tools or strategies to design, implement, and evaluate policies and programs; and (4) the development of management values that foster performance improvement.

What do managers in high-performance organizations do? First, managers in high-performance organizations tend to adopt an achievable performance goal and to develop strategic priorities that may improve organizational performance. Clear and quantifiable strategic goals lead to better organizational outcomes (Boyne and Chen 2007). Second, managers in high-performance organizations are more likely to adopt an administrative decision-making and service delivery structure that facilitates performance improvement activities. A study of independent Texas school districts indicates that organizations with managers who adopt a proactive strategy in initiating interactions with network actors and in actively seeking resources tend to perform better in student academic performances (Goerdel 2006). A study of 500 U.S. school districts finds similar results by linking the extent of a school management's networking activity with the school performance measured by student educational achievement (Meier and O'Toole 2003). The authors suggest that networking allows managers to leverage resources and buffer organizational constraints.

Third, managers in high-performance organizations tend to frequently use managerial strategies and tools to design, to implement, and to evaluate policies and programs. It is consistently found in studies of nonprofit organizations that boards' strategies, structures, working processes, or even reputations are associated with organizational performance (Forbes 1998; Herman and Renz 1998). For example, adoption of needs assessment, strategic planning, measurement of customer satisfaction, cost-cutting management, and revenue exploration strategies may improve organizational performance (Herman and Renz 1998). In a large study of Canadian nonprofit organizations, Bradshaw, Murray, and Wolpin (1992) found that a board's use of certain techniques (such as strategic planning techniques) is positively associated with its financial and reputational measures of organizational performance. A study of Texas school districts indicates that a management's ability to develop strategies to align itself with the environment may have significant impact on organizational performance (Meier et al. 2007).

Managerial practices of diversity and representation may also affect organizational performance. A study of Texas school districts suggests that racial and ethnic diversity of teachers may affect student performance. Additionally, the managers' racial and ethnic representations of students may improve organizational performance measured by student dropout rates and test scores (Pitts 2005). The author attributes this effect to the managers' positions to set policies that encourage performance by all students. Similarly, a study of school districts suggests that administrative representation may also influence performance. Latinos at each level of governance have positive effects on outcomes of Latino students (Meier, O'Toole, and Nicholson-Crotty 2004).

A study of law enforcement agencies indicates that both an agency's active internal and external management actions and strategies contribute to the improvement in the arrest rate. Internal management strategies include establishment of educational requirement, the extent of classroom and field training for new recruits, the presence of a collective bargaining policy for officers, and investment in policing technology. External management strategies include the extent of community policing, networking, and public feedback activities (Nicholson-Crotty and O'Toole 2004).

Finally, managers in high-performance organizations foster a culture supportive of performance enhancement initiatives. A survey shows that federal employees believe that their organizations perform better if their opinions are respected, if teamwork is encouraged, if there is high concern for serving public interests, if employees' interests are protected, and if their supervisors have good supervisory skills (Brewer and Selden 2000; Brewer 2005). The same survey also reveals that organizational performance may also be affected by management's efforts to develop human capitals in hiring, retention, and promotion, and by managers' motivation skills. Another study finds that performance incentive policies may influence performance. Organizations meeting performance incentive standards may have higher performance (Heinrich and Lynn 2000).

A study of Chicago Public Schools indicates that a strategy of setting performance standards and providing extra instructional time to students has a positive impact on student academic performance. The study explains that the improvement occurs because the establishment of performance standards motivates students to work harder and motivates the school and teachers to make significant changes in instruction and in obtaining resource support (Roderick, Jacob, and Bryk 2000).

A study of public school superintendents shows that managerial succession may influence organizational performance. There may be immediate negative impact of managerial succession on student test scores, only if an external hired replacement takes place. The long-term effect of managerial succession on organizational performance is positive. The author attributes this effect to the positive changes in means, motives, and opportunities the new management can bring to an organization (Hill 2005).

What Is Performance Analysis and Why Do It?

What Is Performance Analysis?

Although numerous factors may influence organizational performance, performance causes of your organization can be very different from those of others. Similar to the ways to get a good grade are different for students, each organization faces its own unique external environment and has its own internal management practices, so the causes for performance and ways to improve it are different for organizations. For example, it is conceivable that the cause of underperformance is the lack of resource for one police department, but the poor management skill of its leader is the cause of underperformance for another. Furthermore, the performance cause for a same organization could change over time, contingent on the change of the organization's external environment and internal management practices. Under these circumstances, many managers would like to know what their own organization's performance status is, what causes the performance, and what to do to improve it.

Performance analysis is a managerial tool used by organizations to improve performance through describing, monitoring, understanding, and evaluating organizational performance. The *ultimate organizational goal of performance analysis* is to understand what causes performance and to develop subsequent strategies to improve it. To do that, organizations must obtain performance information first and be able to describe the current performance status and monitor performance change over time. Consequently, there are four specific analytical objectives of performance analysis. *Performance description* is the accurate and meaningful presentation of performance information in order to obtain a good understanding of the current performance status. *Performance monitoring* is the presentation of performance change over time in order to identify the direction and the development of the performance, and more importantly, to detect any sign of underperformance. *Performance understanding* is to specify the causes of performance (or underperformance) and to develop proper strategies of performance improvement. *Performance evaluation* is an assessment on the impact of performance enhancement initiatives, which include policies, programs, or practices designed for performance improvement. Accordingly, performance analysis tools can be classified as tools in performance description, performance monitoring, performance understanding, and performance evaluation. This classification is very important, and this book will use it to present performance analysis tools.

As defined above, performance is either the output or outcome of an organization. Consequently, performance analysis includes the analysis of organizational outputs and outcomes. This book particularly focuses on *outcome analysis*, broadly defined as the use of quantitative outcome performance indicators to systematically analyze organizational performance in order to improve organizational performance and accountability.

Why Performance Analysis?

Why should managers in governments and nonprofits care about performance analysis? The fundamental need for performance analysis stems from the demand of citizens, clients, legislative bodies, or other stakeholders for high-quality public services. It is perhaps true that people care more about performance results rather than the process of how to get them. People feel safe from terrorism only when the threat is detected and removed. Clients are satisfied only when they receive high-quality products or services. Parents are happy only when their children do well in school. The results of performance analysis provide clues on how to provide high-quality products and services.

Good performance protects managers from criticisms of external stakeholders. A budgetary decision made by legislators or grantors is a contract signed by managers to supply a service or product in exchange for legislators' or grantors' agreement of funding. Managers are held accountable for performance. Good performers are in a better position to explain the effectiveness of the funding and to request continual support.

Moreover, performance analysis can help managerial decision making by demonstrating the need or the areas for improvement. With the tool, managers are able to articulate the performance goals and to make decisions to continue improving performance. Finally, performance analysis provides performance guidance and expectations for employees. It helps employees understand the value of their own effort by linking it with an organization's overall performance goal.

What Is the Uniqueness of Performance Analysis in Public and Nonprofit Organizations?

The process of conducting performance analysis is the same for the private and the public or nonprofit managers. They all need to describe, to monitor, to understand, and to evaluate performance. Nonetheless, public or nonprofit managers are judged much less often by their organizations' financial performances in revenue growth, profitability, and net cash flows. Furthermore, some unique aspects of public or nonprofit management in goal setting, decision-making structures, service delivery processes, and external environments result in unique conditions of performance analysis in public and nonprofit organizations. These conditions require the special attention of performance analysts in these organizations. This section briefly discusses these conditions and what a performance analyst should do when facing them. A summary of this discussion is in Table 1–2.

Table 1–2

Unique Aspects of Performance Analysis in Public and Nonprofit Organizations: A Summary

Aspect	Definition	Example
Multiple interests	Performance analysis serves stakeholders who have diverse, inconsistent, and sometimes contradictory interests.	While a high school administration wants high standard testing scores from students, parents want their children to learn skills in school that are not necessarily represented by testing scores.
Short-term funding and decision-making cycle	Performance analysis has to be completed within a year, which is the funding cycle for most governments and many nonprofits.	Most governments in the United States have an annual budgeting cycle, which means that measures used in a performance analysis should be sensitive enough to reflect the policy change and performance improvement within a year.
Intangible and nonfinancial service outputs	Many public services are not tangible commodities that can be exchanged in the market, so their output levels cannot be measured easily.	Public safety such as policing, prosecution, and correction is an intangible service and cannot be sold in market, which creates difficulties to measure the level of its production.
Monopoly of service delivery	Only one or a very limited number of service providers are available in a service region.	Most citizens or clients of public services live in an area that has only one or a very few providers of a public service such as local policing or fire protection.

Multiple Interests

Let us look at a hypothetical but reality-based example. Assume that you are a chief of a local police department. Who may be interested in the performance of your department? There are the citizens who receive your services and pay taxes, the council members who approve funding to pay you, the companies who sell you the policing equipment, employees in your department whose bonuses may be tied to the performance, and of course, yourself and other managers who want to demonstrate what a good job you have done (or have not done). In preparing a performance analysis, you would ask the analyst to pay attention to arrests made because you know that the number of arrests is directly related to the efforts of your department in the sense that, if you make an effort to collect more evidence, you can make more arrests. Because of this effort-driven nature of the arrest rate, you feel a sense of control over your performance, which is pretty reasonable (you have to be able to control it in order to improve it, right?).

The council members probably have different ideas on what should be measured. They would argue that the arrest rate says little about the crime situation in the city, and an increased arrest rate does not necessarily mean a reduction in crimes. So, the council members would like to see a reduction in the crime rates, which for sure would gain them political capitals by simply claiming the reduction. They want to have the bragging right to be the safest city in America by the measure of crime statistics. Nonetheless, a reduction in crimes does not necessarily make happy citizens. You could have a zero-crime community with a bunch of rude police officers writing tickets for every minor traffic offense and greeting people with an attitude. So, residents, who actually pay for police services, want a courteous police force in addition to a safe community.

Realize that there could be many stakeholders who are interested in your organization's performance, and their interests are often diverse and sometimes inconsistent or even contradictory to each other in that the fulfillment of one harms another. For example, stakeholders who are interested to see happy citizens may want more resources in involving community in policing, which likely would drive away the resource for traditional policing techniques that are needed in making arrests. Similarly, a desire to improve students' academic performances measured by standard test scores may be inconsistent with the interest to increase accessibility to an educational service and contradictory to the goal of educational cost control.

Several things may occur to an analyst facing multiple interests. First, the analyst may have multiple analysis questions. Different stakeholder groups want different questions answered in performance analysis. The existence of multiple analysis questions should not be a problem when measures are available and designs are developed properly to answer these questions. However, the analyst should be particularly alert to the requests of inconsistent and contradictory interests in performance analysis and make efforts to explain the possibility that the fulfillment of one performance goal could harm others.

Another problem of multiple interests in performance analysis is that these interests are changing constantly. Analysis questions change either because of the natural progression of the analysis with new data and measures available, or more often, because of stakeholders' changing expectations for the analysis. Oftentimes, stakeholders have expectations that are not articulated at the beginning of the analysis, which results in significant ambiguity in developing the analysis and the possible delay in design and implementation of the analysis.

Changing analysis questions, like a moving target, could lead to a series of changes in measures and designs of a performance analysis and pose new requirements for data analysis. For example, an analysis of a health care educational program originally designed to examine an immediate outcome of psychosocial achievements could later be asked by stakeholders to address issues of participants' educational achievements. As "educational achievements" are outcomes completely different from "psychosocial achievements," this change of analysis questions requires the development of new measures, new data, and new analysis tools.

What could an analyst do to deal with the impact of multiple interests in performance analysis? The key is to stabilize the question–asking process. There may be some truth to the argument that performance analysis is a process for stakeholders to learn their organizations and to raise new questions with the analysis process evolving. However, an analyst needs to have a set of analysis questions constant for a period of time long enough for the completion of an analysis process that consists of the development of analysis questions, measurement, data collection, and data analysis (discussed in the next chapter).

Although it is always a good idea to articulate the questions at the beginning of analysis in order to achieve a consensus among stakeholders about the questions, it may be difficult to do so as stakeholders may be unclear about their expectations of the analysis, or they may be changing their expectations. Nonetheless, some strategies may help the question–asking process. The key is to articulate goals and objectives of an analysis as much as possible before the analysis starts and to be flexible in using measures and analytical tools. Frequent communication should be developed to bring up different expectations of stakeholders before the analysis starts so a compromise of these expectations may be made among stakeholders to arrive at a series of consistent analysis questions. This strategy consists of a few steps as follows.

First, there should be a thorough discussion of the goal, the focus, and the scope of the analysis among stakeholders. Is an analysis for accountability or for management process improvement? A focus on accountability may suggest that the analysis should include more questions on outcomes that stakeholders prefer, while for an analysis focusing on managerial process improvement, more questions on the interrelationship among inputs, outputs, and outcomes may be needed. Is an analysis for performance description, monitoring, and understanding or for performance evaluation? Monthly or even daily observations are required for performance monitoring that focuses on continuous performance improvement. However, this frequency of observations may not be required for a performance description that emphasizes the thoroughness and usefulness of the information presented, often once a year. Is an analysis question-driven? Is data mining possible? Stakeholders may prefer a question-driven process in which they keep raising questions while the analysis process progresses and their understanding of the analysis process evolves. An analysis can be a question-driven process if, and only if, plentiful measures and a large amount of data are available. Abundance of data and measures makes it possible for a data mining process that allows analysts to answer analysis questions raised by stakeholders on an ongoing basis.

Second, demonstrating possible answers to possible performance analysis questions helps identify stakeholders' true interests for the analysis. Stakeholders have a better idea about their expectations for the performance analysis when a possible answer is given to an analysis question. The answer followed by a question of "is this what you want?" is often a powerful tool to find out the real interest of stakeholders. Finally, you can present clearly the cost of a new set of questions. The financial cost of the analysis, as well as the possible political implications, can be made clear to the stakeholders on a regular basis. After a clear understanding of the financial and political implications associated, stakeholders may have second thoughts on changing the direction of an analysis.

Short-Term Funding and Decision-Making Cycle

Most governments and many nonprofits have an annual planning and implementation cycle. Major decisions of resource allocation and service provisions are made annually. Consequently, they are accustomed to looking into their performance on an annual basis. They want performance analyses done annually and fund such analyses on an annual basis. The annual funding cycle means several things for performance analysis.

First, an analysis should be completed within 12 months or less. Performance data should be collected and analyzed, and performance analysis reports should be written long before the annual funding decisions are made. Second, the short funding cycle causes a stakeholder's mindset for quick results; thus, performance measures used in the analysis should be sensitive enough to reflect the policy change and interventional performance improvement actions. For example, an effort to improve student academic performance may take years to see the grade improvement, but it should use less time to see student behavior change in attendance, discipline incidents, and suspensions data. So, the selection of measures sensitive to policy changes and performance interventional activities is important to demonstrate the impact of these changes and activities (measurement selection criteria will be thoroughly discussed in Chapter 2).

Intangible and Nonfinancial Service Outputs

Many governments and nonprofits produce services, not tangible products. The military and law enforcement agencies provide us a safe environment to live. The public education system supplies knowledge and skills. The public health care system (e.g., Medicare and Medicaid) allows access to health care. Realize that the safe environment, the knowledge and skills, and the access to health care are intangible services in their physical shape and form. They are different from tangible products such as vehicles, equipment, and water and power supply.

Production of tangible products allows a straightforward measurement of the production output. The output is simply the sum of products. For example, the output of a vehicle production company at a specific period of time is the total of all vehicles produced during that time. It is, however, not that easy to measure the output of an intangible product or service. For example, what is the output for a local police department? What is the output for the patrol unit? What is an output for police officers who help stranded pedestrians? Lack of a solid and visible product makes it difficult for the police department to use an output that is easily agreed upon and recognized by all stakeholders. To make it even more complicated, like many governments and nonprofits, the police department provides multiple services in patrol, investigation, and community policing, so multiple measures have to be used to accurately assess the output level of the whole department. You will have to use, for example, the number of patrols for the patrol unit and the number of arrests for the investigation unit. Nonetheless, you cannot simply add them to arrive at a total output of the department. It does not make sense to add the number of patrols and the number of arrests because they have different denominators.

Many private businesses also provide intangible services—your travel company plans your travel, your dry cleaner cleans your clothes, your pest control company debugs your home. So, they would have the same problem to measure their output. Right? Wrong. Businesses have a perfect solution for this measurement dilemma of intangible services. They use the market. Because businesses sell their services on the market and because their outputs can be translated to revenues or earnings, it is relatively easy and logical to use financial measures to assess the output of private services.

Public services are not exchanged on the market. They do not generate revenues. There are no price tags on them and no methods to calculate financial gains or loss for them. In other words, we cannot measure their outputs or outcomes by using financial measures. If we have a hard time determining public service outputs, we have an even harder time determining outcomes because outcomes are more likely affected than outputs are by the uncontrollable environmental factors and client characteristics discussed earlier in this chapter.

The absence of tangible products and revenue-generating capability in public services has significant implications for performance analysis. One implication is related to the development of performance measures: governments and nonprofits are forced to use replacement measures of outputs. Two types of replacement measures are often used to assess public service outputs. One is known as *activity measures* (or *workload measures*). There is a difference between activities and outputs. Illustrated in the production process (Figure 1–1), activities are part of the process while outputs are the consequence of the process. For example, the number of courses offered is an activity measure to assess the activity level of an educational program. The number of students graduated is an output measure to gauge how many students are produced in the process. Although activity measures are very close to outputs being measured, they are not output measures. They measure different phases of public service provision.

Another set of replacement measures uses the size of individual service recipients. For example, the number of households served can be used to replace the number of kilowatts of electricity produced in measuring the output of a public utility operation. In this case, the number of service recipients is an output measure of the operation by using the size of service recipients. Similarly, to measure the output of an educational program, the number of students participating in the program can be used to replace the number of courses offered as an output measure. Other popular individual-based measures of outputs include the number of students, the number of clinic visitors, and the number of residents who use a service.

When the size of service recipients is used to surrogate the measure of organizational outputs, "individuals-based" measures are used to replace "organization-based" measures (if you are familiar with the concept of the unit of analysis, it is individuals). Conceivably, individual recipients of a service can be used if they indeed use and benefit from the service; however, caution should be exercised when individual-based data are aggregated to represent organization-wide performance. Limitations in interpretation exist when analysis results of individual-based data are used to infer to organizational performance. Sometimes, the use of individual-based data can lead to an inaccurate estimate of organizational performance. For instance, each household uses a different amount of electricity, so the number of households served may not be as accurate as the number of kilowatts of electricity produced in measuring the output of a public utility operation.

Monopoly of Service Delivery

The production of many public services is monopolized (only one service provider exists in a region). The absence of multiple service providers makes it impossible to conduct interjurisdictional performance comparison of service providers in the region. If the comparison is extended to include the providers in other regions, regional differences become apparent, and the control of demographic differences of regions becomes necessary.

Because regional differences in socioeconomic conditions and customer demographics are so many and often large, controlling all of them in an analysis is difficult and sometimes impossible (think of demographic differences, for instance, between Miami and San Francisco). However, without controlling these differences, the comparison becomes less convincing or sometimes misleading. Even if such a comparison is made, underperformers can always point out this methodology limitation to explain their underperformance or to discredit the analysis ("You cannot compare us with them because we are different"), so the results of comparison are deemed to be less useful.

While the application of interjurisdictional comparison is difficult, the comparison of an organization's own performance over time is perhaps more meaningful and more realistic to implement. Data of an intrajurisdictional trend comparison are relatively easier to obtain because they are from the same organization. Data are likely obtained by the same unit in an organization with the same data collection method, so they often show a high level of reliability. Because data are collected from the same collection method, the task of data recoding and cleaning is minimized.

How Is Performance Analysis Covered in This Book?

Performance analysis can help managers answer several questions. First, it helps them know the current performance status of the organization (Describing Performance—Chapters 3, 4). How well does the organization perform? Does the organization perform better or worse than others? Second, it helps managers trace the performance trend and be able to find underperformance quickly if it occurs (Monitoring Performance—Chapters 5, 6, 7). Is there any trend of performance over time? Is there any trend of underperformance? Third, it help managers understand what may cause underperformance (Understanding Performance—Chapters 8, 9, 10). What factors influence performance? What to do and how to do it to improve performance. Finally, it helps managers evaluate the effectiveness of their performance improvement efforts (Evaluating Performance—Chapters 11, 12, 13). Do these efforts work? How do they improve the performance? What to do to continue performance improvement. The book is concluded with a chapter on how to write an effective performance analysis report (Chapter 14). In the next chapter (Chapter 2), organizational requirements for conducting a performance analysis are discussed.

References

Ammons, D. N., and W. C. Rivenbark. 2008. Factor influencing the use of performance data to improve municipal services: Evidence from the North Carolina Benchmarking Project. *Public Administration Review* 68(2):304–18.

Aristigueta, M. P., and W. Van Dooren. 2007. Toward a performing public sector: The roles of context, utilization, and networks. *Public Performance and Management Review* 30(4):463–8.

Bradshaw, P., V. Murray, and J. Wolpin. 1992. Do nonprofit boards make a difference? An exploration of the relationships among board structure, process, and effectiveness. *Nonprofit and Voluntary Sector Quarterly* 21(3):227–49.

Brewer, G. A. 2005. In the eye of the storm: Frontline supervisors and federal agency performance. *Journal of Public Administration Research & Theory* 15:505–27.

Brewer, G. A., and S. C. Selden. 2000. Why elephants gallop: Assessing and predicting organizational performance in federal agencies. *Journal of Public Administration Research & Theory* 10(4): 685–711.

Boyne, G. A. 2003. Sources of public service improvement: A critical review and research agenda. *Journal of Public Administration Research & Theory* 13(3):367–94.

Boyne, G. A., and A. A. Chen. 2007. Performance targets and public service improvement. *Journal of Public Administration Research & Theory* 17(3):455–77.

Chun, Y. Han, and H. G. Rainey. 2005. Goal ambiguity and organizational performance in U.S. federal agencies. *Journal of Public Administration Research & Theory* 15:529–57.

Forbes, D. P. 1998. Measuring the unmeasurable: Empirical studies of nonprofit organization effectiveness from 1977 to 1997. *Nonprofit and Voluntary Sector Quarterly* 27(2):183–202.

Forbes, M., and L. E. Lynn Jr. 2005. How does public management affect government performance? Findings from international research. *Journal of Public Administration Research & Theory* 15:559–84.

Goerdel, H. T. 2006. Taking initiative: Proactive management and organizational performance in networked environments. *Journal of Public Administration Research & Theory* 16(3):351–67.

Gill, J., and K. J. Meier. 2001. Ralph's Pretty-Good Grocery versus Ralph's Super Market: Separating excellent agencies from the good ones. *Public Administration Review* 61(1):9–17.

Heinrich, C. 2002. Outcomes-based performance management in the public sector: Implications for government accountability and effectiveness. *Public Administration Review* 62(6):712–25.

Heinrich, C., and E. Fournier. 2004. Dimensions of publicness and performance in substance abuse treatment organizations. *Journal of Policy Analysis and Management* 23(1):49–70.

Heinrich, C., and L. E. Lynn Jr. 2000. Governance and performance: The influence of program structure and management on Job Training Partnership Act (JTPA) program outcomes. In *Governance and performance: New perspectives*, ed. Carolyn J. Heinrich and Laurence E. Lynn Jr., 68–108. Washington, DC: Georgetown University Press.

Herman, R. D., and D. O. Renz. 1998. Nonprofit organizational effectiveness: Contrasts between especially effective and less effective organizations. *Nonprofit Management and Leadership* 9(1): 23–38.

Hill, C., and L. E. Lynn Jr. 2004a. Governance and public management: An introduction. *Journal of Policy Analysis and Management* 23(1):3–11.

—. 2004b. Is hierarchical governance in decline? Evidence from empirical research. *Journal of Public Administration Research & Theory* 15(2):173–95.

Hill, G. C. 2005. The effects of managerial succession on organizational performance. *Journal of Public Administration Research & Theory* 15(4):585–97.

Ho, A. T.-K. 2006. Accounting for the value of performance measurement from the perspective of midwestern mayors. *Journal of Public Administration Research & Theory* 16(2):217–37.

Ingraham, P. W., and A. Kneedler Donahue. 2000. Dissecting the black box revisited: Characterizing government management capacity. In *Governance and performance: New perspectives*, ed. C. J. Heinrich and L. E. Lynn Jr., 292–318. Washington, DC: Georgetown University Press.

Jennings, E. T. Jr., and J. A. Ewalt. 2000. Driving caseloads down: Welfare policy choices and administrative action in the states. In *Governance and performance: New perspectives*, ed. C. J. Heinrich and L. E. Lynn Jr., 109–39. Washington, DC: Georgetown University Press.

Julnes, P. L., and M. Holzer, 2001. Promoting the utilization of performance measures in public organizations: An empirical study of factors affecting adoption and implementation. *Public Administration Review* 61(6):693–708.

Kim, S. 2004. Individual-level factors and organizational performance in government organizations. *Journal of Public Administration Research & Theory* 15(2):245–61.

Knott, J. H., and A. A. Payne. 2004. The impact of state governance structures on management and performance of public organizations: A study of higher education institutions. *Journal of Policy Analysis and Management* 23(1):13–30.

Lynn, L. E., C. J. Heinrich, and C. Hill. 2000. Studying governance and public management: Challenges and prospects. *Journal of Public Administration Research & Theory* 10(2):233–61.

Meier, K. J., S. H. Mastracci, and K. Wilson. 2006. Gender and emotional labor in public organizations: An empirical examination of the link to performance. *Public Administration Review* 66(6): 899–909.

Meier, K. J., and L. J. O'Toole Jr. 2003. Public management and educational performance: The impact of managerial networking. *Public Administration Review*, 63(6):689–99.

Meier, K. J., L. J. O'Toole Jr., G. A. Boyne, and R. M. Walker, 2007. Strategic management and the performance of public organizations: Testing venerable ideas against recent theories. *Journal of Public Administration Research and Theory* 17(3):357–77.

Meier, K. J., L. J. O'Toole Jr., and S. Nicholson-Crotty. 2004. Multilevel governance and organizational performance: Investing the political-bureaucratic labyrinth. *Journal of Policy Analysis and Management* 23(1):31–47.

Nicholson-Crotty, S., and L. J. O'Toole Jr. 2004. Public management and organizational performance: The case of law enforcement agencies. *Journal of Public Administration Research & Theory* 14(1):1–18.

O'Toole, L. J., and K. Meier. 1999. Modeling the impact of public management: Implications of structural context. *Journal of Public Administration Research & Theory* 9(4):505–26.

Pitts, D. W. 2005. Diversity, representation, and performance: Evidence about race and ethnicity in public organizations. *Journal of Public Administration Research & Theory* 15(4):615–31.

Provan, K. G., and H. B. Milward. 2001. Do networks really work? A framework for evaluating public-sector organizational networks. *Public Administration Review* 61(4):414–24.

Rainey, H. G., and P. Steinbauer. 1999. Galloping elephants: Developing elements of a theory of effective government organizations. *Journal of Public Administration Research & Theory* 9(1):1–32.

Roderick, M., B. A. Jacob, and A. S. Bryk. 2000. Evaluating Chicago's efforts to end social promotion. In *Governance and performance: New perspectives*, ed. C. J. Heinrich and L. E. Lynn Jr., 34–67. Washington, DC: Georgetown University Press.

Sandfort, J. 2000. Examining the effect of welfare-to-work structures and services on a desired policy outcome. In *Governance and performance: New perspectives*, ed. C. J. Heinrich and L. E. Lynn Jr., 140–65. Washington, DC: Georgetown University Press.

Selden, S. C., and J. E. Sowa. 2004. Testing a multi-dimensional model of organizational performance: Prospects and problems. *Journal of Public Administration Research & Theory* 14(3):395–416.

Selden, S. C., J. E. Sowa, and J. Sandfort. 2006. The impact of nonprofit collaboration in early child care and education on management and program outcomes. *Public Administration Review* 66(3): 412–25.

Yang, K., and J. Y. Hsieh. 2007. Managerial effectiveness of government performance measurement: Testing a middle-range model. *Public Administration Review* 67(5):861–79.

Practices

Key Terms

Performance
Organizational performance
Performance appraisal
Network performance
Inputs
Production process

Outputs
Outcomes
Efficiency
Effectiveness
Quality
Performance management models
Performance causes
The Lynn, Heinrich, and Hill model of public performance management
Environmental causes of performance
Client characteristics causes of performance
Primary work efforts–core work processes–technology causes of performance
Administrative or organizational structure causes of performance
Managerial roles–strategies–actions causes of performance
Performance analysis
Ultimate organizational goal of performance analysis
Specific analytical objectives of performance analysis
Performance description
Performance monitoring
Performance understanding
Performance evaluation
Multiple interests in performance analysis
Short-term funding and decision-making cycle
Intangible and nonfinancial service outputs
Activity measures
Individual-based measures
Organization-based measures
Monopoly of service delivery

Practice Problem 1–1

Locate five performance analysis reports through a search of the Internet or an organization's archives. Notice that the reports may use different names for performance analysis such as performance audits, performance evaluation or assessment, or program evaluation. A performance analysis report is often characterized with several features. First, it focuses on a specific performance issue or a set of performance issues not a general description of performance in an organization. Second, it often targets the performance of one division or one unit in an organization not the performance of the whole organization. For example, it may analyze the issue of slow clean-up efforts after a severe snow storm. It is not the report that depicts the performance of the whole public works department. Performance analysis is not an annual reporting of performance of the whole organization. Service Efforts and Accomplishment reports (SEA) or Performance Reports for Services, often used to showcase the overall performance of all divisions and units in an organization on an annual basis, are not performance analysis reports. You may have to dig deep in an organization's archives, such as in performance auditing reports, to find performance analysis reports. Third, many performance analysis reports present a list of specific recommendations for performance improvement, which is often not included in SEA reports.

After you identify these performance analyses, review them to answer the following questions:

1. Describe the performance issues in analyses and state the performance statuses. For example, if the issue is performance decline, state how much decline is detected in the report.
2. Report the key findings of the performance analysis. Does a report identify any performance causes and any methods of performance improvement? Can you classify these causes using the Lynn, Heinrich, and Hill model?

Practice Problem 1–2

Conduct a literature search for articles in the issues of the most recent 2 years in the following journals: *Journal of Public Administration Research & Theory*, *Public Administration Review*, and *Public Performance & Management Review*. Identify all empirical articles on performance management. Answer the following questions for each article:

1. How is performance defined and measured?
2. Does the article develop a model to identify performance causes and how they affect performance? How do you classify these performance causes based on the Lynn–Heinrich–Hill model described in this chapter?
3. Write a paragraph to briefly describe the key findings of each article.

Practice Problem 1–3

Identify an organization of interest and a performance issue in the organization (e.g., the increase in client complaints about the service, the decline in the number of clients, slow response to service requests, the increase in the number of service errors made).

1. Use the Lynn–Heinrich–Hill model to develop a set of possible reasons that may cause the performance.
2. Explain how these reasons may affect the performance.
3. Suppose that you plan to conduct a performance analysis to find the true causes of performance. Discuss any possible organizational constraints (such as multiple interests or others discussed in this chapter) that may affect the performance improvement.

Practice Problem 1–4

Familiarize yourself with the Web sites in Appendix C of this book, which provide resources and examples of performance management in the public and nonprofit sectors.

CHAPTER 2

What Is Needed for Performance Analysis?

Performance analysis is a tool. To use a tool, you need certain capacities (similar to using a computer in which you should know how to set it up properly, connect it correctly, and work with the right software). This chapter discusses capacities needed for performance analysis. It first introduces the performance analysis process and then examines how to develop organizational capacities for performance analysis. It also details how to obtain a difficult technical capacity in performance analysis—developing performance measures.

Understanding the Performance Analysis Process

Who wants an analysis? Legislators or nonprofit board members may want to know how well the funding is used to support services and whether to continuously fund the services. Service recipients may want to know whether there is room to improve service quality. Tax (or fee) payers or grantors may be interested in how to avoid waste of resources. Performance auditors may want performance information for their specific interests. Most importantly, managers should use performance analysis as a primary tool for performance improvement.

When is a performance analysis needed? It is needed in strategic planning, budgeting, and daily management. In the strategic planning process, a performance analysis helps an agency understand its strategic performance goals and what it takes to achieve them. In budgeting, a performance analysis can demonstrate the effectiveness of resource use in order to make funding decisions. Nonetheless, a performance analysis is most needed when an organization underperforms and performance improvement is expected. Performance analysis helps managers understand their level of performance, track their performance trend, discover the causes of underperformance, and assess the effectiveness of their performance enhancement efforts. A performance analysis can also be done in conjunction with a performance appraisal of individual employees' performances in order to find out how individual workers contribute to an organization's performance.

Who does performance analysis? Analysis can be performed internally by an organization's internal team of managers and analysts or by external consultants or auditors. The internal approach has advantages of ready accessibility to an organization's information, while outside consultants or auditors may be more objective in analysis and in presenting critical recommendations.

Although each analysis is unique in scope and method, they do have several common attributes that can be summarized in the following steps. It is important to note that, because performance analysis is a scientific exploration, the steps below are in fact a description of the scientific research method on specific organizational performance issues. Any book of methodologies should provide a more generic description of the scientific research method.

Step 1: Understanding the Issue

Suppose you are a performance analyst for a nonprofit organization that provides school nursing services to high school students, and suppose board members want an analysis to "assess the outcome of the program in providing quality service to program participants" (a true request from a nonprofit board member in one of my analyses). What exactly do they want to know from the analysis? Whether or how well the outcome has been achieved? Is the outcome being properly tracked and assessed? Or, is there any room to continuously improve the outcome? In other words, what exactly is the objective of the analysis? From the board member's statement, you cannot tell. In fact, it is quite common that a request for an analysis is phrased in vague terms and expressions, which often reflect the complex managerial and decision-making issues in the real world. Thus, an understanding of the issue is necessary before any analysis.

Sometimes, a performance issue is obvious—more customer complaints about slow emergency medical responses, more crimes committed in your area, or more clerical errors in processing documents. You know right away that the issue is to identify the causes of underperformance and to make recommendations for improvement. But, many other times the issue is not that clear. A careful examination of the issue may change it. For example, a concern initially identified as customers' complaints about the higher water–sewer fee may turn out to be an issue of unfair treatment perceived by the customers about unequal increases of the fee among different customer groups. Legislators' expressed intents to provide healthy school lunches may reflect their true concern about the increasing number of overweight children. Nonprofit board members' desires to see improvement in healthy eating behaviors of children in their program may actually reflect their worry about the decline in students' academic performances.

One way to understand a performance issue is to conduct an *analysis of stakeholder interests*. This analysis involves a series of communications with the key stakeholders of the performance analysis to understand who wants the analysis, what exactly they want from the analysis, why they want it, and who the readers of the final analysis report are. It is very common that such an analysis reveals the diversity of interests and intents of stakeholders in performance analysis. For example, an analysis of key stakeholders in a nonprofit health care organization that provides health care to school-age children could reveal that the board members have very different objectives in a performance analysis that "examines the outcome of the program." The medical doctor on the board may want to see the overall improvement of children's health. The school principal may want to know whether the improvement in children's health improves their academic performance in school. The business executive may be concerned about the cost of the program and wants to know more about the chance of continuous funding for the program.

A thorough understanding of a performance issue is the foundation to determine analysis objectives. In the last chapter, analysis objectives are broadly classified as performance description, performance monitoring, performance understanding, and performance evaluation. As the result of the stakeholder analysis, you should be able to determine, in the above example, whether the analysis is for demonstrating the health care achievement of the program (performance description and monitoring), for developing an understanding about how health care affects academic performance (performance understanding), for controlling the program cost (performance monitoring and evaluation), or for exploring key factors that could influence children's health (performance understanding). Realize that an analysis can be conducted for multiple objectives.

Step 2: Starting with Questions

A performance analysis *always* starts with questions that it intends to answer. Though each analysis has its own specific questions, there are some generic forms about how these questions may be asked. If your analysis objective is to simply describe the performance, you are likely to ask the following questions: How well does the organization perform? Does the organization perform better or worse than others? If you are interested in tracking performance, your questions often include the following: Is there any trend of performance over time? Is there any trend of underperformance? Analysts attempting to understand performance causes often ask the following questions: What causes the underperformance? What influences performance? What should be done and how should it be done to improve performance? Finally, if you attempt to evaluate the effectiveness of performance enhancement initiatives, you would likely ask the following: Do these initiatives improve performance? How much improvement does an initiative make? How do these initiatives improve the performance?

A good performance question has to be the *right* question. Clearly, a good question leads to the information an analyst wants. A wrong question results in the information that does not directly and specifically address the interests of the analysis. For example, I used to think that the lack of school parking lots was the cause of some students' tardiness in my classes. So I asked them to tell me how to improve the parking capacity. But, it turned out to be the wrong question to ask because the lack of roads to the parking, not parking itself, is the true cause of students' delay. Moreover, a good question should be *answerable*, which means that the performance and related concepts in the question can be measured and empirically observed with a reasonable level of research efforts. For example, if you analyze what affects students' academic performances, you can use grades to measure academic performance and collect the grade information with a reasonable level of effort. However, a question is less answerable if you ask what affects students' marketabilities after graduation because it is relatively difficult to define, to measure, and to obtain data of students' marketabilities.

Step 3: Developing a Performance Theory

A *theory* is a series of propositions that explain what causes an event to happen. A *performance theory* specifies the causes of a performance. For example, if you believe the reason a student gets a good grade is because he or she studies hard, you theorize that study effort is the cause of academic performance. If you think a fire station has a better record of response time because it has better equipment and its employees are better trained, you theorize that equipment and training status cause response time. In performance analysis, a theory is not required when the analysis objective is to simply describe the performance status or to monitor performance change over time. Nonetheless, a theory is necessary when the analysis objective is to find out the causes of performance (underperformance) or to explain why a performance enhancement initiative should work in performance evaluation.

Why do you need a theory in performance analysis? Imagine that you want to know if group study affects a student's academic performance, and you theorize that group study benefits a student from the information sharing with other group members so the student performs better on tests. By theorizing *how* academic performance is affected by group study, you enhance the plausibility of the cause–effect relationship (or causality) between academic performance and study methods (group study vs. individual study). So, a theory increases the *plausibility of the causality* in a performance analysis. This is why a theory is critical in understanding the causes of performance.

Realize that once a theory is developed, the rejection of it becomes possible. In the above example, it may also be true that group study takes away a student's own study time, so group study actually has no impact or even has negative impact on the student's academic performance. The causality between group study and academic performance is hypothetical until it is proven true and an unproven cause–effect statement is a *hypothesis*. Thus, the development of a theory makes it possible to reject the existence of the causality in performance analysis. Realize that it is this attribute of *rejectability of a hypothesis* that makes the development of alternative explanations of performance causes possible, and searching alternative explanations is a constant task of scientific research that includes performance analysis.

How do you develop a performance theory? There are two sources of a performance theory. One is from a review of the performance management literature that depicts performance relationships in previous studies. The Lynn–Heinrich–Hill performance model introduced in the last chapter can be used as a theoretical basis to develop the performance theory that explains what factors influence your organization's performance. Later in Chapter 8, we will discuss several other theoretical frameworks that should help you understand performance.

Another source is a performance analyst's logical thinking based on his or her knowledge, expertise, and working experiences of the issue and the organization. Of course, it is common that both the literature and the personal experiences are used simultaneously to develop a good performance theory.

Step 4: Developing Performance Measures

How do you assess a student's academic progress? Do you use class grades, the average grade (the grade point average, or GPA), the grade of an important class assignment, the knowledge of whether the student graduates within a certain time or whether the student goes to a graduate school, or the student's standardized test score for graduate school? A *performance measure*, also known as *performance indicator*, is a specific and quantifiable assessment on the level and scope of a performance activity, output, or outcome. It is specific in the sense that a measure assesses only one aspect of the performance. One measure hardly provides a complete and holistic assessment of the performance. For example, the class grade addresses a student's academic achievement, not the student's study efforts, which can be assessed by other measures such as the number of weekly study hours or the number of class attendances. A performance measure has to be *quantifiable*, which means that the data of the measure can be collected to assess the performance. For example, the class grade can be numerically assigned and calculated to assess students' academic performances. So, the class grade can be used as a measure of academic performance.

One of the greatest challenges in performance analysis is to determine what measures to use in an analysis. As discussed in great detail later in this chapter in the "Developing Performance Measures" section, the development of specific measures for a performance analysis depends on the measurement objective and the measurement framework used.

Step 5: Determining the Data Collection Method

Again, suppose you study whether group study affects a student's academic performance, you have a pretty good theory explaining why it should, and you have developed measures of academic performance and group study; your next step is to collect data to prove or disprove this relationship. This process, known as the *empirical observation* of performance, includes the development of a data collection method, data collection, data analysis, and conclusions.

How should data be collected? In the above example, you could design a student survey asking who studies in group and who does not and compare their grades. Or, you could study two classes of students with one requiring group study and the other not, and compare their grades. You could also conduct interviews of students and ask them whether they study in a group and how they perform academically. In this example, surveys, interviews, and academic records (grades) are the *data collection methods* that determine how performance data are collected. There are several popular data collection methods in performance analysis.

Conducting Surveys

Survey data are widely used in performance analysis. One popular way to gauge performance of a service provision is to survey service recipients such as citizens or customers. For example, you can ask residents in a community whether or not they feel safe walking in the street at night and use it as a measure of public safety for the police service. In this case, residents' perceptions replace crime rate, response time, and other archival data in measuring police performance. Because surveys assess subjective perceptions and attitudes of survey respondents on performance, survey measures are sometimes known as *subjective measures* of performance, as opposed to crime rate and response time, which are known as *objective measures* because they are collected from independent observations free of individual perceptions.

In addition to service recipient surveys, surveys of managers and staff can also provide performance information about an organization's operation process, service or production activities, and service outcomes perceived by managers and staff. Forms of surveys include mail, telephone, and electronic surveys through e-mail or the Internet.

Surveys have several advantages as a data collection method for performance information. First, most surveys can be designed easily, and they are universally applied to almost all services in public and nonprofit organizations. Second, surveys directly assess the view of citizens or customers. Because service recipients are the ultimate judges of services, surveys of customer–client satisfaction assess a true outcome of services. Third, a typical survey question is close ended with multiple but limited choices of answers for respondents. This format allows standardized responses, which make classification and analysis of the performance easier than an open-ended question format that is popular in interviews in which respondents offer their own responses. Finally, in comparison with interviews that tend to be in depth and time consuming, surveys may be relatively less costly to do.

Conducting Interviews

Performance data can also be obtained from interviewing stakeholders. For example, interviews can be conducted to solicit service providers' (manager and employees) opinions about the causes of performance in a brainstorm process (the *brainstorm process* is a form of a group interview process). The differences between an interview and a survey are subtle sometimes. In general, interviews allow analysts to ask follow-up questions to gain in-depth understanding about performance, while surveys have limited and standardized responses that are not followed up with further questioning. Realize that both a survey and an interview can be used simultaneously in an analysis. Interviews can be used prior to a survey to develop survey questions or after a survey to understand more about survey responses.

You can interview managers and staff to obtain information about service provision activities and procedures. You can also interview service recipients for their assessment of services. Interviews can take forms of telephone or face-to-face interviews, in a group or with individuals. As a data collection method, one clear advantage of interviews over surveys is that an interview allows analysts to collect richer information. Interviews allow follow-up questions. Also, in the interview, the interviewer and the interviewee have the chance to know each other at a personal level. Skillful interviewers can create an amiable and conducive environment that makes the interviewee feel comfortable to answer questions and to provide more information. Nonetheless, interviews may be expensive to conduct. The large efforts spent on scheduling and organizing for a relatively small number of interviews may make it less preferable for analysts who look for a large sample to analyze. As a result, interviews are often used as a tool supplemental to other data collection methods or are used only when the information needed cannot be obtained from other methods.

Searching Archives

Many organizations have archival documents such as operational, financial, and auditing reports, which can be the sources of performance data for analysis. It is also possible that the performance data can be found in regional, statewide, or national databases, such as the census or the Uniform Crime Reports.

A lot of archival data are collected on a consistent basis so an observation of performance can be developed over time. Also, archival data often include the same information over time, so the data are more consistent than the data from interviews or surveys, which tend to cover different questions each time they are conducted. Also, archival data are often collected with the same or similar data collection procedures and standards, which result in reliable data. However, one major drawback of archival data in comparison with surveys or interviews is, because archival data are often created for various political, legal, and financial reasons other than for the performance analysis per se, they may not provide the exact information needed for a performance analysis.

Creating an Experiment

Again, imagine that you study whether group study affects a student's academic performance in your class. You could assign half of the students in your class to study in a group and the other half to study individually. After the semester is over, you collect and compare grade data of these two groups. Similarly, if a local police department hired more patrol officers to patrol the street this year to crack down on crimes, you can compare crime statistics of this year and last year to assess the impact of the increased patrol activity on crime. In these examples, group study and increased patrol activity are called *performance interventions* or *performance enhancement initiatives* (a term frequently used later in this book). They are created to affect the performance (i.e., academic performance and crime). In an experiment, a performance intervention is created in order to assess its impact on performance.

Strictly speaking, creating an experiment concerns more about when, rather than how, performance data are collected. There are many forms of experiments depending on how a performance comparison is designed and whether a control group is available. The construction of experiments in performance analysis and analysis of experimental performance data will be thoroughly discussed later in Chapters 11 to 13, when the evaluation of performance intervention is discussed.

An experiment allows performance comparison among different performance groups. Performance data can be collected from these performance groups, and these data are valuable in identifying the possible impact of a performance intervention. Nonetheless, experiments are often difficult and expensive to design (Can you really assign two groups in your class with different study methods? How can you be sure that the students who are supposed to study individually really do not talk to each other or study in group?), and ethical dilemmas may be involved in experiments (Is it really fair for the students who study individually?).

Step 6: Collecting Performance Data

Once you know what data to collect and how to collect them, you are ready to start the collection process. In general, the data collection consists of several sequential steps: developing a data collection instrument, obtaining data, entering data, and cleaning data.

Data Collection Instrument Development

Suppose that you want to collect students' grades. You could conduct a survey asking their grades, or you could search their grade records. The survey or the grade records are data collection instruments. A *data collection instrument* is the device used to record or store performance data. Although some organizational records can be used directly in analysis, many instruments need to be developed by analysts themselves. Some popular data collection instruments include the survey instrument, the interview protocol, and the protocol for archive search.

A *survey instrument* is one of the most popular modes of data collection. In general, there are three types of information that should be included in a survey constructed to obtain performance information. First and foremost, the instrument must include items measuring performance. In a survey of service recipients' perceptions about the adequacy of a service, for example, the instrument must include items measuring respondents' assessments about the adequacy. Respondents can be asked whether they receive the service at the adequate level, how satisfied they are with the current level of the service, and/or how much they agree with an item stating that the service is adequately provided. Second, the instrument should include the important socioeconomic, demographic, and personal information of the respondents such as occupation, gender, race, and income. These items help the analyst know who respondents are and may help explain the reasoning of their assessment.

Third, there should be items measuring the reasoning of respondents' assessments. What causes their assessments? These items are important because their answers suggest the ways to improve performance. For example, it can be theorized that residents' assessments about police services are caused by police officers' behaviors. So a survey of police performance should include items on police behaviors such as "how courteous is the police officer to you?" and "how helpful is the police officer to you?" Realize that a performance theory (the above step 3) can be used to guide the development of the items measuring causes of respondents' performance assessments.

An *interview protocol*, developed before an interview, lays out the questions related to the interview. It should include names and affiliations of interviewers and interviewees, dates and times of the interview, and most importantly, the questions asked in the interview about performance and performance causes. The interviewer should be ready to ask follow-up questions that are not in the protocol, which may lead to more insightful explanation and findings.

A *protocol for archive search* should be developed to extract the data in archives. The archival data may be in electronic or paper form. Realize that the archival data can be subjective data from previous surveys and interviews or objective data from documents such as crime reports, response time records, student academic performance records, or financial performance records.

An archive search protocol includes the time and the place of the search, as well as the performance information being searched, such as names of the measures and the data collection method used. In some cases, the original data record sheet can be used to replace the protocol, and there is no need to develop a new protocol. The examples include student academic records sheets for their academic performances, crime reports for police performance, and revenue and expenditure records for financial performance. Nonetheless, in many other cases, the protocol should be developed because either the original record sheet contains unnecessary information or because the data in the sheet are not in the shape or the form needed for the performance analysis. For example, the property appraisal record includes a large amount of information, and a large portion of it may be unnecessary for a performance analysis. A protocol needs to be developed to extract only the necessary information. Daily school attendance records may not be needed in an analysis of monthly attendance. Monthly attendance needs to be calculated and recorded in a newly developed protocol.

Obtaining, Entering, and Cleaning Data

You should always check the availability of data in an organization's archives and other existing data sources before going out to collect new data. If the data exist in the record, there should be a process to transport them and format them for the analysis. Data in paper instruments should be converted to electronic forms for data analysis in the computer. In this book, Microsoft Excel is used in data analysis. Data in other formats should be formatted to the Excel format.

If new data need to be collected, make sure they are entered electronically in the computer for analysis. If the data are initially recorded on paper, they must be reentered electronically. It should be noted that the data security is important in data collection. Personal information is particularly sensitive to security threats of identity crimes and misuses. Laws and practices to safeguard personal information should be followed rigorously to protect the data from such threats.

You should develop a *data entry codebook* during data entry. A codebook lists names of measures in the database and briefly describes each measure. It is particularly useful in databases with a large number of measures. Because the names of measures are always abbreviated to save space in these databases, the codebook helps the analyst recognize the abbreviations in analysis.

Many databases need to be "cleaned" before use. The reasons for the cleaning are many. Different data collection standards may have been used in the past, so data are not comparable. For example, the definition of medical emergencies may have changed over time so some emergencies classified in the past are no longer emergencies with the current standard. Other reasons for data cleaning include: missing values should be coded, data in alphabetical form should be quantified for computer analysis, illegible records of data should be cleared out, and wrong and unnecessary information should be eliminated from the database.

Oftentimes, it is unclear what data are available in an organization at the outset of an analysis. A *data inventory analysis* can be conducted to explore the existence and the quality of the data needed for a performance analysis. Data inventory analysis is a careful examination of the quality of the existing data and their adoptability for the analysis. Its goal is to determine what additional data are needed for the analysis. The analysis consists of a series of interviews with data managers and record search efforts that determine the shape and form of the existing data (e.g., electronic or paper based); the quality of data entry (e.g., the level that is free of data entry errors, legibility of the data); completion of the data (e.g., the sample size); and adoptability of the data for the analysis (whether the data are what is needed for the analysis). The final report of the data inventory analysis describes what data are currently available in the organization, what additional data are needed for analysis, and what data collection methods may be proper to collect the new data.

Step 7: Analyzing Performance

Performance data analysis consists of four sets of tools that quantitatively and analytically describe performance, monitor performance, explore the causes of performance, and evaluate performance enhancement initiatives. These tools are systematically covered throughout this book. The tools in describing performance provide a good knowledge basis on the current performance status, which is the foundation for further in-depth analyses in monitoring a long-term performance trend, understanding causes of underperformance, and improving performance. So, describing performance is the first step of any performance analysis. *Performance description* is a numerical and graphical presentation of the current performance shape and trend. *Performance shape* concerns a static snapshot of the current performance status of an organization, while *performance trend* reveals the direction of the performance development over time by including a time frame of the performance.

The second set of tools in performance analysis are used in monitoring performance change in order to detect whether or not the change is a sign of abnormalities and underperformance from performance benchmarks. Compared with performance description, performance monitoring is a more detailed and more complete observation of performance over time that points out the direction and the development of performance. The multiple data observations collected through the monitoring process also serve the purpose of continuous analysis in understanding what may cause performance and how to improve performance.

The third set of performance analysis tools focus on exploring the causes of performance or underperformance. Tools to empirically detect and model the relationship between performance and performance causes are introduced. Knowing the causes of performance serves the ultimate goal of performance analysis—to improve performance—thus, the result of these analyses provides a foundation for developing policies, programs, and practices to improve performance.

The last set of tools covered in this book concern how to evaluate the impact of policies, programs, or practices that are designed to improve performance. These policies, programs, and practices are collectively called *performance enhancement initiatives* (PEI). This book covers the most important analytical and quantitative tools in identifying and examining the impact of an initiative.

Step 8: Writing a Performance Analysis Report

The analyst is often given significant latitude on what should be presented and how it should be presented in an analysis report. There are occasions where the analysis results are mainly for management's internal use, and no formal reporting is needed for other stakeholders such as legislators, board members, clients or customers, and the general public. In many other cases, however, the key results should be thoroughly presented in a formal report for all stakeholders. This section briefly discusses key elements of such a formal report. A detailed discussion of performance report writing and an example of a report are given in Chapter 14.

First, the report should consist of an accurate title with an executive summary, an introduction that briefly discusses purposes and importance of the analysis, a review of past studies on the same subject to devise a performance theory, a data collection section that explains performance measures used and the data collection process with a discussion of study instrument development, a results section on data analysis and the key findings, and conclusion and recommendations.

The executive summary should not exceed one page. It should start with a brief introduction of the issue and focus on presenting key findings and/or recommendations. The presentation should use straightforward language and avoid technical jargons; it should be written in a way that a layperson of very limited knowledge on management can understand. No discussion of the theory, the methodology, and the measures should be present in the summary.

The introduction should start with the performance issue, the importance of the issue, and the need for the analysis. It should also introduce the organization or the program being analyzed and its activities and operations. If performance enhancement initiatives have been made in the past to improve performance, this section should briefly introduce these efforts. The introduction section should end with the analysis questions.

A theory should be developed for the analysis designed to understand what causes performance (or underperformance). A theory should focus on the reasoning that links the performance causes to the performance. A theory is also important in an analysis that evaluates the impact of a performance improvement initiative in which the theory should elaborate the reasoning why the initiative may improve performance. If a mathematical modeling process is involved in the theory development, it should be placed in an appendix as optional reading.

The data collection section should be a short but lucid coverage on what data collection method is used, why this method (not other methods) is used, what measures are used and why they are used, how a sample is selected if a sample is used, and other data collection issues deemed to be important by the analyst. The methodological details such as the development of specific measures and the detail of data collection steps and processing can be placed in an appendix as optional reading.

The results section should be the focus of the report. The analytical or statistical tools used from which findings are drawn should be discussed briefly before findings are presented. Each significant finding should be presented clearly, accurately, and thoroughly. A logical presentation style is to start with a description of the performance status and trend, followed by (if necessary) an in-depth discussion and presentation of empirical findings on performance causes or on the impact of performance enhancement initiatives. Each empirical finding should be followed by a discussion on its meaning to performance management with a presentation of graphs and tables.

The conclusion and recommendation section summarizes key findings and presents recommendations for performance improvement. It should also identify the limitations of the analysis in methodology and measurement and discuss cautions for the findings when applied to practices.

Developing Organizational Capacities for Performance Analysis

You can always hire someone to do a one-time analysis on a specific performance issue. The difficulty is to incorporate the analysis into your daily management process and to institutionalize the analysis by fostering a culture of performance improvement. What does an organization need in a performance analysis? Why do some organizations fail to use performance analysis? The simple answer is the lack of organizational capacities for the analysis. *Organizational capacities* refer to an organization's possession of political, financial, technical, and cultural competencies to carry out a performance analysis regularly. Development of these capacities is necessary for the success of any performance analysis. This section examines these capacities and discusses the strategies to obtain them.

Political Support

The success of performance analysis requires continual and substantial commitment and support of the general public, elected officials, nonprofit board members, and other interest groups. These political stakeholders not only are the readers of performance analysis reports, but most importantly, they also are the sources of financial support. Either they directly pay for the analysis as taxpayers, or they decide on the funding for the analysis. Their continual support is the most important capacity in performance analysis.

Obstacles exist for obtaining political support. Elected officials and board members often have a short tenure, which makes it difficult to sustain their support over long term. It is not a secret that many performance analysis efforts are initiated by elected officials or nonprofit board members who seek performance improvement strategies and effective uses of the resources. Nonetheless, the departure of a key supportive stakeholder could leave the whole effort in shambles. New political leaders may have different agendas and persuade different initiatives.

Several strategies should be considered to obtain and to sustain political support. The key is to develop a consensus-building process to educate the stakeholders continuously on the value and the need of performance analysis. First, a strategic planning process allows stakeholders to realize the value of performance analysis in achieving an organization's strategic goals and missions. Efforts should be made to involve stakeholders in the strategic planning process and to engage them in using the results of performance analysis in the process. Second, *performance comparison* with other organizations, also known as *benchmarking*, can generate strong interests among stakeholders. Stakeholders are often very curious about how their organizational performance stacks up against others. So, performance comparison can be used to show stakeholders the value of performance analysis in order to gain their support. Third, an analysis on underperformance may allow stakeholders to see the direct benefit of the analysis by revealing the ways to improve performance. Many analyses can be designed to detect underperformance and to improve performance. However, it should be noted that performance analysis should be conducted objectively with careful and unbiased interpretation of performance analysis results. No attempt should be made to fit the results to the need of stakeholders' political agendas.

Financial Support

Stakeholders' political support must transform to sufficient funding for the analysis. Continuous and substantial financial resources should be allocated to hire qualified performance analysts, to develop information databases, and to train managers and employees to use analysis results. The start-up cost for performance analysis can be high because of these new needs to an organization, but the cost can be stabilized or even decreased over time once a performance analysis system is established.

The short-term strategies to enhance financial capacities include an accurate estimation of the cost for performance analysis, inclusion of a line item in budget for the analysis, and the continuous monitoring and assessing of the cost to make necessary budgetary adjustments based on the need of the analysis. In the long run, an understanding should be developed among stakeholders that the cost of performance analysis can be offset eventually by its benefit in performance improvement to an organization. Ideally, an estimate of the benefit as the result of performance analysis should be demonstrated.

Technical Support

A complete performance database, established practices of data management, clearly defined responsibilities of data managers, and frequent use of performance analysis results are all needed in performance analysis. A performance information system should be developed to store performance data with the proper computer hardware or statistical software. The system should be in electronic form and should include sufficient performance information and other information needed for performance analysis. The expectations for data managers' responsibilities to maintain and update the database should be made clear. The effective data management practices should be encouraged and institutionalized.

The strategies to enhance technical support include hiring technical staff and managers capable of developing a performance database and conducting performance analysis. It is also important to let employees understand the need of performance analysis and to request them to assist in the data collection effort. Training can be conducted to help employees understand the technical requirements of a performance analysis, such as different performance measures and performance analysis methods. To increase their willingness to assist or participate in an analysis, employees should be made aware that their individual performances are linked to their organization's performance, and they are accountable for what the organization does or achieves.

Cultural Support

The success of performance analysis also calls for the establishment of an organizational culture that fosters continuous performance improvement. Performance expectations should become a norm in each manager's job description. The communication among stakeholders should be carried on regularly, using the language of performance management. There should be a self-awareness among organization members to relate their individual performances to the overall organizational performance.

To obtain cultural capability of performance analysis, organization members should buy into the value of performance analysis. Leadership plays a pivotal role in advocating the value and use of performance analysis. Managers should act as change agents for an organization that experiences resistance to performance analysis. Workshops should be conducted to increase employees' awareness of performance analysis. Efforts should be made to eliminate the fear or misunderstanding among employees that performance analysis is used to punish them. Instead, performance analysis should be advocated and viewed as a tool to showcase effective practices in performance improvement. Constant feedback through performance analysis should be provided to employees to reinforce the message that their individual performances contribute to organizational performance and that there is an expectation for continual improvement of their individual performances.

Clearly, a successful performance analysis implementation depends on the acquisition of these political, financial, technical, and cultural capacities. Many of these strategies work interactively. The impact of one strategy is often related to the success of the others.

Developing Performance Measures

Numerous measures are available for use in performance analysis. For instance, police performance can be assessed by crime rates, response time to calls, the number of arrests, the number of calls for police services, the number of police patrols, and the number of patrol miles, or residents' satisfaction rates with the police. What measures do you use to measure police performance? The performance of a nonprofit agency that provides nurse services to school-age students can be measured by the number of clinic visits, the number of incidents, the number of students treated, or the percentage of students who are treated and go back to their classes. What measures do you want to measure the performance of the nonprofit agency?

Developing the right measures is a prerequisite for the success of an analysis. Wrong or improper measures lead to the information being useless or even detrimental for performance improvement. For many public and nonprofit agencies, selecting the right measures among many is one of most difficult tasks in performance analysis. This section discusses several key steps in developing proper performance measures.

Understanding the Measurement Objective

The very first step in developing performance measures is to determine what is being measured. Suppose you are asked to analyze the effectiveness of a nonprofit health care agency that provides medical services to the homeless with AIDS. What does the "effectiveness" mean? Does it mean that people receive services that were not provided to them before, they are healthier or happier, or services are provided with less cost? A *measurement objective* is simply the performance being measured. Is it the achievement of an organization's goal or mission, the improvement of the service delivery process, the satisfaction of service recipients, or the efficiency of using resources? Specifically in the above example, is it availability of health care services, improved health of service recipients, or high quality of services with less cost?

What is the measurement objective if you assess students' academic performances in a college class? It could be how much students learn in the class (learning outcome), how much efforts they have put into learning (learning efforts), how much they have enjoyed the learning process (student satisfaction), how effective they have learned with limited resources (learning effectiveness), and of course, it could be a combination of the above.

Adopting a Measurement Framework

The second step in measurement development is to adopt a measurement framework that further specifies the performance objective. The production process, described in Figure 1–1 of the last chapter (Inputs → Process → Outputs → Outcomes), is a basis for a measurement framework in Figure 2–1.

Figure 2–1

A Measurement Framework for the Production Process.

Input Measures ➡ Process Measures ➡ Output Measures ➡ Outcome Measures

Input measures assess the level of resource consumption. *Process (activity or workload) measures* delineate activities or workloads in the production process. *Output measures* evaluate the amount of product produced or the service provided in the production process, while *outcome measures* assess the impact of the product or the service on the desirable goal of the production process. In the above example of the nonprofit health care agency, you may determine that the effectiveness means whether service recipients become healthier, not how much the services cost or what processes and activities are involved in supplying the services. In other words, you are concerned about the outcome of the agency, not its process or output. Consequently, you should develop outcome measures.

Although the input–process–output–outcome measurement framework is popular, it is not the only framework to measure development. From the standpoint of how performance measurement information is collected, measures can be classified as those gathered from documented service records and those obtained from surveying service recipients. The former are often called *objective measures*, while the latter are known as *subjective measures*. The distinction between subjective and objective measures lies in whether the measure is based upon empirical observation, or, alternatively, whether the measure is based on beliefs, perceptions, or attitudes. Another popular measurement framework, the *balanced scorecard*, rooted in a logical model of production process and quality improvement in the private sector, classifies measures into measurement categories of employee learning and growth, production process, service recipients' satisfaction, and financial goals and achievement.

Developing Specific Performance Measures

Once you determine what performance is being measured and what measurement framework to use, you are ready to develop specific measures for the performance. Imagine that you need to assess student academic performance in a college class and the goal of the class is student learning, and you want to know how much students have learned and what factors affect the learning. The measurement objective, therefore, is student learning, and you need to develop specific measures to assess it. Assume that you decide to use the measurement framework of the production process (i.e., input measures–process measures–output measures–outcome measures). What specific measures do you use?

Defined above, an outcome assesses the goal achievement of a production process. Because student learning is the goal of the class, it is an outcome. Before measuring it, let us look at the input and the process leading to student learning. The input is the level of resources consumed in the class that includes time and money spent for study. You could use input measures such as the number of study hours by students, the cost of students to purchase course-related equipment and materials, and the cost for the university to offer the class. The measures of the study process may include the number of lecturing hours, the average number of student attendance in each class, and the average number of pages of reading completed by students. What are output and outcome measures of the class? Recall that, as stated in the last chapter, performance is outputs or outcomes, so performance measures are really just output or outcome measures, as well as their variants—efficiency or effectiveness measures.

Output Measures

Defined before, output is the amount of the product produced or the service provided in a production process. What is a product or a service of the class? Students need to work on assignments required in the class, so the completed assignments are a product of the class, and the percentage of students who have completed all required class assignments is an output measure. Students also need to participate in tests, so the completion of all required tests is a product of the class, and the percentage of students who complete tests required is an output measure.

Many public or nonprofit agencies provide services, not tangible products. For them, the service delivery process itself is (or is very close to) service output, so process measures can be used as output measures. For example, in a local police department, police patrolling is both a process and a product of policing. So the number of patrols is both a measure of the process and a measure of the output. Similarly, the percentage of students who have completed all required class assignments can be seen as both an output measure and a process measure of a class. This is why process and output measures are often used interchangeably in performance analysis.

Outcome Measures

Let us go back to the above example of student learning. What would be an outcome measure of the class? If outcome assesses the impact of a product or a service on the goal established for the production process, what measures should be used to assess the impact of the class on student learning? Arguably, if a student learns better, he or she should get a better grade. So student grade can be an outcome of the class and the percentage of students who complete the class with a passing grade in the class is an outcome measure of the class.

Here is another example. Would the number of crimes per 100,000 residents (the crime rate) be an outcome measure for a local police patrol unit that has a goal to improve public safety? Because an outcome measure must assess the impact of a production (service delivery) process on the achievement of the goal established for the product or service, you should ask "does the crime rate assess the accomplishment of the policing goal of public safety?" Apparently, a lower crime rate means a safer community, so crime rate *is* an outcome measure of the patrol unit. Similarly, the number of arrests by the patrol unit does not directly assess how well the goal of public safety is served (more or less arrests do not mean safer community), so it is *not* an outcome measure.

In some cases of performance analysis, it is useful to distinguish *ultimate outcomes* from *intermediate outcomes*. Ultimate outcomes reflect the long-term impact of the product or the service on the desirable goal, while intermediate outcomes concern the immediate results or achievement of the product or the service. In the case of college education, an ultimate outcome can be career advancement. Student grade is only an intermediate outcome that leads eventually to the ultimate outcome of career advancement. Possible measures of the ultimate outcome include the percentage of graduates who are promoted 5 years after graduation and the annual income growth of the graduates 5 years after graduation.

Efficiency and Effectiveness Measures

As stated in the last chapter, a student who spends 3 hours to complete an assignment is more efficient than a student who uses 4 hours to do so. The number of hours to complete an assignment is an efficiency measure that assesses the level of output (the completion of an assignment) for a given level of input (the number of study hours spent). Similarly, a university that educates 18 students by each faculty is more efficient than one that teaches 15 students per faculty. In this example, the number of students per faculty, commonly known as student–faculty ratio, is an efficiency measure that combines an output (the number of students educated) with an input (the number of faculty). As you can see from these examples, efficiency measures assess the level of output for a given level of input.

Obviously, the number of hours to complete an assignment says nothing about the quality of the assignment completed. The student–faculty ratio does not assess the quality of the students graduated. To evaluate the quality or the outcome of a product or service for a level of resources consumed, we will have to use effectiveness measures. Examples of effectiveness measures in the above examples would be the number of students who successfully complete their studies for each faculty or the number of hours spent for an assignment that receives an acceptable grade. An effectiveness measure combines an outcome and an input measure to assess a level of outcome for a given level of input.

Checking the Goodness of a Measure

Now you have developed a measure; how do you know the measure is good? Assume that you are a college algebra instructor and you are asked to measure student learning in your course. What measure do you use, and how do you know that the measure you use is good? There are a few criteria that can be used to judge if a measure is a good measure.

Measurement Validity

Let us say that you decide to use the attendance data as a measure of student learning. All those who have a perfect attendance record will get an A. Is this a good measure? It probably is not because attendance really does not reflect how much and how well a student learns the materials. Students with perfect attendance records may not read or do exercises or participate in other learning-related activities. Attendance really does not measure student learning. *Measurement validity* refers to the extent a measure assesses what it is supposed to assess. A valid measure of student learning gauges how much and how well a student learns the materials of a study subject.

Let us say that, instead of attendance, you decide to use testing results (the percentage of students who pass tests) to measure the learning outcome. Testing may be much more valid than attendance on student learning. Nonetheless, tests should have proper coverage to be a valid measure. If the instructor gives test questions that are not covered by course materials, the tests do not assess student learning of the materials. Consequently, test results are not a valid measure of student learning. Again, a valid measure has to assess how much and how well students learn the materials introduced in the course.

Measurement Reliability

Now assume that you like neither attendance nor testing in assessing student learning outcome. Instead, you come up with a creative idea of assessment in which you assign each student a grade based on your perception of his or her performance in your class. After all, you are the expert on the subject, and you like to use your authority. There are no tests and no assignments, just your feelings, perceptions, and observations about what and how well a student did in the class. What is wrong with this method of measuring student learning? A student's grade changes each time your perceptions about him or her change. Do these perceptions really reflect the level of learning? They probably do not. The student may act to study hard, sit in the front row to get your attention, and frequently ask questions. The student may visit your office more just to give you a good impression. So, the student's grade changes frequently, reflected in your subjective judgment, although the true level of the student's learning really does not change. A measurement is not reliable when it keeps yielding different results while applied to assess the same object. In the measurement literature, these different results are an estimate of measurement error. *Measurement reliability* assesses the level of measurement error. A reliable measure is free from the measurement error; it yields the same results while applied to assess the same object.

Let us look at another example of measurement reliability. Imagine you live in a community that has very few crimes, and you frequently survey residents to gauge their perceptions on public safety and use it to measure local police performance. A few times a year the community organizes events to attract tourists. After reviewing the survey results, you realize that citizens' concerns about safety are considerably higher during these tourist events even if the actual crime rates really do not change much. In fact, the citizen's perceptions of safety are affected by their observation of increased tourist volume and their perceptions that more tourists may bring more crimes, not whether or not crimes actually happen. Therefore, citizen perception on public safety is not a reliable measure of public safety and local police performance in this case.

Goal Relevance

Measurement validity and measurement reliability are the two most important criteria in selecting measures and judging their goodness. Another important criterion is goal relevance of a measure. As stated in the last chapter, this book largely looks into organizational outcomes. Because outcome measures address the goal achievement of a service or a product, a measure selected must assess the impact on an organization's goal. An organization's goal can be expressed at different levels of generality, using various terms and having various time frames. In this book, a *goal* refers to an abstract, formal, publicly supported statement that reflects an organization's long-term mission and expectations. In a local police department, for example, goals are often expressed as "prevention of criminal activity," "detection of criminal activity," "protection of residents and properties," "creation of a safe and comfortable living environment," or "serving residents' demands for safety." Because goals are generally abstract, they often need to be further specified by key result areas and objectives. A performance measure is goal related when it assesses at least one important aspect of the goal an organization serves. This measurement criterion is known as the *goal relevance of a measure*.

Measurement Affordability and Timeliness

A measure can be valid, reliable, and goal related but extremely costly to get. *Measurement affordability* refers to the cost of obtaining the data for the measure. A measure lacks affordability if it is costly to obtain the data. In general, existing data are more affordable than the data that should be newly collected. There are occasions when the data become available only after the time you need them. If you need the crime statistics every month, but they are collected every year, the measure is not timely. *Measurement timeliness* concerns if the data of a measure are collected timely and frequently enough to meet the need of an analysis. Even the best measure is useless if its data come too late.

Measurement Sensitivity

A measure should be sensitive to the change of performance. Imagine that you conduct a performance analysis for a program that educates adults at risk of obesity on nutrition consumption, and you decide on measuring their body mass index (BMI) change. After 2 months of the program, you find no change to their BMI, and you claim the program fails. What is the problem of your claim? Because it takes much longer than 2 months for any change of BMI to occur, you select a measure that is not sensitive to the program's performance. In this case, you are better off measuring participants' daily food consumptions because its change, if there is any, takes less time to observe. Similarly, response time probably is more sensitive to performance change of a local police department than citizen perception of safety. Students' grades are more difficult to improve than their study behaviors. *Measurement sensitivity* refers to how responsive a measure is to performance change. The short-term decision-making cycle in governments requires the selection of outcome measures sensitive to performance change or interventional activities of policies or programs. Realize that more sensitive measures may require more points of data observations. For example, for a local police department making efforts to improve response times, the collection of monthly response data makes sense because response time data are sensitive to the improvement efforts, while it is less useful to gather monthly data of the citizen satisfaction rating because citizen satisfaction is less sensitive to the efforts.

Measurement Controllability

An issue related to measurement sensitivity is whether the stakeholders of performance analysis have some control over the results of analysis. Say your analysis concludes that older students perform better academically in your class, but you are unable to do anything about this finding because you cannot control the age of the students. Nonetheless, if you also find that group study increases student performance, you can recommend group study as a performance enhancement strategy. Realize that performance analysis results are meaningful only to the extent that they can inform or assist stakeholders in decision making. Thus, an analysis should include measures whose impact can be influenced by decision making. This measurement selection criterion is known as *measurement controllability*. It should be considered in selecting measures of performance analysis in order to make the result of an analysis more meaningful for decision making.

Measurement Levels

Once a specific measure is determined, you should understand the precision of the measure in assessing the level of a performance. Let us say that you measure a person's age. There are two ways to do it. Instead of directly asking how old a person is, you can give the person a set of ranges to choose from: below 30 years, between 31 and 50 years, between 51 and 75 years, and above 75 years. Suppose you ask two persons. Steve is above 75 years, and John is between 51 and 75 years. You know that Steve is older than John, but you do not know exactly how much older Steve is than John. In the other way of measuring age, you ask them their years of birth so you know exactly how old they are. Say Steve is 80 years old, and John is 60 years. With this measure, not only do you know Steve is older than John but also he is 20 years older.

Let us look at another example. Assume you want to measure two students' (Lucy and Bill) academic performances in a college class. You use a letter grade system from A (excellent) to F (failed) for their performances. At the end of the semester, you assign a letter grade A (excellent) to Lucy and a B (very good) to Bill. Lucy knows she is doing better than Bill in the class. How much better? From A to B is one letter grade difference. But exactly how much difference is one letter grade? Lucy is unsure.

However, if your measurement is a scale system of 0 to 100 points with 0 as the lowest score and 100 as the highest score, and if Lucy gets 95 and Bill receives 85, Lucy knows that not only she is doing better but also she is 10 points better than Bill. Moreover, because that 10-point difference is 10% of the 100 maximum possible points, Lucy also knows that her performance is 10% better than Bill's performance.

Realize that a letter grade system detects the performance difference, but it does not tell the degree of the difference (i.e., how much difference). In the measurement literature, the letter grade is said to measure the performance at the ordinal level, and the letter grade is an *ordinal measure*. On the other hand, the 100-point scale measures both the performance difference and the degree of the difference. This measure is known as an *interval measure*. Clearly, an interval measure provides more information about a performance than an ordinal measure does.

The grades in the letter grade system and the numerical points in the 100-point scale system are called *response categories* (or *attributes*). Response categories are A, B, C, D, E, and F in the letter grade system and 0 to 100 in the 100-point scale system. For an ordinal measure, the orders of its response categories can be ranked (e.g., from low to high, from small to large, from young to old, or from bad to good), but the differences among the categories lack a clear meaning. For example, the difference between letter grades A and B is not clear. However, for an interval measure, not only the orders of its response categories can be ranked but also the differences among the categories have clear meanings about the degree of the performance difference. The 10-point difference between Lucy's and Bill's performance is a clear degree of performance difference.

As an exercise, what is the measurement level of a citizen satisfaction rating toward a service that has response categories of very dissatisfied, dissatisfied, satisfied, and very satisfied? Say that Citizen A is very satisfied about the service, and Citizen B is satisfied. Can you *rank-order* their responses (i.e., rank the orders of their response categories)? Sure you can. Citizen A is more satisfied than Citizen B. But, you do not know how much more Citizen A is satisfied than Citizen B. You cannot tell the degree of the satisfaction difference, so this measure is ordinal.

Interval or ordinal measures can detect performance differences, so they are proper measures of performance; however, there are rare cases when a measure is neither ordinal nor interval. Take the example of measuring a person's gender. The two response categories for the measure are female and male. Let us say that Pam is female, and Steven is male. Could you rank-order their responses? You cannot. It does *not* make sense to say that one is greater, higher, larger, or better than the other. Even if you assign numeric values, say 1 for female and 2 for male (Pam = 1 and Steven = 2), you still cannot rank-order the responses of gender. Whenever you have a measure whose response categories cannot be rank-ordered, it is a *nominal measure*. A measure of ethnicity with categories of White, Black, Hispanic, Asian, and Other is a nominal measure. A measure of political party affiliation with categories of democrat, republican, independent, and other is another example of a nominal measure.

Not many performance measures are nominal. Here are several examples. To measure the performance of a government's health and human service division's ability to provide the health insurance coverage, the coverage can be classified as private health insurances and public health insurances. Because it is difficult to judge which type of insurance, private or public, is better, you cannot really rank-order the response categories of the measure; therefore, it is a nominal measure. A local park and recreation department can ask residents whether or not they use local park facilities in order to assess the usage of these facilities. The measure has two categories: using the facilities and not using the facilities. Because it is difficult to rank-order the response categories (which one is better, using the facilities or not using the facilities?), this is a nominal measure.

In sum, an interval measure rank-orders response categories and provides meaningful interpretations on the differences among categories. An ordinal measure rank-orders response categories but does not provide the meaningful information on the difference among categories. A nominal measure does not rank-order response categories. In the spectrum of measurement levels, a nominal measure provides the least information, while an interval measure provides the richest information about the degree of performance differences. An ordinal measure is in the middle. Nominal and ordinal measures are also known as *categorical measures*.

Practices

Key Terms

Performance analysis process
Analysis of stakeholder interests
Right and answerable performance analysis questions
Plausibility of the causality
Hypothesis

Rejectability of hypothesis
Specific and quantifiable performance measures (indicators)
Empirical observation
Data collection methods
Conducting surveys
Conducting interviews
Searching archives
Creating an experiment
Performance interventions
Survey instrument
Interview protocol
Protocol for archive search
Obtaining, entering, and cleaning data
Data entry codebook
Data inventory analysis
Organizational capacities for performance analysis
Political support
Financial support
Technical support
Cultural support
Measurement objective
Measurement framework of an organizational production process
Input measures
Process (activity or workload) measures
Output measures
Outcome measures
Subjective measures
Objective measures
Balanced scorecard measurement framework
Ultimate outcomes
Intermediate outcomes
Efficiency measures
Effectiveness measures
Measurement validity
Measurement reliability
Goal relevance
Measurement affordability
Measurement timeliness
Measurement sensitivity
Measurement controllability
Measurement levels
Ordinal measures
Interval measures
Nominal measures

Response categories (attributes)
Categorical measures

Practice Problem 2–1

Identify a performance issue at your work or school or in your personal life. Examples include signs of unhappy customers, high turnover of employees, tardiness of services, frequent errors in operations, poor school grade, and no or slow response to service requests. Practice all eight steps in a performance analysis, with particular attention to the first four steps: understanding the issue, starting with the right questions, developing a performance theory (if applicable), and developing performance measures.

Practice Problem 2–2

An example is given in the text to measure student learning. Use the measurement framework of an organization's production process to assess the performance of a graduate program (preferably a Master of Public Administration program).

1. Use the program's mission or goals to develop the measurement objective.
2. Develop specific input, output, and outcome measures for the program.
3. Assess the goodness of each measure developed.
4. Determine the measurement level of each measure developed.

Practice Problem 2–3

In an example in the text, I demonstrate how a student's grade based on testing could be an invalid measure of student learning when the materials learned are not covered in the tests. Could you think of any other conditions when a student's grade becomes an invalid measure of student learning?

Practice Problem 2–4

What are measurement levels of the following measures?

1. Response time of medical emergency response units (in seconds)
2. Annual income of a resident surveyed (in dollars)
3. Number of crimes per 100,000 residents in cities
4. Percentage of participants successfully completing an alcohol treatment program
5. Individual citizen's satisfaction ratings on municipal services (response categories: satisfied, neutral, not satisfied)
6. Percentage of citizens rating municipal service excellent or very good
7. Individual worker's ratings on the overall quality of the services provided by a job training program (response categories: excellent, good, fair, poor)
8. Number of workers trained

9. Educational attainment of individuals surveyed (response categories: graduate school, college, high school, middle school, elementary school)
10. Number of years completed in school (i.e., 0, 1, 2, 3, 4, 5 . . .)
11. The mode of transportation to work (i.e., personal car, car pool, bus, motorcycle, bike, others)
12. Amount of donation to nonprofit agencies (in dollars)

Section II
Describing Performance

CHAPTER 3

Describing Performance Shape

I magine you have just come from a basketball game, and your favorite team has won. "How did your team do?" your friend asks. You could say, "They won," or "They won, but it was a very close game," or "They won by 5 points, but the other team hung in there until the last minute of the game." Realize that you are describing the performance of your team. Describing an organization's performance is like describing the outcome of a game. You try to give people an idea of what has happened.

Two criteria are important in performance description. First, you should provide the *complete* information on performance. Because you want your friends to completely understand the outcome of the game, you should try to feed them with ample information about the game. A simple description, "They won," may not be enough. "They won by 5 points" is a better description because it contains more information about the outcome. So the first rule for performance description is to always try to provide more information.

Second, more importantly, you should try to provide the *meaningful* information—the information that helps your friends understand the outcome of the game. "Won by 5 points" probably does not mean much to a person who has no idea that a basketball game can reach as many as 100 points. So it is better if you say "The scores of the game are, say, 100 and 95, and my team won by 5." By saying that, you provide the meaningful information for your friend to understand that it is a close win. *Meaningfulness* in performance description is key for people to understand performance information.

You should always try to describe two aspects of performance. If someone asks you how you (or your children) are doing in school, you can tell them your grades in comparison with your classmates' grades. This is a description of your performance status at a specific time, also known as the *description of performance shape*. You can also talk about how much progress you have made in school by demonstrating the change of your grades over time. This is the *description of performance trend*. This chapter introduces tools to describe performance shape, and the next chapter presents tools of demonstrating performance trend.

Tabular and Graphical Description of Performance

Frequency, Percentage, and Cumulative Percentage of Performance

Table 3–1 shows the monthly number of citizen complaints for the past 24 months in a city's public utility department that provides water and sewer services.

Table 3–1

Monthly Number of Citizen Complaints in a Public Utility Department

20, 25, 23, 17, 26, 26, 22, 33, 31, 19, 29, 13,
23, 25, 26, 26, 25, 28, 28, 33, 14, 31, 21, 24

Table 3–2

Processed Data of Citizen Complaints

Number of complaints	Frequency	Percentage	Cumulative percentage
0 to 20	5	20.8%	20.8%
21 to 25	8	33.3%	54.2% (20.8% + 33.3%)
26 to 30	7	29.2%	83.3% (54.2% + 29.2%)
More than 30	4	16.7%	100.0% (83.3% + 16.7%)
Total	24	100.0%	

What can you say about the performance of the department with just a cursory preview of these data? You should notice that citizen complaints in some months were apparently more than others; 13 is the least and 33 is the largest number of monthly complaints. Beyond that, there is very little you can tell from the data. The truth is that the presentation of the data in its original form provides little meaningful information about performance. Data in the original form are also called *performance raw data*. They are recorded with no or very limited treatment in data processing. Raw data have to be processed thoroughly to obtain meaningful information. In fact, the purpose of performance description is to turn raw data into meaningful explanations.

How do you extract meaningful information from data in Table 3–1? I did a little processing of the data; the result is shown in Table 3–2. Notice that I develop a few *performance ranges* for the number of complaints (i.e., 0 to 20, 21 to 25, 26 to 30, and more than 30), then calculate the number of complaints in each range, also known as *frequency*, and their percentages. I also add up the percentages in each category to arrive at the *cumulative percentage*. For example, there are 5 months when there are citizen complaints equal to or less than 20 times, which is 5/24 = 20.8%.

With the processed data, we have much more to say about the performance of the department. For example, for one-third of the time in the past 2 years (8/24 = 33.3%), the department received citizen complaints between 21 and 25 times a month. The number of monthly complaints was equal to or less than 25 times for most of the time (13 of 24 months or 54.2%). The number of complaints was equal to or exceeded 31 times per month for less than one-sixth (16.7%) of the time. The complaints never exceeded 33 times a month.

We now have a better idea about the performance of the department. Let us now look at what I did. I first determine a few performance ranges in which I can place the citizen complaint numbers accordingly. In this case, the performance ranges are 0 to 20, 21 to 25, 26 to 30, and more than 30. Each range has a lower bound and an upper bound. How are these boundaries determined? There are a few things to keep in mind when you determine performance ranges.

First, you need to have some ideas about the *expected performance targets*. What performance do you expect to see? If you believe you should be warned once the number of citizen complaints exceeds 25 times per month, 25 should be used in determining a performance range. These expected performance targets are also called *performance standards* or *performance benchmarks*. Some of the popular performance targets are used in judging performance in emergency response times, crime statistics, or citizen satisfaction rates. For example, some emergency responders establish the expected response time in the range of 4 to 6 minutes for medical emergencies. Some governments use an 80% citizen satisfaction rate as the performance standard for their services. Any rating lower than that is considered unacceptable.

Also, you can look at the best performance and the worst performance in the raw data to determine boundaries of the range. That is the reason we use 20 as the lower boundary of the performance range and 31 as the upper boundary of the range for the data in Table 3–1, because only a few cases are less than 20 or greater than 31.

Finally, the zero-frequency range should be avoided. There should be no performance range where the frequency of performance is zero. This is because such a range provides little meaningful information about the performance. An example of a zero-frequency range is a 0 to 10 range for the data in Table 3–1.

Microsoft Office Excel

This book uses Microsoft Office Excel in calculations and graphic presentations. The book assumes you have basic knowledge about Excel, which is very popular and easy to use. If you are not comfortable with it, go to Microsoft Office's Web site to take a tutorial or read an introductory guide to the software. You should be ready in no time. All Excel calculations in this book are conducted with either the Data Analysis ToolPak or the Insert Function (f_x) button. Although Excel examples in this book are prepared with Excel 2007, this version has very little difference from Excel 2003 on the Data Analysis and the Insert Function, so the instructions in this book apply to Excel 2003 users as well.

You should be able to easily locate the Insert Function button, labeled with symbol f_x, next to the Formula Bar in an Excel sheet. If your Excel sheet does not show it, click the **View** tab, and check the **Formula Bar** button in the **Show/Hide** group. You should also find it in the **Function Library** group on the **Formulas** tab. For Excel 2003 users who cannot find it in an Excel sheet, click the **Function** button on the **Insert** tab.

To use the Data Analysis ToolPak, you need to load it first. To load it in Excel 2007:

1. Click the **Microsoft Office Button**, often located at the upper left corner of your Excel sheet.
2. Click **Excel Options**.

3. Click **Add-Ins** and select **Excel Add-Ins** in the **Manage** box. Click **Go**.
4. Select the **Analysis ToolPak** check box in the **Add-Ins Available** box, and click **OK**. In case that Analysis ToolPak is not listed in the Add-Ins Available box, click **Browse** to locate it. After you load the Analysis ToolPak, the **Data Analysis** command is available in the **Analysis** group on the **Data** tab.

To load the Analysis ToolPak in Excel 2003:

1. Click **Add-Ins** on the **Tools** menu.
2. Select the check box next to **Analysis ToolPak** in the **Add-Ins Available** box, then click **OK**. If the ToolPak is not listed, click **Browse** to locate it. You may see a message that says that Analysis ToolPak is not currently installed on your computer and asks you to install it. After you load the Analysis ToolPak, the **Data Analysis** command is available on the **Tool** menu.

The Excel Data Analysis Histogram Procedure

To use Excel, you need to open a new Excel sheet. Notice that a sheet is designed for data input in columns and rows. Columns are named by letter; rows are named by number. A particular cell can be located by using a letter and a number such as A1, B2, etc. Let us use the data in Table 3–1 to illustrate how to get frequency and percentage statistics from Excel:

1. Input the revenue data in Column A as shown in Excel Screen 3–1.
2. Click the **Data Analysis** command in the **Analysis Group** on the **Data** tab if you use Excel 2007. If you use Excel 2003, click **Data Analysis** in the **Tool** menu.
3. Select **Histogram** in the **Data Analysis** window.
4. Select the number of complaints in the **Input Range** (i.e., $A$1:$A$25).
5. Determine your performance range and enter it in the **Bin Range**. In Excel, *Bin* is the place to define the performance ranges. You need to enter the upper bound, not the lower bound, of the range because Excel interprets the upper bound of a range as the lower bound of the next range. The performance ranges are shown in column B of Excel Screen 3–1.
6. Select an **Output Range** that does not overlap with the data. If you want your results in a new worksheet, select **New Worksheet Ply** instead of **Output Range**.
7. Click **Label** box. This allows you to show the title of your output. (Important: If you do not select the title cells, A1 and B1 in this case, in the **Input Range** and **Bin Range**, then you do not want to check the **Label** box).
8. Select **Cumulative Percentage** and **Chart Output**.
9. Click **OK**. You should see the output as shown in Excel Screen 3–1.

Excel calculates the frequency and cumulative percentages of the performance ranges. It also presents a *histogram* that graphically demonstrates the percentage of each performance range. However, if you want to see the percentage of each performance range as shown in the last column of the frequency table in Screen 3–1, you need to calculate them yourself with Excel. For example, the percentage in the 0 to 20 range is 5/24 = 20.83%. Because 5 is in B28, we want the percentage in D28. Place the cursor in D28, then type = *B28/24* and hit the **Enter**

Screen 3–1

The Histogram Procedure: Citizen Complaint Data.

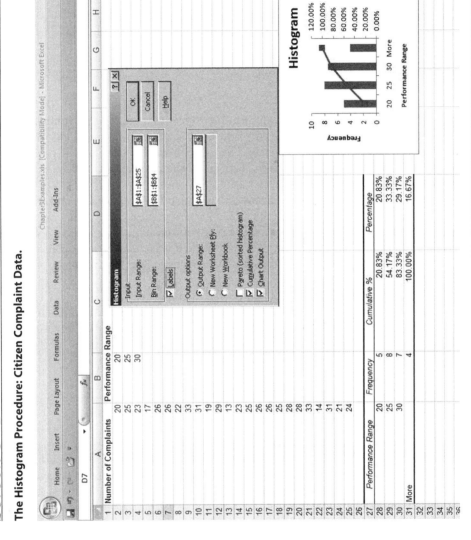

Table 3–3

Satisfactions of 20 Residents

(3 = very satisfied, 2 = satisfied, 1 = dissatisfied)
3, 2, 3, 2, 2, 1, 3, 3, 1, 3, 1, 2, 1, 1, 3, 3, 2, 2, 2, 3

key. You should get 20.83% in D28. Notice that the equal (=) sign is required for the numerical calculation.

To convert cell D28 (0.2083) to the percentage format (20.83%) in Excel 2007, place the cursor in D28. Click the **Home** tab and select the **Percentage** (%) in the **Number** group. If you use Excel 2003, after placing the cursor in D28, select **Format** and **Cells**, then choose **Percentage** on the **Number** tab. You can use the same method to calculate the percentages of the other three performance ranges, or you can make the calculation a little easier by using Autofilling, introduced later in this chapter.

Let us look at another example. Citizens' surveys are often used to gauge citizens' satisfaction for services, and survey results can be used to assess performances of an organization. In an example of a citizen survey of police services, 20 citizens are asked whether they are very satisfied, satisfied, or dissatisfied with police services. Realize that these response categories (very satisfied, satisfied, dissatisfied) are performance ranges. The satisfaction responses of 20 residents are presented in Table 3–3.

The results are presented in Excel Screen 3–2. It shows that 25% of survey respondents are dissatisfied with police services, compared with 35% who are satisfied, and 40% who are very satisfied. Of the respondents, 75% (35% + 40%) are either satisfied or very satisfied with police services.

Numerical Description of Performance

The Average Performance

Assume you are a high school math teacher, and there are 5 students in your class. In a recent test, they score 50, 60, 70, 80, and 90 on a 100-point scale. If you are asked to use one figure to present the performance of the class, what would that be? You would probably average these numbers to get 70.00 [(50 + 60 + 70 + 80 + 90)/5]. This number, known as the *mean* in statistics, is the arithmetic average of a series of numbers. If $\bar{Y}$ is the mean, N is *the number of cases* or observations, and Y_1, Y_2, Y_3 ... Y_n are *individual cases* from 1 to N, then

$$\bar{Y} = \frac{(Y_1 + Y_2 + Y_3 \ldots Y_n)}{N} = \frac{\sum Y_i}{N}.$$

The summation symbol, Σ, indicates all elements should be added together. The mean is a popular measure in performance analysis. It is particularly useful when you use a single number to represent a group of numbers and when you conduct performance comparison.

Screen 3–2

The Histogram Procedure: Citizen Satisfaction Data.

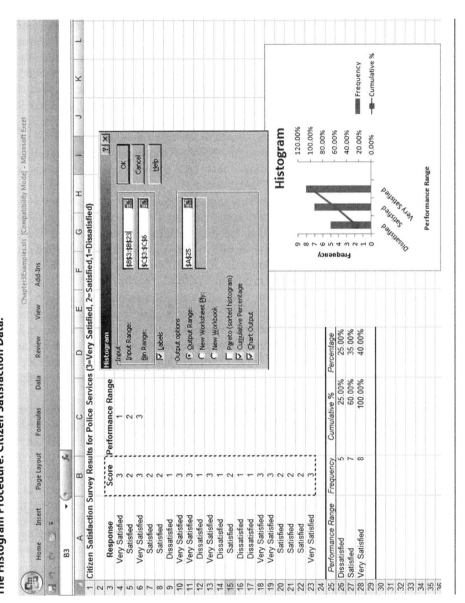

Imagine you teach a second math class now, and you want to know which class performs better. You can give the second class the same test that you gave to the first class, average students' scores, and compare the result with the 70.0 points from the first class.

Nonetheless, the mean has a few limitations in performance data presentation. First, it is applicable to interval measures but not to nominal measures. It applies to ordinal measures only if their response categories are well defined and quantified and if these categories have equal ranges. For example, let us say you conduct a citizen survey on police performance, and you ask respondents whether they are satisfied with the performance of their local police services. You use very satisfied, satisfied, neutral, not satisfied, and not satisfied at all to categorize their responses. To use the mean for this ordinal measure, you can assign a numerical value to each of the five categories in the following order: very satisfied = 5, satisfied = 4, neutral = 3, not satisfied = 2, not satisfied at all = 1.

Suppose that you survey 5 residents, and they give the responses found in Table 3–4. With the numerical value assigned to each of the responses, you have a series of values 5, 5, 3, 1, and 2. The mean is 3.2 [(5 + 5 + 3 + 1 + 2)/5]. What does that mean? It indicates that the average residential assessment is between satisfied (4) and neutral (3). This calculation of the mean is done with an assumption that the response categories have equal ranges when numerical values are assigned. It is assumed that, for instance, a resident's intensity of satisfaction from satisfied to very satisfied is equal to that from neutral to satisfied. As another example, the response categories of the age measured with young (below 25 years old), middle age (26 to 66 years), and mature (above 66 years) have unequal ranges because the age difference in the young category (25 − 0 = 25) is different from that in the middle-age category (66 − 26 = 40) and the mature category. Therefore, the mean does not apply to this ordinal measure of age.

Another limitation of the mean is that it is often biased to represent data with extreme values. Assume that you want to look into the performance of a fire and rescue unit in your city. The unit got 6 calls last week, and the response times in chronological order were 2.0, 1.0, 2.0, 5.0, 20.0, and 4.0 minutes. The 20-minutes response was for a trip to a remote area. The mean of the response times is 5.7 minutes. Is this an accurate representation of the performance? Realize that all but one response are less than 5.7 minutes. The mean is largely skewed by the 20-minute trip; it misrepresents the overall performance of the unit. In

Table 3–4

Satisfactions of Five Residents

Residents	Response
Resident A	Very satisfied
Resident B	Very satisfied
Resident C	Neutral
Resident D	Not satisfied at all
Resident E	Not satisfied

performance analysis, this 20-minutes case is known as a *performance outlier*. The mean may not be an accurate representation of performance data that have outliers. This point is particularly true when the number of cases is small.

The Middle Performance

If the mean is not accurate, what do you use? In the above response time example, you can choose the value in the middle. Let us say that you rank these values in an ascending order to get: 1.0, 2.0, 2.0, 4.0, 5.0, and 20.0. There are 6 numbers in this series. The number in the middle is between the third number (2.0) and the fourth number (4.0). The average of these 2 figures is 3.0 [(2.0 + 4.0)/2].

The *median* falls in the middle of an ordered series of numbers in a fashion where half of the numbers are smaller, and the other half are greater than it. When we have an odd number of cases in the data, the median is the number right in the middle. For example, if we only used the first 5 cases in the fire response time example (i.e., 1.0, 2.0, 2.0, 4.0, and 5.0), the median would be 2.0. If we have an even number of cases in the data, the median is the midpoint between the 2 middle cases (i.e., the average of these 2 middle cases).

The median is more appropriate when the mean is highly skewed by performance outliers. Clearly, the median of 3.0 minutes is more accurate than the mean of 5.7 minutes to represent the performance of the fire fighters in our example. Nonetheless, the median also has a few limitations in data presentation. First, it does not apply to nominal measures. It does not make sense to calculate the median for measures such as gender or race. Second, the calculation of the median excludes performance outliers, but outliers may contain the important information that deserves close examination. For example, the 20-minute trip in the above example may indicate a need to improve the response time in the remote area by mapping it out more carefully. Sometimes, performance analysts conduct *analysis of performance outliers* to exclusively focus on extreme performances.

The Typical Performance

In the response time example, what is a typical performance for the unit? Realize that, among the response times, only 2.0 minutes occurs twice. The rest happen only once. So, it is reasonable to say that a 2.0-minute response time is a more typical representation of the performance than the others. The value that occurs most frequently in a data series is called the *mode*.

One good thing about the mode is that it applies to all interval, ordinal, or nominal measures. Let us look at the case in Table 3–5. Residents' insurance types are used to assess the performance of the public health department in a city. The insurance types are insured with public insurance plans (Medicare or Medicaid), insured with private insurance plans, insured with both, or uninsured. The city collects the data from clinic visits this year, found in Table 3–5.

Even if you are able to assign numerical values to response categories, it does not make sense to calculate the average for the data. For instance, if you assigned 1 to 4 to the 4 categories in Table 3–5, you would have an average of 1.34, which contains no meaningful interpretation of the performance. The median is not much useful either. You will find that the middle

Table 3–5

Insurance Statuses of Clinic Visitors

	This year
Visitors with public insurances	324,458
Visitors with private insurances	421,673
Visitors with both	12,045
Visitors without insurance	17,211

is in the category of visitors with private insurance. It really does not make any sense unless you can rank these categories in order. So the mean and the median do not provide much information on the performance of the department. The mode is the only meaningful and useful measure in this case. It is visits with private insurances, which means that the most frequent visitors to clinics have private insurances.

The Excel Data Analysis Descriptive Statistics Procedure

Excel makes it very easy to calculate and present the mean, the median, and the mode. You can use either the Insert Function (f_x) or the Descriptive procedure in the Data Analysis ToolPak. While this chapter covers the Data Analysis ToolPak, Chapter 5 introduces the use of the Insert Function exclusively. Let us use the above response time example in illustration.

1. Input response time data in Column A in a new Excel sheet, as shown in Screen 3–3.
2. Click the **Data Analysis** command in the **Analysis Group** on the **Data** tab if you use Excel 2007. If you use Excel 2003, click **Data Analysis** in the **Tool** menu.
3. Select **Descriptive Statistics** in the **Data Analysis** window.
4. Select the data in A1 to A7 of Response Time in the **Input Range** (i.e., $A$1:$A$7).
5. Click the **Label in First Row** box to show Response Time as the title of your output.
6. Select an **Output Range** that does not overlap with the data ($A$11 in this example). If you want your results in a new worksheet, select **New Worksheet Ply** instead of **Output Range**.
7. Select **Summary Statistics**.
8. Click **OK**. The results are shown in Screen 3–3. Notice that the mean, the median, and the mode are highlighted for your convenience of reading.

Some Important Excel Procedures

Though Excel is not new to many people, it is important to take some time here to learn or to refresh several very important Excel procedures that will surely save you time later.

Screen 3–3

The Descriptive Statistics Procedure: Response Times.

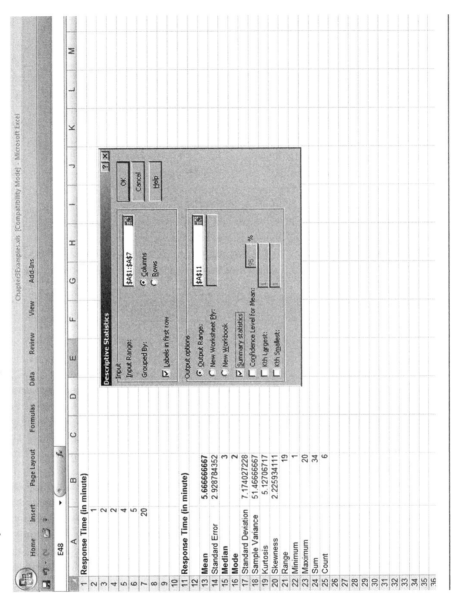

Formulas and Autofilling

Screen 3–4 shows the number of traffic accidents in an urban city in the past 3 years. What is the total number of accidents each year, and what is the grand total of all 3 years? One very useful Excel procedure is the formulas. If you want to create a formula to calculate the total number of accidents this year, one way is to enter = *B2 + C2 + D2* into **cell E2**. Recall that a formula starts with the equal sign (=). Press **Enter**, and the total appears in E2.

To put that formula into cells E3 through E5, you can position the cursor on the lower-right corner of E2 until the cursor changes to a plus sign (+). Hold down the left mouse button and drag the mouse through the cells. The plus sign is called the *cell's fill handle*. When you complete dragging, release the mouse button, and the row totals appear. This procedure is called *Autofilling*. It saves you a lot of time because you do not have to reenter the formula multiple times.

Similarly, the way to create the formula that sums up the numbers in the first column (fatal accidents) is to enter = *B2 + B3 +B4* into **cell B5**. Position the cursor on B5's fill handle, drag through row 5, and release in column E; you autofill the totals into C5 to E5.

Another way of autofilling is to Copy and Paste. In the above example of autofilling row totals, move your cursor to E2, which now is = B2 + C2 + D2. Right-click your mouse; you should see a Copy symbol. **Click** the symbol, then position the cursor in E3, hold down the mouse button, and drag down through column E. Release the mouse in row 5 to select cells E3 through E5. Right-click the mouse to select the **Paste**. You can use the same method to autofill the column totals.

Referencing

Another important Excel procedure is Referencing. Realize that each autofilled formula is different from the original one. In cell E2, the formula is = B2 + C2 + D2. In cell E3, it is = B3 + C3 + D3. In cell E4, it is = B4 + C4 + D4. Excel adjusts the formula accordingly and automatically when you autofill from row 2 to row 3 and row 4. You do not need to change the formula yourself. This is called *relative referencing*. The formula gets adjusted relative to where it is originated.

Relative referencing saves you a lot of time, but it has a drawback. Let us say that you want to know each row total's proportion of the grand total (73 in E5); you create a formula (= E2/E5) in F2. Now, if you position the cursor on the fill handler and drag through column F and release in F5, you will see cells F3 to F5 filled with invalid "#/DIV/0" (a number divided by 0), as shown in Screen 3–5.

This occurs because of relative referencing. For example, in cell F3, you expect to see = E3/E5. Instead, relative referencing makes it = E4/E6. Because there is no value in E6, it results in an invalid number. To avoid this, you need to use *absolute referencing* in which you fix the E5 by placing dollar signs ($) in F2 as = E2/$E$5. Now, you can position the cursor on the fill handler, drag through column F, and release in F5 to obtain correct proportions.

A Case Study

The Health and Human Service Department in the city of Karlton (population 320,000) houses a medical emergency division (MED) that provides emergency medical service (EMS) to

Screen 3–4

Number of Accidents in Urban City (per 1000 populations).

	A	B	C	D	E	F
1		Fatal	Serious Non-fatal	No Serious	Total	Porportion
2	This year	3	6	12		
3	Last year	4	7	15		
4	Two years ago	3	10	13		
5	Total					

Screen 3–5

Excel Referencing.

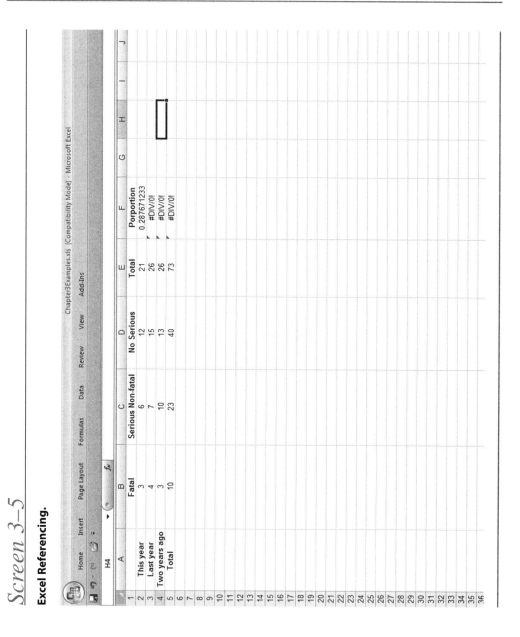

	A	B	C	D	E	F
1		Fatal	Serious Non-fatal	No Serious	Total	Porportion
2	This year	3	6	12	21	0.28767123
3	Last year	4	7	15	26	#DIV/0!
4	Two years ago	3	10	13	26	#DIV/0!
5	Total	10	23	40	73	#DIV/0!

residents. The city also has a fire department that provides fire protection and rescue services. The fire department is managed separately from MED.

An emergency medical incident begins when a person or bystander recognizes that emergency medical care is needed. To access the EMS system, people need to call 911. Police department dispatchers answer 911 calls. From the information provided by the caller, the dispatcher determines what type of emergency service is needed—police, fire, or medical. The dispatcher then initiates a police response or transfers the call to the fire department for fire emergencies or to MED for medical emergencies. Once MED receives the call, a paramedic confirms the address to dispatch an ambulance, asks a series of questions set by the medical protocol to determine the nature and severity of the problem, and may provide instructions to the caller on what to do before help arrives. For life-threatening incidents or incidents where special equipment or expertise is required, MED notifies the fire department to respond as first responders. The steps of conducting a performance analysis are first introduced in Chapter 2. This case study illustrates these steps in a performance analysis in MED.

Step 1: Understanding the Issue

The city sets a response time standard of at least 80% of responses within 8 minutes for medical emergencies. The response time is from the moment of receipt of a 911 call to the time an ambulance reports the arrival at the scene. MED prepares quarterly response time reports to the city manager's office.

Recently, a local television crew reported 2 cases of death that might be caused by slow responses of the city's medical services. Also, the city received a number of calls from residents complaining about slow response times for medical services. In a recent city commission meeting, the commissioner also raised the issue of the slow responses and asked the city manager to investigate. The city manager noticed that 90% of the citizens in a recent survey were happy with the emergency medical services, and this satisfaction rate was consistent with results of previous surveys. So the city manager was unsure about the level and prevalence of the slow response times. The manager suspected that a few isolated cases got extensive TV coverage, which makes the city look worse than it really is. Tracey Riley is a management analyst for the city. The city manager asked Tracey to conduct a performance analysis to find out the recent performance of MED.

Tracey understands that objectives of the analysis include performance description, performance monitoring, performance understanding, and performance evaluation. Her conversations with the commissioner and the city manager indicated that they wanted to know the performance shape of MED in response time, so the objective of this analysis is a performance description.

Step 2: Asking Questions in the Performance Analysis

An important step in performance analysis is to ask the right and answerable questions that guide the analysis process. It is apparent that the stakeholders (i.e., residents, media, commissioner, and city manager) are interested in whether there is a deteriorating performance of MED services. So Tracey asks the following questions: How has MED performed recently? Has there been a deterioration of response time in MED?

Step 3: Contemplating a Performance Theory

One step in performance analysis, introduced in Chapter 2, is to develop a performance theory. A theory is very important in performance understanding when the objective is to discover the causes of underperformance or in performance evaluation when the objective is to explain why a performance enhancement initiative should work. Because the analysis objective in this case is to simply describe the performance shape, there is no need to develop a performance theory. However, Tracey understands that, if a deteriorated response time is discovered in this analysis, she will need to provide some theoretical explanations on the possible causes.

Step 4: Determining Performance Measures and Collecting Performance Data

The city collects several performance measures for EMS. In addition to the above mentioned survey results and the response time, it also gathers information on the number of medical runs, the percentage of complaints responded to within 30 days, and the number of defibrillation saves. Because the stakeholders are clearly concerned about slow responses, Tracey decided to focus on the response time with an understanding that she may need other measures in the future for a complete picture of the MED performance.

The response time consists of answer speed, talk time, and dispatch time. Answer speed is the time from the receipt of a 911 call to the moment a police department dispatcher picks it up. Talk time is the time the dispatcher uses to take the call. Dispatch time is the period from the dispatch of the medical crew to the arrival at the scene. Tracey gathered the following raw data for the response time of emergency calls for the medical services. Table 3–6 shows the response times to 94 medical emergency calls during January of the year when the incidents on TV occurred. The data are presented in the form commonly known as the *stem and leaf plot* in which the stem is the response time range, and the leaf is the response times in seconds. The stem and leaf plot is a useful presentation tool for interval and ordinal data.

Step 5: Analyzing the Performance

MED has used a few performance standards to evaluate its response time. In addition to the above mentioned standard that at least 80% of responses are within 8 minutes for medical emergencies, it also requires that more than 50% of responses are within 6 minutes. Excel histogram results from Screen 3–6 show that 84.0% (79 of 94) of responses were less than the 8 minutes, 59.6% (56 of 94) responses were less than 6 minutes, and 25.5% (24 of 94) of responses were less than 4 minutes. Also, 32/94 = 34.0% of responses were within the 4 to 6 minute range.

The Excel Descriptive Results in Screen 3–6 show that the mean of the response times in January was 332 seconds or 5.5 minutes. The median was 322 minutes or 5.4 minutes, where half of the responses took more time, and the other half took less. The most frequent occurring response was 280 seconds or 4.7 minutes; it happened 3 times.

Table 3–6

Response Times to Calls for EMS in January

Response time range	Response times (in seconds)
Less than 30 seconds	
30–60 seconds	56
61–90 seconds	80
91–120 seconds	110
121–150 seconds	123, 144
151–180 seconds	154, 159, 167, 173, 175, 178
181–210 seconds	185, 189, 193, 199, 200, 204
211–240 seconds	213, 218, 220, 230, 235, 235, 239
241–270 seconds	241, 245, 245, 247, 250, 253, 270
271–300 seconds	275, 278, 280, 280, 280, 290, 290, 293, 294, 295, 297
301–330 seconds	303, 309, 310, 311, 320, 324, 327
331–360 seconds	332, 339, 341, 345, 347, 353, 358
361–390 seconds	367, 369, 374, 379, 386, 389, 389
391–420 seconds	393, 395, 397, 411, 416, 417
421–450 seconds	423, 423, 437, 443, 447
451–480 seconds	453, 455, 467, 469, 478
481–510 seconds	486, 489, 491, 493, 501
511–540 seconds	512, 516, 517, 520, 523
541–570 seconds	543, 543, 546
571–600 seconds	577, 582
More than 600 seconds	

Step 6: Drawing Conclusions in a Performance Report

MED uses 2 performance targets to evaluate its performance. The performance analysis results show that MED meets the performance standard that at least 80% of responses are within 8 minutes for medical emergencies. In fact, 84.0% of trips had response times less than 8.0 minutes. MED also meets the second standard, which requires 50% of trips have response times less than 6.0 minutes; 59.6% of trips had a response time less than 6.0 minutes.

Both MED performance standards were met. So Tracey concludes in her report that the performance of MED has not deteriorated, and the response time of MED is in an acceptable range of performance standards. Nonetheless, Tracey also indicates that her conclusion is based on the data in a single month, and the continuous monitoring of the response time is needed.

Screen 3–6

Histogram and Descriptive Procedures: The EMS Case.

	A	B	C	D	E	F	G	H
	Response time (in second)	Performance Range (in second)						
2	56	240						
3	80	360						
4	110	480						
5	123							
6	144							
7	154	*Performance Range (in second)*	*Frequency*	*Cumulative %*				
8	159	240	24	25.53%				
9	167	360	32	59.57%				
10	173	480	23	84.04%				
11	175	More	15	100.00%				
12	178							
13	185							
14	189	**Descriptive Statistics**						
15	193							
16	199	Mean	332.0957447					
17	200	Standard Error	12.84925775					
18	204	Median	322					
19	213	Mode	280					
20	218	Standard Deviation	124.5781759					
21	220	Sample Variance	15519.72192					
22	230	Kurtosis	-0.789766337					
23	235	Skewness	0.068909548					
24	235	Range	526					
25	239	Minimum	56					
26	241	Maximum	582					
27	245	Sum	31217					
28	245	Count	94					
29	247							
30	250							
31	253							
32	270							
33	275							
34	278							

Histogram

Practices

Key Terms

Two criteria in performance information description (completeness and meaningfulness)
Description of performance shape
Description of performance trend
Performance raw data
Purpose of performance description
Performance range
Frequency
Percentage
Cumulative percentage
Performance targets (standards or benchmarks)
Average performance (mean)
Number of cases or observations
Middle performance (median)
Typical performance (mode)
Performance outliers
Analysis of performance outliers
Stem and leaf plot
Microsoft Excel
Excel Data Analysis ToolPak
Excel Insert Function (f_x)
Excel Data Analysis Histogram Procedure
Excel Data Analysis Descriptive Procedure

Practice Problem 3–1

Table 3–7 shows the number of tons of trash collected by 10 units in a city's sanitation division last year.

1. Use the Excel Histogram Procedure to calculate frequency, cumulative percentage, and percentage. (Note that the Histogram Procedure does not give you the percentages. You should use Excel to calculate percentages from frequencies). Use performance ranges of 0 to 30,000 tons, 30,001 to 40,000 tons, 40,001 to 50,000, and above 50,000 tons to describe the performance of the units. Write a paragraph to report about your findings.
2. Use the Excel Descriptive Procedure to calculate the mean, the median, and the mode. What do these statistics tell you?

Practice Problem 3–2

The Department of Parks and Recreation in the town of Winter Holiday operates a small park near to its city hall. The department uses the attendance to measure its workload in determining

Table 3–7

Number of Tons of Trash Collected

Unit	Tons of trash collected
1	34,000
2	27,000
3	54,000
4	43,000
5	19,000
6	37,000
7	46,000
8	35,000
9	48,000
10	39,000

Table 3–8

Number of Park Visitors of 25 Days

5, 3, 10, 1, 2, 3, 4, 3, 5, 100, 4, 3, 2, 4, 25, 150, 3, 3, 5, 4, 8, 7, 10, 15, 30

the budget for the park. The city manager has long believed that the park has too few visitors, and the department should reach out to more customers, or its budget would be reduced. You are a performance analyst for the city. The city manager has asked you to prepare a performance analysis for the park to determine whether the budget request for the park is justified in the city's budget proposal. You randomly selected 25 days in the past year and calculated the park attendance data, as shown in Table 3–8.

1. Use the Excel Descriptive Procedure to get the mean, the median, and the mode for the performance data. Write a paragraph to explain the meaning of these performance statistics. Do you recommend the use of the mean in your performance presentation? Why or why not? Do you recommend the use of the median or the mode? Why or why not?
2. Use the Excel Histogram Procedure for the attendance data with performance ranges of your choice? Interpret the results.
3. Prepare a performance analysis report to discuss budgetary recommendations to the city manager.

Practice Problem 3–3

The nonprofit Dover Human Service Foundation provides health care services to children. The foundation operates a clinic providing services to after-school children whose parents are still

Table 3–9

Daily Number of Clinic Visitors

Daily number of clinic visitors	Number of days
0	0
1	0
2	1
3	1
4	10
5	7
6	8
7	10
8	20
9	15
10	8
11	10

Table 3–10

Student Satisfactions Toward Services

Student ID	Satisfaction rating	Gender
1	Very dissatisfied	Male
2	Very satisfied	Male
3	Satisfied	Female
4	Neutral	Female
5	Neutral	Male
6	Very satisfied	Female
7	Satisfied	Female
8	Dissatisfied	Female
9	Very dissatisfied	Male
10	Satisfied	Male
11	Satisfied	Female
12	Satisfied	Male
13	Dissatisfied	Female
14	Satisfied	Female
15	Satisfied	Male
16	Dissatisfied	Male
17	Very satisfied	Male
18	Very satisfied	Female
19	Very satisfied	Female
20	Neutral	Female

at work. The foundation has a performance measurement system to track its performance. Two licensed nurses alternate the office hours in the clinic. The data of last year indicated that the clinic had 6 to 9 visitors daily for 70% of the time, and it had 9 or fewer visitors daily for 90% of the time. Recently, one nurse claimed an increase in clinic visits this year and made a request for additional hiring. You are asked to assess the validity of this claim. You assembled the data of the past 90 days of this year, shown in Table 3–9.

1. What are the mean, the median, and the mode of this performance data?
2. Use the Excel Histogram Procedure for the clinic visit data with performance ranges of your choice.
3. Do you recommend hiring? Prepare a performance analysis report to justify your recommendation.

Practice Problem 3–4

Table 3–10 shows the satisfaction ratings of 20 students toward the services of the Registrar's Office at a public university. The ratings are recorded on a scale of very dissatisfied, dissatisfied, neutral, satisfied, and very satisfied. The gender information of the students is also provided. Use what you have learned so far to provide as much information as you can to describe these two measures.

CHAPTER 4

Describing Performance Trend

S uppose you are concerned about your child's academic performance in school. There are two ways to find that out. You compare your child's grades with the grades of peer students, or you track your child's grade change over time. We learned how to present the peer comparison of performance in the last chapter. In this chapter, we study the tools to describe performance change over time.

Why is it important to describe performance over time? A time dimension gives a sense of direction, development, and change of performance activities. It provides a context to tell a performance story that has a beginning and an end, while the peer comparison is just a static snapshot of performance at a specific time. The presentation of performance over time is known as the *performance trend presentation.*

There are a few things you should prepare for a trend presentation. First, you should determine the time frame of data in presentation. Are they yearly, quarterly, monthly, or daily data? Oftentimes, the purpose of the presentation provides clues about the time frame. If you present performance in an annual budget request, you probably need annual data for the annual budget cycle. If you present the information in a strategic planning process, you likely need annual data as well as data of a longer time. If you are interested in tracking everyday performance changes, you likely need daily and monthly data.

Moreover, you should select proper performance measures in a trend presentation. In addition to the principles discussed in Chapter 2 ("Developing Performance Measures"), the arithmetic form of measures should also be considered in presentation.

Forms of Measures

A measure of organizational performance can take one of these arithmetic forms: the aggregate, the average, the percentage, or the per capita. Say that a local nonprofit health agency organizes a campaign to encourage school-age children to eat more fruits and vegetables, and the campaign emphasizes the proper nutrition consumption of fruits and vegetables in the school lunch program. You want to demonstrate the performance trend of the agency by presenting how well children eat after participating in the campaign.

You could measure how many servings of fruits and vegetables children in the program consume. Number of fruit and vegetable servings is an *aggregate measure* of performance. An aggregate measure is an assessment of performance data in their very rudimental form. It simply adds all counts of individual performance cases. The specific forms of an aggregate measure often start with the words the "number of." Examples include number of arrests in a local police department, number of credit hours earned by students in a high school, and number of tons of solid waste collected in a local solid waste department, among many others.

Oftentimes, the presentation of an aggregate measure is simply not enough or not adequate. You will have to use other forms of measures. For example, instead of saying "98 students have 666 servings of fruit and vegetables daily," you can say "students consume an *average* of 6.8 servings of fruit and vegetables daily." We discuss this *average measure* of performance in Chapter 3 (the mean). It is the result of dividing the value of an aggregate measure by the number of individual cases. Other examples of average measures of performance include average daily number of crimes for a police department, average response time for emergency incidents for an emergency response division, and average grade point averages of a high school class. Average measures are popular in performance trend presentations.

Suppose, after a few months of implementation, you want to know whether the healthy eating campaign has had any impact on students' weights. You have tested 100 students and discovered that 90 of them have the normal body weight measured by body mass index (BMI) scores; the normal BMI percentage is 90. This is a *percentage measure*. Percentage measures, also known as *proportion measures*, are very popular forms in performance analysis because they are applicable to all nominal, ordinal, and interval measures, while average measures are limited to interval and occasionally ordinal measures. For example, to describe the effort to attract female or minority workers, a human resource department can use percentage of female workers and percentage of minority workers. Both are created from nominal measures of gender and race. An instructor can apply percentage of students who pass a test, a measure created from an ordinal grade measure of pass or fail. The use of percentage measures was also discussed in Chapter 3.

Suppose that you measure the revenue collection performance of a city's finance department, and you find that the city's total revenue has increased by 10% this year. Could you conclude that the revenue collection performance improves by 10%? You probably could not if you know that city's population also has increased by 10% this year. Because population growth also brings revenue, and it has nothing to do with the department's revenue collection effort, the use of total revenue would inflate the department's performance. To rule out the impact of population growth on the revenue for a more accurate portrayal of the revenue collection performance, you can choose revenue per capita (total revenue/population) instead of total revenue. A *per capita measure* is used when there is a need to control the impact of the population or other events on the performance. Other popular per capita measures of performance include crime rates (i.e., the number of crimes per 100,000 population); number of arrests per police employee; number of clients served per full-time employee; and student/teacher ratio (number of students/number of teachers).

Measuring the Trend

Once the form of a measure is determined, you are ready to select *trend performance measures*. This chapter introduces 3 popular trend measures: the growth rate, the percentage difference, and the percentage ratio. Table 4–1 shows the number of students passing a state exam over the last 3 years in a public high school. The measure is used to assess the school's instructional performance.

Growth Rate

Last year, 530 students passed the test, and 550 did it this year. So the number of students who passed the exam has grown by 3.8% [(550 − 530)/530] this year. The *growth rate* assesses the degree of performance change over a previous period. It can be calculated for aggregate measures, average measures, or per capita measures. It is generally not used for percentage measures.

$$\text{Growth Rate} = (P_t - P_{t-1})/P_{t-1}$$

The performance at a term is P_t, and P_{t-1} is the performance of a term prior to P_t. Notice that the growth rate can be negative when P_t is smaller than P_{t-1}. The interpretation of a negative growth rate depends on the measure used. It does not necessarily mean a worse performance. For example, a 5% decline (−5%) in crimes indicates a performance improvement.

You can average the growth rates to get an *average growth rate*. In the state exam data, the growth rate last year was 6.0% [(530 − 500)/500]. So the average growth rate for the last 2 years is 4.9% [(3.8% + 6.0%)/2], which means that the number of students passing the state exam has increased by an annual average of 4.9% for the last 2 years. The average growth rate can be used as a performance benchmark to assess performance growth. For example, the growth rate this year (3.8%) is significantly lower than the average rate (4.9%), indicating a below-average growth in the number of students passing the test.

Percentage Difference

In Table 4–1, the percentage of students passing the exam was 550/620 = 88.7% this year, and 530/610 = 86.9% last year. The percentage difference is 1.8% (88.7% − 86.9%). The *percentage difference* (R_d) is defined as

$$R_d = R_t - R_{t-1}.$$

Table 4–1

Number of Students Passing a State Exam

	Number of students passing the exam (column 1)	School enrollment (column 2)	Pass percentage (column 1/column 2)
2 years ago	500	600	83.3%
Last year	530	610	86.9%
This year	550	620	88.7%

A performance measured in percentage at a term t is R_t, and R_{t-1} is the performance measured in percentage at a previous term $t - 1$. The percentage difference assesses the performance change measured in percentage. It is useful when measures of performance are percentage measures.

The percentage difference and the growth rate have different meanings. In the above example, the school enrollment data are used in calculating the percentage difference, but they are not used in the growth rate calculation. The percentage difference indicates that the percentage of students passing the exam increases from 86.9% last year to 88.7% this year; however, the growth rate of the students passing the exam has slowed down from 6.0% last year to 3.8% this year.

It is important to know that the use of different measures can give different impressions about a performance trend, so a presenter needs to know precisely the correct interpretation of a performance trend. Moreover, the use of multiple measures is always better than a single measure in presentation, as long as the presenter understands different interpretations of the measures presented.

Percentage Ratio

Like the percentage difference, this ratio also applies to percentage measures. In Table 4–1, the percentage of students passing the exam was 88.7% this year and 86.9% last year. The *percentage ratio* is 102.1% (88.7%/86.9% = 1.021), indicating that the chance of a student passing the exam this year is 2.1% (102.1% – 100.0%) greater than that of last year. The percentage ratio (θ) can be calculated from the following equation:

$$\theta = R_t / R_{t-1}.$$

In another example, if 30% of students received As in a math class this year and only 20% of students had As last year, the percentage ratio is 150% (30%/20% = 1.50), which indicates that the chance of a student getting an A this year is 50% (150.0% – 100.0%) higher than that of last year or that a student is 50% more likely to get an A this year than last year. On the other hand, if only 15% of students received As this year, the percentage ratio is 75% (15%/20% = 0.75). You would say that the chance of a student getting an A this year is only 75% of last year or that the chance of a student getting an A this year is 25% less than that of last year (i.e., 75% – 100% = –25% and a negative percent ratio translates into "less" in description).

Notice that the interpretation of the percentage ratio is very different from that of the percentage difference because the percentage ratio is a measure of *likelihood* in statistics, and the percentage difference is not. A detailed discussion of concepts in probability or likelihood will be seen later in this book.

Let us look at another example to illustrate the use of these performance trend measures. Return to Class Rate (RTC) is used to assess the performance of a school-based health care clinic. After a student visits the clinic for health care attention and treatment, the student is either sent home, sent to a hospital, or returned to class if the student is restored to health. RTC assesses the extent that clinic visitors receive proper treatments and return to class. A higher

Table 4–2

Return to Class

	Number of clinic visitors (column 1)	Number of visitors returned to class (column 2)	RTC (column 2/column 1)
2 years ago	1455	1254	86.2%
Last year	1579	1331	84.3%
This year	1694	1350	79.7%

Table 4–3

Return to Class Percentage Difference and Percentage Ratio

	RTC	Percentage difference	Percentage ratio
2 years ago	86.2%		
Last year	84.3%	84.3% − 86.2% = −1.9%	84.3%/86.2% = 97.8%
This year	79.7%	79.7% − 84.3% = −4.6%	79.7%/84.3% = 94.5%

RTC indicates more students return to class with little interruption of education and thus a better performance for the clinic. Table 4–2 shows RTC statistics for the last 3 years.

The number of visitors returned to class has increased for the last 2 years. The growth rate was 6.1% [(1331 − 1254)/1254] last year and 1.4% [(1350 − 1331)/1331] this year. So if you just looked at the growth rate, you could conclude that the clinic's performance has improved over the last 3 years; however, the RTC percentage difference and percentage ratio in Table 4–3 tell a different story.

RTC declines by 1.9% last year and by 4.6% this year, indicating a deterioration of performance 2 years in a row, as well as a worse performance decline this year than last year. Clinic visitors were 2.2% less likely (i.e., 97.8% − 100%) to be returned to class last year than 2 years ago and 5.5% less likely (i.e., 94.5% − 100%) to be returned to class this year than last year. These results indicate that, although more visitors have been returned to class for the past 3 years, the RTC rate has actually declined.

Describing the Trend

Once you collect performance data over a relatively long time, you can observe the change of performance over the time with multiple data points. How many data points do you need to demonstrate the trend? In our example of the state exam, we use 3 data points for the past 2 years to constitute 2 time periods—from Year 1 to Year 2 and from Year 2 to Year 3 (the current year). These time periods are known as *performance intervals* in performance trend analysis.

To detect a performance trend, you need at least 2 consecutive performance intervals, and ideally, the intervals are equal in time. For example, the intervals from data points in Years 2004, 2005, and 2006 are equal in time (1-year distance in the intervals), while the intervals from Years 2004, 2005, and 2007 are not. Equal intervals make the interpretation of the trend easier and more accurate. Also, you should try to collect the data at the same time in an interval. For example, if you measure the citizen satisfaction rate annually and you want to present it in a trend, you should try to measure it at approximately the same time of the year to rule out the possible impact of time on the satisfaction rate.

There are different standards as to when a trend occurs. In this book, a performance trend is said to exist if two or more consecutive performance intervals move toward the same direction. There are two types of performance trends: the *positive performance trend* and the *negative performance trend*. Of course, there are cases when no clear performance direction is detected.

A Positive Performance Trend

A positive performance trend shows a continual performance improvement over time. As defined above, a trend exists if 2 consecutive performance intervals point to the same direction. For example, if the citizen satisfaction rate has been 80%, 85%, and 90% for the last 3 years, we have seen a positive performance trend with 2 consecutive intervals of 80% to 85% and 85% to 90%.

In this example, the citizen satisfaction rate has increased over time. When the increase in value of a measure indicates performance improvement, we call it a *measure of positive performance*. Examples include number of students passing an exam, percentage of students in the normal category of BMI, and daily average consumption of fruits and vegetables by school-age students. A greater value in these measures indicates a performance improvement, and a smaller value is a sign of performance deterioration. A positive performance trend is identified when a measure of positive performance shows an *upward trend*.

Excel can be used to demonstrate a performance trend graphically. Here is an example. The Global Assessment Functioning (GAF) score is used to assess school-age children's psychosocial functioning. The value of the score goes from 0 to 100, with a larger score indicating a better psychosocial status. A school-based counseling program, funded by a nonprofit health care agency, has been implemented for the past 3 years to target school-age children diagnosed with a variety of psychosocial problems in a local school. Table 4–4 shows the GAF scores of the participating students.

Use the following steps in Excel to demonstrate the trend:

1. Enter the data in the first three columns in an Excel sheet. Use column A for time: *Two Years Ago*, *One Year Ago*, and *This Year*; column B for *GAF scores of each year*; and column C for the *growth rate*. You do not need to enter the number of cases. Use the first row for the labels: *Year*, *Average GAF Score*, and *Growth Rate*.
2. Press and hold the mouse to select the data area A1 through C4.

Table 4–4

Global Assessment Functioning (GAF) Test Results

Year	Number of cases	Average GAF score	Growth rate (%)
2 years ago	1002	53.42	
1 year ago	976	56.97	6.65
This year	1004	60.94	6.97

Figure 4–1

Global Assessment Functioning Scores.

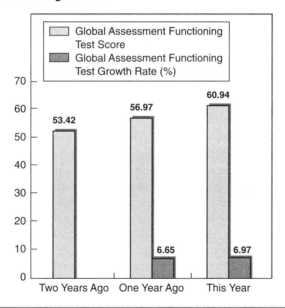

3. Click the **Column** command in the **Charts** group on the **Insert** tab. (Note: If you use Excel 2003, click the **Chart** button on the **Insert** tab or click **Chart Wizard**, and you are shown a list of chart types.)
4. Select the **Clustered Column** (the first graph) in the 2-D column on the **Column** tab. You should see a graph similar to Figure 4–1. (Note: If you use Excel 2003, choose **Column** in the **Chart Type** window and **Clustered Column** in the **Chart Sub-Type** window. Click **Next**.)
5. Use the **Design** menu and the **Layout** menu to edit the graph. (Note: For Excel 2003 users, Excel allows a few graphical options in Titles, Axes, Gridlines, Legend, Data Labels, and Data Table. Try each of them to select the graphical effects you prefer.)

Note that an upward graph does not necessarily indicate a positive performance trend. For example, an upward trend in crime rate (i.e., the number of crimes per 1000 population) indicates a negative performance development. A declining trend of crimes shows performance improvement. In fact, when a decline in its value indicates a performance improvement, it is a *measure of negative performance*. Other examples of such measures include the percentage of students failing an exam, the percentage of overweight children, and the response time.

Some measures are difficult to be classified as either positive or negative performance measures. Examples include number of arrests, number of repairs made, and number of traffic tickets. Many of them are measures of activities or outputs. There is no clear guidance to classify them as either positive or negative, but an upward trend does indicate an increased level of activities or outputs.

A Negative Performance Trend

A negative performance trend is present when performance deterioration occurs for 2 or more consecutive performance intervals. Citizen satisfaction ratings of 90%, 85%, and 80% for the last 3 years constitute such a trend. Because the satisfaction rating is a measure of positive performance, a downward trend reflects a negative performance trend. For a measure of negative performance, such as the crime rate, a negative performance trend occurs when an upward trend is present.

Clearly, the selection of measures is important in a performance trend demonstration. For the presentation purpose, it is always better to choose a measure of positive performance to show a performance trend because it has a distinctive upward trend for performance improvement and a downward trend for performance deterioration, which should be easily recognized by a general audience not trained in performance measurement. For example, the graduation rate is a better choice of measure in presentation than the dropout rate for school performance. The employment rate is a better presentation measure than the unemployment rate, though the use of the latter is more common.

Let us work on another example with Excel. School counselors are asked to assess the psychological status of students in a nonprofit counseling program that targets depression. The program is offered continually through the academic year to students with psychological problems that could be related to depression. Students in the program go through a 12-week counseling session. At the end of the session, counselors conduct a thorough evaluation of a student and determine whether and how much the depression-related psychological problems persist. Table 4–5 shows the status of students who have participated in the program for the past 3 years after counseling.

The percentage of students without presenting problems is a measure of positive performance. It has declined for the last 3 years from 51.52% [34/(34 + 32)] to 33.82% [23/(23 + 45)], suggesting a deteriorating performance trend of the program. Percentage differences and percentage ratios also show the same result. Program participants are 22.13% less likely (i.e., 77.87%–100%) to be without presenting problems of depression this year than last year. Use the following steps in Excel to show this worsening performance trend:

Table 4–5

Presenting Problems of Depression After Counseling

Year	Number of students without presenting problems (column 1)	Number of students with presenting problems (column 2)	Percentage of students without presenting problems [column 1/(column 1 + column 2)]	Percentage difference	Percentage ratio
2 years ago	34	32	51.52%		
1 year ago	43	56	43.43%	−8.08%	84.31%
This year	23	45	33.82%	−9.61%	77.87%

1. Use the first three columns of an Excel sheet to enter data exactly as shown in the first three columns of Table 4–5.
2. Press and hold the mouse to select the data area A1 through C4.
3. Click the **Column** command in the **Charts** group on the **Insert** tab. (Note: If you use Excel 2003, click the **Chart** button on the **Insert** tab, and you are shown a list of chart types in the **Chart Wizard** window.)
4. Select the **100% Stacked Column** in the 3-D column on the **Column** tab. You should see a graph similar to Figure 4–2. (Note: In Excel 2003, choose **Column** in the **Chart Type** window and the **100% Stacked Column with a 3-D Effect** in the **Chart Sub-Type** window.)
5. Use the **Design** menu and the **Layout** menu to edit the graph. In Figure 4–2, I select **Show Data Table** in the **Labels** group on the **Layout** menu. (Note: Excel 2003 also allows a few graphical options in Titles, Axes, Gridlines, Legend, Data Labels, and Data Table.)

In Figure 4–2, each column represents 100% of the performance data in a specific year, showing all the students participating in the counseling program in that year. The percentage column is split by the dark color of "no presenting problems" and the light color of "presenting problems." The graph shows a clear downward trend for the percentages of "no presenting problems," indicating a worsening performance by this measure.

A Nontrend Performance

A nontrend performance occurs when there is no *distinctive indication of performance trend*. There are two types of nontrend performances: a flat performance and an up-and-down performance. A flat performance reflects a graphic presentation of constant or almost constant performance data points over time (a flat line). Citizen satisfaction rates of 90%, 90%, and 90% for the last 3 years constitute an example. The visual of the data shows no change in the performance.

Figure 4–2

Participants with or Without Presenting Problems of Depression.

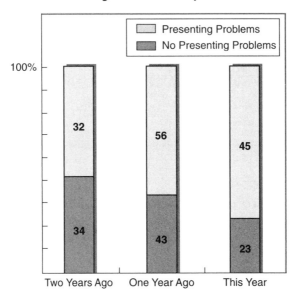

It is arguable about what constitutes a distinctive indication of a trend. In the above example, is 90.5% distinctive from 90.0%? What about 90.6% from 90.0%? Because it is often rare to have 2 identical performance data points (what is the chance that the satisfaction rates are exactly the same 2 years in a row?), we always have to make a judgment call. I often use what I call the *0.5 percent rule*. I define 2 performance points distinctive if they are 0.5% or greater apart. For example, a 90.5% is distinctive enough from 90.0%, but 90.4% is not. Similarly, a performance score of 503 is distinctive from 500, because 503 is 0.6% (503/500 − 100%) different from 500, but a score of 502 is not distinctive from 500 because 502 is only 0.4% (502/500 − 100%) different from 500.

Another nontrend performance is an up-and-down performance. A series of performance data points of 90%, 95%, and 89% is an example in which the first performance interval shows an increase while the second indicates a decline. With this up-and-down performance series, it is impossible to establish a performance trend. More performance data points are needed. Table 4–6 shows crime statistics and the population information in a major U.S. city for the past 6 years.

The total number of crimes for the city has increased from 80,833 to 88,932. The growth rate is about 10% [(88,932 − 80,833)/80,833] for the period. If this measure were used to assess the police performance of the city, we would conclude that the police performance has declined for the period. At the same time, however, the population of the city has also increased; therefore, the crime rate (the number of crimes per 100,000 population) has fluctuated during this time.

Table 4–6

Crime and Population Statistics of a Major U.S. City

Year	Number of crimes	Population	Number of crimes per 100,000 population
5 years ago	80,833	1,484,224	5446.15
4 years ago	82,391	1,543,228	5338.87
3 years ago	83,452	1,553,211	5372.87
2 years ago	85,431	1,584,324	5392.27
Last year	86,389	1,614,321	5351.41
This year	88,932	1,642,341	5414.95

Figure 4–3

Crime Rates in a Major U.S. City.

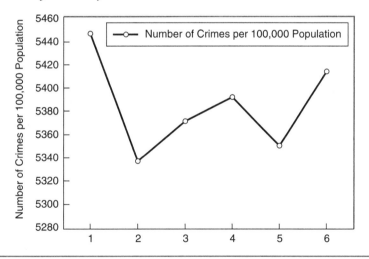

Figure 4–3 clearly shows the up-and-down fluctuation. The time includes a 3-year period when the crime rate increased from 5338.87 to 5392.27, but, overall, there has been no distinctive indication of performance trend during this time. The following steps in Excel can be used to create Figure 4–3:

1. In an Excel sheet, use the first column to enter the Number of Crimes per 100,000 Population as displayed in Table 4–6.

2. Press and hold the mouse to select the data A1 to A7.
3. Click the **Line** command in the **Charts** group on the **Insert** tab. (Note: If you use Excel 2003, click the **Chart** button on the **Insert** tab, and you are shown a list of chart types in the **Chart Wizard** window.)
4. Select the **Line with Markers** on the **Line** tab. You should see a graph similar to Figure 4–3. (Note: In Excel 2003, choose **Line** in the **Chart Type** window and the **Line with Markers Displayed at Each Data Value** in the **Chart Sub-Type** window.)
5. Use the **Design** menu and the **Layout** menu to edit the graph. (Note: For Excel 2003 users, follow the Excel instructions to finish the graph.)

A Case Study

LIVEWELL, Florida, is a nonprofit agency that provides low-income HIV positive (AIDS) people with accessibility to services in transportation, temporary housing, food, emergency medical supplies, and AIDS education. The core activities include the provision of a free bus pass to people in need of transportation, door-to-door services for medical or food supplies, and temporary housing for people in need.

The agency locates its users through visits and an agency outreach program. Once a potential user is located, an eligibility assessment is conducted to determine the person's qualification for the program. During the past 12 months, LIVEWELL has provided 912 people with bus passes, 288 people with door-to-door services, and 56 people with temporary housing.

The agency has 9 employees that include 1 manager, 1 assistant manager, 3 case managers, 2 medical staffers, and 2 case management assistants. It had a total program expense of $755,000 last year. Ms. Christina Ferguson, the executive director of LIVEWELL, has 12 years of managerial experience and has been working in LIVEWELL for 4 years.

Step 1: Understanding the Issue

There have been an increasing number of AIDS cases in the area served by LIVEWELL. Christina has observed a growth in users served by LIVEWELL. Nevertheless, the revenue sources for LIVEWELL were limited. For a long period of time, LIVEWELL relied on a state grant and several relatively small business and personal donations. To meet the increase in the workload, about 3 years ago Christina applied for and was able to secure a federal grant of $1.5 million over a 3-year period. The grant is used to provide AIDS-related services with a possibility of renewal after successful implementation.

The federal government will evaluate the effectiveness of the grant at the end of the 3-year period. Christina wants to ensure the agency is ready for the evaluation. She wants the evaluation to go well so that she can apply for its renewal. She needs a preliminary analysis of the agency's performance in providing services with the grant.

Christina understands that analysis objectives of a performance analysis include performance description, performance monitoring, performance understanding, and performance evaluation. With her limited resources, Christina is unable to conduct a full-fledged performance evaluation. Her communication with a federal auditor indicates that LIVEWELL needs to provide the data that describe how the federal grant has helped the agency to achieve its goal. So Christina decides to focus her assessment on *describing* LIVEWELL performance for the past 3 years after receiving the grant—she wants a performance trend presentation.

Step 2: Asking the Questions in Performance Analysis

Christina wants to know how well the federal grant has been spent to help achieve or sustain the agency's goal—to provide eligible people accessibility to services. Because LIVEWELL services include a provision for bus passes, door-to-door visits for medical services and food, and temporary housing services, accessibility to services can be further specified as accessibilities to the public transportation system, to medical services, and to temporary housing services.

Based on this specification of the goal, a proper set of assessment questions can include the following: Has the agency increased or sustained accessibility to the public transportation system for the last 3 years? Has the agency increased or sustained accessibility to medical services for the last 3 years? Has the agency increased or sustained accessibility to temporary housing services for the last 3 years?

Step 3: Contemplating a Performance Theory

Because the analysis is a simple description of the performance trend, there is no need to provide a performance theory. A significant performance improvement in the past 3 years can result from the federal grant. However, Christina should be ready to explain any large performance deterioration that may be uncovered in the trend presentation.

Step 4: Determining Performance Measures and Collecting Performance Data

Measures must be developed to assess the agency's goals and to answer the analysis questions. Data must be available or collectible within the time frame of the analysis. After a data inventory analysis of the agency's database, Christina decided to use number of bus passes issued to assess the goal of accessibility to the public transportation system. She also decided to use number of doctor referrals issued to assess the goal of accessibility to medical services and number of people assigned temporary housing to evaluate the goal of accessibility to temporary housing. All these measures are aggregate performance measures.

LIVEWELL has a user information database that includes the personal information of users (e.g., race, gender, age); their diagnostic information (e.g., HIV symptoms); and the service information (e.g., referral status, issuance of bus passes, assignment of temporary housing status). The personal information is entered when a person first enters the LIVEWELL service system and his or her eligibility for services is assessed. The information is updated each time a person uses LIVEWELL services.

Step 5: Analyzing the Performance

Christina assembled the data of the last 3 years and developed Table 4–7, which shows that number of bus passes issued has increased for the past 3 years for an average annual growth rate of 12.7% [(11.1% + 14.3%)/2]. Number of doctor referrals issued increased last year by 8.6%, but declined this year by 13.7%. Christina suspected that the decline was caused by the agency's recent increase in door-to-door visits by the agency's medical staffers. These visits might reduce users' needs to visit doctors for illnesses that were treated on site by the medical staffers. Number of users assigned temporary housing has not changed much for the past 3 years, suggesting that the need for such a service may have stabilized. Figure 4–4 visualizes these performance changes.

Table 4–7

Service Accessibility Statistics in LIVEWELL

Year	Bus passes	Growth rate: Bus passes	Doctor referrals	Growth rate: Doctor referral	Temporary housing	Growth rate: Temporary housing
2 years ago	718		128		57	
Last year	798	11.1%	139	8.6%	57	0%
This year	912	14.3%	120	−13.7%	56	−1.8%

Figure 4–4

Service Accessibility in LIVEWELL.

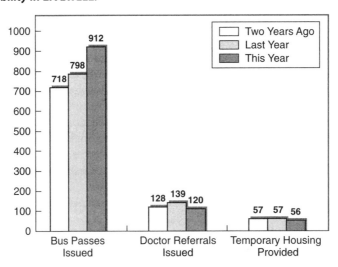

Step 6: Drawing Conclusions in a Performance Report

Christina concludes that the federal grant has increased qualified people's accessibility to transportation and sustained their accessibility to temporary housing. Christina has the empirical evidence showing that the federal grant has made a significant positive impact on service accessibility. She is prepared to argue in her grant renewal proposal that eliminating the grant would significantly hinder the agency's mission.

Christina also discusses the limitation of her analysis in the proposal, which is that she only uses the aggregate measures (i.e., total numbers of bus passes, doctor referrals, and temporary housing users) and their growth rates. Further effort should be made to present the performance trend with other forms of measures such as the percentages of eligible LIVEWELL clients who received bus passes, doctor referrals, or housing. The presentation of more measures will give a more complete and accurate picture of LIVEWELL performance.

Practices

Key Terms

Performance trend presentation
Aggregate measures
Average measures
Percentage measures (proportion measures)
Per capita measures
Trend performance measures
Growth rate
Average growth rate
Percentage difference
Percentage ratio
Performance intervals
Positive performance trend
Negative performance trend
Nontrend performances
Measures of positive performance
Upward trend
Downward trend
Measures of negative performance
Distinctive indication of performance trend
0.5 percent rule
Excel graphing

Practice Problem 4–1

Table 4–8 shows the average response time of the police department in the city of Oldcastle for the past 5 years.

Table 4–8

Average Response Time in Oldcastle (in minutes)

Year	1	2	3	4	5 (this year)
Most urgent incidents	5.28	5.48	5.17	5.07	4.55
Urgent incidents	7.13	7.20	7.10	8.69	8.25
Nonurgent incidents	12.08	12.60	13.01	11.51	11.62

Table 4–9

Alcohol Treatment Program Statistics in Mulluck County

Year	1	2	3	4	5 (this year)
Success rate (%)	40	42	55	53	54
Program staff	5	8	8	10	10
Program budget (in million dollars)	1.6	2.3	2.6	2.5	2.5

1. Determine and calculate the trend performance measure(s) to identify any performance trend.
2. Use Excel to present the data graphically.
3. Write a brief report of analysis to summarize your findings from a performance trend analysis, knowing that the city's goal is to keep average response time within 6 minutes for most urgent incidents, within 8 minutes for urgent incidents, and within 11 minutes for nonurgent incidents.

Practice Problem 4–2

The Department of Community Justice in Mulluck County has an adult alcohol treatment and rehabilitation program. The program, started 5 years ago, offers educational classes, alcohol treatment, and rehabilitation services. Success in treatment and rehabilitation is defined as a participant remaining alcohol free for 12 months after the treatment. Table 4–9 shows the success rate of the program and other program-related statistics.

1. Determine and calculate trend performance measure(s) to identify any performance trend.
2. Use Excel to present the data graphically.
3. Write a brief report to summarize your findings from the performance trend analysis.

Practice Problem 4–3

Sometimes, analysts put together several performance measures to create an index measure of performance. For example, a quality of life index may consist of performance measures of public safety, transportation, parks and recreation, economic development, education, and human services. These index measures, also known as composite measures, are often intervallic.

The Department of Transportation in Deland County uses a Pavement Condition Index (PCI) to measure distress of the road. PCI data are collected from visual inspection of a roadway by the department's inspectors. The value of index goes from 0 (the worst) to 100 (the best). Table 4–10 shows PCI, citizen satisfaction with the road pavement condition, and related cost statistics.

1. Determine and calculate the trend performance measure(s) to identify any performance trend.
2. Use Excel to present the data graphically.
3. Write a brief report to summarize your findings from the performance trend analysis.

Table 4–10

Road Pavement Condition Statistics in Deland

Year	1	2	3	4	5 (this year)
PCI	51	74	75	76	80
Citizen satisfaction rate (%)	57	60	63	58	55
Cost per lane mile resurfaced ($)	70,793	87,375	80,607	70,006	75,182

Citizen satisfaction rate is the percentage of citizens responding to a survey who say that they are satisfied or very satisfied with the pavement condition of local roads. Cost per lane mile resurfaced includes the cost of seal coat, thin overlay, and structural overlay.

Table 4–11

Medical Response Times in City of Deerland

	Cumulative percentage						
	Jan.	**Feb.**	**Mar.**	**April**	**May**	**June**	**July**
Less than 4 minutes	26%	26%	24%	24%	21%	17%	18%
Less than 6 minutes	60%	60%	57%	61%	54%	48%	48%
Less than 8 minutes	84%	84%	81%	83%	79%	73%	74%

Practice Problem 4–4

Table 4–11 shows medical emergency response times during the first 7 months of the year for the Department of Fire and Rescue in the city of Deerland. The city's performance standards are 25% of the response times within 4 minutes, 60% within 6 minutes, and 80% within 8 minutes.

1. Conduct a performance trend analysis to demonstrate any performance trend.
2. Use Excel to present the data graphically.
3. Write a report to summarize your findings about the city's compliance with performance targets.

Section III

Monitoring Performance

CHAPTER 5

Performance Monitoring Basics

Here is an example to illustrate the need of monitoring. You want a mortgage loan with a 6.0% interest, but the bank insists on a credit score of 750. Your score is 690, which would get a loan with a 7.0% interest rate. If you want a better rate, you need a better credit score. That 1% difference in the interest rate would cost you more than $70,000 dollars in payment for a $300,000 loan over 30 years.

What Is Performance Monitoring and Why Do It?

Why keep tracking your credit score? First, it provides an ongoing check on your financial performance records. You may find unusual financial irregularities and misdeeds such as signs of identity thefts or mistakes in your financial transaction records. Second, it helps you uncover inefficient practices and operations that lead to poor finance performance. You may discover that your low credit score is a result of overspending and late payments of credit card bills. To improve the score, you need to cut back the spending level and pay the debts on time. Third, the monitoring also helps you establish the need for services. For example, after reviewing the credit report, you may realize that you need credit consulting and financial planning to develop a healthy financial life and to achieve your financial goals.

Finally, perhaps most important, the monitoring helps you uncover underperformance quickly to avoid the further deterioration of the performance. Imagine that your low credit score is caused by the tardiness to pay credit card bills, and this tardiness goes unnoticed long enough for you to have trouble getting any credit lines. The result may be declamation of insolvency for your personal finance that directly and significantly affects your life.

Performance monitoring is a systematic and periodic observation of performance over time in order to develop or verify performance records, to uncover inefficient and ineffective practices, to identify needs for services, and most important, to detect underperformance timely to avoid the further deterioration of performance. It is a systematic tracking and ongoing examination of an organization's performance by weighing it against established performance standards.

Performance monitoring is different from once-in-a-while performance auditing or evaluation in that it is conducted more frequently, and it is more focused on tracking daily operations. Performance monitoring is aimed at identifying the symptom of underperformance quickly and responding timely.

Performance monitoring should apply to all services in public and nonprofit organizations. Some services need it more than others because the underperformance of these services needs swift and timely responses, and a delay in response could have devastating consequences. Crimes need to be observed frequently by the police to detect criminal patterns and to develop proper strategies to save lives and properties. Emergency supply during natural or man-made disasters should be tracked closely to avoid the shortages that could cause the loss of lives. Traffic accidents need to be watched carefully to minimize fatalities and loss of properties. Response times to emergencies should be monitored closely to avoid or to reduce the loss of lives. The availability of cash to pay off financial obligations should be tracked frequently to prevent financial insolvency. This chapter introduces the steps in performance monitoring and basic monitoring tools. Chapters 6 and 7 present two specific monitoring tools.

Developing a Performance Monitoring System

The steps in a performance analysis in Chapter 2 apply to the development of a performance monitoring system: understanding the issue for monitoring, asking the right monitoring questions, developing a theory for monitoring, developing measures for monitoring, determining data collection methods, collecting data for monitoring, conducting performance monitoring through analyzing data with monitoring tools, and writing the monitoring report. These sequential steps are shown in Figure 5–1.

Understanding the Issue for Monitoring

Imagine that a police department has recently received an increasing number of citizen calls for police assistance and wants to know if this is a seasonal surge due to the temporary influx of visitors for the college spring break or a more permanent increase in criminal activities. Imagine that an emergency response unit piles up food and water for hurricanes only to find out what people really need is medicines and medical supplies. Imagine that the financial director in your city has just told you that the city lacks cash to pay for its bills because a few large taxpayers have not paid their shares of taxes on time.

The very first step in developing a performance monitoring system is to identify a *monitoring need*. It is quite common that the need starts with an issue in everyday management operations and decision making. Increasing citizen complaints about tardiness in garbage collection indicate a need to monitor the garbage collection operation. More frequent requests for

Figure 5–1

Performance Monitoring Steps.

Understanding the issue for monitoring ▷ Asking questions ▷ Developing monitoring theories ▷ Developing measures for monitoring ▷ Determining data collection methods ▷ Collecting data ▷ Conducting performance monitoring ▷ Writing the monitoring report police assistance call for a possible monitoring of crime activities. A rising number of traffic accidents suggest a need to monitor and improve traffic control. The appearance of large and constant budget deficits requires the monitoring of revenue collection efforts and spending patterns.

A clear monitoring need helps you determine the *monitoring goal(s)*: what you want to achieve in the monitoring. Stated above, performance monitoring can help you develop and verify performance records, discover inefficient or ineffective practices and operations, identify service needs, and/or uncover underperformance quickly to avoid further deterioration of performance. A performance monitoring often has multiple goals.

For your specific monitoring issue, the goal can be further specified as, for example, to meet residents' needs for emergency supplies during disasters (identification of service needs); to increase the chances of timely garbage collection (timely discovery of inefficient or ineffective operations and underperformance); to improve police response to crimes (timely discovery of underperformance); to reduce traffic accidents in rush hours (timely identification of service need patterns, discovering inefficient practices, and uncovering underperformance); or to reduce budget deficits or to balance the budget (discovery of inefficient practices).

A good understanding of the monitoring need and goals helps you accurately determine what should be monitored—*the monitoring subject(s)*. Should you track organizational inputs, outputs, or outcomes? Should you monitor revenues and manpower consumed for the production (efficiency) or for goals achieved (effectiveness)? Determination of a monitoring subject will be discussed again later in this chapter when the key components of a monitoring flow and monitoring measures are discussed.

Determining Monitoring Questions

A good understanding of the monitoring need and goal should help the development of the *monitoring questions*. Facing a growth in citizens' calls for services and a goal to improve responses, a police department may want to ask the following questions: Is the growth unusual, compared with data in the past? Has there been an increase in crimes committed since last year? Has there been an increase in crime-fighting activities in the police department? With an increase in traffic accidents and a goal to reduce traffic congestion, a transportation authority may want to know the following: Is the recent increase in traffic fatalities unusual? Has there been an increase in traffic volume? Has the city's plan to ease traffic congestion been implemented properly and timely?

Although every monitoring has its own specific questions, the following is a list of generic forms of performance monitoring questions. They should help you develop your own monitoring questions.

- Are performance goals being met?
- Has the performance plan been implemented effectively?
- Have operations been implemented according to the plan?
- Are the intended services being delivered to the intended clients?
- How good is my performance compared with others' performances, my previous performance, and the performance standard?

- Has the agency performed better or worse? Has the agency underperformed?
- Are there any signs of underperformance?
- Is there any room for performance improvement?
- Is my performance unusually poor, compared with data in the past?

Developing a Theory of the Monitoring Flow

Say you are a police chief in a city government who has heard many citizen complaints about crimes recently, and you want to know if there has been a significant increase in criminal activities in your jurisdiction. To respond swiftly to any surge of crimes, you want a system to monitor police response to crimes. You articulate that the monitoring goal of the system is to improve police response to crimes. The monitoring subject is police response to crimes. What is it? How do you measure it?

One way to understand police response is to specify its role in the production process discussed in Figure 1–1 of Chapter 1 (Inputs → Process → Outputs → Outcomes). The inputs are resources consumed in providing police response, which can be the budget amount allocated for the police patrol or the manpower designated for police response. The process concerns the activities and operations in providing police response. The outputs are police responses directly generated from the process such as arrests, while the outcomes are the results expected from police response such as crime reduction. This flow of inputs to outcomes in performance monitoring is the *monitoring flow*, shown in Figure 5–2. Monitoring subjects can be inputs, outputs, process, and/or outcomes in the monitoring flow.

Thus, a well-developed theory of the monitoring flow should help you specify the monitoring subject and its role in the production process—a critical step for developing proper monitoring measures and for applying the monitoring results to address any underperformance in the production process. It is important to note that a monitoring system should emphasize the monitoring of outputs and outcomes, although the system may also track inputs and the process that lead to the output and the outcome. Monitoring inputs and the process may provide clues on how to develop proper strategies to improve the output and outcomes.

Developing Measures for Monitoring

Once the monitoring flow and monitoring subjects are determined, monitoring measures should be developed accordingly. Table 5–1 lists possible measures in the police response example, along with their monitoring subjects and their roles in the production phases.

Figure 5–2

The Monitoring Flow: A Case of the Production Process of Police Response.

Inputs (Resources) → Process (Activities, Operations) → Outputs (Arrests) → Outcomes (Crime Reduction)

Table 5–1

Developing Measures for Monitoring Police Response

Production phase	Inputs in police response
Monitoring subject	Resources consumed in police response
Measure example	The number of sworn officers on duty per 1000 populations
Production phase	Process in producing police response
Monitoring subject	Activities and operations in police response
Measure example	The number of calls for services dispatched
Production phase	Outputs of police response
Monitoring subject	Products of police response generated from the process
Measure example	The number of arrests made
Production phase	Outcomes of police response
Monitoring subject	Desirable results of police response
Measure example	The reported number of violent crimes per 1000 populations

What measures should be used in monitoring? Because numerous measures are available for each possible monitoring subject, using all of them would be too costly and time consuming. Selecting limited measures is necessary. In addition to the criteria discussed in the "Developing Performance Measures" section in Chapter 2 (e.g., measurement validity, measurement reliability), consider the following in the selection.

First, measures selected should meet monitoring goals. To ensure swift police response to crimes, the response time and crime rates may be monitored. To discover residents' needs for a police service, the number of calls for the service may be monitored. To ensure availability of sufficient resources to support police response, the police budget amount may be monitored. If you are concerned about the possibility of resource waste in operations, measures of efficiency of police operations, such as the number of arrests per police employee, may be monitored.

Second, indicators selected should address specific monitoring needs. For example, an increase in users' complaints for water and sewer services may indicate a need to improve user services. Monitoring the number of user complaints may become necessary. A surge in traffic accidents may suggest a need to improve the transportation system, so monitoring the measures of transportation practices such as the miles of newly paved roads and the miles of existing roads widened or maintained in good condition may be needed.

Collecting Data for Monitoring

Data for performance monitoring come from surveys, archival documents or data, or interviews of related persons. A key component in data collection is to determine *monitoring frequency*—how often a measure should be monitored. Monitoring frequency dictates how often performance data should be collected. In the above case of police response, how frequently should we monitor the number of calls, the number of arrests, or the crime rate statistics: every day, every month, every 2 months, or even longer? Monitoring goals determine monitoring frequency. Daily monitoring of data is unnecessary for a monitoring intended to produce police response information for an annual budget request; monthly collection of the data may be enough. Monthly or annual data should be enough to demonstrate the trend of police response for planning or legislative oversight. Similarly, daily or monthly monitoring may be unnecessary for constructing a 5-year strategic plan. Nonetheless, if the monitoring is for improving day-to-day police operations, daily monitoring and collection of the response information are needed.

The monitoring cost is another consideration in determining monitoring frequency. It could be costly in money and manpower to conduct daily or even monthly monitoring. The cost incurred in frequent monitoring could exceed the benefits of the information yielded in the process.

Conducting Performance Monitoring and Writing the Monitoring Report

Conducting performance monitoring is to use *performance monitoring tools* to discover service need patterns, inefficient–ineffective practices, and underperformances. The essence of these tools is a systematic comparison of a performance with established performance standards, performance variations, or standardized performance. Thus, performance monitoring tools can be classified into three categories: tools in monitoring against performance standards, tools in monitoring performance variation, and tools in monitoring standardized performance. This chapter presents basic monitoring tools, while Chapters 6 and 7 cover two advanced tools of monitoring.

Once the monitoring is completed, the results should be presented in a monitoring report that follows the format discussed in Chapter 2 ("Writing a Performance Analysis Report"). It is a good practice to write a monitoring report for the record even if no warning trend of underperformance is detected.

Monitoring Against Performance Standards

Let us continue our police response example. Say that you, the police chief, want a system to monitor police response to crimes. You want to respond swiftly to any surge of crime activities in your city, articulating that the monitoring goal of the system is to improve police response to crimes, the monitoring subject is the outcome of police response, and the monitoring question is has there been an unusual increase in crimes recently.

You specify the outcome of police response by developing a monitoring flow like that described in Figure 5–2, selecting measures like those in Table 5–1. One outcome measure is the crime rate, the reported violent crimes against people (number of crimes per 1000 populations). Table 5–2 presents the crime rate for the past 2 years up to October of this year. Monthly data are monitored for timely police response.

The core analysis in performance monitoring is a process of using monitoring tools to consistently and systematically conduct performance comparison. One basic tool is the *comparison with the past performance* in which the current performance is weighed against

Table 5–2

Number of Reported Violent Crimes Against People per 1000 Populations

Monitoring Goal: To improve police response to crime
Monitoring Subject: Crime-responding outcomes
Monitoring Question: Has there been an unusual increase in crimes recently?
Outcome Measure 1: Reported violent crimes against people (number of crimes per 1000 populations)
Reporting Date: November 1, this year

	Monthly this year (column 1)	Monthly last year (column 2)
January	0.2120	0.1753
February	0.1541	0.2568
March	0.2561	0.2624
April	0.3184	0.3115
May	0.3154	0.3762
June	0.3306	0.2950
July	0.3863	0.3444
August	0.2172	0.1438
September	0.3110	0.2558
October	0.1619	0.1954
November	Not Available (or NA)	0.1429
December	NA	0.2326
Annual		2.9920

the past performance in order to discover any performance difference like that shown in Table 5–3.

Monthly crimes last year and this year until October are put side by side and analyzed. The data indicate that the crimes were relatively low from January to March, gradually increased and reached the highest during the summer months from April to July, then started to decline from August.

Also shown in Table 5–3 is the month-to-month comparison of the crimes. Of the 10 first months this year, 6 had a crime increase and 4 saw a decline from the same months last year. The data show a clear trend of monthly increase during the summer months from June to September, when the largest monthly increase was in August from 0.1438 last year to 0.2172 this year, for a stunning $0.0734/0.1438 = 51.0\%$ increase! Also, the September increase of 0.0552, the second highest monthly surge for a $0.0552/0.2558 = 21.6\%$ increase, is also really alarming. The monthly comparison shows a clear trend of crime increase in the summer, which constitutes a *warning sign of underperformance* of police response.

Table 5–3

Crime Rate: Comparison with the Past Performance

	Monthly this year (column 1)	Monthly last year (column 2)	Monthly difference (column 3 = column 1 − column 2)
January	0.2120	0.1753	0.0366
February	0.1541	0.2568	−0.1027
March	0.2561	0.2624	−0.0062
April	0.3184	0.3115	0.0069
May	0.3154	0.3762	−0.0607
June	0.3306	0.2950	0.0357
July	0.3863	0.3444	0.0419
August	0.2172	0.1438	0.0734
September	0.3110	0.2558	0.0552
October	0.1619	0.1954	−0.0336
November	NA	0.1429	NA
December	NA	0.2326	NA
Annual		2.9920	

In the above example, we compare crimes of the same months for the past 2 years. This same-period comparison is important in crime rate monitoring because crimes often show seasonal differences. Other examples of performances associated with seasonal fluctuations include unemployment rates, revenues generated from economic activities (such as sales taxes), traffic volumes, and attendances of park and recreation facilities. The same-month comparison is important in monthly monitoring.

In addition to the same-period comparison, you can also compare the performances of 2 consecutive months. The crime rate this February was 0.1541, a significant decline from that in the previous month (0.2120). Because the crimes tend to gradually increase from the start of a year, this large February decline indicates an anomaly in the crime pattern. In performance analysis, a performance data point that unusually departs from the existing data pattern is known as a *performance outlier* (see also Chapter 3). Outliers often occur due to particular events, which could be that the city's weather was particularly cold this February and that led to fewer criminal activities on the street, the city intensified its efforts in patrols and arrests in that month that drove criminals out of the city, or a change in the crime reporting method resulted in some crimes previously reported in February are now reported in January or March.

The examination of outliers helps discover these particular events that cause performance change and thus provides insights about the performance. However, one also should not read too much into outliers in performance monitoring because outliers, by definition, are unlikely to happen again. For example, if it is known that the remarkable low crime rate in February was a result of some specific events that are unlikely to happen frequently in the future, there should be little concern about the large crime rate difference between February and March (0.2561 − 0.1541 = 0.102 or about 10 more crimes per 10,000 populations).

One statistical way to alleviate the impact of outliers in performance monitoring is the *comparison with the average performance*. In the police response example, you can compare the March crime rate this year (0.2561) with the average of the first 3 months of the year [(0.2120 + 0.1541 + 0.2561)/3 = 0.2074]. Table 5–4 shows the comparison between a monthly crime rate and the average crime rate of the months so far this year. For example, the average in February is 0.1830 [(0.2120 in January + 0.1541 in February)/2]) in the second column of Table 5–4. Notice that the average performance can be replaced or complemented by the median performance or the mode performance.

Shown in column 3 in Table 5–4 of the 10 months in the comparison, the crimes are lower than the average in 3 months and equal to or above the average in 7 months. The comparison shows a trend of crimes higher than the average from March to September except a slight decline in August, which is indicated by all positive figures in column 3 from March to September except that in August, constituting a sign of underperformance during this period.

In addition to comparing with the past and the average, you can measure the performance up against the national, the state, or the regional standards or benchmarks. This is called the *comparison with established performance standards* (or *benchmarks*). The benchmarks could be national, state, or regional averages; the performance of similar organizations; or any established or acceptable performance standards. In the police response example in Table 5–5, the monthly performance is compared with the last year's average crime rate (0.2767) in the cities of similar population sizes in the same geographic region. The 0.2767 is the annualized monthly average obtained by dividing the annual rate by 12 (the actual monthly data of the regional average is not available). The monthly crime rate is also compared with last year's national monthly average (0.3445).

Table 5–4

Crime Rate: Comparison with the Average Performance

	Monthly this year (column 1)	Mean this year (column 2)	Difference from the mean (column 3 = column 1 − column 2)
January	0.2120	0.2120	0.0000
February	0.1541	0.1830	−0.0290
March	0.2561	0.2074	0.0487
April	0.3184	0.2351	0.0833
May	0.3154	0.2512	0.0642
June	0.3306	0.2644	0.0662
July	0.3863	0.2818	0.1045
August	0.2172	0.2738	−0.0566
September	0.3110	0.2779	0.0331
October	0.1619	0.2663	−0.1044
November	NA		
December	NA		
Annual			

Table 5–5

Crime Rate: Comparison with Performance Standards

	Monthly this year (column 1)	Monthly regional average (last year) (column 2)	Difference from regional average (column 3 = column 1 – column 2)	Monthly national average (last year) (column 4)	Difference from national average (column 5 = column 1 – column 4)
January	0.2120	0.2767	−0.0647	0.3445	−0.1325
February	0.1541	0.2767	−0.1226	0.3445	−0.1904
March	0.2561	0.2767	−0.0206	0.3445	−0.0884
April	0.3184	0.2767	0.0417	0.3445	−0.0261
May	0.3154	0.2767	0.0387	0.3445	−0.0291
June	0.3306	0.2767	0.0540	0.3445	−0.0139
July	0.3863	0.2767	0.1097	0.3445	0.0418
August	0.2172	0.2767	−0.0595	0.3445	−0.1273
September	0.3110	0.2767	0.0344	0.3445	−0.0335
October	0.1619	0.2767	−0.1148	0.3445	−0.1826
November	NA	0.2767	NA	0.3445	NA
December	NA	0.2767	NA	0.3445	NA
Annual		3.3200		4.1340	

The results indicate that the city's crime rate is higher than the regional average in 5 of the 10 months. Nonetheless, except in the month of July, the city's crime rate is lower than the national average. The city's crimes were higher than the regional average from April through September except August, suggesting a sign of underperformance during this period. This result is consistent with that from the above comparison with the average performance in Table 5–4.

In sum, the current performance can be compared against the past performance, the average performance, and the established performance standards in performance monitoring. These comparisons apply to all forms of performance measures including percentage measures, aggregate measures, average measures, and per capita measures as well as trend measures of growth rate, percentage difference, and percentage ratio.

Monitoring Performance Variation

Table 5–6 shows performances of 2 garbage collection teams by the tons of the garbage collected in the past 5 days. Which team performs better?

Measured by the average performances, both teams perform at the sample level—30 tons of collection a day. However, which team would you like to pick up your garbage? A closer look at the data shows that there is a larger day-to-day performance difference by Team A,

Table 5–6

Tons of Garbage Collected

Day	Team A	Team B
1	10.00	28.00
2	20.00	29.00
3	30.00	30.00
4	40.00	31.00
5	50.00	32.00
Mean	30.00	30.00

from 10 tons to 50 tons a day, while the difference by Team B is much smaller, from 28 to 32 tons a day, at around 30 tons a day. The performance of Team B is much more consistent and predictable.

Performance variation concerns the difference or the disparity of the performance. Statistically, it reflects the degree of the departure of individual performances (e.g., the ton of garbage collected each day) from the average performance. Monitoring performance variation reveals *performance predictability* and *performance consistency*. Statisticians also use the term *reliable* to describe a consistent and predictable performance. A performance is said to be reliable if the individual performances center closely around the average performance. A performance lacks reliability if individual performances scatter all over so they depart greatly from the average performance. As you can imagine, monitoring performance variation is important because you want to ensure reliable services delivered to residents or customers.

Here is another example. Table 5–7 shows the response times of 2 fire and rescue stations in an urban city. The response times (in minutes) of the recent 10 incidents for each station are presented. Which station performs better? Which station would you like to respond to your emergencies?

The average response time is the same for both stations, 7.4 minutes, but Station B appears to have a larger performance variation, while Station A's performance is more predictable and consistent around 7.4 minutes. Exactly how much variation does each station have? Statisticians use variance, standard deviation, and range to measure performance variation.

Variance (σ^2 or s^2)

$$\sigma^2 = \frac{\sum (X_i - \mu)^2}{N}$$

Each of the individual performance cases ($i = 1,2,3 \ldots N$) is represented by X_i. In Table 5–7, for example, the cases for Station A are the 10 response times. The mean is μ, N is the number of cases, and Σ is the summation symbol where every element in it should be added. The above formula is used when you include *all* performance cases of the study subject. In statistics, a data set that includes all cases of a study subject is known as the *population* (the concepts of

Table 5–7

Response Times of Two Fire and Rescue Stations (in minutes)

Responses of last 10 incidents	Station A	Station B
1	8.00	3.00
2	7.00	12.00
3	8.00	7.00
4	6.00	4.00
5	6.00	4.00
6	9.00	6.00
7	7.00	3.00
8	9.00	9.00
9	8.00	11.00
10	6.00	15.00
Mean	7.40	7.40

population and sample will be discussed with more detail in Chapter 7). For example, if you study all 24,500 students in a university, these 24,500 students constitute a population for your study. However, if you merely draw a sample from the population, the sample variance is

$$s^2 = \frac{\sum (X_i - \bar{X})^2}{n-1}.$$

Individual performance cases ($i = 1,2,3 \ldots n$) are represented by X_i in the sample, $\bar{X}$ is the sample mean, and n is the number of cases in the sample (while the capital letter N represents the number of cases in the population). Notice that the *variance* essentially estimates the distance of each individual performance case from the mean performance (i.e., $X - \bar{X}$). A smaller variance indicates that there is a smaller distance from each individual performance to the mean performance, or in other words, individual performances center more closely on the mean, resulting in a more predictable (close to the mean) and consistent (around the mean) performance.

In our example in Table 5–6, the mean of the daily collections for Team A is 30 [(10 + 20 + 30 + 40 + 50)/5]. The numerator of the formula for the sample variance, 1000 [(10 − 30)² + (20 − 30)² + (30 − 30)² + (40 − 30)² + (50 − 30)²], is divided by the denominator 4 ($n − 1 = 5 − 1$) to arrive at a variance of 250. The variance for Team B's performance is 2.50, much smaller than Team A's variance, so Team B's performance is more predictable, consistent, reliable, and thus better than Team A's performance.

Standard Deviation (σ or s)

The *standard deviation* is simply the square root of the variance. The population standard deviation is symbolized by σ, while the sample standard deviation is denoted by s. In the above example, the sample standard deviations are 15.81 ($\sqrt{250}$) for Team A's performance and 1.58 ($\sqrt{2.5}$) for Team B's. The standard deviation has similar interpretation of the variance. A larger standard deviation indicates a larger performance variation. The standard deviation is used more often as a measure of variation than the variance.

Maximum, Minimum, and Range

You can identify the largest numerical value of the performance (maximum) and the smallest value (minimum). The difference between them (i.e., maximum − minimum) is called the *range*. In the above example of garbage collection, the maximum, the minimum, and the range are 50, 10, and 40 for Team A, and 32, 28, and 4 for Team B. Note that the range is different from the performance ranges defined in Chapter 3. The former is a statistical concept, and the latter is a management concept. There can be multiple performance ranges for a group of data, but there is only one range for the data.

Excel Insert Function (f_x)

Chapter 3 introduces the Excel Data Analysis Descriptive Statistics procedure to obtain a group of descriptive measures such as the mean, the median, or the mode. If you want just one measure, the mean for example, Excel Insert Function (f_x) provides a much easier and more convenient way. For those who do not see the Insert Function symbol (f_x) in your Excel sheet, review Chapter 3 (section "Microsoft Office Excel") on how to load it. Let us say that you want to calculate the mean for the crime rate in Table 5–2.

1. Input the crime data in an Excel sheet, shown as the data array from B3 to B12 in Screen 5–1 and select a cell for the result of the average (B14 in this case).
2. Click the **Insert Function** button (f_x), next to the **Formula** bar, to open the **Insert Function** dialog box, shown in Screen 5–2.
3. Type the name of the function you want to use in the **Search for a Function** window in the **Insert Function** dialog box. If you do not know the name, select a category of formulas you want to work with from the **Select a Category** window. If you are not sure which category you should use, select the **All** category then click a function from the **Select a Function** window and read the definition of the function given below the window.
4. Select the **Average** function because you want to calculate the average of the data. Click **OK**.
5. Select data in cells from B3 to B12 (i.e., B3:B12) in the **Number 1** window (the only calculation in this example) in the **Function Arguments** box. You should be able to see the 0.2663 in the **Formula Result**, shown as in Screen 5–3.
6. Click **OK**. The result should appear in cell B14. You should also see the =AVERAGE (B3: B12) in the **Formula Bar**. In other words, you can use the Formula Bar directly to get your answer if you know the name of the function and the location of the data. Make sure you type the equal sign "=" each time you use the Formula Bar and place a bracket "( )" for the data.

Screen 5–1

Excel Insert Function.

	A	B	C
1		Monthly This Year (t)	
2			
3	January	0.2120	
4	February	0.1541	
5	March	0.2561	
6	April	0.3184	
7	May	0.3154	
8	June	0.3306	
9	July	0.3863	
10	August	0.2172	
11	September	0.3110	
12	October	0.1619	
13			
14	Average		

Screen 5–2

Insert Function Dialog Box.

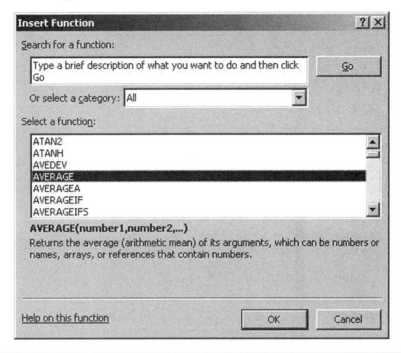

The Excel Insert Function is a very useful calculation tool. Many calculations in this book use it. So knowing how to use it is very important to get through this book. For the convenience of the reader, Table 5–8 shows the names of some popular Insert Functions. A full list of Insert Functions used in this book is provided in Appendix A with related statistical topics covered.

Let us use the police response example to practice the above Excel Insert Function. Table 5–9 shows the measures of performance variation for crimes. For example, the variance so far this year in February (0.0017) is the variance of the crimes in the first 2 months (0.2120 in January and 0.1541 in February). The results show a steady increase over time in the variance and standard deviation, indicating that the crimes have fluctuated more over time, and they have become more unpredictable.

Monitoring Standardized Performance

Let us look at a simple example first. An academic department in a university uses both Graduate Record Exam (GRE) and Graduate Management Admission Test (GMAT) scores in the

Screen 5-3

Insert Function Argument Box.

	A	B
1		Monthly This Year (1)
2		
3	January	0.2120
4	February	0.1541
5	March	0.2561
6	April	0.3184
7	May	0.3154
8	June	0.3306
9	July	0.3863
10	August	0.2172
11	September	0.3110
12	October	0.1619
13		
14	Average	=(B3:B12)

Function Arguments

AVERAGE

Number1 B3:B12 = {0.211961704357026;0.1540567491...

Number2 = number

= 0.266294855

Returns the average (arithmetic mean) of its arguments, which can be numbers or names, arrays, or references that contain numbers.

Number1: number1,number2,... are 1 to 255 numeric arguments for which you want the average.

Formula result = 0.266294855

Help on this function

OK Cancel

Table 5–8

Some Useful Excel Insert Functions (*f_x*)

Function	Name of function in Excel
Mean	AVERAGE
Median	MEDIAN
Mode	MODE
Population variance	VARP
Sample variance	VAR
Population standard deviation	STDEVP
Sample standard deviation	STDEV
Maximum	MAX
Minimum	MIN

Table 5–9

Crime Rate: Measures of Performance Variations

	Monthly this year (column 1)	Variance so far this year (column 2)	Standard deviation so far this year (column 3)	Maximum so far this year (column 4)	Minimum so far this year (column 5)	Range so far this year (column 6 = column 4 − column 5)
January	0.2120					
February	0.1541	0.0017	0.0409	0.2120	0.1541	0.0579
March	0.2561	0.0026	0.0512	0.2561	0.1541	0.1021
April	0.3184	0.0048	0.0695	0.3184	0.1541	0.1643
May	0.3154	0.0049	0.0701	0.3184	0.1541	0.1643
June	0.3306	0.0050	0.0706	0.3306	0.1541	0.1766
July	0.3863	0.0063	0.0792	0.3863	0.1541	0.2323
August	0.2172	0.0059	0.0768	0.3863	0.1541	0.2323
September	0.3110	0.0053	0.0729	0.3863	0.1541	0.2323
October	0.1619	0.0061	0.0779	0.3863	0.1541	0.2323
November	NA					
December	NA					
Annual						

graduate admission. Student A has a GRE of 1050, and Student B has a GMAT of 550, and the department can only accept one student. Which student should be accepted based on the test scores?

The GRE and GMAT scores cannot be compared directly because they use different scoring systems. GREs have a maximum score of 1600, while the maximum score in GMAT is only 800. So you have to use standardized scores for comparison. The standardized scores, also known as z-scores, put 2 different scores in the equal footing for comparison. The z-score of a population with a mean of μ and a standard deviation of σ is

$$z = \frac{X - \mu}{\sigma}.$$

Individual cases are represented by X. The z-score for a sample with a mean of $\bar{X}$ and a standard deviation of s is

$$z = \frac{X - \bar{X}}{s}.$$

In the above example, if the mean of GRE is 1000 with a standard deviation of 100, Student A's z-score is 0.5 [(1050 − 1000)/100]. If the mean of GMAT is 500 with a standard deviation of 50, the z-score of Student B is 1.0 [(550 − 500)/50]. Student B has a higher standardized score and therefore should be accepted by the department.

Standardization of performances allows the tracking and comparing of performances with different measures. For example, a police department can compare standardized crime rates with standardized response times to discover which measure shows a more severe sign of underperformance. Similarly, standardized scores make it possible to compare the performances of a fire department with that of a police department.

Table 5–10 shows the crime rate and the average response time in a police department for the past 10 months, from January to October. The z-scores of both measures are calculated

Table 5–10

Standardized Police Performances

	Number of crimes per 1000 populations	z-Score	Average response time	z-Score
January	0.2120	−0.6973	5.7000	−0.4675
February	0.1541	−1.4405	4.0000	−1.7536
March	0.2561	−0.1307	6.9000	0.4403
April	0.3184	0.6687	8.9000	1.9533
May	0.3154	0.6304	7.4000	0.8186
June	0.3306	0.8255	6.5800	0.1982
July	0.3863	1.5404	5.8000	−0.3919
August	0.2172	−0.6302	6.8000	0.3646
September	0.3110	0.5740	5.4000	−0.6945
October	0.1619	−1.3403	5.7000	−0.4675
Mean	0.2663		6.3180	
Standard Deviation	0.0779		1.3218	

Screen 5–4

Insert Function for *z*-Scores.

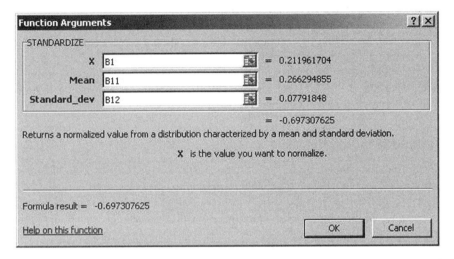

with the mean and standard deviation of the data. The result shows that both crime rates and the response time had best standardized performance in February when the crime rate was low ($z = -1.4405$), and the response time was short ($z = -1.7536$). Nonetheless, the police performance measured in the response time was better than that measured in the crime rate in February (-1.7536 is smaller than -1.4405). The worst police performance in the crime rate was in July ($z = 1.5404$), and the worst performance in the response time occurred in April ($z = 1.9533$), while the response time in April is worse than the crime rate in July from the comparison of their *z*-scores (i.e., 1.9533 is larger than 1.5404).

The *z-scores* can be easily calculated from the Excel Insert Function. The function name is Standardize. For example, the *z*-score of the crime rate in January (-0.6973) is calculated in Excel, shown in Screen 5–4. Notice that you can use Excel autofilling and absolute referencing introduced in Chapter 3 to generate *z*-scores of other months.

A Case Study

Many governmental services are outsourced to business or nonprofit contractors, creating a need to monitor the performance of the contractors to ensure the fulfillment of contractual requirements. The services likely to be contracted out at the local government level include, but are not limited to, air traffic control, legal services, fire protection, trash collection, health care, snow plowing, building maintenance, bill collection, data processing and analysis, street cleaning, steer repair, and recycling. The goals of contracting are usually high service quality and low service cost.

However, if poorly managed, outsourcing could go sour quickly. A government may fail to recognize all costs it should assume in outsourcing decisions. Also, outsourcing can cause a government's over reliance on external suppliers that results in a possible loss of control over critical activities and cost management. Most importantly, a government may lose control over the quality of service provided by a contractor.

The city of St. Stevenson (population 145,000) has used a private company to collect the waste of residents and businesses. Five years ago, the city signed a contract with the company to collect the solid waste and recycled materials from residents and businesses in the city. The contract specifies that the city should assign a full-time performance inspector to enforce the fulfillment of contractual terms with the company.

Step 1: Understanding the Issue

Mr. Eddie Jones is appointed as the performance inspector for the city. One of his very first responsibilities is to examine the contractual terms and to assess the need to regularly monitor the contractor's performance in the solid waste collection, the recycled materials collection, and the cleaning of the streets. He identifies several reasons that make the monitoring necessary.

First, waste collection is one of the most important services to the residents of the city. According to a recent citizen survey, street cleaning along with public safety are the important factors that influence residents' overall satisfaction toward the city government. Continual high performance in waste collection is expected by residents.

Second, waste collection contracts are often long term; contracts longer than 3 years are common. The contract in St. Stevenson was signed for 5 years. A long-term contract may result in less motivation and momentum for the company to improve services. Consistent monitoring may serve as a stimulus for the contractor to improve performance.

Third, waste collection in the city is a supplier market in which only two companies are qualified for and capable of providing the service for the city. Because of the limited competition, the cost to switch to another company if the current contractor performs poorly is very high. It saves taxpayers money if the city regularly monitors the performance of the current provider and provides swift feedback for performance improvement.

Bearing the monitoring need in mind, Eddie believes that the monitoring goals are (1) to frequently and systematically review the progress toward the completion of the contractual terms, (2) to identify areas of underperformance, and (3) to recommend proper performance improvement actions. He also determines that the monitoring subject should be the outcome of solid waste collection services, defined as the satisfaction of users (including residential and business users of the services) and a clean environment of streets, roads, and communities.

Eddie met with the city manager and the finance director to discuss the role of performance monitoring in management and to solicit support from them. He argued that contractual performance monitoring should be a critical part of the city's managerial control process, and the city should integrate the monitoring in its ongoing strategic planning and budgeting process, as well as in its performance measurement and reporting practice.

Step 2: Starting with Questions

Eddie's idea has strong support from the city manager and the finance director. The performance inspector position is secured and is specified as a full-time position to monitor the streets and collection services. Based on the monitoring goals, several monitoring questions have been developed by Eddie:

■ Are the performance goals established for the waste collection met?
■ How good is the performance compared with performance benchmarks?
■ Are there any warning signs of underperformance?
■ Is there any room for performance improvement?

Step 3: Developing a Theory for Monitoring

The success of the monitoring depends on the inspector's knowledge on the production process of the waste collection. Eddie must have an acute understanding of the production flow of waste management and the critical factors that influence the flow. He must use this knowledge to develop a proper measurement process that captures the resources used, the operational elements in which wastes are collected, the outputs of the process on how much waste is collected, and most important, the outcome in user satisfaction and clean environments.

Eddie should develop a theory on how the outcome is affected by the waste collection inputs, process, and outputs, as well as other nonperformance factors such as weather, which may affect the outcome of user satisfaction and clean environments. Using this theory, Eddie can identify the causes of an underperformance quickly and respond properly. He can discover whether the underperformance is *minor* (e.g., waste overflows from containers) that can be fixed quickly with a minor change of the process or *major* (e.g., constant delay in time for waste pickup) that requires structural adjustment of the production process.

Step 4: Developing Measures for Monitoring

The city has collected a total of 20 inputs, outputs, and outcome measures related to the waste collection services. These measures assess the inputs (e.g., the annual total expenses for waste collection, the number of full-time employees involved in waste collection contracting–monitoring–evaluation); the outputs (e.g., the average number of users served per month, the number of tons of waste collected, the percentage of collections made on schedule, the percentage of user complaints handled within 24 hours); and outcomes (e.g., the average response time to a user complaint for a follow-up, the daily number of user complaints, the percentage of complaining users who are satisfied with the follow-up—the user satisfaction rate).

Step 5: Collecting Data and Monitoring Performance

It is impossible to regularly monitor all 20 measures, so Eddie decides to monitor the 2 most important outcome measures: the daily number of user complaints and the percentage of complaining users who are satisfied with the follow-up. Both assess user satisfaction.

Eddie tracks down the number of complaints daily. The follow-up satisfaction rate data were assembled monthly, prior to his monthly meeting with the contractor. In practice, the majority of user complaint calls are received in the city and transferred to the inspector's office. Eddie contacts the contractor to convey the complaints daily by e-mail or phone. Once a complaint is resolved or an explanation is provided, the contractor informs Eddie, who then could call the users to conduct a follow-up survey of satisfaction. Table 5–11 shows the number of user complaints for the past 2 weeks.

Although Eddie communicates with the contractor daily to exchange information, he uses a 5-day period (from Monday to Friday) to decide on whether there is a sign of underperformance based on the number of complaints. He tallies and analyzes the following information every Friday in his monitoring practice:

- the daily number of complaints
- the daily average of this week vs. the daily average of this month until now
- the daily average of this week vs. the daily average of last month
- the daily average of this week vs. the daily average of last year

Comparisons are made for the total number of complaints and, more importantly, for the number of major complaints. From past experience, Eddie knows that a possible warning sign of underperformance is detected if one of the following occurs:

- An increase in the daily number of complaints 5 days in a row.
- An increase in the number of major complaints 5 days in a row .
- The daily average of complaints this week is larger than the daily average of complaints this month until now (or last month or last year).
- The daily average of major complaints this week is larger than the daily average of major complaints this month until now (or last month or last year).

If a warning sign is detected and Eddie finds the need for possible structural changes for the operation, he will call for a face-to-face meeting with the contractor to discuss potential changes needed for performance improvement. In this case, there were a daily average of 15.20 complaints for the week ending on April 6, higher than the daily average of March (14.60) but lower than the daily average of last year (15.32). Wednesday, April 4, saw the largest number of complaints. There were 8 major complaints during the week for a daily average of 1.60. Eddie has asked the contractor to provide a follow-up within a week on the corrective actions made on these major complaints.

There was a daily average of 10.80 complaints for the week ending on April 13, a decline compared with the daily average this month until now (13.00). Nonetheless, there were 9 major complaints this week instead of 8 last week. Eddie decides to raise his concern about this increase in the next meeting with the contractor.

Step 6: Preparing the Performance Monitoring Report

The key monitoring results are prepared by Eddie in a monthly report that is delivered to the city's management and the contractor. Eddie also prepares an annual monitoring report used in the city's annual budgeting process to make contracting and funding decisions.

Table 5-11

Number of User Complaints for Waste Collection in St. Stevenson in April

Date	Minor	Major	Total	Daily average this week (total)	Daily average this month until now (total)	Daily average last month (total)	Daily average last year (total)	Daily average this week (major)	Daily average this month until now (major)	Daily average last month (major)	Daily average last year (major)
Monday, April 2	11.00	3.00	14.00		14.00	14.60	15.32		3.00	3.30	3.60
Tuesday, April 3	17.00	3.00	20.00		17.00	14.60	15.32		3.00	3.30	3.60
Wednesday, April 4	25.00	2.00	27.00		20.33	14.60	15.32		2.67	3.30	3.60
Thursday, April 5	11.00	0.00	11.00		18.00	14.60	15.32		2.00	3.30	3.60
Friday, April 6	4.00	0.00	4.00	15.20	15.20	14.60	15.32	1.60	1.60	3.30	3.60
Monday, April 9	7.00	1.00	8.00		14.00	14.60	15.32		1.50	3.30	3.60
Tuesday, April 10	11.00	2.00	13.00		13.86	14.60	15.32		1.57	3.30	3.60
Wednesday, April 11	10.00	3.00	13.00		13.75	14.60	15.32		1.75	3.30	3.60
Thursday, April 12	10.00	1.00	11.00		13.44	14.60	15.32		1.67	3.30	3.60
Friday, April 13	7.00	2.00	9.00	10.80	13.00	14.60	15.32	1.80	1.70	3.30	3.60

Practices

Key Terms

Performance monitoring
Performance monitoring steps
Monitoring needs
Monitoring goals
Monitoring questions
Monitoring flow
Monitoring subjects
Monitoring frequency
Performance monitoring tools
Monitoring against performance standards
Comparison with the past performance
Comparison with the average performance
Comparison with established performance standards
Warning sign of underperformance
Monitoring performance variation
Performance variation
Performance predictability, consistency, and reliability
Variance
Standard deviation
Maximum, minimum, range
Excel Insert Function (f_x)
Monitoring standardized performance
z-Scores

Practice Problem 5–1

The department of transportation in a state government has four vehicle registration offices in a metropolitan area. The department recently conducted a series of examinations to find out the number of mistakes made in issuing or renewing driver licenses. Twelve tests were conducted in each of these four agencies, and the results are shown in Table 5–12. Input the data in an Excel file.

1. Calculate the mean, the sample variance, the sample standard deviation, the maximum, the minimum, and the range for each agency. Discuss the performances of these agencies. Which agency is the best performer? Which is the worst? What makes you draw these conclusions? If the state decides to retrain agencies one at a time, what would be your priority list of retraining?
2. Use the mean and standard deviation of the all cases to calculate z-scores for all test results.

Table 5–12

Number of Errors in Vehicle License Offices (per 100 licenses issued)

	Office A	Office B	Office C	Office D
Test 1	3.00	6.00	9.00	9.00
Test 2	7.00	3.00	4.00	9.00
Test 3	8.00	2.00	2.00	7.00
Test 4	5.00	5.00	2.00	6.00
Test 5	5.00	2.00	6.00	4.00
Test 6	5.00	9.00	2.00	1.00
Test 7	1.00	6.00	10.00	2.00
Test 8	9.00	4.00	5.00	9.00
Test 9	10.00	8.00	6.00	10.00
Test 10	5.00	2.00	7.00	4.00
Test 11	3.00	2.00	7.00	1.00
Test 12	4.00	1.00	8.00	2.00

Table 5–13

Performance Monitoring of Police Outputs

Monitoring Goal: To improve police response to crime

Monitoring Subject: Crime-responding activities or outputs of police department

Monitoring Question: Has there been an unusual increase in police crime-responding activities recently?

Output Measure 1: Number of calls for services dispatched (911 calls and officer initiated calls included)

Reporting Date: November 1, this year

	Monthly this year	Monthly last year
January	2764	2261
February	2201	2130
March	2029	2458
April	2815	2361
May	3769	3740
June	3917	3928
July	3726	3462
August	3798	3221
September	3193	3520
October	2277	2345
November	NA	2871
December	NA	2347
Total	30,489	34,644

Practice Problem 5–2

An ideal performance monitoring system should track not only outcomes but also inputs, process, and outputs. In the police response example in this chapter, we use a case of outcome monitoring on the crime rate. Table 5–13 shows the data of an output measure of that department: the number of calls for services dispatched. (Note that the measure can be treated as a process measure as well.)

1. Conduct a performance monitoring of the output using the tools of monitoring against performance standards and monitoring performance variation.
2. Write a brief paragraph to discuss whether there is a warning sign of underperformance.

Practice Problem 5–3

Conduct an outcome performance monitoring in an agency of your choice.

CHAPTER 6

Performance Monitoring Chart

I magine that you direct a nonprofit nursing clinic in a high school that provides various health care services to students, and on a regular day, you treat about 10 to 15 students. You could have as many as 20 visitors on a busy day or as little as 5 on a quiet day. You can handle the load as long as it is somewhere between 5 and 20 visitors daily. However, recently, you have seen many days of more than 20 visitors, which makes you wonder what caused the surge and if you should increase the staffing level. On the flip side, if you often had less than 5 visitors a day, you would want to know if you should reduce the staffing level and relocate the resource to other needs.

What Is a Performance Monitoring Chart and Why Do It?

In this example, 2 performance benchmarks, 20 and 5 visitors daily, are used to create a performance range in monitoring the performance variation. Any variation within the range is normal, and no specific action is needed; the variations out of the range are signs of performance warnings that may potentially cause disruptions or redundancies of the services.

A *performance monitoring chart* (PMC) specifies a normal, or acceptable, level of performance variation. It can be used to identify an abnormal performance variation for performance improvement actions. A PMC has been successfully used in the private sector to monitor and control the quality and the cost of products and services. It can be used in the public and nonprofit sectors for the same purposes.

A PMC is particularly important for public services that require intensive and frequent monitoring and timely response to drastic performance decline, such as services in areas of public safety, emergency management, and financial management. Terrorist activities, crimes, traffic conditions, emergency responses, and cash balances are examples in which the warning signs of underperformance need to be identified quickly, and corrective actions need to be taken immediately.

A Little More on Performance Variation

Let us say that, during your drive to work every day, you take the same route, use the same car, and drive at the same time of day. The trip took 30 minutes yesterday but 32 minutes today.

Let us say that the causes of the difference are the normal routines: the traffic was a little worse today, you drove a little slower today (you just cannot keep the same speed all the time so the driving speed has to be a little different from time to time), you made a call to a friend during the drive, or you listened to your favorite but slower rhythm music during the drive. There is really nothing out of the ordinary that causes the 2-minute difference. Statisticians like to call this 2-minute difference the *random variation*, and these causes of random variation the *common causes*.

There can be many common causes for the random variation, and any one of them results in only a small amount of variation. Nonetheless, when added together, the total amount of variation can be large. As stated in the last chapter, a large performance variation is an indication of unreliable or unpredictable services; so, you intend to eliminate it. How much do you do to eliminate common causes? A lot. You would have to stop talking on the phone, stop listening to the music, and start driving at the same speed (is that even possible?). In other words, you would have to completely change the way you drive.

Because there are so many common causes, eliminating them all is very difficult and costly. The complete change of the whole system (your driving behavior in this case) is often needed. So we usually manage to live with the random variation caused by common causes. We accept the fact that random variations of performance are a common occurrence, and nonspecific actions of performance improvement are needed. We say that performance variation from common causes is a product of a stable system.

Now, let us change our example a little. Let us say that you decide to make some changes today. Maybe you became bored driving in the same route again and again, so you tried a new road. Maybe you changed the driving time of day to avoid rush hour traffic, or maybe you cruise controlled for a faster speed. You got there in 20 minutes—10 minutes faster than yesterday. This 10-minute difference was a result of several *specific causes*, and the variation from specific causes is known as the *nonrandom variation*.

You probably realize that specific causes are relatively easy to identify, so they can be addressed relatively easily. In the above example, if you want to eliminate the nonrandom variation in driving time, you need to go back to your old driving routines. In the real management world, the specific causes may be addressed by frontline managers without completely changing the management system.

As you can see from the above example, a good understanding of the difference between random variations and nonrandom variations is the key for performance control. A PMC can help us identify nonrandom performance variations and distinguish them from random performance variations so proper actions can be taken to identify the specific causes of nonrandom performance variations for performance improvement actions.

Creating a Performance Monitoring Chart

In general, three steps are involved in creating a PMC. First, you need to determine the performance measure being monitored. All forms of measures can be used for a PMC (see Chapter 4 for the forms of measures). Although multiple measures can be monitored, it is recommended that one PMC is used for each measure for clarity of presentation. The second step involves the collection of performance data. Data for PMCs are collected frequently, often daily, weekly, or monthly.

Last and most important, a performance range that comprises an *upper performance limit* (UPL) and a *lower performance limit* (LPL) should be specified. These performance limits can be any performance benchmarks or standards deemed to constitute an acceptable performance range by PMC designers or service stakeholders. In other words, PMC must specify a performance range that represents a normally functioned system in which no performance improvement actions are needed. Let us see an example. The data in Table 6–1 reflect the daily number of user complaints received at a solid waste collection service in a local government for the past 20 days.

The average number of daily complaints is 17.80. Suppose you want to be warned when the number exceeds 25, then 25 is the UPL. Any performance above that is an indication that the nonrandom variation may occur. Suppose there are days with no complaints reported at all, so you can set zero as the LPL (see Table 6–2 for the data). Visually, the UPL is the higher monitoring level in a PMC graph, and the LPL is the lower level (shown in Figure 6–1 with the average performance). The PMC shows that the daily number of complaints exceeded the

Table 6–1

Daily Number of User Complaints for Solid Waste Collection Service

Day	Number of complaints
1	18.00
2	14.00
3	21.00
4	26.00
5	26.00
6	29.00
7	9.00
8	19.00
9	25.00
10	15.00
11	17.00
12	12.00
13	11.00
14	15.00
15	16.00
16	9.00
17	17.00
18	18.00
19	21.00
20	18.00

Table 6–2

**Data Needed for Creating a Performance Monitoring Chart:
An Example of Solid Waste Collection Service**

Day	Number of complaints	Average	LPL	UPL
1	18.00	17.80	0.00	25.00
2	14.00	17.80	0.00	25.00
3	21.00	17.80	0.00	25.00
4	26.00	17.80	0.00	25.00
5	26.00	17.80	0.00	25.00
6	29.00	17.80	0.00	25.00
7	9.00	17.80	0.00	25.00
8	19.00	17.80	0.00	25.00
9	25.00	17.80	0.00	25.00
10	15.00	17.80	0.00	25.00
11	17.00	17.80	0.00	25.00
12	12.00	17.80	0.00	25.00
13	11.00	17.80	0.00	25.00
14	15.00	17.80	0.00	25.00
15	16.00	17.80	0.00	25.00
16	9.00	17.80	0.00	25.00
17	17.00	17.80	0.00	25.00
18	18.00	17.80	0.00	25.00
19	21.00	17.80	0.00	25.00
20	18.00	17.80	0.00	25.00

LPL = lower performance limit; UPL = upper performance limit.

UPL in days 4, 5, and 6; inquiry should be made to explore the causes of this performance decline, and subsequent performance improvement actions should be taken.

The key to create a PMC is to determine the performance limits UPL and LPL, which can be performance standards or benchmarks commonly accepted by stakeholders. Best or worst performances can also be used. As a performance analyst, you may use any performance levels with which you feel comfortable.

What if you do not have a good idea on how to determine the performance limits? This chapter introduces a statistical method to help. To understand the concept of the *empirical rule*, say that you examine the response times to fire emergency calls in your city last year. Among thousands of calls received, the fire trucks got there between 4 to 8 minutes most of the time. There were some incidents of responses less than 4 minutes or more than 8 minutes, but rarely did it take less than 2 minute or more than 10 minutes. There were fewer cases as the responses got shorter or longer. If you can visualize this, most responses stack up in the middle of an axis that represents the number of cases of responses with fewer and fewer cases at each end of the axis, forming a bell-shaped histogram just like that shown in Table 3–6 in Chapter 3 or a smoother curve in Figure 6–2. In fact, the data of many performances have bell-shaped

Figure 6–1

Performance Monitoring Chart for Daily Number of User Complaints in Solid Waste Collection Service.

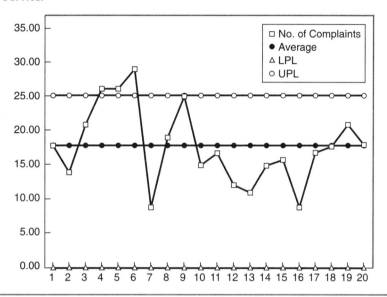

Figure 6–2

Response Times (in minutes).

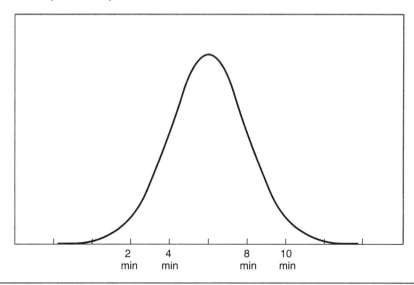

histograms. Examples include the number of daily citizen complaints, college students' GPAs, the number of daily arrests, and the number of crimes daily.

Basically, the empirical rule says that if you know the average (μ) and the standard deviation of the data (σ) and if the histogram of the data is approximately bell shaped, then

- about 68% of the data fall between $\mu - \sigma$ and $\mu + \sigma$;
- about 95% of the data fall between $\mu - 2\sigma$ and $\mu + 2\sigma$; and
- nearly all data (99.7%) fall between $\mu - 3\sigma$ and $\mu + 3\sigma$.

So, if you know that the average response time in your fire department is 6.0 minutes and the standard deviation of response times is 2.0 minutes, about 68% of the responses are between 4.0 ($6.0 - 1 \times 2.0$) and 8.0 ($6.0 + 1 \times 2.0$) minutes, and about 95% of the responses are between 2.0 ($6.0 - 2 \times 2.0$) and 10.0 ($6.0 + 2 \times 2.0$) minutes. Almost all of the responses (99.7%) are between 0.0 ($6.0 - 3 \times 2.0$) and 12.0 ($6.0 + 3 \times 2.0$) minutes.

Because it is very rare for a performance to go above or below three standard deviations of the average, when that does happen, it can be a nonrandom variation caused by specific events that deserve close examination. The following criteria are recommended to discover possible cases of nonrandom variations:

- A single point falls outside the three standard deviations.
- At least two out of three successive values fall on the same side of—and more than two standard deviations away from—the average.
- At least four out of five successive values fall on the same side of—and more than one standard deviation away from—the average.
- At least eight successive values fall on the same side of the average.

Table 6–3 shows the number of traffic accidents reported daily in an urban city for the past 30 days. The average number of traffic accidents is 30.10 with a standard deviation of 6.28. Based on the empirical rule, a performance monitoring chart is created with the performance limits determined by 3σ. The LPL is 11.27 ($30.10 - 3 \times 6.28$), and the UPL is 48.93 ($30.10 + 3 \times 6.28$).

Figure 6–3 visualizes the control chart. The number of accidents is within the performance limit for all the days except day 20 when there were 49 accidents. According to the criteria recommended above, this is a possible case of nonrandom variation that deserves close investigation.

You should exercise several cautions when applying the empirical rule. First, the empirical rule requires that the shape of performance data is either bell curved or close to bell curved. Otherwise, the assumption of using the empirical rule is broken, and the results are not accurate. Moreover, the data that use the empirical rule in this chapter are interval. It is possible to apply the empirical rule for nominal or ordinal data to create monitoring charts, but that coverage requires advanced statistical knowledge, which is beyond this book. Second, efforts should be made to collect sufficient data points in calculating the mean and the standard deviation. The use of a small number of data points could result in an inaccurate estimation of the mean and the standard deviation.

Table 6–3

Daily Number of Traffic Accidents

Day	Number of accidents	Average	LPL	UPL
1	32.00	30.10	11.27	48.93
2	29.00	30.10	11.27	48.93
3	30.00	30.10	11.27	48.93
4	30.00	30.10	11.27	48.93
5	22.00	30.10	11.27	48.93
6	27.00	30.10	11.27	48.93
7	36.00	30.10	11.27	48.93
8	31.00	30.10	11.27	48.93
9	34.00	30.10	11.27	48.93
10	28.00	30.10	11.27	48.93
11	24.00	30.10	11.27	48.93
12	38.00	30.10	11.27	48.93
13	32.00	30.10	11.27	48.93
14	29.00	30.10	11.27	48.93
15	33.00	30.10	11.27	48.93
16	22.00	30.10	11.27	48.93
17	37.00	30.10	11.27	48.93
18	20.00	30.10	11.27	48.93
19	28.00	30.10	11.27	48.93
20	49.00	30.10	11.27	48.93
21	30.00	30.10	11.27	48.93
22	30.00	30.10	11.27	48.93
23	17.00	30.10	11.27	48.93
24	27.00	30.10	11.27	48.93
25	33.00	30.10	11.27	48.93
26	38.00	30.10	11.27	48.93
27	36.00	30.10	11.27	48.93
28	28.00	30.10	11.27	48.93
29	27.00	30.10	11.27	48.93
30	26.00	30.10	11.27	48.93

LPL = lower performance limit; UPL = upper performance limit.

Finally, the empirical rule provides a rational way to identify nonrandom performance variations, but it should not replace human judgment based on careful observation of performance data. A performance analyst should always use his or her experience and combine it with opinions of other stakeholders in determining the performance limits. Also, the performance limits should be determined on a trial-and-error basis before they are adopted, and they should be modified when new data are available.

Figure 6–3

Performance Monitoring Chart for Daily Number of Traffic Accidents.

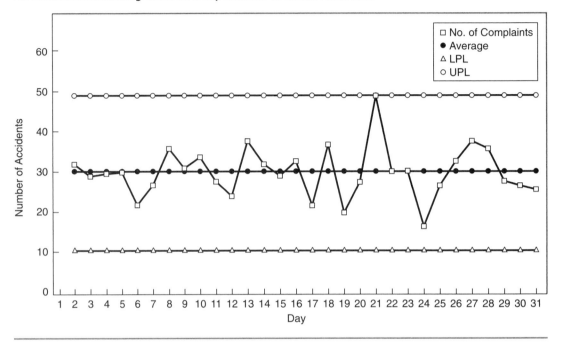

A Case Study

One very important use of a PMC is to respond rapidly to emergencies. The Health and Human Service Department (HHSD) in Greenville County has attempted to develop a performance monitoring system to track reported cases of influenza-like illness (ILI). The purpose of the system is to provide early warnings for any possible outbreaks of influenza in the area. Clearly, identifying a possible outbreak is the first step to control it. The system is also designed to discover any possible cases of avian influenza due to growing global concerns over a potential avian influenza pandemic from a novel strain of bird flu. Ms. Lisa Walsh, the department's performance analyst and statistician, is responsible for the development of the monitoring system.

Step 1: Understanding the Issue

Cases of ILIs have been reported daily in the seven area hospitals. Data are aggregated and reported to HHSD on a monthly basis. It has become clear to Lisa that monthly monitoring is not enough to achieve the monitoring goals stated above. Daily monitoring is needed. The department does have a monitoring system in place, so the cost to update the system from monthly reporting to daily reporting may be manageable. To prepare for the reporting, Lisa proposed to hire a data analyst to collect the data and to conduct the analysis. She also requests a line item in the budget for data collection and analysis.

Since the ILI cases are reported from seven area hospitals, one critical issue in monitoring is how quickly a hospital should enter the information of a case into the system. A consensus has been reached between the department and the hospitals that the information of all new ILI cases should be reported to the department within 24 hours of a patient visit.

It has also been established that daily monitoring data and weekly monitoring reports are available to all related persons in the hospitals and the county's medical emergency response team. In case a warning of a possible outbreak is issued, the county medical emergency response team is ready for immediate responses, all area hospitals are informed immediately, and resources used to respond are mobilized.

Step 2: Developing Monitoring Questions, Theory, and Measures

Because the goal of the system is to provide early warnings, the monitoring question should be the following: Are there any warning signs of a possible influenza outbreak in the county? Other related questions include geographical areas of outbreak in the county, patients' ages and gender compositions, and possible causes of the potential outbreaks. Answers to these questions help the county effectively distribute its resources in the outbreaks.

The monitoring should be a learning experience to understand the patterns and trends of ILIs in the county. A theory that explains what may cause the patterns and trends of ILIs should help the county develop proper strategies to rapidly respond to possible outbreaks or even to avoid future outbreaks. The theory should examine how demographic factors (e.g., population growth) and health care factors (e.g., residents' health care knowledge of the population, health care preventive activities) may influence the patterns and trends of ILIs in the county so that strategies in prevention, preparedness, and response can be developed accordingly.

The number of ILI cases should be a primary measure in the monitoring. The number of cases by hospital (indicating the specific geographic areas of the county), by age, and by gender should help HHSD and the hospitals develop a complete picture of the patterns and trends of ILI cases and gain the knowledge on how to respond effectively to a potential outbreak.

Step 3: Collecting Data and Monitoring Performance

Lisa understands that the key to successful monitoring is to determine what constitutes a warning sign of a possible outbreak. Because reporting a warning will trigger the mobilization of the county's resources in emergency responses, overreporting of ILI warnings when they do not eventually develop into outbreaks will drain the county's resources, and underreporting of warnings when there are real outbreaks will cause delay in response and inflict pain in patients.

After intensive consulting with the hospitals and the county medical emergency response team, Lisa decides to use the following criteria to guide her monitoring. A warning is issued to HHSD and the area hospitals when

- the number of reported ILI cases exceeds by 2 standard deviations for 2 consecutive days, or
- the number of reported ILI cases exceeds by 3 standard deviations.

Lisa has the data of reported ILI cases from the 7 area hospitals in the past 2 years. The data show a mean of 5.30 per day and a standard deviation of 2.13. A warning is issued when the number of reported cases is nearly equal to 9 (5.30 + 2 × 2.13) for 2 consecutive days or when the number of reported cases is nearly equal to 11 (5.30 + 3 × 2.13) cases a day. Moreover, the lower limit of the reported cases should also be established for possible under-reporting of cases. An investigation should be triggered for possible underreporting if the number of reported cases is equal to or less than nearly 1 (5.30 − 2 × 2.13) case daily for 2 consecutive days.

Lisa has notified these monitoring limits to the hospitals and the county medical emergency response team, acknowledging that these limits will change frequently to reflect the data from new cases. She has also promised them that she will keep constant communication with all related parties on her monitoring practice to ensure a high-quality monitoring system of ILI cases.

Practices

Key Terms

Performance monitoring chart (PMC)
Random variation
Nonrandom variation
Common causes
Specific causes
Upper performance limit (UPL)
Lower performance limit (LPL)
Empirical rule
Application of the empirical rule in developing a PMC
Recommended criteria to judge possible nonrandom variation based on the empirical rule

Practice Problem 6–1

Assume that you took a math test and scored 86 out of 100 points, and a few months later you retook the same test. Also assume that your math level has not changed during that time. Is your chance of getting exactly 86 points great? Assume that you got 85 in the repeat. What could cause the variation of your performance? Are they common causes or specific causes?

Practice Problem 6–2

Like the above exercise, this question also helps you understand the concepts of random and nonrandom variations. First, identify a repeated activity or process you do daily in your personal life (e.g., eating lunch, driving to work, spending money on lunch). Second, develop a measure of the activity or process (e.g., the duration of the lunch by minutes, amount of money spent on lunch). Third, measure the activity daily over a month. Report the data in an Excel sheet. Use this case to explain the concepts of the random variation and the nonrandom variation. Do you observe any possible nonrandom variations? What may cause the random variation of the activity measured (i.e., the common causes)? What may cause the nonrandom variation of the activity measured (i.e., specific causes)?

Now, repeat the above practice on a performance in a public or nonprofit organization of your choice. Examples of measures could be the number of daily resident (or customer) complaints, the number of requests received daily for information, the number of daily errors made on a specific procedure, or the number of minutes spent on a specific repeated task.

Practice Problem 6–3

Medical emergency response times consist of call-taking time and dispatch time. Call-taking time is the time from the receipt of the call until dispatch, and dispatch time is the time from dispatch to arrival at the scene. So, any effort to improve response times should include strategies to improve call taking as well as strategies to improve dispatch. Table 6–4 reflects 20 responses by a city's emergency response team during last week.

Table 6–4

Emergency Medical Response Times (in seconds)

Call	Call-taking time	Dispatch time
1	48	320
2	60	480
3	60	456
4	60	234
5	90	483
6	98	563
7	60	390
8	30	360
9	48	360
10	60	340
11	90	459
12	55	348
13	60	290
14	45	267
15	56	356
16	90	457
17	98	239
18	148	453
19	70	480
20	60	397

Table 6–5

Number of ILI Cases Reported in Greenville

Day	Number of ILI cases	Day	Number of ILI cases
1	2	16	4
2	6	17	2
3	3	18	6
4	8	19	3
5	4	20	8
6	5	21	9
7	7	22	3
8	2	23	5
9	10	24	7
10	12	25	4
11	3	26	1
12	5	27	9
13	1	28	3
14	14	29	5
15	7	30	6

ILI = influenza-like illness.

Create PMC charts for the call-taking times, dispatch times, and response times. Use two standard deviations above the mean (e.g., the mean + two standard deviations) to judge if there is a warning sign of performance deterioration.

Practice Problem 6–4

Refer to the case study in this chapter, the data in Table 6–5 show the actual number of ILI cases in the past 30 days. Use these data to calculate the mean and the standard deviations to develop a PMC(s). Do you find any dates when warnings should be issued? What criteria do you use to determine a warning sign?

CHAPTER 7

Statistical Performance Monitoring

L et us say you manage a city of a half million residents, and once a year you ask residents how well they like the city's services. Because it is too costly to survey all residents, you draw a small portion of them to ask. In this example, the city's residents are the *subjects of the study*, the small portion is a *sample of the subjects*, and the half million residents are the *population of the subjects*. In many cases of performance analysis, obtaining the population is either too costly or impossible. Even a small nonprofit operation could serve hundreds of customers. A small or midsize city could serve thousands of residents. An emergency response team could respond to hundreds of requests for assistances. When the subjects of the study are many, we often rely on samples in performance analysis. This chapter introduces a tool to monitor performance based on samples.

Important Statistical Concepts

Populations, Samples, Parameters, and Statistics

The *population* is the total set of the subjects in a performance analysis. A *sample* is a portion or subset of the population. A sample is studied when the population is not available. Let us say you survey 1000 residents out of the half million in the above example. One thing you want to find out is residents' average age because you believe that the age may have something to do with residents' assessments on the city services—older residents may rate more favorably on city services.

Getting the true average age of all residents is too costly because it requires a survey of every resident in the city. So you decide to go with an estimate from the sample. Suppose the average age of the 1000 residents in the sample is 40.1. This sample average, the sample mean, can be used as an estimate for the average age of all residents. Similarly, a sample can be used to estimate the median, the mode, the variance, or the standard deviation of a population. The numerical estimates from a sample are known as *statistics*, while the population characteristics being estimated are called *parameters*.

Because the purpose of statistics is to estimate parameters from a sample, a fundamental question in statistics is how accurate the estimation is. That is, in the above example, how close the sample average of 40.1 is to the true average age of the half million residents in the city.

Statistical methods that use samples to estimate population parameters are known as *inferential statistics*.

Probability and Probability Distributions

Let us say you asked the sample of 1000 residents how happy they were with city services. Suppose that, out of the 1000 in the sample, 600 (or 60%) said they were happy, and the other 400 (or 40%) said they were unhappy. If you are about to ask one more person (your 1001st subject), what is the chance, or probability, that person is happy about the services? It is 60%. So, what is the probability? By definition, the *probability* of a particular result (being happy in this case) is the proportion of times that result would occur in a long run of repeated observations. The probability value goes from 0 to 1. A value of 0 indicates the result does not occur, while 1 means it occurs for sure.

Why is the concept of probability critical in statistics? Realize that, although 60% of respondents in your survey are happy with the city services, you cannot really say that 60% of *all residents* in your city are happy with the services. This is because the 60% is an estimate from a sample, and there is *always* a difference between a sample estimate and the true population parameter being estimated. Think about this: What is the chance that the true percentage of all residents who are happy about services is exactly 60%? It is very slim if there is any. So there is a difference between the 60% and the true percentage. This difference, also known as the *estimation error*, always exists when a sample is used to estimate the population. This is the reason why we have to use probability, not certainty, in statistical analyses. We have to use the language of probability to describe the results of the analyses based on samples.

What does a probability look like? One way to visualize the probability is through the *probability distribution*. In our example, there are two results (happy or unhappy with services) of residents' satisfaction for city services. The probability distribution of the citizen satisfaction is shown in Table 7–1, which presents all possible results along with their probabilities.

Notice that the probability of each result falls between 0 and 1, and the total probability of all results *always* equals 1 (or 100%). The probability distribution can also be presented in a histogram shown in Figure 7–1.

Notice that there are only two results of the citizen satisfaction rate in the histogram (happy or unhappy). It is an ordinal measure that has two values (see Chapter 2 for the concept of measurement level). What does the probability distribution of an interval measure look like?

Table 7–1

Probability Distribution of Citizen Satisfaction

Result	Probability
Happy with the services	0.6 (or 60%)
Unhappy with the services	0.4 (or 40%)
Total	1.0 (or 100%)

Figure 7–1

Probability Distribution of Citizen Survey Results: A Histogram.

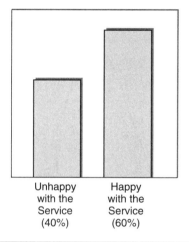

An interval measure often has continual numeric values such as residents' ages in the citizen survey example if respondents are asked to provide their ages in years (e.g., 23, 35, or 67 years of age).

Let us say the probability distribution of the residents' ages in the city has a symmetric and bell-shaped distribution with a mean of μ and a standard deviation of σ; then we say the ages are normally distributed or the age measure has a *normal probability distribution* or a normal distribution. As discussed in Chapter 6, the empirical rule applies when a performance is normally distributed with about 68% of data falling within 1 standard deviation of the mean, as shown in Figure 7–2. About 95% and more than 99% of all cases fall within 2 and 3 standard deviations, respectively.

For example, if the average age of the residents is 40 years, and the standard deviation is 15, then about 68% of residents have ages between 25 (40 − 15) and 55 (40 + 15) years, about 95% between 10 (40 − 30) and 70 (40 + 30) years, and more than 99% (99.7%) between nearly equal to 0 (40 − 45) and 85 (40 + 45) years. The normal probability distribution is the most important distribution in statistics because it approximates well the distributions of many interval performance measures such as individuals' annual incomes, the number of years of school completed, heights, weights, and traffic times to the work.

Basic Concepts of Statistical Estimation

Suppose the average age of our sample of 1000 residents is 40.1 years. How close is it to the true average age of all residents? In other words, how accurate is the sample mean to the population mean? To answer this question, we need to introduce the concepts of the sampling

Figure 7–2

Probability Distribution of Age.

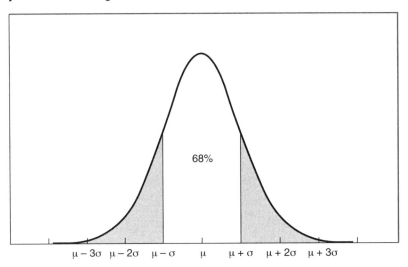

distribution and the central limit theorem. Let $\bar{X}$ represent the sample mean, and μ be the population mean.

I want you to imagine a situation that only exists in a hypothetical world. Assume that you *constantly* draw samples from a population and calculate their means. The probability distribution of these sample means is called the *sampling distribution*. The *central limit theorem* basically says that when the sample size is large enough (equal to or greater than 30), the sampling distribution of these sample means is approximately normal, with a mean equal to the population mean μ. How close a sample mean is to the true population mean is measured by something called the *standard error*, $\sigma_{\bar{x}}$, calculated from

$$\sigma_{\bar{x}} = \frac{\sigma}{\sqrt{n}}.$$

The standard deviation of the population is σ, and n is the *sample size*, which is the number of cases in the sample (1000 residents in our example). The standard error can be seen as a measure of accuracy of estimation. As the sample size (n, the denominator in the standard error equation) increases, the standard error $\sigma_{\bar{x}}$ is smaller. So a sample mean is closer to the population mean for a larger sample. Also, for a large sample ($n \geq 30$), the sample standard deviation s is approximately equal to the population standard deviation σ. So the standard error can be estimated from

$$\sigma_{\bar{X}} = \frac{s}{\sqrt{n}}.$$

The central limit theorem is true even if the population distribution is far from normal. Now, come back to our original question of how close our sample mean of 40.1 is to the population mean. Of course, we are never going to know the true average age unless we ask every resident in the city. However, if we are able to say something like "it is very likely that the true average age is between 37.0 and 43.0 years," it is still a pretty good achievement in estimation. In this case, an interval (37.0, 43.0) is established so the true population age will fall in it. This is called the *confidence interval* estimation. The next section focuses on creating a confidence interval.

Statistical Estimation Processes

Large-Sample Confidence Intervals for a Mean

If the sample size is equal to or larger than 30, you can use the following equation to estimate a confidence interval for a population mean:

$$\bar{X} \pm z\sigma_{\bar{x}} = \bar{X} \pm z\left(\frac{s}{\sqrt{n}}\right).$$

The sample mean is $\bar{X}$, the standard error is $\sigma_{\bar{x}}$ that can be estimated from $\sigma_{\bar{x}} = \frac{s}{\sqrt{n}}$, while s is the sample standard deviation, and n is the sample size. What is z? Remember that we introduced the z-score in Chapter 5 while studying standardized performance. z-Scores are standardized scores, and each z-score has a corresponding probability that represents how likely a confidence interval includes the true population mean. What does that mean? Think this way. If we could keep drawing samples 100 times and create 100 confidence intervals, and if 95 of these 100 confidence intervals include the true population mean, we are 95% confident that these confidence intervals include the true population mean, and these are *95% confidence intervals*. What is the z-score for a 95% confidence interval? The NORMSINV process in the Excel Insert Function (f_x) calculates that easily (shown in Screen 7–1). The NORMSINV procedure assumes a *standard normal distribution* for its calculation. This is a specific normal distribution with $\mu = 0$ and $\sigma = 1$.

The result shows that the z-score for a 95% confidence interval is 1.96. Notice that, in the probability window, I type in 97.5% (0.975), not 95%. Why? Shown in Figure 7–3, z-scores are normally distributed, and their probability distribution is symmetric with one side of the normal probability curve mirroring the other side. Keep in mind that the total probability of all z-scores is 100%, so one side of the curve is 50%. Also shown in Figure 7–3, the 95% probability takes the middle space in the curve, leaving 5% (100% − 95%) that is not covered under the 95% probability in the 2 tails of the curve (one on each side of the curve). Because the curve is symmetric, the probability in each tail is 2.5%.

Screen 7–1

The z-Score for the 95% Confidence Interval.

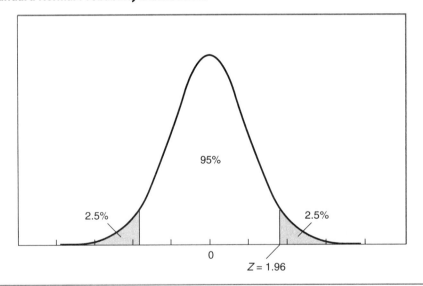

Figure 7–3

The Standard Normal Probability Distribution.

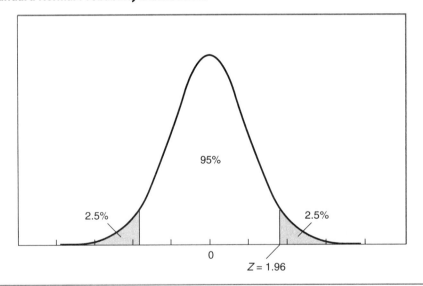

The NORMSINV procedure uses a cumulative probability for a *z*-score, which is the probability to the left area of the *z*-score that includes the 95% probability and the tail on the left side of the curve (2.5%). This is why you should type 97.5% (2.5% + 95%) in the NORMSINV procedure to calculate the probability for a 95% confidence interval. Similarly, you can calculate the *z*-score for a *99% confidence interval*. It should be 2.58. Make sure you type in a probability of 99.5% (0.5% + 99%) or 0.995 in the Excel NORMSINV window for the probability.

Now, let us see an example. A university administration wants to estimate students' average GPAs, which is scored from 0 to 4 (the highest); 250 students are selected. The average GPA in the sample is 2.751 with a standard deviation of 0.50. Create a confidence interval to estimate the average GPA of all students in the university.

We know $\bar{X} = 2.751$ and $\sigma_{\bar{x}} = s/\sqrt{n} = 0.50/\sqrt{250} = 0.50/15.81 = 0.0316$. Calculated from the confidence interval equation above, the lower bound of a 95% confidence interval is $\bar{X} - z\sigma_{\bar{x}}$ = 2.751 − 1.96 × 0.0316 = 2.751 − 0.0619 = 2.689. The upper bound of the interval is $\bar{X} + z\sigma_{\bar{x}}$ = 2.751 + 0.0619 = 2.813. So the 95% confidence interval is (2.689, 2.813), which means that we are 95% confident that the GPA average of all students at the university is between 2.689 and 2.813. The lower end of a 99% confidence interval is $\bar{X} - z\sigma_{\bar{x}}$ = 2.751 − 2.58 × 0.0316 = 2.669. Its upper end is $\bar{X} + z\sigma_{\bar{x}}$ = 2.751 + 0.0815 = 2.833. We are 99% confident that the GPA average of all students is between 2.669 and 2.833.

A 99% confidence interval gives you a better chance to include the average than the 95% interval, but it comes with a cost. Realize that a 99% confidence interval is always wider than a 95% confidence interval for the same estimation, and a wider interval is less accurate and less insightful in estimation. A very wide interval does not tell us much. We learn little from a finding, say, that there is a very good chance that the GPA average of all students is between 0.5 and 3.5. You pretty much can guess that without any calculation. By using a 99% confidence interval instead of a 95% interval, you gain a greater probability (for the true mean to fall in) at the cost of a less accurate estimate. It is like shooting a target. The bigger the target sign is, the more likely you'll hit it. However, hitting a larger target does not mean that you are as accurate a shooter as hitting a smaller one.

Among numerous confidence intervals that can be created, the 95% and 99% confidence intervals are most popular, so I recommend you memorize the *z*-scores for them. The *z*-scores for the 95% interval (1.96) and for the 99% interval (2.58) are also known as the *critical values* associated with these 2 probabilities (95% and 99%). We will learn later in the book that these probabilities are necessary in making decisions and drawing conclusions in hypothesis testing. Moreover, remembering these 2 critical values can save you time in calculation, although it should be easy to use Excel to get the *z*-score for any confidence interval of your interest.

Small-Sample Confidence Intervals for a Mean

When the sample size is smaller than 30, the *z* distribution (i.e., the normal distribution) is replaced by something called the *t distribution*. The confidence interval with a *t* distribution is

$$\bar{X} \pm t\sigma_{\bar{x}} = \bar{X} \pm t\left(\frac{s}{\sqrt{n}}\right).$$

The t distribution is also bell shaped and symmetric. Nonetheless, compared with that of the z distribution, the bell-shaped curve of the t distribution is flatter. This is because the small sample size reduces the accuracy in estimation. How flat the shape of the t distribution curve is really depends on something called the *degrees of freedom*, which is $n - 1$ in the confidence interval estimation. A smaller sample size leads to a flatter bell shape of the curve. The larger the degree of freedom, the closer the t distribution is to the z distribution.

When the sample size is large, the t distribution is approximately the z distribution, and the t-score is approximately the z-score. For example, recall that the z-score for a 95% confidence interval is 1.96. When the sample size is 1000 (a large sample size), the t for a 95% confidence interval is 1.96, shown in the Excel Insert Function (f_x) TINV procedure in Screen 7–2. Realizing that TINV gives the inverse of the probability, I type in 0.05 or 5% (100% − 95%) in the probability window instead of the 95%. The degrees of freedom are 999 (1000 − 1).

Here is an example of how to use the t distribution to create a confidence interval. A fire chief in a large urban city wants to know the average response time of the city's fire emergency response team. Because there are thousands of responses every year, it is very difficult to have the average of them all. A sample of 25 responses was randomly selected. The sample mean is 6.40 minutes with a standard deviation of 1.20 minutes. Create a confidence interval to estimate the average response time of the response team. First, the t value with degrees of freedom of 24 (25 − 1) for a 95% confidence interval is 2.064, shown in Screen 7–3.

We know $\bar{X} = 6.400$ and $\sigma_{\bar{x}} = s/\sqrt{n} = 1.20/\sqrt{25} = 1.20/5.00 = 0.240$. The lower bound of a 95% confidence interval is $\bar{X} - t\sigma_{\bar{x}} = 6.400 - 2.064 \times 0.240 = 6.400 - 0.495 = 5.905$. The

Screen 7–2

The *t*-Score for the 95% Confidence Interval with a Large Sample (*n* = 1000).

Screen 7–3

The *t*-Score for a 95% Confidence Interval with *n* = 25.

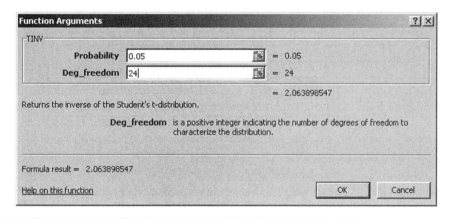

upper bound of the interval is $\bar{X} + t\sigma_{\bar{X}} = 6.400 + 0.495 = 6.895$. We are 95% confident that the average response time of all responses is between 5.905 and 6.895 minutes.

Similarly, you should be able to use Excel to obtain a *t* score of 2.797 for a 99% confidence interval with a sample size of 25. The lower end of a 99% confidence interval is $\bar{X} - t\sigma_{\bar{X}} = 6.400 - 2.797 \times 0.240 = 6.400 - 0.671 = 5.729$. The upper end is $\bar{X} + t\sigma_{\bar{X}} = 6.400 + 0.671 = 7.071$. We are 99% confident that the average response time is between 5.729 and 7.071 minutes.

There is an important point for confidence interval estimations. The *t* distribution should be used for small-sample estimations, and the *t* distribution is approximately the *z* distribution for large samples, so the *t* distribution can be used for both large-sample and small-sample estimations. In other words, the *t* distribution is more applicable than the *z* distribution for constructing confidence intervals. You can always use *t*-scores to create confidence intervals.

Confidence Intervals for a Proportion (Percentage)

So far we deal with the confidence interval estimation for a mean. How do you estimate a proportion? Recall that, at the beginning of this chapter, we use an example of citizen satisfaction rate for city services. How can we estimate the confidence interval for that rate? Let $\hat{\pi}$ be the sample proportion. The confidence interval for a population proportion can be obtained from

$$\hat{\pi} \pm t\sigma_{\hat{\pi}}.$$

The standard error of the proportion, $\sigma_{\hat{\pi}}$, can be estimated from

$$\sigma_{\hat{\pi}} = \sqrt{\frac{\hat{\pi}(1-\hat{\pi})}{n}}.$$

Let us say we survey 1000 residents and 60% of them are happy with services ($\sigma_{\hat{\pi}} = \sqrt{(0.60)(1-0.60)/1000} = \sqrt{0.24/1000} = 0.0155$). The lower bound of the 95% confidence interval is $0.60 - 1.96 \times 0.0155 = 0.600 - 0.0304 = 0.5696$. The upper bound is $0.600 + 0.0304 = 0.6304$. We are 95% confident that the citizen satisfaction rate is between 56.96% and 63.04%. Could you use the same method to calculate a 99% confidence interval for the satisfaction rate?

A Case Study

One important use of performance monitoring is to track the need of residents. The Women Resource Foundation (WRF), a nonprofit organization in an urban city of about 1 million residents, provides emergency human services to women and others. Most of its clients are victims of domestic and other violence who desperately need help with emergency medical supplies, shelters, and food. The foundation has 20 employees, including 8 full-time administrative staff and case managers and 12 part-time volunteers, and is funded by grants from the state and the federal government as well as business donations. The foundation is governed by a board of 8 members from local communities.

Services of the foundation include a temporary shelter, food supply, and medical referral and assistance. The foundation's operation of food supply is teamed up with a major local grocery chain. The grocery provides perishable food items such as breads, soups, and pastry products. The food supply is sufficient enough to meet the need of WRF clients, but the grocery wants to know how much food is needed from WRF so it can plan its supply line.

Step 1: Understanding the Issue

The grocery needs to know on a weekly basis how much food is needed by WRF so it can minimize the potential waste of foods that are left unconsumed. Because these foods are perishable items that last only a short time, the grocery wants a relatively accurate estimate for the amount of consumption for perishable food items by WRF clients.

Mark Blunt, the performance analyst hired by WRF, is responsible for conducting the analysis. Mark realizes that the foundation receives hundreds of requests for assistance every day, and it is very difficult to gather the information of all these requests, so the sample information is needed and confidence intervals for estimation should be created.

Step 2: Developing Monitoring Questions and Measures

Evidently, the monitoring question is how much perishable food is needed weekly by WRF clients. To answer this question, Mark first needs to know how many WRF clients need perishable food, which can be calculated from

The average weekly number of clients who need perishable food = the average weekly number of clients × the percentage of clients who need perishable food.

Thus, the estimation consists of two elements: the weekly number of clients and the percentage of clients who need perishable food. They are the measures used in the estimation.

Step 3: Estimating the Average Weekly Number of Clients

The foundation uses an intake assessment process to determine the qualification of clients and their needs. Mark tallied a sample of the intake assessment logs for the past 20 weeks to obtain the weekly number of clients, shown in Table 7–2.

The Excel Insert Function is used to calculate the average weekly number of clients (132.850) and the standard deviation (32.993). The standard error of the sample is 7.378. Because the sample size is 20 (smaller than 30), the t distribution and $\bar{X} \pm t\sigma_{\bar{X}}$ are used to

Table 7–2

Weekly Number of Clients of WRF

Week	Number of clients
1	132
2	143
3	167
4	121
5	176
6	123
7	89
8	145
9	165
10	133
11	156
12	93
13	98
14	188
15	176
16	84
17	75
18	127
19	123
20	143
Mean	132.850
Standard deviation	32.993
Standard error	7.378

Screen 7–4

The *t* for a 95% Confidence Interval with *n* = 20.

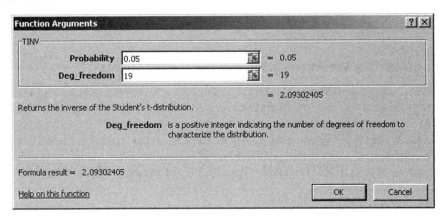

create the confidence interval. With degrees of freedom of 19 (20 − 1), the *t*-score for a 95% confidence interval is 2.093, as shown in Screen 7–4.

The lower bound of the interval is 117.408 (132.850 − 2.093 × 7.378 = 132.850 − 15.442), and the upper bound is 148.292 (132.850 + 15.442). So Mark is 95% confident that the average weekly number of clients is between 118 and 149 (numbers rounded up to integers).

Step 4: Estimating the Percentage of Clients Who Need Perishable Food

To estimate the percentage of clients who need perishable food, Mark selected a sample of 50 clients who are qualified for the services in the intake assessment process. Once a client was identified, a simple survey was filled out by the receptionist to specify whether the client needed perishable items. The survey shows that 42 clients need perishable food, so $\hat{\pi} = 42/50 = 0.84$. The confidence interval for a population proportion can be obtained from $\hat{\pi} \pm t\sigma_{\hat{\pi}}$. The standard error of the proportion is $\sigma_{\hat{\pi}} = \sqrt{(0.84)(1 - 0.84)/50} = \sqrt{0.1344/50} = 0.0519$. The *t* for a 95% confidence interval with degrees of freedom of 49 (50 − 1) is 2.009, calculated from the Excel TINV procedure.

The lower bound of the 95% confidence interval is 0.736 (0.840 − 2.009 × 0.0519 = 0.840 − 0.104). The upper bound is 0.944 (0.840 + 0.104). So Mark is 95% confident that between 73.6% and 94.4% of the clients need perishable food.

Step 5: Reporting the Monitoring Results

From the above estimations, Mark concludes that the average weekly number of clients is between 118 and 149 and between 73.6% and 94.4% of them need perishable food, so the average weekly number of clients who need perishable food is between nearly equal to 87 (118

× 73.6%) and nearly equal to 141 (149 × 94.4%). After listening to Mark's findings, the foundation decided to base its request on the upper end, 141 clients per week, to be on the safe side of the estimation for sufficient perishable foods. The foundation also asked Mark to continue the estimation on a monthly basis in order to modify the request with the new information.

Practices

Key Terms

Subjects of the study
Sample of the subjects
Population of the subjects
Parameters
Statistics
Inferential statistics
Probability
Estimation error
Probability distribution
Normal probability distribution
Sampling distribution
Central limit theorem
Standard error
Sample size
Confidence intervals
95% confidence intervals
99% confidence intervals
Standard normal distribution
Two critical values
t distribution
Degrees of freedom
Confidence intervals for a mean
Confident intervals for a proportion

Practice Problem 7–1

The authority in a school district is very concerned about a recent newspaper report of the high absence rate among students in the district. The report says that the absence rate of the district may be well above the state average of 11.30 days a year per student. The authority wants to closely monitor the absence rate trend. To start, a sample of 250 students in the district was drawn to develop a baseline performance target for the performance tracking. The average absence rate of the sample is 11.90 days per student with a standard deviation of 3.90. Create a 95% and a 99% confidence interval to estimate the absence rate of the district.

Practice Problem 7–2

A citizen satisfaction survey on policing services was conducted in a city of about 100,000 residents. Of 1934 residents in the sample who returned the survey, 895 said they were either "happy" or "very happy" with the services, and 1039 said that they were "unhappy" or chose "don't know." Create a 95% and a 99% confidence interval to predict the percentage of residents who are "happy" or "very happy" about the police services.

Practice Problem 7–3

The number of vehicle accidents is sampled from a city's 20 major traffic intersections and their adjacent areas several times a day to assess traffic congestion. The police department uses the information to allocate resources of traffic control. A performance standard of an average of 2.0 accidents per hour per area is established. A traffic emergency control system is mobilized and resources are directed to traffic control once the traffic condition is equal to or worse than the standard. Table 7–3 shows the accident information taken between 7:00 am and 8:00 am today. Should the police department mobilize the traffic emergency control system? Why or why not?

Table 7–3

Number of Accidents in an Urban City

Areas	Number of accidents
1	0
2	3
3	1
4	2
5	0
6	0
7	2
8	3
9	1
10	3
11	2
12	2
13	5
14	1
15	2
16	0
17	2
18	1
19	0
20	2

Screen 7–5

Simple Random Sampling.

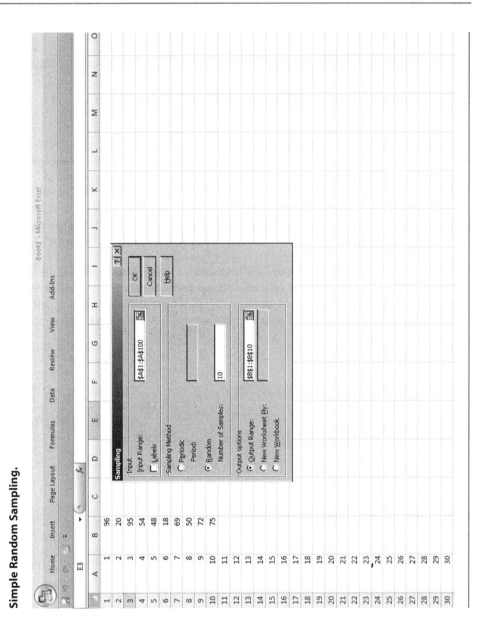

Practice Problem 7–4

The theories of sampling are beyond the coverage of this book but should be discussed in any research methodology texts. This practice shows you how to use Excel Data Analysis to select a random sample by the simple random sampling technique.

1. Click **Data Analysis** in the **Analysis** group on the **Data tab** (for Excel 2003 users, click the **Data Analysis** tab on the **Tools** menu).
2. Select the **Sampling** dialog window. Excel allows you to sample randomly from an input range, which means that every case in the input range has the same chance to be chosen. Screen 7–5 shows an example in which 10 numbers in Column B are selected from an input range of 100 numbers (the sampling frame) coded as 1 through 100 in Column A. If the same number is selected more than once, repeat the process to select more numbers. Use the **Help** button in the dialog window if you need assistance in this procedure.

Additionally, the **Random Number Generation** in **Excel Data Analysis** allows you the choices of selecting the number of variables, the number of random numbers, the probability distribution used in selecting the random numbers, and sometimes, the parameters used in defining your selection based on the distribution you choose. Use the **Help** button in the random number generation if you have any questions about these choices.

Section IV

Understanding Performance

CHAPTER 8

Performance Understanding Basics

S uppose you took a college math class and scored poorly. You figure that the reason for the poor performance was your study method—you were studying alone on a difficult topic. When you retook the class, you worked in a group with other students and did much better. You conclude that studying in a group improves your math performance. In this simple example, you experience an underperformance manifested by your poor math score, you identify a need to improve performance, you empirically discover the cause of the underperformance—the studying method—and you draw a lesson that you will need to study in a group to improve the performance.

What Is Performance Understanding and Why Do It?

Performance understanding is a process to discover the causes of underperformance. It is a systematic approach to explore the issue of underperformance, to understand what may cause the underperformance, and to empirically determine the causes of underperformance. Performance understanding starts with an issue of underperformance and ends with suggestions to improve the performance.

Performance understanding is the essential link among the steps in the logical model of performance improvement: performance description → performance monitoring → performance understanding → performance evaluation. *Performance description* specifies the performance status; *performance monitoring* identifies underperformance; *performance understanding* discovers causes of underperformance and suggests performance improvement strategies; *performance evaluation* assesses the results of performance improvement strategies.

What is *underperformance*? The term underperformance is defined broadly in this book as any performance not up to expectation. It is any performance deemed to have room for improvement. It can be a trend of performance deterioration over time, a large undesirable performance variation such as that away from plus or minus three standard deviations, or a performance inferior to established performance standards.

Why performance understanding? Discovering causes of underperformance is a necessary first step for performance improvement, which is the ultimate goal of performance analysis. A performance analysis serves a much lesser value if it is not for performance improvement. Moreover, discovering causes of underperformance is perhaps the most difficult aspect of performance analysis. It can be conceptually exhaustive because it requires a comprehensive exploration of the production or the service delivery process to discover key causes of an underperformance; it can be technically challenging because it often asks for a complex empirical examination on how performance is affected by these key causes. Additionally, it often is a long and continuous process because the causes of underperformance change over time, and identifying these causes is needed for long-term and *sustainable* performance improvement.

Finally, there is a practical reason to understand causes of underperformance. For agencies to make resource requests in budgets, in grant applications, or in strategic plans, discovering causes of underperformances strengthens their rationale of the resource requests to improve performance.

What questions should be asked in performance understanding? The generic forms of questions in performance understanding include the following: What causes underperformance? Why does an organization underperform? What is the relationship between the performance and possible causes of the performance? How is the performance affected by the causes? What can be done to improve performance?

There are several steps in performance understanding, modified from the generic steps of performance analysis in Chapter 2, to focus on the issue of discovering underperformance:

- defining the issue of underperformance
- understanding underperformance
- determining causes of underperformance
- eliminating the causes of underperformance and monitoring the performance improvement

This chapter introduces these steps. Chapters 9 and 10 present tools to determine the causes of underperformance.

Defining the Issue

Chapter 2 introduces eight generic steps in the performance analysis process. You may want to review the first two steps (understanding the issue and starting with questions), which also apply to performance understanding. The discussion here specifically focuses on the issue of underperformance. Let us start with an example. Suppose you teach in a college, and lately you have seen an increasing number of students coming late for your class. You have made class announcements that you wanted to see punctuality, but the tardiness continued. You wonder what might cause the tardiness and what you can do to correct it.

The first step in performance understanding is to recognize that there is a problem of underperformance and something needs to be done about it. If the situation is normal, there is no need to improve it. Performance description and monitoring tools introduced in the previous chapters can be used to identify the symptoms of underperformance.

After recognizing the problem, you need to define the problem clearly as an issue of underperformance. In the above example, you need to specify what tardiness is—how late is tardy: 1 minute, 5 minutes, or 10 minutes after a class starts. You also should articulate the consequence of underperformance and the need to address the underperformance—disruption of lecturing, disruption of students' learning, and negative impact on student academic performances.

Also important is that the parties involved in the performance analysis agree on the issue. In our example, it helps you develop effective strategies to correct tardiness if students agree that tardiness affects them negatively and should be addressed and if other instructors and the department chair agree on the need to address the issue so you have academic and administrative support to conduct the analysis.

Finally, preliminary knowledge and information about the possible causes of underperformance should give you some ideas as to how feasible your solutions may be. An analysis is less useful if its solutions are not feasible. For example, the tardiness may be caused by lack of parking spaces for students driving to the campus. To correct that problem, the university would need to increase parking spaces. Until that happens, there is very little you can do individually. The solution lacks feasibility.

Understanding Underperformance

The importance of a theory in performance analysis is established in Chapter 2. Here, we focus on how to develop a theory to understand underperformance. What may cause students' tardiness in our example? Reasons could include students' lack of interest in the class, their extracurricular activities, their class schedule conflicts, or the cases when students simply forget about the time of the class. Tardiness could also result from the change of the class schedule, the change of classroom location, the closure for maintenance of a major road to the classroom, or the lack of nearby parking for student drivers.

Realize that, in this example, we classify all potential reasons into one of two categories: reasons related to individual students or reasons related to the class. By this classification, we attempt to capture all potential causes of tardiness systematically and comprehensively. This systematic and comprehensive attempt to recognize all key potential causes of underperformance is called the *theory of performance understanding*.

Why do we need a theory to understand underperformance? Sometimes it is easy to figure out the reasons of underperformances. Missing classes will lead to poor academic performance. Traffic congestion will result in longer travel time. In other times, however, the cause of underperformance is difficult to discover. Some students do poorly in math for many possible reasons: the lack of previous exposure to the subject, the lack of study effort, the improper learning style and methods, or the instructor's difficult lecturing approach. Because there could be many causes of underperformance, there should be a systematic way to identify them and to explain how they may affect the performance. A theory does just that. It provides a structured way to identify all key potential causes of underperformance and to explain how they may influence performance.

It is important to note that a good theory not only captures all key potential causes of underperformance but also speculates *how* these causes may affect performance—the relationship between the causes and underperformance. For example, you may speculate that less motivated students plan less but use more travel time to the classroom and, consequently, have a greater possibility of being late. The lack of parking spaces near the classroom forces students to use parking lots far away, resulting in longer travel time to the classroom.

How do you develop a theory of performance understanding? A good theory often stems from a thorough understanding about the circumstances and processes that result in the underperformance. Brainstorming by a group of experts who understand the issues of the production process is an important source of a theory. If necessary, these experts can be asked to write down individually what they believe are the key causes of the underperformance, discuss these causes in a group, then come to a consensus on a list of key potential causes agreed by all experts. This process of *brainstorming and consensus building* also gets key parties on board to solve the problem of underperformance. Moreover, you may also want to review the empirical literature on what affects performance in Chapter 1 and use the related empirical findings to generate possible causes of the underperformance in your organization.

The following section presents three theoretical frameworks in management to help you develop a theory of your own performance analysis. These theories should specify the potential managerial causes of underperformance and how they may affect performance.

The Production Process Theory

The organizational production process introduced in Chapters 1 and 2 (Input → Process → Output → Outcome) can be used as a theoretical framework to identify potential causes of underperformance during the production process. According to this framework, the underperformance of an organization's outcome is the result of factors in inputs, the process of converting the inputs to outputs, and the outputs. For example, a student's poor academic performance (an underperformance outcome) could result from insufficient resources and time (input), inefficient study process and methods (the process), and insufficient study efforts (output).

This theory emphasizes the importance of the production process that converts inputs into outputs. As an example, let us say that there have been increasing citizen complaints about slow response time in a metropolitan city. The director of the fire and rescue service suspects that something is not going well in the emergency response process, described in Figure 8–1.

The response time is affected by how quickly a 911 call for emergency is initiated; how quickly, accurately, and properly the call center places the call for the emergency response units; and how quickly the emergency dispatch team arrives at the scene. The possible causes of slow responses (underperformance) include the slow initialization of an emergency call, the slow and/or inaccurate information taken by call takers in the call center, the placement of the call to an incorrect response unit (e.g., a call of medical emergency is erroneously placed to a fire protection unit), and the slow emergency dispatch. Figure 8–1 is known as a *flowchart* that is commonly used in identifying problems in a process of operation. After developing the chart, the director decides to investigate all the possible causes to identify the true causes of slow response.

The Context-Design Theory

The production process theory focuses on an organization's *internal* operations, applying to the cases in which a clear flowchart of production phases can be established, and the performance outcome can be seen largely as the result of the organization's internal operations.

Figure 8–1

The Flowchart of Emergency Responses.

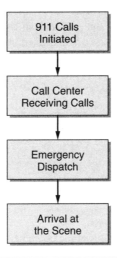

Figure 8–2

The Context-Design Theory of Underperformance.

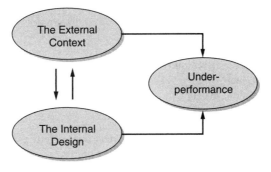

Alternatively, the context-design theory is more applicable when an organization's *external* factors in its environment play an important role in causing underperformance. As discussed in Chapter 1, these factors reflect the political, legal, and economic context in which an organization has to work. Some salient examples include the income or education levels of citizens or clients and the performance of the local economy.

The context-design theory specifies that there are two types of factors that influence an organization's performance, as shown in Figure 8–2. *The contextual factors* concern the external environment of an organization such as the socioeconomic condition of the community and characteristics of its residents. An organization's *internal design factors* refer to its production process, organizational structure, managerial roles, and strategies.

For example, a higher crime rate (underperformance) can be caused by contextual factors as well as internal design factors, as illustrated in Table 8–1. Many organizational outcomes are significantly influenced by contextual factors, so the context-design theory can be used properly to identify causes of underperformance of many organizational outcomes.

Table 8–1

Possible Causes of Crime Increase

Contextual causes

- Socioeconomic characteristics of the community
  - slow economic growth
  - sunset industries
  - seasonal influx of tourists
- Residential characteristics of the community
  - low income
  - high unemployment
  - low education
- Crime-related contextual causes
  - historical high crime trends
  - lack of neighborhood communities' efforts to fight crimes
- Other contextual causes

Internal design causes

- Resources allocated for preventing and fighting crimes
  - lack of financial resources
  - lack of manpower
  - lack of new technology
- Processes to prevent and fight crimes
  - lack of patrols in some crime-rampant areas
  - sluggish efforts in investigating certain types of crimes
  - slowness of arrests for certain types of crimes
- Decision making
  - lack of administrative discretion and flexibility in directing and relocating financial resources and manpower in crime fighting
- Managerial behaviors
  - ineffective leadership styles of management
  - slow adoption of proactive crime prevention strategies such as community-oriented policing
  - lack of an effective merit system to award high-performance employees
- Other internal design causes

The Balanced Scorecard Theory

This theory coherently connects four distinctive perspectives of organizational functions: finance, learning and growth, internal operation, and citizens' (service users') needs. The *financial perspective* concerns the health of an organization's finance and the availability of financial resources in providing services. The *internal operation perspective* is related to how effective a production or service delivery operation is to deliver high-quality services to citizens or service users. The effort to sustain organizational growth through strengthened workers' capabilities and motivation, as well as enhanced information and knowledge capabilities, is reflected in the *learning and growing perspective*. The *citizen (user) perspective* concerns the level of satisfaction of citizens or service users.

The *balanced scorecard theory* helps a performance analyst identify the causes of under-performance that occur in these organizational functions. This theoretical framework is particularly useful when the goal of the analysis is to improve citizen or user satisfaction (the citizen–user perspective). An analyst can use this theory to identify the factors in an organization's finance, operations, and learning and growth areas that may influence citizen or user satisfaction. Table 8–2 is an example of what may cause the dissatisfaction of

Table 8–2

Potential Causes of User Dissatisfaction for Water–Sewer Service

User dissatisfaction is the result of the following:
- Financial perspective
  - lack of available resources to provide quality water–sewer service
  - inefficient use of resources in providing the service
  - wasteful spending in providing the service
  - other causes from the financial perspective
- Internal operation perspective
  - unreliable service delivery processes
  - slow responses to delivery problems
  - lack of coordination of different work groups
  - administrative inflexibility in relocating resources to meet users' needs
  - use of outdated technology in service delivery
  - other causes from the internal operation perspective
- Learning and growth perspective
  - lack of trained workers to provide quality services
  - lack of motivated workers to provide quality services
  - ineffective teamwork
  - inaccurate information and outdated knowledge
  - other causes from the learning and growth perspective

users (underperformance) in a water–sewer service of a local government, using a balanced scorecard theory.

Because the balanced scorecard theory was initially developed for private organizations, it is important to realize that the purpose and the application of the theory are very different for the public and nonprofit organizations. In a private business whose desire is to maximize financial performance, the theory is used to assess organizational functions that serve the goal in financial perspective, while in a public or nonprofit organization, the theory should be used to enhance the quality of services to citizens or service users (the citizen–user perspective) through identifying effective management strategies in the organization's finance, operations, and learning and growth perspectives.

Determining Causes of Underperformance

Once all key potential causes of underperformance are identified from the theory, the next step is to collect data and to conduct an analysis to prove empirically *whether* these potential causes are the true causes of underperformance, and if they are, *how* they affect underperformance. This section presents a simple tool of gathering expert opinions on causes of underperformance. The more complex analytical and statistical methods will be discussed in the next two chapters (Chapters 9 and 10).

The tool can start with the brainstorm–consensus building process described above to discover the potential causes of underperformance. Experts, with keen knowledge about the production or service delivery process, are gathered and asked to rank the importance of each cause in affecting the underperformance. Because the ranking is based on how important the cause is in relation to other causes, it is known as the ranking of *relative importance* of the cause. A total score from the rankings of all experts can be assigned to the cause, then all causes are assessed and ranked by their relative importance, and decisions are made to address these causes based on their relative importance.

Let us take the above example on crime increase. Suppose that 10 experts (could be ones who have good knowledge on the crime issues in the city) are identified, and each is asked to rank the relative importance of each cause listed in Table 8–1 ("other causes" are excluded). A scale system of 1 to 5 is used with 1 = not important cause and 5 = very important cause. With 10 experts ranking each cause, the maximum score of each cause is 50 (5×10) points, and the minimum is 10 (1×10) points. Table 8–3 shows the tallied results of expert opinions on the causes of higher crimes.

The results in Table 8–3 indicate that experts believe that the crime increase is caused mostly by internal design causes, although some of contextual causes may also contribute to the increase. The most important causes include the lack of resources and technology in crime prevention–fighting, the slow adoption of proactive crime prevention strategies, the sluggish efforts in investigating crimes, and a slow economy. There is a word of caution in interpreting these results though. Realize that these results are the *perceived* causes of higher crimes. There may be a difference between these perceptions and the true causes of higher crimes. If strategies developed to reduce crimes are based on these opinions, there is a need to constantly monitor the effect of these strategies and make necessary modifications of the strategies.

Table 8–3

**Causes of Crime Increase Ranked by Experts on
Relative Importance**

Causes	Score
Contextual causes	
Slow economic growth	38
Sunset industrial bases	32
Seasonal influx of tourists	25
Low income of population	35
High unemployment of population	30
Low education of population	35
Historical high crime trends	35
Lack of neighborhood communities' efforts to fight crimes	25
Internal design causes	
Lack of financial resources	45
Lack of manpower	45
Lack of new technology	40
Lack of patrols in some crime-rampant areas	30
Sluggish efforts in investigating certain types of crimes	38
Slowness of arrests for certain types of crimes	30
Lack of administrative flexibility in relocating resources	30
Ineffective leadership styles of management	35
Slow adoption of proactive crime prevention strategies	43
Lack of an effective merit system for employees	35

Eliminating Causes of Underperformance

Once the causes of underperformance are identified, the next step is to eliminate them by developing and implementing a *performance improvement strategy*. The strategy should include the performance improvement goals, the specific performance enhancement initiatives (PEI) to attack causes of underperformance, the resources designated for the strategy, the time frame that allows the strategy to work, and the assessment plan to evaluate the effectiveness of the strategy.

It is imperative to develop clear performance improvement goals in a performance improvement strategy. The goals should be challenging but achievable. Although large and drastic improvement is desired, a gradual improvement should also be encouraged. A viable strategy often consists of different phases of improvement with different levels of the improvement goal designed and expected in these phases.

It should be realized that some performance enhancement initiatives may take longer than others to implement. Resources can be added annually in the budget; but it takes longer to change leadership behaviors, to establish an effective merit system, and to develop a proactive culture of crime prevention through developing community-oriented crime preventive programs. It is also important to estimate the cost of each initiative and to allocate sufficient resources for each initiative. Some initiatives cost more than others, although more expensive initiatives are not necessarily more effective in eliminating the causes of underperformance.

Frequent monitoring and assessment on the effectiveness of the performance improvement strategy are needed. Modifications of the strategy are necessary when it shows no or marginal effect on performance. Importantly, efforts should be made to solicit political and technical supports needed to sustain the performance improvement strategy, and constant monitoring and assessment play a role in ensuring such support (review Chapter 2 on "Developing Organizational Capacities for Performance Analysis"). The tools to assess the effectiveness of performance enhancement initiatives will be presented in Chapters 11 to 13.

A Case Study

The Health Education and Learning Center (HEAL) provides nutrition education and psychosocial counseling services to 15 schools in a school district of a metropolitan area. The center is funded by the nonprofit Stone Foundation as well as grants from the state. Occasionally, it also receives donations from private donors. One of the center's two major services is psychosocial counseling to students diagnosed with various psychosocial behaviors in schools.

At the start of each school year, a screening process is conducted to identify students who may suffer from a variety of psychological problems such as anxiety, depression, and impulsive or abusive behaviors. The screening process consists of an initial interview and a series of tests on a student's psychosocial functions, and it lasts 4 weeks. Once a student is diagnosed with having a psychosocial problem, he or she will be admitted into a 12-week counseling program in which weekly individual or group sessions aimed at improving their conditions are conducted. At the end of the program, tests will be conducted to measure the improvement of the participants' psychosocial functions. The counseling program is built on the premise of the social cognitive theory that the improvement in a student's psychosocial status enhances his or her academic performance.

The counseling division of HEAL hires 15 licensed counselors. Each counselor is assigned to a school in the program. The counseling services are provided on site in schools. Besides the job of conducting counseling sessions, a counselor is also responsible for collecting related data for assessing participants' improvements, as well as to attend a monthly meeting in the HEAL headquarters to exchange the program information.

Step 1: Defining the Issue

In addition to results of the psychosocial testing, HEAL uses a measure of user satisfaction to assess the performance of the counseling service. The satisfaction measure consists of 10 items in a survey sent out annually to school teachers and principals. The items ask respondents for their satisfaction levels on whether the counseling program has created a healthier school environment, a better academic environment for participating students, and a better educational environment for teachers. The scale of these 10 items is from 1 = very dissatisfied to 5 = very satisfied.

For the past 3 years, the average satisfaction score has been 4.1, 4.0, and 4.1. Although the score leans to the end of being satisfied, there is room for improvement. Considering that the program has been in place for more than 3 years and the significant amount of resources poured into the program, a score of 4.5 is not an unrealistic performance goal. Compared with that target, the current performance score of around 4.1 is clearly an underperformance.

The view that there is a need to improve the performance of the counseling program is shared among the HEAL management and Stone Foundation board members. Even the HEAL counselors agree that there is need for continual improvement of the program performance measured by the satisfaction measure, because they know that teachers and principals are key stakeholders of the program and their support is critical in seeking continual funding for the program. Thus, the analysis questions should be the following: What affects the satisfaction of teachers and principals for the counseling program? How should the satisfaction be improved?

Step 2: Understanding the Underperformance

What may cause the dissatisfaction of teachers and principals? It is clear that many factors may contribute to their dissatisfaction. They include ones related to the program operation as well as ones associated with individual counselors. Discussed above, the balanced scorecard theory is particularly useful to identify factors that influence the satisfaction of citizens or users.

According to the balanced scorecard theory, users' satisfaction for a service may be affected by three perspectives of a service: the operation process of how the service is provided to them (the internal operation perspective), how well the employees in the organization are trained and motivated (the learning and growth perspective), and how healthy the organization's finance is (the financial perspective). In this particular case, among all three perspectives, the finance of the HEAL probably is unlikely to cause teachers' or principals' dissatisfaction on the quality of the counseling service because teachers and principals are not directly involved in determining the financial resources and capabilities of the counseling program.

However, 2 other perspectives should influence the level of the satisfaction significantly. After a brainstorming and consensus building session with a group of principals and teachers who have participated in the program for the last 3 years, the foundation's analysts develop a list of potential causes based on these 2 perspectives, shown in Table 8–4.

Step 3: Identifying and Eliminating the Causes of Underperformance

After the above analysis, a decision is made by the HEAL management to include all the above possible causes in the future survey of teachers and principals. The results of the survey will be used to identify the true causes of the dissatisfaction to improve the performance of the counseling program.

Table 8–4

Possible Causes of Dissatisfaction for the HEAL Counseling Program

Internal operation perspective

- Too few individual sessions.
- Too few group sessions.
- Sessions conducted on days that are not convenient for teachers.
- The 12-week program should be replaced by the 16-week program.
- Many students having problems are not identified from the screen process.
- Many students having problems are not seen by counselors on time.
- Seeing the counselor once a week is not enough for participating students.
- The classroom presentations of the counselor do not give much information.
- The classroom intervention of the counselor does not help much.

Counselor (learning and growth) perspective

- The counselor is not accessible.
- The counselor is not competent.
- The counselor is unwilling to help.
- The counselor does not help lessen my students' discipline problems.
- The counselor is not responsive to the needs of my students.
- The counselor is not responsive to the needs of students' families.
- The counselor is not responsive to my needs.
- The counselor is not a good source of information.
- The counselor does not act as a team member at my school.
- The counselor is not courteous.
- The counselor is not open and available to help the school with student needs.
- It is difficult for me to communicate with the counselor.
- The counselor does not work collaboratively with me on scheduling.

Practices

Key Terms

Performance understanding
Underperformance
Potential causes of underperformance
Theory of performance understanding
Brainstorming and consensus building process
Production process theory
Flowchart
Context-design theory
Contextual factors

Internal design factors
Balanced scorecard theory
Finance perspective
Internal operation perspective
Learning and growth perspective
Citizen (user) perspective
Expert opinions in identifying causes of underperformance
Relative importance of a cause of underperformance
Performance improvement strategy

Practice Problem 8–1

Some college students have poor or undesirable grades. What causes academic underperformance in a college class? Define the issue of academic underperformance. Use a theory to identify all key potential factors that may cause a student's underperformance in a college class (any class of your choice). What is your theory? What are the causes?

Moreover, if you are a college student, find a group of your classmates and conduct a brainstorm and consensus building session to come up with a list of causes of academic underperformance agreed by all; then rank the causes in the list to find out the relative importance of each cause in leading to the academic underperformance.

Practice Problem 8–2

Identify and define an issue of underperformance in a public or nonprofit organization of your choice. Use a theory to identify all key potential causes of underperformance. What is your theory and what are the causes of underperformance?

Find a group of experts on the issue and conduct a brainstorm and consensus building session to come up with a list of causes of underperformance agreed by all. Then, ask the group to rank the causes in the list to find out the relative importance of each cause.

Practice Problem 8–3

As you may have realized, a theory is a method of thinking that helps you to understand the nature of the underperformance and to identify the causes of underperformance. With limited spaces, this chapter only discusses three generic theoretical frameworks in management: the production process, the context-design theory, and the balanced scorecard. There are many other theories that can also help you understand an issue of underperformance. One such theory is used by economists to look into the relationship between the output and inputs of a product (or service), attempting to discover the so-called *production function* to maximize the output. For example, a police patrol unit can try different combinations of inputs in capitals (e.g., vehicles and equipment); labors (e.g., patrol officers); and technologies (e.g., communication and networking) in order to maximize the patrol miles (the output).

The theory of the production function employs different combinations of inputs in order to optimize (or maximize) the output. The theory of the production process puts an emphasis on the flowing steps of the production process that converts inputs to outputs. Still, the balanced scorecard theory looks into the production process with a focus on integrating distinctive organizational functions.

In fact, all these theories are just different lenses looking at the same thing (the performance) but with each lens having a different focus point. Now, identify and define an issue of underperformance in a public or nonprofit organization of your choice. Use at least two of the theories discussed in this chapter to identify all key potential causes of underperformance. What are your theories and what are the causes of underperformances?

CHAPTER 9

Determining Causes of Underperformance: Relationship Analysis

Y ou are a police chief in an urban city, and you recently have witnessed an increase in violent crimes in your city. You have a theory that attributes the increase mainly to a growing undereducated and unemployed population, a slow local economic growth, and an insufficient policing workforce. You talked to a few people in your department and they all agreed with you. But, are you right? Are these truly the causes of the crime increase? How confident are you about your theory? After all, it is only the opinion of a few people. To prove (or disprove) this theory, you need to get your hand on the crime and the other data.

In the last chapter, we learned how to use theories to identify potential causes of underperformance, and we also study a simple tool of using expert opinion to determine the causes of underperformance. This chapter continues the discussion on discovering the causes of underperformance, focusing on more complex but objective statistical and analytical tools of developing a performance relationship.

Some Important Concepts

Relationship

Does an insufficient policing force cause crimes? To establish the *causality* that one thing causes another, you should first establish a relationship between them. So, to say that the level of the policing force causes crimes, you have to prove that they are related first. The relationship between a performance and its potential cause is called *performance relationship*.

Although we use the term *relationship* all the time, it is hard to clearly define it; however, several principles apply when it comes to interpreting a relationship. First, if Event A happens, Event B also happens, therefore, we say A and B are perfectly related. For example, if the data of the last 10 years show that crimes declined during years when there were growths in the policing force and that crimes increased during years when the policing force decreased, then crimes and policing force are perfectly related.

Second, if Event A happens while Event B does not happen, we say A and B are not related. If crimes have increased 10 years in a row during which the policing force has not changed, then crimes and the policing force are unrelated. Third, if Event A happens, Event B may or may not happen. Crimes have increased every year for the last 10 years, while the policing force increased in some years but declined in others. Then, crimes and the policing force *may* be related.

Why is a relationship important in performance analysis? A relationship is a prerequisite for causality. A relationship *must* exist for causality to happen. In our example, the relationship between crimes and insufficient policing force must be established before we can say that insufficient policing force causes crimes. If the relationship does not exist, neither does the causality. If the two events are not related, they are not causal. Therefore, though the proof of a relationship does not necessarily mean the existence of causality, a relationship analysis does help us rule out the factors that are not causes of underperformance.

Variables

There are two concepts, crimes and the policing force, in our example. In order to empirically examine their relationship, we need to measure them first. Let us say that the policing force is measured by the number of uniform police officers and crimes are assessed by a crime rate measure, the number of crimes per 100,000 residents. Realize that crime rate is different from year to year and the number of police officers also change over time. In statistics, a measured concept is a *variable* when its response categories (i.e., the attributes) can change. All performances and their causes in performance analysis are variables (if a performance cannot be changed and improved, what is the point of analyzing it?).

When we theorize that insufficient policing force causes crimes, we specify a possible cause–effect relationship. The possible cause is policing force, and the effect is crime. A possible cause in a performance analysis is measured by the *independent variable*, and the effect is represented by the *dependent variable*. By definition, the dependent variable is the one that is being affected, and the independent variable is the one that affects the dependent variable. It is important to remember that the dependent variable always measures the performance in a performance analysis. This is why the dependent variable is also known as the *performance variable*, and the dependent (performance) variable should be the center of discussion in any performance analysis.

Crimes can be affected by more than one cause. There are often multiple causes for a performance, so there are multiple independent variables for a dependent variable. However, this chapter presents analytical tools that examine the relationship of one independent variable with the dependent variable. The joint impact of multiple independent variables will be discussed in the next chapter.

Measurement Levels

It is imperative that you completely understand the concept of measurement levels introduced in Chapter 2. As a summary, the response categories of an *interval variable* (i.e., a variable measured by an interval measure) can be rank-ordered, and the differences among categories are meaningful. Examples include a person's age measured by the number of years after birth, response times measured by minutes or seconds in time, a person's education measured by the number of years in school, and a family's income measured by earnings in dollars.

The response categories of an *ordinal variable* can be rank-ordered, but the differences among the categories bear little or no meaning. A measure of a person's education by the highest school level completed with categories of high school or below, college, or graduate school is an example. Finally, it is impossible to rank-order the response categories of a *nominal variable*. Examples include gender (male or female), race (Black, White, Hispanics, Asian, etc.), and political party affiliations (Democrat, Republican, and Independent). Nominal and ordinal variables are also known as *categorical variables*, because their response categories are often clearly defined. For example, the response categories of gender are female and male. The response categories of the ordinal measure for a person's education by the highest school level are clearly defined (i.e., high school or below, college, graduate school).

A good grasp of these concepts in measurement levels is necessary to understand the materials in this book, particularly the analytical tools in the chapters hereafter. This chapter introduces three analytical tools that examine performance relationship:

- categorization analysis: the relationship between one categorical variable and one interval variable
- contingency table analysis: the relationship between two categorical variables
- correlation analysis: the relationship between two interval variables

This chapter also introduces an important statistical procedure—hypothesis testing—and presents hypothesis tests related to relationship analyses.

Categorization Analysis

A *categorization analysis* involves an interval variable and a categorical variable. The categorical variable can be either a nominal or an ordinal variable. In this section, tools for an interval dependent (performance) variable are discussed first, followed by a presentation of tools for a categorical dependent (performance) variable.

Interval Dependent (Performance) Variables

What tools of relationship analyses should be used if the dependent variable is interval? Table 9–1 shows 20 response times by three fire response teams. How well do the teams perform? Do they perform differently? In this example, the dependent variable (response times) is an interval variable, and the independent variable is a nominal variable (teams). We want to know the relationship between teams and their response times. A relationship exists if different teams perform differently, or one team performs better than others. The relationship is absent if no team performs better, or in other words, all teams have the same response times.

Table 9–1

Performance of Fire Response Teams

Responses ID	Response time (in minute)	Team
1	6.4	1
2	7.5	2
3	6.8	2
4	7.0	3
5	8.2	1
6	8.6	2
7	6.7	2
8	3.6	3
9	4.2	1
10	6.2	1
11	5.1	1
12	8.1	3
13	5.8	2
14	7.5	2
15	9.0	1
16	3.7	3
17	7.5	3
18	6.9	2
19	5.5	1
20	6.5	3

A simple method to examine this relationship is to calculate the average response time of each team. With the help of Excel, you can rearrange the data and make the calculation easier by sorting the response times by team as shown in Screen 9–1. To sort the data:

1. Highlight the data you want to sort.
2. Choose **Sort** in the **Sort & Filter** group on the **Data** tab. (For Excel 2003 users, simply choose **Sort** from the **Data** tab.)
3. Select the variable to sort the data, which is the team in this example, using the drop-down button in the **Sort By** window. With an ascending order of smallest to largest values, the sorted data are shown in Screen 9–1. Realize the sorted data allow you to rearrange the response times by each team.

Now, you can easily calculate the average response of each team with the average from the Excel Insert Function (*fx*) (review Chapter 5), shown in Screen 9–2. The average response times are 6.4, 7.1, and 6.1 minutes for Teams 1, 2, and 3, respectively. The total average of all responses is 6.5 minutes. Clearly, teams perform differently. Team 3 responds much more quickly (6.1 minutes) than Team 2 (7.1 minutes). Being a different team makes a difference.

Screen 9–1

Response Time Data Sorted by Team.

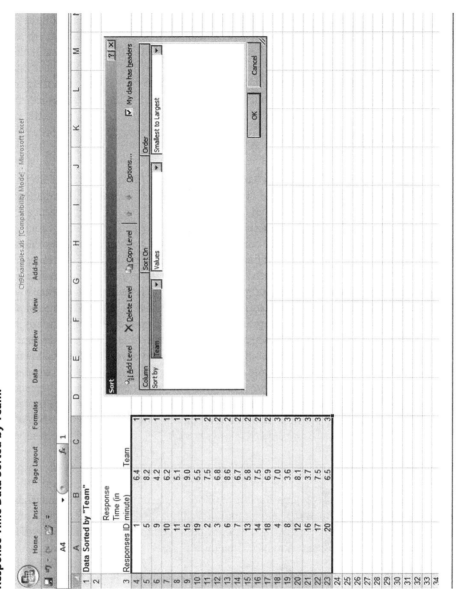

Screen 9–2

Response Time Averages by Team.

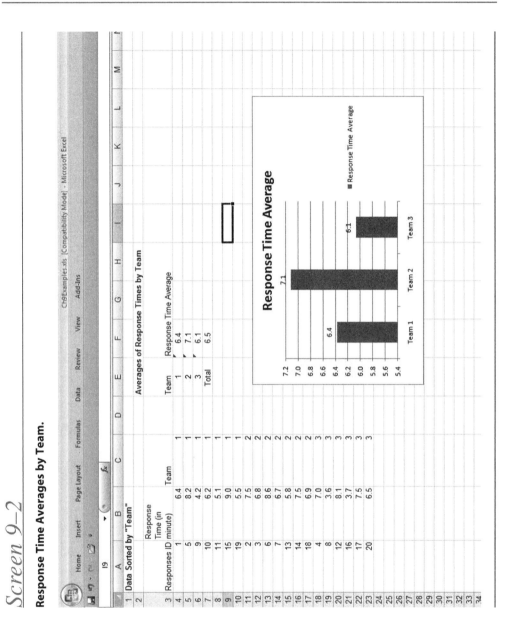

There is a relationship between teams and response times. Screen 9–2 also shows a graph of this relationship.

Let us look at another example. Psychosocial Condition Score (PCS) is used to assess the psychosocial status of school-age students. The score has a range of 60 to 100 with a higher score indicating a better psychosocial status. It is an interval measure. PCS is used by a non-profit agency to assess the performance of its school counseling program. One variable that may influence students' PCSs is counselors' performances, measured by students' satisfaction about the counseling service. Each counselor is assessed on a 3-point scale of fair, good, or very good, for an ordinal measure.

Do counselors' performances affect students' PCSs? Is better psychosocial status associated with higher counseling performance? What is the relationship between counselors' performances and PCSs? In the past school year, twenty 12-week counseling sessions were conducted. The average PCS and counseling performance of each session are shown in Table 9–2.

To assess how counseling performance is related to PCSs, we can compare PCSs of different counseling performance categories. Using the Excel procedures described above, as shown in Screen 9–3, we can easily obtain the average PCSs for fair counselor performances

Table 9–2

Psychosocial Condition Scores (PCS) and Counseling Performance

Session	Session average PCS	Counselor performance
1	85	Very Good
2	65	Good
3	76	Very Good
4	67	Fair
5	86	Fair
6	83	Very Good
7	67	Good
8	64	Good
9	72	Very Good
10	48	Fair
11	55	Fair
12	70	Very Good
13	69	Very Good
14	50	Good
15	67	Very Good
16	41	Fair
17	57	Fair
18	61	Good
19	73	Good
20	76	Very Good

Screen 9–3

Psychological Condition Scores (PCS) and Counselor Performance.

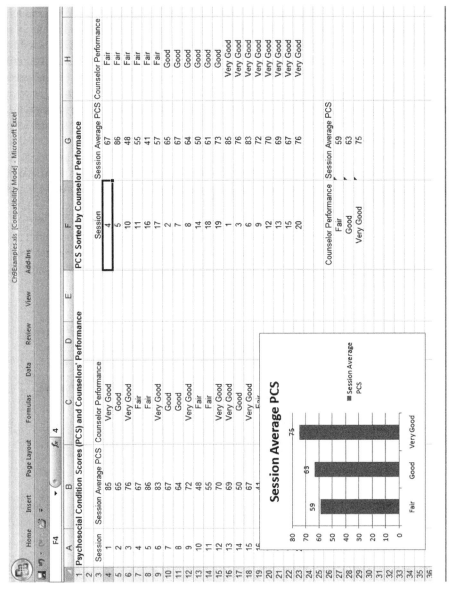

(59), for good performances (63), and for very good performances (75). Clearly, counselor performance and PCS are related—a higher counselor performance is associated with a higher PCS.

Categorical Dependent (Performance) Variables

Suppose you use citizen satisfaction to assess the performance of a city's services. You suspect that citizens' satisfaction is related to their ages—older people tend to be happier about services. Citizen satisfaction is measured on a 3-point scale in a survey with categories of very satisfied, satisfied, or dissatisfied toward the services. Age is measured by a respondent's year of birth. A survey of 20 residents is conducted, and the age and satisfaction information are collected. In this case, the dependent variable (citizen satisfaction rate) is categorical. It is an ordinal measure. The independent variable (age) is interval.

We can calculate the average age for each satisfaction category to assess the relationship. The results in Screen 9–4 show that dissatisfied residents have an average age of 42.4, and the average ages of satisfied and very satisfied residents are 38.7 and 41.0. There is no clear evidence to suggest that age and satisfaction are related. Older citizens do not appear happier with the city's services.

Contingency Table Analysis

What tools should apply to the relationship of two categorical variables? Say that you are interested in the relationship between students' class participation and their academic performances. You suspect that class participation improves academic performance. You use fail or pass to measure academic performance and no or yes to measure class participation. Both variables are ordinal. Table 9–3 shows the data from 20 students in your class.

A cursory count shows that there are 9 nonparticipating and 11 participating students. If there is a relationship between participation and performance, nonparticipating students should be more likely to fail the class, and participating students should be more likely to pass the class. So, the relationship can be assessed by the failure rate (the percentage of students who fail the class) and/or by the pass rate (the percentage of students who pass the class). A *contingency table* does just that. Table 9–4 shows a completed contingency table based on the information from Table 9–3.

Of the 9 nonparticipating students, 7 fail the class for a failure rate of 77.8%, shown in the cell at the upper left corner of the table. Only 2 nonparticipating students pass the class for a pass rate of 22.2% (the rate at the lower left corner). On the other hand, of the 11 participating students, only 3 fail the class for a failure rate of 27.3%, and the other 8 pass the class for a pass rate of 72.7%. These results show that participating students perform better academically. Participation and performance are related. Participation may improve academic performance.

A contingency table presents the information for each and every response category of the two variables in analysis. It applies only to relationships of two categorical variables. It would be very difficult to use it on an interval variable that has numerous response categories. Several steps are involved in creating a contingency table.

Screen 9–4

Age and Satisfaction.

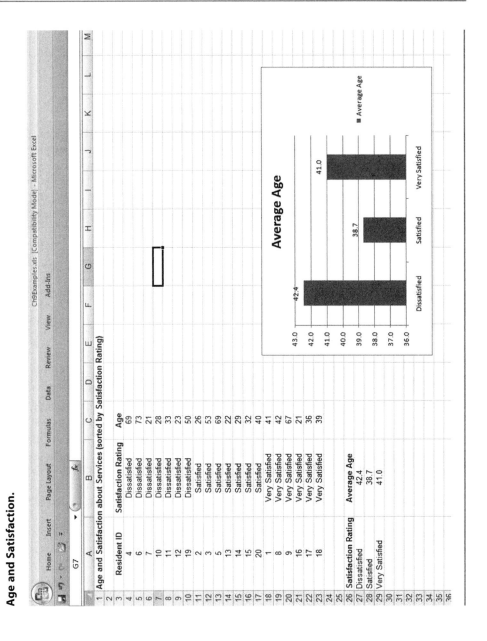

Table 9–3

Participation and Class Performance

Student ID	Participation	Performance
1	No	Fail
2	No	Pass
3	Yes	Pass
4	No	Fail
5	Yes	Pass
6	No	Pass
7	No	Fail
8	Yes	Pass
9	No	Fail
10	Yes	Pass
11	No	Fail
12	Yes	Fail
13	Yes	Pass
14	No	Fail
15	Yes	Pass
16	Yes	Pass
17	Yes	Fail
18	Yes	Fail
19	No	Fail
20	Yes	Pass

Table 9–4

Participation and Performance: A Contingency Table Analysis

	Participation		
	No	**Yes**	**Total**
Performance			
Fail	7 (77.8%)	3 (27.3%)	10
Pass	2 (22.2%)	8 (72.7%)	10
Total	9	11	20

Step 1: Position Variables Correctly

You need to clearly identify the dependent (performance) variable and the independent variable. (In the example, the dependent variable is academic performance, and the independent variable is class participation.) Then, make sure to position the dependent variable as the row variable, whose categories of fail and pass should be aligned as rows as shown in Table 9–5.

Table 9–5

Positioning Variables in Contingency Table Creation

	Participation		
	No	Yes	Total
Performance			
Fail			
Pass			
Total			

Also, you should position the independent variable as the column variable to align the categories of no and yes as columns, shown again as in Table 9–5. Also important is to include a row for column totals and a column for row totals, and a cell for the grand total at the right bottom corner of the table. Table 9–5 is a completed table without numbers in it.

Step 2: Determining Row, Column, and Grand Totals

Now, you need to fill in the row and column totals in the table. First, how many nonparticipating students are in the data? In our example, you can count them easily from the 20 students; however, the counting would be much more difficult for a much larger database, which is often seen in real-life analyses. Fortunately, the COUNTIF in the Excel Insert Function can make the counting very easy. COUNTIF counts the number of cells within a range that meet a certain criterion. The process is shown in Screen 9–5. After selecting students' participation data in the **Range** (B4:B23 in this case), type in *no* in the **Criteria** window to indicate the nonparticipating students and click **OK**. The result shows that there are 9 nonparticipating students in the data.

Because there are 20 students in the data, if 9 of them are nonparticipating, 11 are participating. We can use the COUNTIF process to count the number of students who fail the class (10) and the number of students who pass (10). Table 9–6 shows the column totals (9 and 11), the row totals (10 and 10), and the grand total (20).

Step 3: Determining the Number in Each Cell

Let us first try the number in the upper left cell of the table—the number of nonparticipating students who fail the class. You can sort the data by participation to align all nonparticipating students together, as shown in Table 9–7, where the 9 nonparticipants are listed in the first 9 cells in the participation column.

Then, use COUNTIF to select all nonparticipating students who fail the class, as shown in Screen 9–6. The result is 7, which should be put in the upper left cell of the table, shown in Table 9–8.

Screen 9–5

The COUNTIF Procedure.

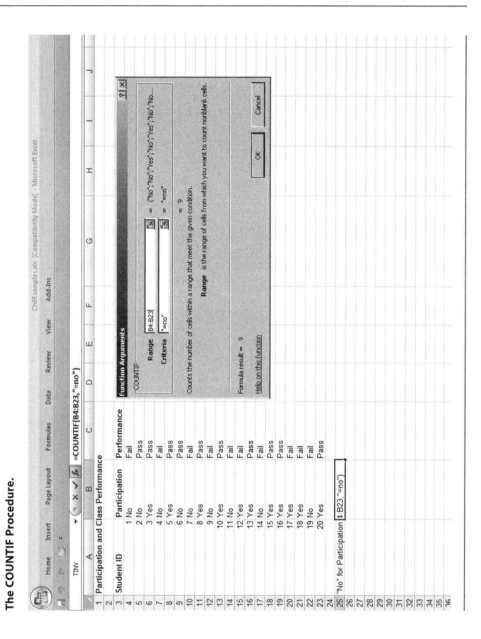

Table 9–6

Row, Column, and Grand Totals in a Contingency Table

	Participation		Total
	No	**Yes**	**Total**
Performance			
Fail			10
Pass			10
Total	9	11	20

Table 9–7

Participation and Performance (sorted by participation)

Student ID	Participation	Performance
1	No	Fail
2	No	Pass
4	No	Fail
6	No	Pass
7	No	Fail
9	No	Fail
11	No	Fail
14	No	Fail
19	No	Fail
3	Yes	Pass
5	Yes	Pass
8	Yes	Pass
10	Yes	Pass
12	Yes	Fail
13	Yes	Pass
15	Yes	Pass
16	Yes	Pass
17	Yes	Fail
18	Yes	Fail
20	Yes	Pass

Because there are a total of 9 nonparticipating students, if 7 of them fail, 2 should pass. That is the number at the lower left cell of the table. Similarly, there are 10 students who fail; if 7 of them are nonparticipating, then 3 should be participating. This is the number in the upper right cell. Similarly, you should be able to determine that there are 8 participating students who pass. Table 9–9 shows a contingency table with completed cell numbers.

Screen 9–6

Calculating Nonparticipating Students Who Fail.

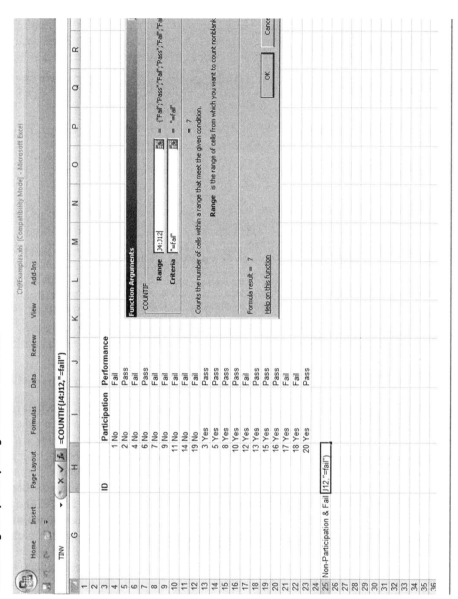

Table 9–8

Determining a Number for a Cell in a Contingency Table

	Participation		
	No	**Yes**	**Total**
Performance			
Fail	7		10
Pass			10
Total	9	11	20

Table 9–9

A Contingency Table with Completed Cell Numbers

	Participation		
	No	**Yes**	**Total**
Performance			
Fail	7	3	10
Pass	2	8	10
Total	9	11	20

Step 4: Calculating the Column Percentage of Each Cell

The percentage of nonparticipating students who fail the class is $7/9 = 77.8\%$. This calculation requires you to use the total in the first column (9) in the table; it is called the *column percentage* of a cell. You can calculate the column percentages for the rest of the cells of the table. The percentage of nonparticipating students who pass the class is $2/9 = 22.2\%$. The percentage of participating students who fail the class is $3/11 = 27.3\%$, and the percentage of participating students who pass the class is $8/11 = 72.7\%$. Table 9–4 above is a completed contingency table with column percentages.

Notice you can also calculate the row percentages if you want. Nonetheless, because we place the dependent variable in rows and the independent variable in columns, it makes more sense to obtain column percentages for the meaningful relationship information.

Step 5: Conducting the Analysis and Drawing Conclusions

From the column percentages, you can easily draw a conclusion that participation and performance are related. You can also calculate percentage difference and percentage ratio, two measurement forms introduced in Chapter 4. In this example, the pass rates are 72.7% for participating students and 22.2% for nonparticipating students, for a percentage difference of

50.5% (i.e., 72.7% − 22.2%). Participating students are 227% (i.e., 72.7%/22.2% − 100%) more likely than nonparticipating students to pass the class.

Realize there are 2 rows and 2 columns in the example (excluding the row and the column for the totals). It is called a 2 × 2 table. In many other cases, contingency tables have more than 2 rows and 2 columns. The construction of contingency tables with more rows and columns becomes a little more complex, but the above steps and Excel programming still apply.

Correlation Analysis

Correlation analysis applies to the relationship between two interval variables. This section presents necessary steps in conducting correlation analysis and in visualizing the relationship.

Key Steps in Correlation Analysis

A university administration uses the graduation rate to assess educational effectiveness of its academic programs. The graduation rate is the percentage of students who have graduated within a period of time defined by an academic program. For example, an 85% graduation rate indicates that 85% of students in the program have graduated within a time defined by the program. A study of the graduation rate is conducted annually. The university administration wants to find out what academic or administrative variables may affect the graduation rate. Obviously, the dependent (performance) variable is the graduation rate, and the academic or administrative variables are independent variables. Table 9–10 shows the data of 15 academic programs this year.

Let us first look at the relationship between budget and the graduation rate. Because both variables are interval, their relationship can be assessed by a measure known as the *correlation coefficient* or the *Pearson correlation coefficient*, represented by the letter *r*. The value of a correlation coefficient can be obtained from either the CORREL or the Pearson procedure in the Excel Insert Function (*fx*). In the CORREL procedure, shown in Screen 9–7, Array 1 and Array 2 are used for the data of the two variables in the analysis. In our example, the graduation data in cells B4 to B18 are placed in Array 1, and budget data in cells C4 to C18 are selected for Array 2.

The correlation coefficient value is .543. What does that mean? Two pieces of information are needed in interpreting a correlation coefficient—its direction and its magnitude. A positive value of a coefficient indicates that both variables move toward the same direction. That is, when the value of one variable increases, the value of the other increases too. A negative value of a coefficient indicates that the variables move in the opposite direction. The magnitude of a relationship is measured on a scale from −1.000 to 1.000. A zero (0) would mean no relationship between the two variables, 1.000 is a perfectly positive relationship, and −1.000 is a perfectly negative relationship.

There is no universally agreed interpretation for an *r* value between 0 and ±1.000. I consider any value between ±.500 and ±.999 as a strong relationship, any value between ±.250

Screen 9–7

Budget and Graduation Rate: A Correlation Analysis.

	A	B	C	D	E
			=CORREL(B4:B18,C4:C18)		
1	What May Affect Graduation Rate?				
2					
3	Program ID	Graduation Rate	Budget (in million)	Average Class Size	No. of Scholarships
4	1	0.65	2.13	23.12	17
5	2	0.54	1.34	21.13	18
6	3	0.74	1.6	27.25	19
7	4	0.86	2.47	28.05	29
8	5	0.85	2.19	19.5	41
9	6	0.88	1.96	19.63	43
10	7	0.51	1.53	37.66	15
11	8	0.66	1.15	32.76	27
12	9	0.84	1.83	36.73	40
13	10	0.56	2.49	36.55	19
14	11	0.6	1.88	32.95	22
15	12	0.52	0.8	32.92	16
16	13	0.51	1.16	25.25	16
17	14	0.57	1.37	22.25	20
18	15	0.59	1.82	27.12	22

Function Arguments

CORREL

Array1   B4:B18   = {0.65;0.54;0.74;0.86;0.85;0.88;0.5...

Array2   C4:C18   = {2.13;1.34;1.6;2.47;2.19;1.96;1.53;...

    = 0.542687652

Returns the correlation coefficient between two data sets.

    Array1   is a cell range of values. The values should be numbers, names, arrays, or references that contain numbers.

Formula result =   0.542687652

Help on this function   OK   Cancel

Table 9–10

What May Affect the Graduation Rate?

Program ID	Graduation rate	Budget (in million $)	Average class size	Number of scholarships
1	0.65	2.13	23.12	17
2	0.54	1.34	21.13	18
3	0.74	1.6	27.25	19
4	0.86	2.47	28.05	29
5	0.85	2.19	19.5	41
6	0.88	1.96	19.63	43
7	0.51	1.53	37.65	15
8	0.66	1.15	32.76	27
9	0.84	1.83	36.73	40
10	0.56	2.49	36.55	19
11	0.60	1.88	32.95	22
12	0.52	0.80	32.92	16
13	0.51	1.16	25.25	16
14	0.57	1.37	22.25	20
15	0.59	1.82	27.12	22

and ±.4999 as a moderate relationship, and any value between ±.001 and ±.249 as a weak relationship. So, the relationship between budget and the graduation rate ($r = .543$) is positively strong. Another way to interpret the r is to compare it with other r values. For example, a relationship of .900 is stronger than that of .800.

Similarly, you can calculate the r between the class size and the graduation rate. Class size is measured by the average number of students in the classes of a program. The r value of $-.271$, shown in Screen 9–8, indicates that the relationship between the graduation rate and class size is negative—a smaller class size is related to a higher graduation rate—and that it is weaker than the one between the graduation rate and budget. Budget may have a larger impact on the graduation rate than class size.

Finally, the relationship between the number of scholarships and the graduation rate is examined. The r value is .879, indicating a strong positive relationship. The programs with more scholarships tend to graduate more students, and the relationship is strongest among all three examined so far in this example, suggesting the impact of scholarships on graduation is largest among the three independent variables.

Now, we have done three correlation analyses and calculated three correlation coefficients. Excel Data Analysis presents a process to calculate them all together to create a *correlation matrix*. You may want to review Chapter 3 on how to load Data Analysis ToolPak in Excel. Recall that the **Data Analysis** is in the Analysis group on the Data tab (for Excel 2003 users, it is on the Tools menu). In the **Data Analysis** window:

Screen 9–8

Calculating the *r* Between Class Size and Graduation Rate.

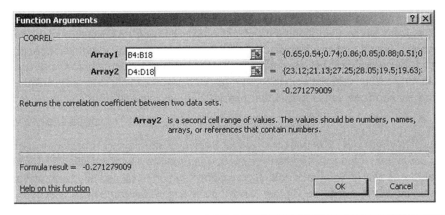

1. Click **Correlation** in the **Data Analysis** window. Make sure that you select data in the Input Range properly and check **Labels in the First Row** if you include the variable names in the Input Range.
2. Select an Output Range that does not overlap with the inputted data. Screen 9–9 shows the process.
3. Click the **OK** button.

You will see the correlation matrix as shown in Table 9–11. Realize that the matrix not only presents the *r* values between the graduation rate and the independent variables, but also the *r* values among the independent variables. For example, the relationship between budget and the number of scholarships is .401. A moderate positive relationship indicates that programs with larger budgets offer more scholarships. The diagonal elements of the matrix are equal to 1.000, because the relationship of a variable with itself is always perfectly positive.

Visualizing the Relationship—The Scatter Chart

Many people like to visualize a relationship. With help of the Excel Scatter Chart function (in the Charts group of the Insert menu or in Chart Wizard), Figure 9–1 is created for the relationship between budget and the graduation rate. The chart, known as a *scatter chart*, shows a slight upward pattern of the data, visually demonstrating the relationship pattern that a larger budget is related to a higher graduation rate, with a few points of exceptions.

Figure 9–2 shows the relationship between the graduation rate and class size. Realize the weak relationship between these two variables is demonstrated as the data points spread out loosely.

Screen 9–9

Excel Data Analysis Process: Creating a Correlation Matrix.

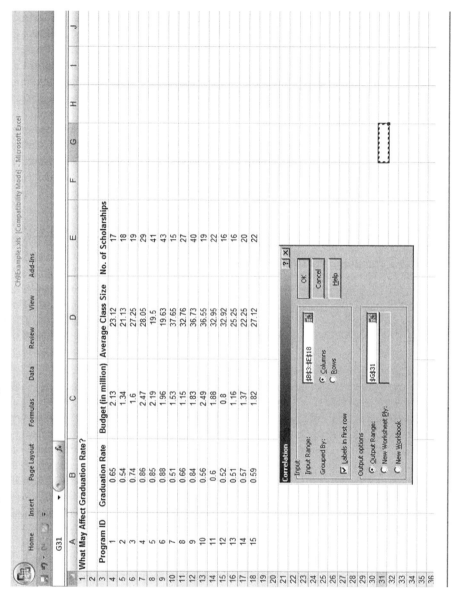

Program ID	Graduation Rate	Budget (in million)	Average Class Size	No. of Scholarships
1	0.65	2.13	23.12	17
2	0.54	1.34	21.13	18
3	0.74	1.6	27.25	19
4	0.86	2.47	28.05	29
5	0.85	2.19	19.5	41
6	0.88	1.96	19.63	43
7	0.51	1.53	37.65	15
8	0.66	1.15	32.76	27
9	0.84	1.83	36.73	40
10	0.56	2.49	36.55	19
11	0.6	1.88	32.95	22
12	0.52	0.8	32.92	16
13	0.51	1.16	25.25	16
14	0.57	1.37	22.25	20
15	0.59	1.82	27.12	22

Table 9–11

What May Affect the Graduation Rate? A Correlation Matrix

	Graduation rate	Budget (in million $)	Class size	Number of scholarships
Graduation rate	1			
Budget (in millions)	.542687652	1		
Class size	−.271279009	−.056978061	1	
Number of scholarships	.878724793	.401426553	−.235559607	1

Figure 9–1

Scatter Chart for Budget Graduation Rate.

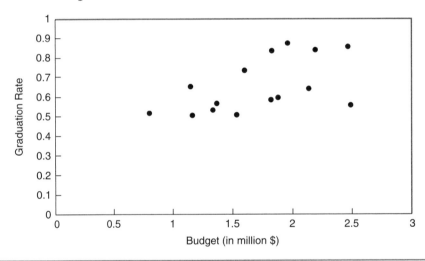

Figure 9–3 shows the strong positive relationship between the number of scholarships and the graduation rate. Compared with the above two, the upward pattern of the data in the chart shows a clearer positive relationship between the graduation rate and the number of scholarships. A higher graduation rate is related to a larger number of scholarships.

In addition to its visual effect in demonstrating a relationship, a scatter chart can help you determine the shape of a relationship. The correlation coefficient works best to determine a relationship when the shape of the relationship is linear, which means that the values of the two variables change proportionally. If the relationship is not linear, the use of the correlation coefficient may be improper, and the use of a scatter chart helps you identify the nonlinear

Figure 9–2

Scatter Chart for Class Size and Graduation Rate.

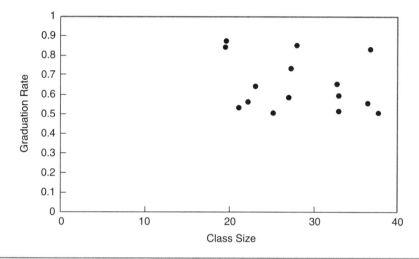

Figure 9–3

Scatter Chart for Number of Scholarships and Graduation Rate.

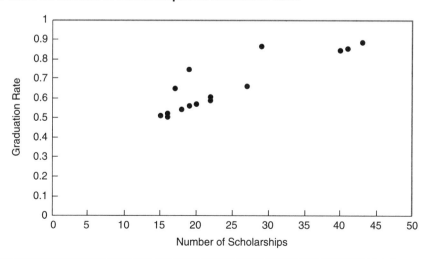

nature of the relationship. A discussion of nonlinearity will be seen in the next chapter in performance modeling.

Hypothesis Testing Basics and Testing for the Correlation Coefficient

So far in this chapter we have assumed that the population information is available for analysis. What happens if only samples are available? Let us say that, in the above example of the graduation rate, the 15 programs in the study are a sample selected from a population of, say, more than 100 academic programs in the university. Is there still a relationship between budget and the graduation rate for all these programs, as that demonstrated by the sample ($r = .543$)? Because the sample size is small (15 programs or $n = 15$), how much confidence do we have to say that the relationship still holds true for all the programs?

This section answers these questions by introducing a statistical tool known as *hypothesis testing*. A hypothesis test helps us discover how confident we are to draw a conclusion from a sample about the population. Specifically in a hypothesis test of a relationship, it tells how confident we are to declare that a relationship truly exists in a population. This section introduces hypothesis testing basics. It presents a *hypothesis test for the correlation coefficient*, which applies to the relationship of two interval variables. The next section demonstrates a hypothesis test for the relationship of two categorical variables—the chi-square test.

There are a few things you should know before conducting a hypothesis test. First of all, you conduct a hypothesis test *only when* you have a sample and you want to use the sample to draw inferential conclusions about the population. If your data are the population information already, you do not need hypothesis tests (review Chapter 7 for the difference between a population and a sample). Also, the tests presented in this book require probability sampling that ensures the proper representation of the sample for the population. In addition, for some tests in this book, the population form of the variable must have a particular form of distribution. For example, the t test in this book requires a normal or an approximately normal distribution of the variable. This is particularly true for small sample tests. Finally, a larger sample size improves the validity of a test. There are several steps involved in hypothesis testing. This section will use the hypothesis testing of the correlation coefficient to illustrate these steps.

Step 1: Setting Up Hypotheses

A hypothesis test starts with two mutually exclusive hypothesis statements. The *null hypothesis (Ho)* concerns the status quo, no effect, no change, or no relationship. This is usually a statement that the population parameter has the value that shows *no effect*. In the case of the correlation coefficient test, the null hypothesis is that there is *no* relationship between the dependent (performance) variable and the independent variable. Specifically for the relationship between budget and the graduation rate in our example, the null hypothesis is that there is *no* relationship between budget and the graduation rate.

The *alternative hypothesis (Ha)* in our example is that there *is* a relationship between budget and the graduation rate. As you see, the alternative hypothesis contradicts the null hypothesis. It is called alternative because it asserts that the population parameter falls in some alternative set of values to what the null hypothesis specifies. The alternative hypothesis is judged acceptable if the sample data are inconsistent with the null hypothesis.

Why are hypotheses created this way? In our criminal justice system, a person is presumed innocent until proven guilty. Sufficient evidence is needed to convict a person for a crime. Hypothesis tests are fashioned in a similar manner: sufficient evidence is required to prove the alternative hypothesis. Without sufficient evidence, the status quo of the null hypothesis is kept. In our example, you suspect that budget and the graduation rate are related (the alternative hypothesis is true). But, unless sufficient evidence is provided from the sample to support that, no relationship is assumed. Statisticians use the following symbols for hypothesis statements of a correlation coefficient test:

$$Ho: \rho = 0,$$

$$Ha: \rho \neq 0.$$

In the equations, ρ (a Greek letter pronounced as rho) is the population correlation coefficient between the two variables tested. So *Ho*, the correlation coefficient $\rho = 0$, means that there is no relationship between the two variables, and *Ha: $\rho \neq 0$* means that there is a relationship between them.

Step 2: Calculating the Test Statistic

Test statistic is a numeric value calculated from the sample to test the hypotheses. This statistic typically involves an estimate of the population parameter to which the hypotheses refer. The test statistic for testing *Ho: $\rho = 0$* is a *t* statistic that has a *t* distribution (review Chapter 7 for this distribution):

$$t = \frac{r\sqrt{n-2}}{\sqrt{1-r^2}}.$$

In the equation, *r* is the sample correlation coefficient and *n* is the sample size. This test has $n - 2$ degrees of freedom. For the relationship between budget and the graduation rate, $r = .543$, $n = 15$:

$$t = \frac{.543\sqrt{15-2}}{\sqrt{1-.543^2}} = \frac{1.9578}{.8397} = 2.3315.$$

Step 3: Determining the *P*-value

The P-*value* is one of most important concepts in statistics. What is it? There are two possible results for our test of the relationship between budget and the graduation rate. Either the result shows the relationship exists, or it does not. Let us say that the result shows that there is a relationship, but in reality there is not. In other words, we have made an error to predict a relationship. How could that happen? Remember that we use a sample to estimate the population parameter, so we always have a chance to make an error in estimation (review the concept of probability in Chapter 7). The *P*-value is the probability of that error. In our example, it is the probability that we conclude there is a relationship, but in reality there is not.

Many hypothesis tests require us to determine whether a test is *one-tailed* or *two-tailed*. That depends on how the alternative hypothesis *Ha* is set up. In our example, there are two different ways to state the *Ha*. In the first way, we can say that there is a relationship between budget and the graduation rate. In this statement, we do not specify whether the relationship is positive or negative. In other words, this statement contains two possibilities: a positive relationship or a negative relationship. This is why this test is two-tailed. It includes two possibilities. It leads to two possible conclusions.

Another way to state the *Ha* is that the relationship is positive. Then, we have a one-tailed test because this statement consists of just one possible result. Similarly, a test is one-tailed if we state that the relationship is negative in the *Ha*. In sum, a test is one-tailed if the *Ha* specifies the *direction of a relationship* (i.e., positive or negative in our example). The test is two-tailed if the *Ha* does not indicate the direction of the relationship. A *P*-value in a two-tailed test is twice as large as the *P*-value in a one-tailed test for a test statistic of the normal or approximately normal distribution (such as the *t* distribution). For example, if the *P* for a two-tailed test is .02, the one-tailed *P* is .02/2 = .01. If you could not determine whether your test is one-tailed or two-tailed, use the two-tailed *P*-value, because it is less likely to reject the null hypothesis in a two-tailed test, which makes it more rigorous than the one-tailed test.

To calculate the *P*-value in the test of correlation coefficient, you can use the TDIST process in Excel Insert Function (*fx*). Screen 9–10 shows how to obtain the *P*-value in our

Screen 9–10

Calculating the *P*-value from a *t* Distribution.

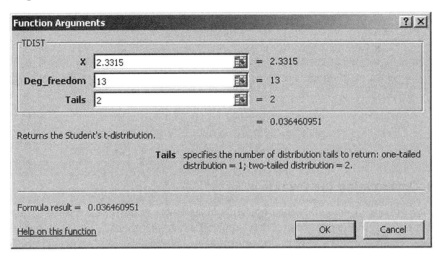

example of budget and the graduation rate. Place the t statistic (2.3315) in the x window (x means the test statistic). The degrees of freedom are $n - 2 = 15 - 2 = 13$. I choose a two-tailed test so I type 2 in the **Tails** window. If you choose a one-tailed test, put 1 there. The P-value is .0365.

Step 4: Setting the Significance Level (*the α-level*)

Recall that in Chapter 7, we construct a 95% confidence interval to estimate the true population parameter. We say that we are 95% confident about our estimation, which is equivalent to saying that we tolerate a 5% estimation error. In the case of a 99% confidence interval, we tolerate a 1% estimation error. The significance level α is the probability of the estimation error tolerated by the researcher. It can be seen as the highest probability level of estimation error a researcher can stand, and an error probability greater than that is considered unacceptable. Different from the P-value, which is calculated from test statistic, α has to be determined by you, the analyst. You decide on how much error you would allow for an estimation. Obviously, for very important decisions, you want a small chance of error, then you set a very small α. For most performance analysis tests, I would recommend a 5% (.05) or a 1% (.01) α-level. In our example, I choose an α-level of .05.

Step 5: Drawing Conclusions

If P is smaller than α (i.e., $P < \alpha$), we reject the null hypothesis and conclude that there is sufficient evidence to indicate that the alternative hypothesis is true. In our example, because $P = .0365$ and $\alpha = .05$, P is smaller than α, we reject the null hypothesis and conclude that there is sufficient evidence to indicate that the relationship is not equal to zero, which is the same as saying that there is a relationship between budget and the graduation rate. Some statisticians like to describe this conclusion as the relationship *does not happen by chance*, indicating that the same conclusion should be drawn from other samples from the population. Another way to state this conclusion is that the relationship is *statistically significant* at the .05 level.

Let us see why this conclusion makes sense. That P is smaller than α means the actual error probability P is smaller than the tolerated error probability α. When that happens, we know our chance of making an estimation error when concluding a relationship exists is within the range of our tolerance; so we conclude there is a relationship.

If P is equal to or larger than α (i.e., $P \geq \alpha$), we fail to reject the null hypothesis, and we conclude that there is *no* sufficient evidence to indicate that the alternative hypothesis is true. In a relationship test, this means that there is no sufficient evidence to indicate that the relationship exists or that the relationship is not statistically significant. Realize that this conclusion does *not* mean that there is no relationship. It simply says that there is no sufficient evidence of such a relationship, which is as close as saying that we do not really know whether there is a relationship or not.

As an exercise, conduct a hypothesis test on the relationship between the graduation rate and class size. The null hypothesis, *Ho*, is there is no relationship between the graduation rate and class size. The alternative hypothesis, *Ha*, is there is a relationship between them. The t

statistic should be close to −1.016. Notice that the *x* window in the Excel TDIST process does not take negative values for some reason. So each time you have a negative *t*, change it to the positive value. In this case, you should type in 1.016 in the *x* window. This treatment of *t* statistic is acceptable because the *t* distribution is symmetric with one side mirroring the other so the replacement of the negative sign of the *t* does not affect the result of the probability. With 13 degrees of freedom, a two-tailed *P*-value is .328. Because it is larger than the α-level of .05, we fail to reject the null hypothesis, and we conclude that there is no sufficient evidence to indicate there is a relationship between the graduation rate and class size at the .05 level. This is an interesting result. The sample correlation coefficient −.271, a weak relationship based on a sample of 15 programs, does not provide sufficient evidence to indicate that the graduation rate and class size are related for all programs at the university.

Similarly, conduct a hypothesis test on the relationship between the graduation rate and the number of scholarships. *Ho* is there is no relationship between these two variables, and *Ha* is there is a relationship between them. The two-tailed *P* = .0000016166. (Excel gives a 1.16166E-05, indicating that there are five zeros after the decimal point.) Because *P* is smaller than α (set at .05), you should reject the null hypothesis and conclude that there is sufficient evidence to indicate that a relationship between these two variables is present at the .05 level.

Chi-Square Test

If you have two categorical variables (either nominal or ordinal), you can perform a *chi-square* (χ^2) *hypothesis test*. Below are the steps involved in the test, illustrated with the case in the contingency table analysis on participation and class performance (data in Tables 9–3 and 9–4).

Step 1: Setting up Hypotheses

Ho is there is no relationship between the two variables, and in our example, there is no relationship between participation and class performance. *Ha* is there is a relationship between the two variables, and in our example, there is a relationship between participation and class performance.

Step 2: Calculating the Test Statistic

The test statistic is chi-square, denoted by the Greek letter χ^2 (pronounced as kai square). You need to know a few things to calculate it. First, you should know the *observed* number in a cell (also known as *Fo*). Let us look at the data in Table 9–4. Cell numbers in the table are observed numbers of the cells. For example, the observed number of nonparticipating students who fail the class is 7, the number at the upper left cell. Second, you should also know the *expected* number in a cell (known as *Fe*), calculated from the following equation:

$$Fe = (Row\ Total \times Column\ Total)/Grand\ Total.$$

Table 9–12 contains the necessary information for the calculation. The expected number in the cell for nonparticipating students who fail the test is $(10 \times 9)/20 = 4.5$. Highlighted in Table 9–12 are the numbers used to arrive at this figure. The row total for this cell is 10, and the column total is 9. The grand total is 20. The expected number in the cell for participating students who fail the test is $(10 \times 11)/20 = 5.5$, highlighted in Table 9–13.

Table 9–14 shows the expected numbers of all four cells. χ^2 is calculated from the following equation:

$$\chi^2 = \sum \frac{(Fo - Fe)^2}{Fe}.$$

In our example, $\chi^2 = (7.0 - 4.5)^2/4.5 + (3.0 - 5.5)^2/5.5 + (2.0 - 4.5)^2/4.5 + (8.0 - 5.5)^2/5.5 = 5.05$. The degrees of freedom for a chi-square test are (number of rows − 1) × (number of columns − 1). It is $(2 - 1) \times (2 - 1)$, which is 1 in this example.

Table 9–12

The Expected Number for Nonparticipating Students Who Fail the Class

	Participation		
	No	**Yes**	**Total**
Performance			
Fail	**4.5**		**10**
Pass			10
Total	**9**	11	**20**

Table 9–13

The Expected Number for Participating Students Who Failed the Class

	Participation		
	No	**Yes**	**Total**
Performance			
Fail		**5.5**	**10**
Pass			10
Total	9	**11**	**20**

Table 9–14

The Completed Table with Expected Numbers

	Participation		
	No	Yes	Total
Performance			
Fail	4.5	5.5	10
Pass	4.5	5.5	10
Total	9	11	20

Screen 9–11

Using CHIDIST to Obtain the *P*-value.

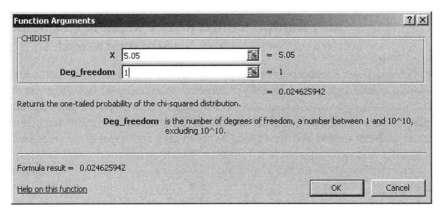

Step 3: Determining the *P*-value

Recall that the *P*-value is the probability that we reject the null hypothesis, but it is true. In the chi-square test, it is the probability that we conclude that two variables are related, but in reality they are not. *P* is determined by χ^2. Realize that χ^2 cannot be negative (all differences in the χ^2 are squared, so they are all positive). The minimum possible value, $\chi^2 = 0$, occurs when *Fo* = *Fe* in each cell, indicating that the two variables are completely independent to each other. χ^2 has a probability distribution skewed to the right. The precise shape of the distribution depends on the degrees of freedom.

There are two ways to calculate *P* in Excel. First, it can be obtained from Excel Insert Function (*fx*) CHIDIST command, as shown in Screen 9–11 for our example. In the *x* window:

1. Type the χ^2 statistic (5.05 in our example).

2. Type 1 in the **Deg_freedom** window. *P* is .0246.

Another way to obtain the *P*-value is to use the CHITEST procedure in Excel Insert Function. CHITEST uses observed and expected numbers of cells directly, as shown in Screen 9–12 with our example. Make sure that you place observed numbers in the **Actual_Range** and expected numbers in the **Expected_Range** in Excel, as shown in the screen. The *P*-value (.0246) is shown as the Formula Result. Notice that you do not need to calculate χ^2 statistic in the CHITEST procedure, so it is easier than the CHIDIST procedure.

Step 4: Determining the Significance Level (α)

Let us set α at .05.

Step 5: Drawing Conclusions

Because *P* (.0246) is smaller than α (.05), we reject the null hypothesis and conclude that there is sufficient evidence to indicate that there is a relationship between participation and class performance or that the relationship is statistically significant at the .05 level. Realize, if the α is set at .01, we will fail to reject the null hypothesis, and we will conclude there is no sufficient evidence to indicate the relationship exists. The conclusion depends on the α-level given in this example.

A Case Study

Step 1: Defining the Issue

Riverdale is a large urban city in a populated metropolitan area. The department of public works in the city operates a mechanical shop that is responsible for maintaining the city's vehicles. The work orders are largely issued for the police department's patrol vehicles and the fire department's emergency response vehicles. To maintain an immediate response to a work order on a 7-days-a-week 24-hour-a-day schedule, the workforce is divided into three service teams with each on an 8-hour schedule. Each service team has five mechanics and a supervisor. Their working hours alternate by week so no team works constantly on the night shift when the workload is less.

Recently, there have been an increasing number of complaints from the city's employees, mainly from patrol officers in the police department about the slow response to service calls for vehicle repairs and maintenance. The city uses a recommended performance standard that requires service calls be responded to within 4 hours, defined as a vehicle status update made by the supervisor of a service team.

Step 2: Determining the Analysis Question

The director of the mechanical shop, Sam Stevenson, understands that several factors could contribute to the slow response of the mechanical shop. According to the flowchart of a typical

Screen 9–12

Using CHITEST to Calculate the *P*-value.

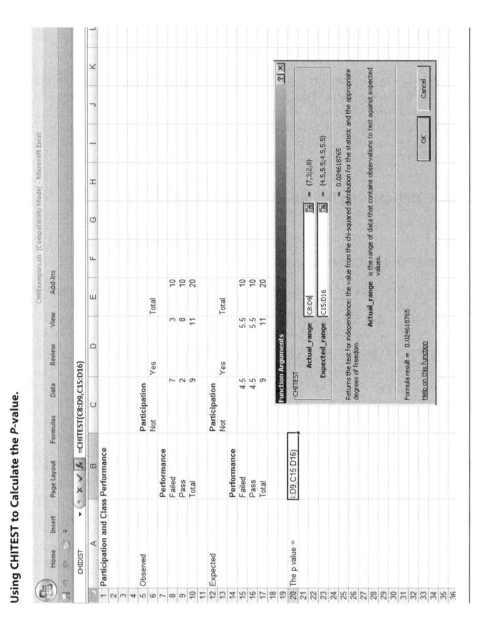

vehicle repair and maintenance process, these factors include the initial location of the vehicle that needs repairs or maintenance, the diagnostic time of the problem (depending on the nature of the problem), the accuracy of problem diagnosis, the estimation time on the cost and the process of repair or maintenance, and the time to file the status update report.

After talking to a few experts in the department and several police officers, Sam comes to believe that, in addition to these procedural factors, teamwork and team dynamics also play an important role in service responses. Mechanics are often required to work in teams, so the communication among them and between mechanics and their supervisor significantly influence the speed and quality of the service. There have been cases in the past when a supervisor could not find the diagnostic reports filed by workers due to miscommunication.

Sam suspects that Team A has the worst performance record because of anecdotal stories about the team's slow responses. So, before launching a complete analysis on all possible causes of slow responses, Sam requests an examination on each team's performance and his question is, do teams perform differently in service responses?

Step 3: Conducting the Analysis

The service response data are collected. Because the computer system in the department only keeps limited information on service records and because of the relatively large number of service requests, Sam has to use a sample. He randomly collects records of 50 service responses for each team at the same period of time during a day. Failures and successes in meeting the standard (the 4-hour limit) are reported. The data are shown in Table 9–15.

The data show that, of 150 responses, 115 (or 115/150 = 76.7%) were responded to within 4 hours (defined as success), and the other 35 did not meet the 4-hour standard (defined as failure). Team A has a success rate of 70% (35/50), less than that of Team B (39/50 = 78%) or Team C (41/50 = 82%), which seems to suggest that Team A has an inferior performance record. However, because only a relatively small sample of calls (150 calls) is analyzed, a hypothesis test is needed to find out if different teams really have different success rates, or in other words, if there is a relationship between teams and their responses.

Both the dependent variable (the success rates) and the independent variable (teams) are categorical, so the chi-square test is proper. The null hypothesis is there is no relationship between teams and their success rates, or teams have the same success rates. The alternative hypothesis is there is a relationship between teams and their success rates, or teams have different success rates.

Table 9–15

Service Responses in Riverdale's Mechanical Shop

	Team A	Team B	Team C	Total
Failure	15	11	9	35
Success	35	39	41	115
Total	50	50	50	150

The P-value of the test is .352, shown in Screen 9–13. At an α-level of .05, because P is larger than α, Sam fails to reject the null hypothesis, and he concludes that there is no sufficient evidence to indicate that the teams have different success rates. In other words, if Sam concludes that the teams have different success rates, the chance is 35.2% that he has a wrong conclusion.

Step 4: Drawing Conclusions

The result of the hypothesis test does not indicate that Team A is a poorer performer. The evidence derived from the sample of 150 cases is not sufficient for Sam to conclude that Team A performs differently. He is left with two options. One is to investigate the factors rather than the teams' performances that could cause slow responses. The other option is to collect more data on the teams' performances. The result of a hypothesis test is influenced by the sample size. Everything else being equal, a larger sample leads to a greater likelihood to reject the null hypothesis and to conclude that a relationship exists.

Practices

Key Terms

Causality
Performance relationship
Relationship
Variables
Independent variable
Dependent (performance) variable
Interval variable
Ordinal variable
Categorical variable
Categorization analysis (key steps)
Contingency table analysis (key steps)
Column percentage
Correlation analysis (key steps)
Correlation coefficient (the Pearson Correlation Coefficient)
Correlation matrix
Scatter chart
Hypothesis testing (key steps)
Null hypothesis
Alternative hypothesis
Test statistic
P-value
One-tailed or two-tailed test

Screen 9–13

Chi-Square Test of Service Responses in Riverdale's Mechanical Shop.

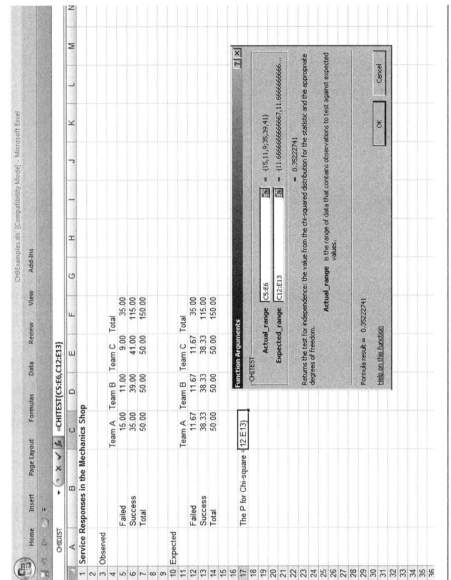

Direction of the relationship
P-value for one-tailed or two-tailed test
α-level (significance level)
Conclusions in hypothesis testing
Hypothesis testing steps for a correlation coefficient
Hypothesis testing steps in a chi-square test
Sorting data in Excel
Excel Insert Function (f_x) COUNTIF procedure
Excel Insert Function (f_x) CORREL procedure
Excel Data Analysis Correlation procedure
Excel Insert Function (f_x) TDIST procedure
Excel Insert Function (f_x) CHIDIST procedure
Excel Insert Function (f_x) CHITEST procedure

Practice Problem 9–1

The city of Newport needs to hire facility maintenance employees. Because the job has had a high turnover rate in the past, the speed of new hiring is critical for the continuity of the work. The hiring process consists of several steps: announcing the job, receiving a candidate application, reviewing the candidate qualification, conducting the interview, and making the decision of hiring. To speed up the process, an idea has been proposed to change the interview mode from face-to-face to telephone. You are the performance analyst for the city. You experiment the idea by conducting 10 telephone interviews and compare them with the length of 10 recent face-to-face interviews. Table 9–16 shows the comparison. Conduct a categorization analysis to examine the relationship between the interview mode and the interview length defined as the number of days from the time of scheduling an interview to its completion. Also, present your result visually.

Practice Problem 9–2

The department of economic development in a county government serves customers in business and nonprofit sectors. The director suspects that the satisfaction of these customers is affected by, among other things, how long they have received the service from the department. The director believes that long-time customers are happier because they know the department's operation better, and thus, they are more understanding. Table 9–17 shows the satisfaction rate and the length of services of the 30 customers from a recent survey. Perform a contingency table analysis to prove or disprove the suspicion of the director. Present your findings visually.

Practice Problem 9–3

Table 9–18 shows student performance in a performance analysis course. What are the dependent (performance) variable and the independent variables? Conduct a correlation analysis to

Table 9–16

Interview Mode and Length

Interview ID	Interview mode	Interview length (number of days)
1	Face-to-face	4
2	Phone	3
3	Face-to-face	5
4	Phone	4
5	Phone	7
6	Phone	7
7	Face-to-face	2
8	Face-to-face	4
9	Face-to-face	7
10	Phone	3
11	Phone	4
12	Face-to-face	3
13	Face-to-face	3
14	Face-to-face	3
15	Phone	3
16	Phone	2
17	Face-to-face	4
18	Face-to-face	4
19	Phone	5
20	Phone	4

Table 9–17

Service Length and Satisfaction

ID	Length with the department	Overall satisfaction	ID	Length with the department	Overall satisfaction
1	3	2	16	4	3
2	4	3	17	3	2
3	2	1	18	1	1
4	4	2	19	1	1
5	3	3	20	3	2
6	3	1	21	1	1
7	3	3	22	3	2
8	3	2	23	2	2
9	4	3	24	2	2
10	4	2	25	2	2
11	1	1	26	3	3
12	2	1	27	3	3
13	3	2	28	3	2
14	2	1	29	1	2
15	3	1	30	1	2

Length: 1 = less than 3 years; 2 = 3 to 6 years; 3 = 7 to 10 years, 4 = more than 10 years. Satisfaction: 1 = dissatisfied; 2 = somewhat satisfied; 3 = satisfied.

Table 9–18

Student Performance in a Performance Analysis Course

Student ID	Class score	Weekly study hours	Age	Number of classes taken in the program
1	89	4	35	4
2	92	3	20	5
3	74	2	50	4
4	83	4	62	6
5	95	3	45	6
6	67	1	19	3
7	93	3	39	2
8	80	2	28	3
9	73	3	57	4
10	91	4	44	1
11	78	2	42	5
12	86	3	25	4
13	73	3	27	2
14	93	4	33	4
15	85	3	34	4

examine the relationships between the dependent (performance) variable and each of the independent variables. Use scatter charts to visualize these relationships.

Practice Problem 9–4

Assume that the data in Table 9–18 are from a sample. Conduct a hypothesis testing on the relationships in Problem 9–3.

Practice Problem 9–5

Assume that the data in Table 9–17 are from a sample. Conduct a hypothesis testing on the relationship between the two variables.

Practice Problem 9–6

Identify a performance issue in a public or nonprofit organization of your choice. Specify a performance relationship that includes a dependent (performance) variable and at least one independent variable. Collect the data to conduct a relationship analysis. If necessary, perform a hypothesis test.

CHAPTER 10

Determining Causes of Underperformance: Performance Modeling

I n the last chapter, we learned how to discover performance relationship. Let us say that a correlation analysis shows that students' study times are related to their grades. The correlation coefficient between the number of weekly study hours and class grades is .750, indicating that study time is positively associated with the grades. So we know that a student who spends more time studying gets a better grade. What we still do not know, however, is how much more time is needed for the student to get an A in the class. In other words, we do not know *the exact form of the relationship*—how much change of a performance is in response to the change in a possible cause. In this chapter, we learn how to specify the exact form of a relationship by performance modeling. We want to establish that, for example, a student has to put in 5 hours a week to get an A.

Performance modeling serves two *purposes*. First, it provides a meaningful interpretation of a performance relationship so that a useful recommendation of performance improvement can be made. Performance modeling specifies the level of effort needed to achieve an expected level of performance. In the above example, we can tell a student with a B grade precisely how much more study time is needed to get an A. This recommendation is much more useful than simply saying that you should study harder.

Second, a performance model can be used to predict a performance level. We can use study time to predict a student's grade if we know the exact form of the relationship. *Performance predication* helps us rationalize the level of inputs (or outputs) needed for an expected level of performance in the planning and the budgeting processes. For example, if we know that building a new fire station will reduce the response time by 1 minute, we can base our request for additional budgetary resources on this relationship.

Performance modeling can be done in several ways. The exact form of a relationship can be developed from theories. For example, a measure of financial performance, earnings, is specified in theory as follows: Earnings = Revenues − Costs. This simple model illustrates that financial performance is affected by revenue collection efforts and cost control efforts. The exact forms of many other performance relationships can be theorized through more complex mathematical modeling processes.

This chapter presents a *statistical modeling process* that uses statistical estimations to develop the exact form of a performance relationship. Presented first in the chapter is a modeling process that has one independent variable—the simple regression—followed by a discussion on a regression model of multiple independent variables. The assumptions of the regression models will also be examined in the chapter.

Simple Regression Modeling

The Basic Model

Let us say that we examine how study efforts affect academic performance. Assume that study efforts consist of two parts: attending the lectures and studying at home. Also assume that a student will earn 50 of the maximum 100 points if he or she attends lectures. For each additional study hour the student spends at home weekly, the score improves by 10 points. Table 10–1 shows the relationship between the study effort and the academic score.

The relationship can be expressed algebraically as

$$Score = 50 + 10 \, (study \; hour).$$

In this example, the score is the dependent (performance) variable, and study hour is the independent variable (the cause). A generic form that describes how a performance is affected by an independent variable is

$$Performance = \alpha + \beta \, (the \; cause).$$

In the equation, a and β are population parameters that need to be estimated from the data. If we use Y for the dependent variable and X for the independent variable, the above equation becomes

$$Y = \alpha + \beta X.$$

This equation is the *basic performance model*. Realize that, in the above example, study hour and the score are perfectly associated (the correlation coefficient is 1.000). Visually, it is a straight line in a scatter chart shown in Figure 10–1.

In reality, however, a perfect relationship is hard to find for several reasons. First of all, not every student has the same learning curve. It is very likely that two students spending the

Table 10–1

Study Effort and Academic Performance

Number of weekly study hours	0	1	2	3	4	5
The score	50	60	70	80	90	100

Figure 10–1

A Perfect Relationship.

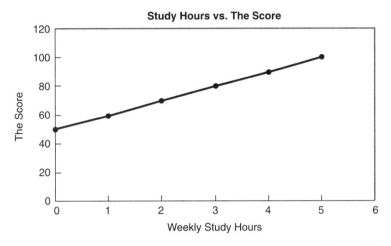

same amount of study time have different scores. So the relationship between study hour and the score is different for different students, which means that a performance model cannot perfectly predict performance for every student and that there is an error in predicting a student's performance. Figure 10–2 shows a more realistic relationship between study times and the scores of 20 students.

Also, population data are often unavailable; samples have to be used to estimate population parameters. Because of these and other reasons, the population parameters α and β in $Y = \alpha + \beta X$ are unknown, and they have to be estimated from a sample in the following manner:

$$\hat{Y} = a + bX.$$

This is the *performance prediction model* or the *simple regression model*. While $\hat{Y}$ represents the predicted mean values of the dependent variable, X is the values of the independent variable. The *intercept* ("a" in the equation) is estimated for α in the basic performance model, and the *slope* ("b" in the equation) is an estimate for β. The slope is also known as the *regression coefficient* of the regression model.

One key task in regression is to estimate the intercept and the slope. A popular method of the estimation is the *method of least square*, which minimizes the *prediction errors* of the equation defined as the *sum of squared errors* or $\Sigma(Y - \hat{Y})^2$; $(Y - \hat{Y})$ is the prediction error between an actual (observed) performance value Y and a predicted performance value $\hat{Y}$; $\Sigma(Y - \hat{Y})^2$ is the summation of prediction errors for all the data used in the prediction. Minimizing $\Sigma(Y - \hat{Y})^2$ means that the equation has the least prediction error or the most accurate prediction

Figure 10–2

A Realistic Relationship.

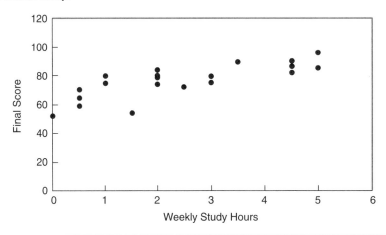

Figure 10–3

A Model $\hat{Y} = a + bX$ for the Data in Figure 10–2.

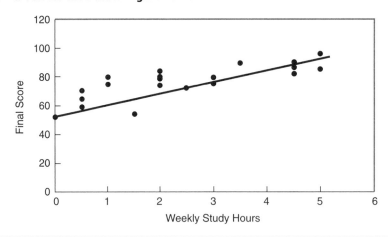

in estimating the performances. Shown in Figure 10–3 for data in Figure 10–2, the model $\hat{Y} =$ $a + bX$ is a straight line (linear) estimate in the figure.

Used to illustrate the estimation process, the data in Table 10–2 show the processing speed of 20 randomly selected case applications in a federal immigration processing agency. The number of processing days is the period from the receipt of an application to the day when a

Table 10–2

Immigration Case Processing Speed

Case ID	Number of processing days	Error rate
1	903	0
2	768	0
3	1006	3
4	1152	3
5	1145	4
6	1180	0
7	727	0
8	916	4
9	1134	5
10	787	0
11	838	0
12	742	0
13	736	1
14	799	1
15	825	2
16	728	0
17	857	0
18	885	0
19	986	2
20	892	1

decision of its approval or denial is made. A case can be declared as incomplete if it lacks necessary information. In most incomplete cases, a request is mailed out to the client or the client's attorney for the additional information.

The average processing speed of these 20 cases is 900 days; it is too long, and the agency is under pressure to reduce it. One theory is that the error rate of an application significantly affects the processing speed (i.e., the number of processing days). The error rate is the number of errors in filing or processing a case. Errors can be caused from missing important documents or from the inconsistent, inaccurate, or erroneous information. Though many errors are caused by either clients or their attorneys, others result from mistakes of processing officers. What is the relationship between the error rate and the processing speed?

The correlation coefficient between the error rate and the processing speed is .632, and it is statistically significant at the .05 level. The error rate and the processing speed are associated. A higher error rate is related to a longer processing period. What is the exact form of the relationship? How does the change in the error rate affect the processing speed? To answer these questions, you can formulate a performance prediction model in the following fashion:

$$Number\ of\ Processing\ Days = a + b\,(error\ rate).$$

Excel Data Analysis can help us estimate the intercept (*a*) and the slope (*b*) in the model (again, review Chapter 3 on how to load Analysis ToolPak).

1. Select the **Data Analysis** command in the **Analysis** group on the **Data** tab.
2. Click **Regression** from the **Data Analysis** window. As shown in Screen 10–1, the dependent variable *Y* is the number of processing days. The independent variable *X* is the error rate.
3. Check the **Labels** box if you include variable names (i.e., number of processing days, error rate) in your data ranges.
4. Select an output range that is not overlapping with the data. Click **OK**.

There are three tables in the Excel Summary Output, as shown in Screen 10–2. We will discuss all these statistics in this chapter. Now, to obtain the performance prediction model, go to the column of the last table that includes Coefficients of Intercept and Error Rate. The intercept of the equation is 824.86. The coefficient of the error rate is the slope 58.03. So, the performance prediction model is

$$Number\ of\ Processing\ Days = 824.86 + 58.03\,(error\ rate)$$

Interpretation of the Model

What does this model mean? The *interpretation of a model* should focus on the intercept and the slope. The intercept is 824.86 in this example. It is the number of processing days when the error rate is zero (i.e., no processing error or *b* = 0). The number of processing days is 824.86 if there is no error in filing and processing the case. Visually, it is the point where the prediction model intercepts with the *Y* axis in the scatter chart of the prediction.

The interpretation of the slope is a little more complex. It is 58.03 in our example. To understand it, assume that there is one error in applications (i.e., the error rate = 1). According to the regression model, number of processing days = 824.86 + 58.03 (error rate), the predicted processing speed is 824.86 + 58.03 (1) = 882.89 processing days when the error rate is 1. We know that the number of processing days is 824.86 when there is no error (i.e., 824.86 + 58.03 (0) = 824.86). The difference between these two results is 882.89 − 824.86 = 58.03, the slope. This is the change of the processing speed when the error rate changes from 0 to 1. Similarly, the processing speed changes by 58.03 days when the error rate changes from 1 to 2, 2 to 3, 3 to 4, 4 to 5, etc. That is, for each additional error made, the number of processing days increases by 58.03. So the slope is the change of the number of processing days in response to the change of the error rate. The change in the error rate is also known as a one-unit change, because it reflects the change in days from 0 to 1, from 1 to 2, from 2 to 3, etc. Therefore, the slope is defined as the change of value in the dependent variable (*Y*) for a one-unit change in the value of the independent variable (*X*).

In sum, the regression model, number of processing days = 824.86 + 58.03 (error rate), indicates that an immigration case takes 824.86 days to process when there is no error. With each additional error, the processing speed increases by 58.03 days. Clearly, this is a much more accurate and insightful explanation than the finding from the correlation analysis, which simply says that the error rate and the processing speed are related.

Screen 10–1

Immigration Case Processing: A Simple Regression Process.

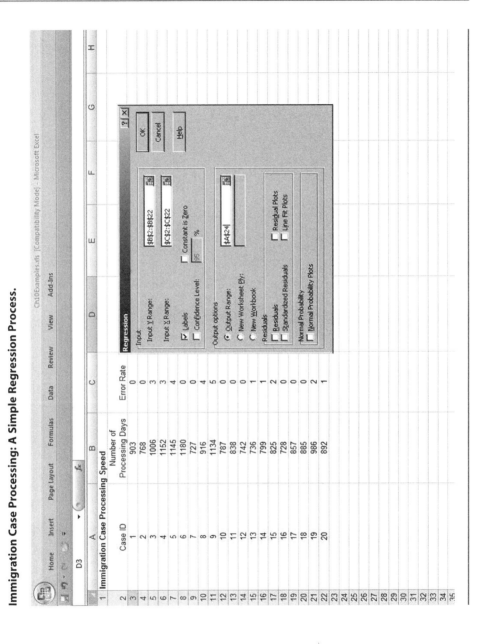

Screen 10–2

Summary Output of Simple Regression.

SUMMARY OUTPUT

Regression Statistics	
Multiple R	0.63282422
R Square	0.400466493
Adjusted R Square	0.367159076
Standard Error	120.9149726
Observations	20

ANOVA

	df	SS	MS	F	Significance F
Regression	1	175786.449	175786.449	12.0233428	0.00274816
Residual	18	263167.751	14620.43061		
Total	19	438954.2			

	Coefficients	Standard Error	t Stat	P-value	Lower 95%	Upper 95%
Intercept	824.8601533	34.70396193	23.76847217	4.7999E-15	751.9497783	897.7705282
Error Rate	58.03065134	16.73573654	3.467469221	0.00274816	22.87014637	93.19115631

How Good Is the Model?

There are several ways to judge how good a performance prediction model is. They all measure the accuracy of a model in predicting the actual (observed) performance Y. A model is deemed better if it predicts the actual performance more accurately.

Coefficient of Determination (r²)

The first table in the Excel Regression Summary Output presents regression statistics. Multiple R is the correlation coefficient introduced in Chapter 9. Recall, in Chapter 9, the correlation coefficient is denoted by the letter r. Shown in Table 10–3, the r for the processing speed and the error rate is .6328.

Excel Summary Output also gives R square, also known as the coefficient of determination. Although the capital letter R is used in Table 10–3, the small letter r is more proper in simple regression models when there is one independent variable. R should be used in multiple regression models that have multiple independent variables.

r^2, as it is called, is the squared r or the squared correlation coefficient. Because $r = .6328$ in this example, $r^2 = (.6328)^2 = .4005$, shown in Table 10–3. r^2 is one of the most important measures to assess how good a model is. What does it mean? Imagine that you are a processing officer and you are about to process your next case. I would ask you to predict the processing speed, the number of processing days, for that case. What will it be? Let us also assume you know the processing speeds of the 20 cases in Table 10–2, but you do not know their error rates. Statisticians say that the best prediction you can get under these conditions is the mean, the average number of the processing days—900 days in this case. So you would predict that your next case will take 900 days to process. Is that an accurate prediction? Probably not, because the mean is just the average speed of all the cases, and these cases have very different processing speeds. What is the prediction error if you use the average? Let Y be the actual number of processing days for your next case and $\bar{Y}$ be the average number of processing days. Your prediction error will be $Y - \bar{Y}$ if you use the average in the prediction.

Now, suppose you know the error rates of the 20 cases, and you use them to create a regression model to predict the number of processing days. If you know the error rate of your next case, you can use it to predict the processing speed of the case. Realize that, because the

Table 10–3

Regression Statistics: The Immigration Case Processing Example

Regression statistics	
Multiple R	.63282422
R square	.400466493
Adjusted R square	.367159076
Standard error	120.9149726
Observations	20

error rate is highly associated with the number of processing days ($r = .633$), this new prediction based on the error rate information should be more accurate than the prediction by using the mean (the 900 days). Exactly how much more accurate is your new prediction compared with the one using the mean? Let $\hat{Y}$ represent your new prediction, the number of predicted processing days from the regression model that includes the error rate information. Your prediction error from the actual processing speed is $Y - \hat{Y}$. Recall that the prediction error is $Y - \bar{Y}$ if you use the mean. So, using the regression model instead of the mean, you reduce the prediction error by $(Y - \bar{Y}) - (Y - \hat{Y}) = (\hat{Y} - \bar{Y})$, which leads to a reduced prediction error by $(\hat{Y} - \bar{Y})/(Y - \bar{Y})$ proportionally.

Realize that this is the prediction rate improvement for just one case. If you add the prediction rate improvements of all cases (20 in our example) and square them to avoid that positive and negative values cancel out each other, you have the definition of r^2 in the following fashion:

$$r^2 = \frac{\sum(\hat{Y} - \bar{Y})^2}{\sum(Y - \bar{Y})^2}.$$

In the equation, Σ is used to sum up all cases in prediction and square is used to arrive at a positive value. As you can see, r^2 is the proportion of the prediction error reduced by using the regression model $\hat{Y}$ instead of the mean $\bar{Y}$. A larger r^2 indicates a better prediction of the model. In our example of the immigration processing speed ($r^2 = .4005$), we say that 40.05% of prediction errors is reduced by the regression model. The values of r^2 go from 0 and 1, and there is no negative r^2 value.

Table 10–3 also gives a measure called adjusted r^2. It will be discussed later in the multiple regression modeling. Right now, all you need to know is that r^2 and adjusted r^2 have the same meaning. The number of cases (Observations in the Excel Output) is also listed in Table 10–3.

Standard Error of the Estimate
This statistic is called standard error in the Excel Regression Summary Output (Table 10–3). It is a measure of the variation of the predicted values from the actual values ($Y - \hat{Y}$). The standard error of the estimate, represented by $\hat{\sigma}$, is defined as

$$\hat{\sigma} = \sqrt{\frac{\sum(Y - \hat{Y})^2}{n - 2}}.$$

In the equation, $\Sigma(Y - \hat{Y})^2$ is the sum of squared errors defined earlier in this chapter; n is the number of cases (observations). The standard error of the estimate is 120.91 in our example. A smaller standard error indicates a smaller variation of the predicted values from the actual values and, therefore, a more accurate prediction.

This measure can be used to create a confidence interval for the estimation. In our example of immigration processing, if there is one processing error, the predicted number of processing days is 824.86 + 58.03 (1) = 882.89. How confident are we about the accuracy of this estimate?

From the knowledge in Chapter 7, we can form a confidence interval $\hat{Y} \pm t\hat{\sigma}$. The predicted value $\hat{Y}$ is 882.89. The t statistic with $n = 20$ (degrees of freedom $= 20 - 1 = 19$) is 2.093 for a 95% confidence interval (use the Excel TINV process introduced in Chapter 7 for the t). So the confidence interval is from 630 (i.e., $882.89 - 2.093 \times 120.91$; rounded) to 1136 (i.e., $882.89 + 2.093 \times 120.91$; rounded). Hence, we are 95% confident that the true average number of processing days for all cases with one processing error is between 630 and 1136.

F *Test*

Recall from Chapter 7 that statistical inference is necessary when sample data are used to estimate population parameters. Hypothesis testing should be conducted when population parameters are inferred from samples. Chapter 9 describes basic steps in hypothesis testing. The Excel Regression Summary Output provides several inferential statistics. First, an F test of the regression model is presented in the analysis of variance (ANOVA) table. The null hypothesis of this test is the dependent variable is unrelated to any of the independent variables in the model. In the simple regression, because there is only one independent variable, the null hypothesis can be stated as the dependent variable and the independent variable are unrelated. The alternative hypothesis is these two variables are related. Realize that, if these two variables are unrelated, there is no reason to construct the regression model. In other words, the construction of the regression model is meaningful *only if* the null hypothesis is rejected. The null hypothesis of the F test in the immigration processing example is that the processing speed and the error rate are unrelated. The alternative hypothesis is that they are related. Table 10–4 shows the F test results.

To understand how to get these results, you need to know the concepts of *sums of squares* (SS) and *mean squares* (MS), which are somewhat related to the concept of variance. Defined in Chapter 5, the variance is the distance from individual cases to the mean of the data. Think of one specific variance in a regression model as the distance from the actual values (Y) to the mean value ($\bar{Y}$). This variance is measured by something called the total sum of squares or SS_{Total}; SS_{Total} is defined as $\Sigma(Y - \bar{Y})^2$ to include all individual cases in analysis.

Realize that SS_{Total} consists of two parts in a regression model: the distance from actual values (Y) to predicted values ($\hat{Y}$) based on the regression model and the distance from the predicted values ($\hat{Y}$) to the mean value ($\bar{Y}$). That is $(Y - \bar{Y}) = (Y - \hat{Y}) + (\hat{Y} - \bar{Y})$, and therefore,

Table 10–4

The F Test in the ANOVA Table

			ANOVA		
	df	**SS**	**MS**	**F**	**Significance F**
Regression	1	175786.449	175786.449	12.0233428	.00274816
Residual	18	263167.751	14620.43061		
Total	19	438954.2			

$\Sigma(Y - \bar{Y})^2 = \Sigma(Y - \hat{Y})^2 + \Sigma(\hat{Y} - \bar{Y})^2$ for all cases. Recall from an earlier discussion that $\Sigma(Y - \hat{Y})^2$ measures the prediction error (residual) of the regression model, and it is also known as the sum of squared errors (residuals) or $SS_{Residual}$. $\Sigma(\hat{Y} - \bar{Y})^2$ represents the gain in prediction due to using the regression model rather than the mean, so it is called $SS_{Regression}$.

Table 10–4 shows that $SS_{Regression}$ is 175786.45, and $SS_{Residual}$ is 263167.75 in the immigration processing example. $SS_{Regression}$ has k degrees of freedom, and k is the number of the independent variables in the model; $SS_{Residual}$ has $n - (k + 1)$ degrees of freedom (n is the number of cases). Table 10–4 also shows the degrees of freedom (df) for different sums of squares in a relationship that $df_{Regression} + df_{Residual} = df_{Total}$. In our example, $df_{Regression} = 1$ and $df_{Residual} = 20 - (1 + 1) = 18$ and $df_{Total} = 1 + 18 = 19$.

When a sum of squares takes account of degrees of freedom, it becomes a mean square or MS. $MS_{Regression} = SS_{Regression}/df_{Regression}$, which is $175786.45/1 = 175786.45$ in our example. $MS_{Residual} = SS_{Residual}/df_{Residual} = 263167.75/18 = 14620.43$. Both are shown in Table 10–4. The F statistic is defined as

$$F = \frac{MS_{Regression}}{MS_{Residual}}.$$

A larger F value reflects a large $MS_{Regression}$ in relation to $MS_{Residual}$, indicating that a larger portion of the total variance is accounted for by the regression model. Therefore, a larger F value is more likely to transform to a conclusion in favor of the alternative hypothesis that the variables in the regression model are related.

In our example, the F value is $175786.45/14620.43 = 12.02$. The P-value is called the significance F in the Excel output. It is .002748. Recall from Chapter 9 that the P-value is the probability that we reject the null hypothesis, but it is true. In this example, it is the probability that we conclude the processing speed and the error rate are related, but they are truly not. In other words, it is the probability that we make a mistake to draw that conclusion.

Let us set the significance level at .05 ($\alpha = .05$). This is the highest probability level of a mistake we can tolerate (the α here is the significance level, not the parameter intercept in the basic performance model). Because $P < .05$, indicating that the probability of making an estimation error is smaller than our tolerated level, we reject the null hypothesis and conclude that there is sufficient evidence to indicate that the processing speed and the error rate are related. This result indicates that it is meaningful to construct this performance prediction model.

t Tests

Also presented in the Excel Regression Summary Output is a t *test for the intercept (α) and the slope (β)*. The null hypothesis for the test of the intercept is $\alpha = 0$, and the alternative hypothesis is $\alpha \neq 0$. From the basic performance model $Y = \alpha + \beta X$, we know that when $\alpha = 0$ and $\beta \neq 0$, $Y = \beta X$. So the result from this test of the intercept really determines the form of the relationship between variables X and Y.

Table 10–5 shows the test results for our example. The coefficient of the intercept is $a = 824.86$. The standard error of the intercept, represented by $\hat{\sigma}_a$, is 34.70. The test statistic (t) is calculated from $t = a/\hat{\sigma}_a = 824.86/34.70 = 23.77$, also shown in Table 10–5. The test has degrees of freedom $df = n - 2 = 20 - 2 = 18$. The P-value is very small 4.7999E-15 (there are 15 zeros

Table 10–5

t Tests for the Intercept and the Slope

	Coefficients	Standard error	*t* stat	*P*-value	Lower 95%	Upper 95%
Intercept	824.8601533	34.70396193	23.76847217	4.7999E-15	751.9497783	897.7705282
Error rate	58.03065134	16.73573654	3.467469221	.00274816	22.87014637	93.19115631

after the decimal point). Let the significance level be .05. Because $P < .05$, we reject the null hypothesis and conclude that the intercept $\alpha \neq 0$. If you are interested in calculating the *P*-value by yourself, use Excel Insert Function TDIST. Type the *t* value of 23.76847 in the *x* window, 18 in the degrees of freedom window, and 2 for a two-tailed probability.

The *t* test for the slope (β) is a very important test in regression analysis. The null hypothesis in this test is $\beta = 0$, indicating that the independent variable X and the dependent variable Y are unrelated or that the error rate is unrelated to the processing speed in the example. The alternative hypothesis is $\beta \neq 0$, or X and Y are related. Realize, when $\beta = 0$, $Y = \alpha + \beta X = \alpha + 0X = \alpha$; $Y = \alpha$ means that Y is a constant value α regardless of any X value, and X has no impact on Y. In a scatter chart, $Y = \alpha$ is a straight line parallel with the X axis, indicating variable Y is a constant value for any given X value. So $\beta = 0$ is equivalent to saying that X and Y are unrelated. On the other hand, when $\beta \neq 0$ and then $\beta X \neq 0$, X is related to Y, in a way that $Y = \alpha + \beta X$; thus, $\beta \neq 0$ can also be interpreted as Y and X are related.

The slope (b) is 58.03 in our example. Its standard error ($\hat{\sigma}_b = 16.74$) is also presented in Table 10–5. The test statistic, the *t* value, is calculated from

$$t = \frac{b}{\hat{\sigma}_b}.$$

So $t = 58.03/16.74 = 3.467$ in our example; $P = .002748$. At the .05 significance level, because $P < .05$, we reject the null hypothesis and conclude that there is sufficient evidence to indicate that $\beta \neq 0$ or that the error rate X is related to the processing speed Y. From the above tests, we know that the intercept $\alpha \neq 0$ and the slope $\beta \neq 0$ for our example. Therefore, it is meaningful to construct and estimate the model $Y = \alpha + \beta X$: the number of processing days = 824.86 + 58.03 (error rate).

The Excel output also provides 95% *confidence interval estimates for the intercept and the slope*. The estimate ensures a 95% confidence that the estimated value falls within the interval. In our example, the lower bound of the interval for the intercept is 751.95, and the upper bound is 897.77, so we are 95% confident that the true (population) intercept (α) is between 751.95 and 897.77. Similarly, we are 95% confident that the slope (β) falls within 22.87 and 93.19. Remember that, according to our prediction equation, the number of processing days = 824.86 + 58.03 (error rate), we estimate that an increase in each additional error will result in an increase in the number of processing days by 58.03. This confidence interval indicates that we are 95% confident that the true increase in the number of processing days for each additional error is between 23 (rounded) and 94 (rounded) days.

Multiple Regression Modeling

So far we have only dealt with the regression model that has one independent variable. In reality, however, few performances are affected by only one variable. Multiple causes influence performance simultaneously or consecutively. A poor academic performance may result from a combination of a student's poor study efforts and the instructor's inadequate teaching quality. Slower responses to emergencies may be a result of poorly trained dispatchers and increasingly congested traffic routes. Numerous socioeconomic and organizational factors can affect crime rates. A *multivariate analysis* concerns the impact of multiple independent variables on the performance, while the analysis that examines the impact of one independent variable on the performance is a *bivariate analysis.*

This section presents a modeling process that assesses the simultaneous impact of multiple possible causes on a dependent (performance) variable. For a performance possibly affected by multiple possible causes, this multivariate modeling process has several clear advantages over a bivariate process that analyzes the impact of one possible cause at a time. First, it allows an examination on the *joint impact of multiple causes* on the performance. For example, if both study efforts and instructional effectiveness affect a student's academic performance simultaneously, how well will a student perform if he or she makes good efforts *and* also has a good teacher? This joint impact is considered in a multivariate analysis, but not in a bivariate analysis.

Second, the multivariate analysis examines the impact of each possible cause while *controlling* the impact of other possible causes on the performance. To illustrate the concept of the control, suppose that a bivariate analysis shows that there is a relationship between home Internet access and students' academic performances. Students with home Internet access have higher academic scores. However, it is also found that students having home Internet access come from wealthier families. In fact, family income affects both home Internet access and academic performance. While controlling family income, the relationship between home Internet access and academic performance does not exist. Family income, not home Internet access, is proven to be associated with academic performance. In this example, a multivariate analysis process is used to examine the relationship between home Internet access and academic performance while controlling the impact of family income. In a multivariate analysis, a variable is said to be controlled when its impact on other variables is removed. This process is known as the *statistical control*. The statistical control helps us find out the true impact of a possible cause on the performance. This advantage of the multivariate analysis in statistical control cannot be overstated, because performance analysis often involves multiple possible causes and it is critically important to discover the true causes.

The Basic Model

In a multivariate model that involves k number of independent variables, the basic model can be expressed as

$$Y = \alpha + \beta_1 X_1 + \beta_2 X_2 + \ldots \beta_k X_k.$$

In the equation, Y is the dependent variable, and X_1, X_2, . . . X_k represent the independent variables; α, β_1, β_2 . . . β_k are population parameters. This equation is known as a *multivariate performance model*. The estimated prediction equation for the model is

$$\hat{Y} = a + b_1 X_1 + b_2 X_2 + \ldots b_k X_k.$$

This equation is the *multivariate performance prediction model* or the *multiple regression model*. While $\hat{Y}$ represents the predicted mean values of the dependent variable, X_1, X_2, . . . X_k are the values of the independent variables. The intercept ("a" in the model) should be estimated for α. Also, b_1, b_2, . . . b_k, the slopes, are estimates for β_1, β_2, . . . β_k. A slope in the multiple regression models, also known as the *partial regression coefficient*, represents the impact of an independent variable on the dependent variable $\hat{Y}$ while controlling other independent variables.

Let us work on an example. Recall that, when we build the simple regression model based on the immigration processing data, the error rate is identified as the sole independent variable. Now, the management believes that the processing speed is also affected by two other variables: a processing officer's work experience measured by how long he or she has worked in the agency as well as the officer's case experience measured by how long he or she has been processing the same type of cases. It is reasonably assumed that an officer who stays in the agency longer and works on the same type of cases longer should possess better knowledge on the processing procedure and therefore should process cases more quickly. Table 10–6 shows the processing data of the 20 selected cases.

A multivariate performance prediction model can be formulated in the following fashion:

$$Number\ of\ Processing\ Days = a + b_1\ (Error\ Rate) + b_2\ (Work\ Experience) +$$
$$b_3\ (Case\ Experience).$$

The regression process in the Excel Data Analysis estimates the *intercept and the slopes* in the model. The estimation process uses the least square method introduced above. As demonstrated in Screen 10–3:

1. Select **Regression** in the **Data Analysis** window.
2. Select the number of processing days in the Y variable range, and the error rate, the work experience, and the case experience in the X variable range.
3. Check the **Labels** box if you include variable names while selecting the data.
4. Select an output range that is not overlapping with the data. Click **OK**.

Similar to the Excel simple regression output, the Excel multiple regression output also presents three tables, shown in Screen 10–4. To obtain the prediction model, go to the column of the last table that shows coefficients of intercept and slopes. The intercept of the equation ("a" in the prediction model) is 906.68. The coefficient of the error rate, 49.45, is the slope of that variable (b_1 in the prediction equation). This estimate is noticeably different from that in

Screen 10-3

Immigration Case Processing: A Multivariate Analysis.

Immigration Case Processing Speed

Case ID	Number of Processing Days	Error Rate	Officer's Work Experience. Length at Job (in Year)	Officer's Case Experience. Length at the Same Type of Cases (in Year)
1	903	0	9	8
2	768	0	8	8
3	1006	0	2	1
4	1152	3	2	1
5	1145	3	1	1
6	1180	4	4	2
7	727			
8	916			
9	1134			
10	787			
11	838			
12	742			
13	736			
14	799			
15	825			
16	728			
17	857			
18	885			
19	986			
20	892			

Regression

Input
Input Y Range: $B$2:$B$22
Input X Range: $C$2:$E$22
☑ Labels   ☐ Constant is Zero
☐ Confidence Level: 95 %

Output options
◉ Output Range: $A$24
○ New Worksheet Ply:
○ New Workbook

Residuals
☐ Residuals   ☐ Residual Plots
☐ Standardized Residuals   ☐ Line Fit Plots

Normal Probability
☐ Normal Probability Plots

OK
Cancel
Help

Screen 10–4

Summary Output of Multiple Regression.

Ch10Examples.xls [Compatibility Mode] - Microsoft Excel

| | Home | Insert | Page Layout | Formulas | Data | Review | View | Add-Ins | | | |

	A	B	C	D	E	F	G	H	I	J
24	SUMMARY OUTPUT									
25										
26	*Regression Statistics*									
27	Multiple R	0.754338701								
28	R Square	0.569026876								
29	Adjusted R Square	0.488219415								
30	Standard Error	108.7363391								
31	Observations	20								
32										
33	ANOVA									
34		*df*	*SS*	*MS*	*F*	*Significance F*				
35										
36	Regression	3	249776.7371	83258.91236	7.04176162	0.003118964				
37	Residual	16	189177.4629	11823.59143						
38	Total	19	438954.2							
39		*Coefficients*	*Standard Error*	*t Stat*	*P-value*	*Lower 95%*	*Upper 95%*			
40	Intercept	906.6832206	101.0333737	8.974096252	1.21135E-07	692.5020846	1120.8644			
41	Error Rate	49.45083171	20.30778512	2.435067705	0.026966058	6.400260135	92.501403			
42	Officer's Work Experience	12.32576479	12.47880955	0.987735629	0.337984793	-14.12812371	38.779653			
43	Officer's Case Experience	-32.77973325	13.10681676	-2.500968302	0.023628148	-60.56493729	-4.9945292			
44										

Table 10–6

More Data for the Immigration Case Processing Example

Case ID	Number of processing days	Error rate	Officer's work experience—length at work (in year)	Officer's case experience—length at processing the same type of cases (in year)
1	903	0	9	8
2	768	0	8	8
3	1006	3	2	1
4	1152	3	1	1
5	1145	4	4	2
6	1180	0	9	2
7	727	0	9	7
8	916	4	7	7
9	1134	5	1	1
10	787	0	7	5
11	838	0	5	5
12	742	0	10	2
13	736	1	3	3
14	799	1	8	6
15	825	2	6	6
16	728	0	7	7
17	857	0	7	6
18	885	0	10	5
19	986	2	10	5
20	892	1	7	5

the simple regression model (58.03). The slopes for the work experience (b_2 in the prediction model) and the case experience (b_3 in the prediction model) are 12.33 and −32.78, respectively, constituting the multiple regression model as follows:

$$Number\ of\ Processing\ Days = 906.68 + 49.45\,(Error\ Rate) + 12.33\,(Work\ Experience)$$
$$-32.78\,(Case\ Experience).$$

Interpretation of the Model

Like the simple regression, the *interpretation of a multiple regression model* should also focus on the intercept and the slopes. The intercept is 906.68 in the example, indicating that the number of processing days is 906.68 when the error rate is zero (i.e., no error or $b_1 = 0$), and the processing officer has no work experience in the agency ($b_2 = 0$) and no experience in processing the same type of cases ($b_3 = 0$).

The slope for the error rate is 49.45, indicating that for each additional error made in the processing, the number of processing days increases by 49.45 for the officers with the same work and case processing experience (i.e., controlling the work experience and the case experience). The slope for the work experience is 12.33, indicating the number of processing days increases by 12.33 for each additional year of the work experience a processing officer gains while controlling the error rate and the case experience. This result is counterintuitive because increased work experience should reduce the processing time. We will learn later that this finding is not statistically significant, suggesting the impact of this variable on the processing speed does not exist while considering the impact of the case experience.

The slope for the case experience, −32.78, shows that the number of processing days declines by 32.78 for each additional year of case experience an officer has. This result supports the management's belief that that the increased experience in processing the same type of cases should improve the processing speed.

How Good Is the Model?

The measures to judge a multiple regression model are similar to those in simple regression modeling. They include the coefficient of multiple determination R^2 (the capital letter R is used in the multiple regression models), the standard error of the estimate, and several inferential statistical measures.

The Coefficient of Multiple Determination R²

The interpretation of R^2 is the same as that of the coefficient of determine r^2 in the simple regression. It is the percentage of errors reduced by using the multiple regression model $\hat{Y} = \alpha + b_1X_1 + b_2X_2 + \ldots b_nX_n$ to predict Y instead of using the mean $\bar{Y}$. R^2 is a measure of the joint impact of multiple independent variables on the dependent variable. Table 10–7 shows that R^2 is .569 in our example, indicating that 56.9 % of prediction errors have been reduced by using the multiple regression model: *Number of Processing Days* = 906.68 + 49.45(*Error Rate*) + 12.33(*Work Experience*) − 32.78(*Case Experience*).

Clearly, a larger R^2 indicates a better prediction of the model.

Another popular interpretation of R^2 is that it measures the proportion of the total variation in the dependent variable Y that is explained simultaneously by the predictive power of all the independent variables in the multiple regression model. In our example, we can say that 56.9% of variation in the processing speed is explained by the three independent variables in the regression model.

Realize that R^2 is the square of the *multiple correlation coefficient* or the multiple R of .754 in Table 10–7 (i.e., $.754^2 = .569$). The multiple R is a measure of the relationship between the dependent variable and all independent variables. It is the Pearson correlation coefficient between the actual (observed) Y values and the predicted $\hat{Y}$ values.

Though R^2 is a popular measure, it has a few undesirable features in some circumstances. First, the addition of independent variables in the model, even if these independent variables

Table 10–7

**Regression Statistics in a Multiple Regression Model:
The Immigration Case Processing Example**

Regression statistics	
Multiple R	.754338701
R square	.569026876
Adjusted R square	.488219415
Standard error	108.7363391
Observations	20

have no relationship with the dependent variable, will artificially inflate the value of R^2. Second, R^2 may be inaccurate when the number of cases (the sample size) is small. These are the reasons why *adjusted* R^2 is used. The adjusted R^2 has the same interpretation as that of R^2 but is probably a better measure when the number of independent variables is many and the number of cases is small. Nonetheless, while the values of R^2 go from 0 to 1, the value of adjusted R^2 could be negative when $R^2 <$ (the number of independent variables)/(the number of cases $- 1$). If this happens, treat adjusted $R^2 = 0$.

Standard Error of the Estimate

The standard error in Table 10–7 is an estimate of variation of the predicted values $\hat{Y}$ from the actual values Y. In our example, the standard error of the estimate is 108.74. This measure can be used to construct a confidence interval for a predicted value. For example, what is the predicted number of processing days for an application that has one processing error and that is processed by an officer with 2 years work experience and 1 year case experience? From the prediction model, it is number of processing days = 906.68 + 49.45(1) + 12.33(2) − 32.78(1) = 906.68 + 49.45 + 24.66 − 32.78 = 948.01.

The t statistic for a 95% confidence interval with $n = 20$ (degrees of freedom = 20 − 1 = 19) is 2.093 (use Excel TINV for the t). The boundaries of the confidence interval are 720 (i.e., 948.01 − 2.093 × 108.74; rounded) and 1176 (i.e., 948.01 + 2.093 × 108.74; rounded). So we are 95% confident that the true average number of processing days is between 720 and 1176 days for the cases that meet these conditions.

Some Inferential Statistical Measures

The Excel output provides several inferential statistical measures of multiple regression models. The math processes to obtain these measures are similar to those for inferential statistics in the simple regression model introduced before. So I skip the math derivation and focus on the interpretation of results.

First, an F test is presented in the ANOVA table. The null hypothesis is the dependent variable is unrelated to any of the independent variables in the model (i.e., *Ho*: $\beta_1 = \beta_2 = \dots \beta_k$ = 0). If this happens, there is no basis to construct the multiple regression model. In other words, the construction of the model is meaningful only if the null hypothesis is rejected. The

Table 10–8

The *F* Test for the Multiple Regression Model

			ANOVA		
	df	SS	MS	F	Significance *F*
Regression	3	249776.7371	83258.91236	7.04176162	.003119
Residual	16	189177.4629	11823.59143		
Total	19	438954.2			

alternative hypothesis is the dependent variable is related to at least one independent variable in the model (i.e., *Ha*: at least one $\beta_i \neq 0$).

The null hypothesis of the *F* test in the immigration processing example is that the processing speed is unrelated to any independent variable in the model. The alternative hypothesis is that the processing speed is related to at least one independent variable in the model. Table 10–8 shows the result of the *F* test. The *P*-value of the *F* test is the significance *F* in the Excel printout, which is .003119 in our example. Let us set the significance level at .05. Because *P* < .05, we reject the null hypothesis and conclude that there is sufficient evidence to indicate the processing speed is related to at least one independent variable in the model. This result demonstrates that it is reasonable and meaningful to construct this multiple regression model.

Also presented in the Excel output is a *t* test for the intercept (α) and the slopes (β). The null hypothesis for the intercept is the intercept = 0, and the alternative hypothesis is the intercept $\neq$ 0. The *P*-value is a very small value 1.21135E-07 (7 zeros after the decimal point), as shown in Table 10–9. Let the significance level be .05. Because *P* < .05, we reject the null hypothesis and conclude that the intercept $\neq$ 0.

The testing for individual slopes (β) in the multiple regression is the same as that in the simple regression. The null hypothesis is that an individual population parameter $\beta_i = 0$, and the alternative hypothesis is $\beta_i \neq 0$. Let X_i be any of $X_1, X_2 \ldots X_k$ in the multiple regression model $Y = \beta_1 X_1 + \beta_2 X_2 + \ldots \beta_k X_k$. When $\beta_i = 0$, $\beta_i X_i = 0 X_i = 0$, indicating that the dependent variable Y is unrelated to the independent variable X_i. The test statistic has a *t* distribution with the degrees of freedom = $n - (k + 1)$; n is the number of cases (observations), and k is the number of independent variables.

In our example, let the slope of the error rate be β_1. The null hypothesis for testing β_1 is that the error rate and the processing speed are unrelated or $\beta_1 = 0$. The alternative hypothesis is that they are related or $\beta_1 \neq 0$. The *t* value is calculated from a comparison of the slope (b_1) with its standard error ($\hat{\sigma}_{b1}$) in a fashion that $t = b_1/\hat{\sigma}_{b1}$. The slope for the error rate is 49.45, and its standard error is 20.31, so $t = 49.45/20.31 = 2.435$, also shown in Table 10–9. The *P*-value is .02697, smaller than the significance level set at .05. So we reject the null hypothesis and conclude that the error rate and the processing speed are related. This test result provides evidence that the error rate affects the processing speed significantly. A reduced error rate likely leads to a shortened processing speed. You can calculate the *P*-value yourself by using Excel

Table 10–9

t Tests for the Intercept and the Slopes in a Multiple Regression Model

	Coefficients	Standard error	*t* stat	*P*-value	Lower 95%	Upper 95%
Intercept	906.6832206	101.0333737	8.974096252	1.21135E-07	692.5021	1120.864
Error rate	49.45083171	20.30778512	2.435067705	.026966058	6.40026	92.5014
Work experience —length at job (in year)	12.32576479	12.47880955	0.987735629	.337984793	−14.1281	38.77965
Case experience —length at processing the same type of cases (in year)	−32.77973325	13.10681676	−2.500968302	.023628148	−60.5649	−4.99453

Insert Function TDIST. Type the *t* value of 2.435 in the *x* window with degrees of freedom = $20 - (3 + 1) = 16$, and the *P*-value should be .02697 for a two-tailed probability.

The null hypothesis for the slope β_2 is that a processing officer's work experience and the processing speed are unrelated or $\beta_2 = 0$. The alternative hypothesis is that they are related or $\beta_2 \neq 0$. The calculation for the *t* is the same as described above in the test for the error rate. The *P*-value is .33798, shown in Table 10–9, larger than the significance level set at .05. We therefore fail to reject the null hypothesis. There is no sufficient evidence to indicate that an officer's work experience affects the processing speed. The result of the next test shows that it is the officer's case experience, not the work experience, that impacts the processing speed.

The null hypothesis for the slope β_3 is that a processing officer's experience of processing the same type of cases (the case experience) is unrelated to the processing speed or $\beta_3 = 0$. The alternative hypothesis is that they are related or $\beta_3 \neq 0$. The *P*-value for the test is .02363, smaller than the significance level set at .05. We therefore reject the null hypothesis and conclude that there is sufficient evidence to indicate that an officer's case experience is related to the processing speed. The increase in case experience may reduce the number of processing days.

Finally, the Excel output also provides a 95% confidence interval estimate for the intercept and the slopes. The interpretation of these estimates is the same as that in the simple regression model. For example, we are 95% confident the interval for the true (population) intercept (a) is between 692.50 and 1120.86, and the true slope for the error rate (β_1) is between 6.40 and 92.50.

The Final Model and Performance Predictions

Because the work experience is unrelated to the processing speed, it should be removed from the model. Only the error rate and the case experience should be included in a final model to predict the processing speed, and the Excel Data Analysis for regression should be rerun to construct the model that consists of only these two independent variables. The Excel Summary output is shown in Screen 10–5 and the model is

$$Number\ of\ Processing\ Days = 975.92 + 38.81\,(Error\ Rate) - 27.41\,(Case\ Experience)$$

The R^2 of the model is 54.27%, indicating that about 54% of variation of the processing speed is explained by the model. The F test of the model shows that at least one independent variable is related to the dependent variable at the .05 significance level so that the model is statistically significant at that level, indicating that it is reasonable and meaningful to construct this model.

The tests of the slopes show that both the error rate and the case experience are statistically significant at the .05 level, suggesting that they have significant impact on the processing speed. This result indicates that it is reasonable and meaningful to construct a performance prediction model in which both the error rate and the case experience are used to predict the processing speed.

According to the model, the number of processing days is 975.92 when there is no error in a case processed by an officer who has no case processing experience (i.e., the error rate = 0 and the case experience = 0). Each processing error can lead to a delay of 38.81 days in processing, and each year of the case experience gained by the processing officer can speed up the processing by 27.41 days.

You can use the final model to predict the processing speed. For example, for an immigration application that has 2 processing errors and that is processed by an officer with 5 years of case experience, the predicted processing speed is number of processing days = 975.92 + 38.81(2) − 27.41(5) = 975.92 + 77.62 − 137.05 = 916.49 days.

Model Assumptions

This section discusses the underlying assumptions of regression models and common forms of violations of the assumptions. The impact of violations and the methods of correction will also be presented.

Linearity

The models discussed in this chapter assume a linear relationship between the independent variables and the dependent variable. Although this assumption hardly is perfectly satisfied,

Screen 10–5

The Final Model of the Immigration Case Processing Example.

Ch10Examples.xls [Compatibility Mode] - Microsoft Excel

	A	B	C	D	E	F	G	H
25	SUMMARY OUTPUT							
26								
27	*Regression Statistics*							
28	Multiple R	0.736714128						
29	R Square	0.542747706						
30	Adjusted R Square	0.488953318						
31	Standard Error	108.6583461						
32	Observations	20						
33								
34	ANOVA							
35		*df*	*SS*	*MS*	*F*	*Significance F*		
36	Regression	2	238241.385	119120.6925	10.08929984	0.001292186		
37	Residual	17	200712.815	11806.63617				
38	Total	19	438954.2					
39								
40		*Coefficients*	*Standard Error*	*t Stat*	*P-value*	*Lower 95%*	*Upper 95%*	
41	Intercept	975.921425	72.70786564	13.42250135	1.78061E-10	822.5210232	1129.321827	
42	Error Rate	38.81326328	17.20452474	2.255991599	0.037534428	2.514838278	75.11168829	
43	Officer's Case Experience: Length at the Same Type of Cases (in year)	-27.40840592	11.91690519	-2.29996056	0.034389775	-52.55091323	-2.265898602	
44								
45								
46								
47								
48								
49								
50								
51								
52								
53								
54								
55								

results from linear models that badly violate it could be very misleading. Table 10–10 shows data of the population growth rate and revenues per capita for a major urban city for the past 20 years. Revenues per capita is a measure of financial performance for the city's revenue collection efforts.

A regression model based on the data is revenues per capita = 1589 − 4.037 (population growth rate). The *P* for the *F* test is .681, and the *P* for the slope of the population growth is .681. We therefore conclude that there is no sufficient evidence to indicate that population growth is related to revenues per capita at the .05 significance level.

However, a scatter chart of the variables, shown in Figure 10–4, indicates that there is an ∩-shape relationship between them. (Note, the visual presentation is often a very effective way to identify the shape of a relationship.) Revenues per capita increase when the population growth increases until around 7%, and then revenues per capita start declining while population growth continues. This relationship suggests that the population growth brings revenues only to a certain point.

This example illustrates that results of a regression model could be misleading when the assumption of linearity is violated. A conclusion of no relationship may be drawn from a regression model while in fact there is a relationship between the variables. How do you deal

Table 10–10

Population Growth and Revenue Collection

Year	Population growth rate (%)	Revenue per capita ($)
1	4.8	1639
2	3.8	1364
3	6.1	1693
4	3.8	1480
5	5.1	1573
6	9.2	1539
7	4.1	1496
8	8.9	1684
9	8	1654
10	7.2	1728
11	7.8	1700
12	9.5	1614
13	4.5	1480
14	10.5	1563
15	11.2	1503
16	12.6	1305
17	4	1483
18	10	1503
19	6.7	1722
20	11.9	1453

Figure 10–4

Population Growth and Revenue Collection: a Scatter Chart.

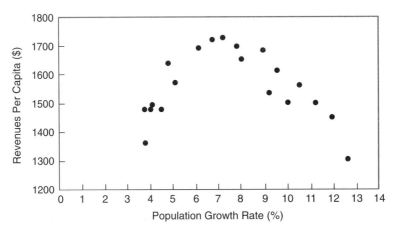

with the violation of linearity? In the above example, you could run two regression models using population growth rate = 7% as the splitting point. The data of population growth less or equal to 7% are used in one model, while the data greater than 7% are used in another model to predict the revenues. From Figure 10–4, we know that the relationships in these two models are approximately linear.

The nonlinear relationship in Figure 10–4 is a form of a *curvilinear relationship* in which the relationship of the variables follows a specific pattern of nonlinearity. If the form of a curvilinear relationship is identified, the variables may be transformed to make the relationship more linear. An independent variable can be transformed to its square root, quadratic, power, or logarithmic forms to alleviate the degree of curvilinearity. Excel Insert Functions make it easy to conduct these transformations. Practice Problems 10–3 and 10–4 in this chapter allow you to experience two popular forms of the curvilinear relationship and the ways to transform the variables.

Homoscedasticity

Defined before, the difference between a predicted value $\hat{Y}$ and the actual (observed) value Y (i.e., $Y - \hat{Y}$) is the prediction error (or the prediction residual). Regression analysis assumes that the variation of prediction errors is equally distributed with the values of the independent variables, a condition known as *homoscedasticity*. Once it is violated, *heteroscedasticity* exists. Table 10–11 shows average response times to emergencies (Y) and the populations covered (X) in 18 fire districts of a major metropolitan area. Figure 10–5 visualizes the relationship between these two variables. The figure shows that the response times in the districts with

Table 10–11

Response Times and Populations in 18 Metro Fire Districts

Districts	Populations served	Average response times (in minute)
1	61772	5
2	37403	4.1
3	85900	9
4	83988	4.3
5	74359	6.9
6	71760	8.4
7	58844	5.9
8	64782	5.1
9	35400	3.9
10	53780	4.8
11	54786	4.5
12	53245	4.7
13	54039	4.9
14	55890	5
15	55437	4.5
16	77380	5.3
17	65430	5.9
18	52030	5.1

Figure 10–5

Response Times and Populations Served.

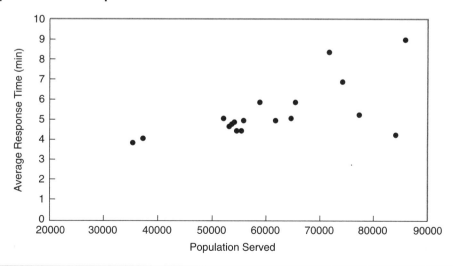

Screen 10–6

The Excel Procedure for Residual Plots in Regression.

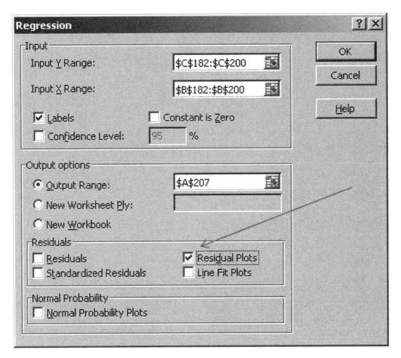

populations less than 70,000 appear to be consistent around 4 and 5 minutes, and the response times appear to vary largely for the districts with populations greater than 70,000.

The larger variation in more populated districts may reflect the fact that these districts have larger geographic areas to cover so the response times to locations of various distances vary largely. The Excel Regression process in Data Analysis allows creation of a graph that shows the independent variable against the prediction error (the residual). In the Regression window, make sure to check the Residual Plots box as shown in Screen 10–6.

This Excel command allows you to plot an independent variable against the prediction error $(Y - \hat{Y})$, as shown in Figure 10–6 of the district population against the prediction error (residual) of the response time. It shows clearly that the error (residual) becomes larger for larger populated areas. The relationship suffers heteroscedasticity.

The existence of heteroscedasticity may cause inaccurate estimation and hypothesis testing results for the intercept and the slopes. The logarithmic transformation of the dependent and independent variables is often used to treat heteroscedasticity because a log transformation reduces values of a variable, hence reducing its variation. Both the based-10 log (Excel Insert

Figure 10–6

The Residual Plot of the Response Time Example.

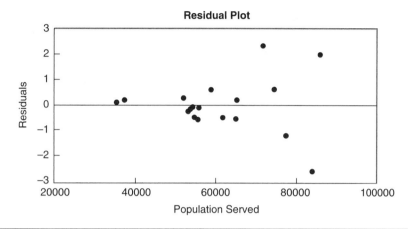

Function LOG10) and the natural log (Excel Insert Function LN) can be found in the Excel Insert Function (*fx*).

Multicollinearity

The phenomenon that two or more independent variables in a multiple regression model are highly associated is called *multicollinearity*. If multicollinearity occurs, the estimation of the intercept and the slopes may be misleading. For example, both study time and reading volume are used in a model to predict academic performance of students in a college English literature class. Study time is the number of weekly study hours, and reading volume is the number of pages of recommended reading materials. You can imagine that study time and reading volume are highly associated—students who spend more study time are more likely to read more. If both variables are included to predict students' academic performances, the impact of one variable on academic performance while controlling the other may not be statistically significant. This could happen because the estimated standard errors of regression coefficients (the slopes) in a model that suffers multicollinearity tend to be large so that coefficients are less likely to be statistically significant.

How high should the association be for multicollinearity to become a problem? It is recommended by some literature that a correlation coefficient greater than +.6 or smaller than −.6 deserves a close examination for possible multicollinearity. How do you correct it if multicollinearity is a concern? One commonly recommended method is to remove the collinear variables from the model. In the above example, you can remove either study time or reading volume (but not both) from the model to eliminate the problem. Another method is to combine the collinear variables to create a sole variable in the model.

Model Specifications

With readily available computer software programs capable of regression analysis, such as Excel, it is tempting to throw in some data in a test drive of modeling. It should be noted though that any modeling process without a thorough thinking process and a well-developed theory is prone to incorrect model specifications, which means that wrong variables and/or variables with inappropriate measurements are included in the model. The signs of incorrect model specifications include the model has a very low R^2 (<20%), its F test result is not statistically significant, and/or none of the t test results for slopes is statistically significant.

Measurement Level

In general, variables in regression analysis should be measured at the interval level. If an independent variable is ordinal or nominal with more than two response categories, it needs to be converted into a dichotomy variable with a coding of 0 and 1. An ordinal variable with ζ number of response categories should be converted to $\zeta - 1$ number of dichotomy variables in a regression model. For example, an ethnicity variable coded as White = 1, Black = 2, Hispanics = 3, and Others = 4 ($\zeta = 4$) can be converted to $\zeta - 1 = 4 - 1 = 3$ dichotomy variables, with the first dichotomy variable being coded as White = 1 and all other groups = 0, the second variable coded as Black = 1 and all other groups = 0, and the third variable coded as Hispanics = 1 and all other groups = 0. Without this coding conversion, the result of a regression analysis is hard to explain. You can use Excel to sort the multiple response categories of a variable, making the coding conversion easier.

A Case Study

The city of Greenfield (population 14,000) is located in a major metropolitan area that consists of 24 cities and a county. The major municipal services in Greenfield include policing, local transportation (local road construction and maintenance), two municipal parks, recreation services, and a garbage collection service. The city relies on the county, a major adjacent city, and business contractors for other municipal services.

Step 1: Defining the Issue

Situated in an area that has multiple service providers from governments, nonprofits, and businesses, the city faces competition to improve its services. A recent citizen survey of the 24 cities and the county ranks the city the 13th in a comprehensive service quality index that is based on respondents' perceptions of municipal services. The local realtors' Quality of Living index ranks the city the 10th among the 24 cities. In many people's minds, Greenfield is one of those ordinary places where it is hard to associate it with the best or the worst of anything.

The city's strategic service plan stresses the importance of attracting more residents and businesses to enlarge the city's revenue base. It is clear to the management that the city's image of mediocrity in service delivery must be improved and that quality services are the key for a good reputation. So in the past few years, considerable efforts have been made to improve service quality. The budget has been increased to hire more workers, to purchase the latest technologies, and to improve daily operations. The managerial concepts of performance management, process management, and cost control have been implemented. Nevertheless, there has been no immediate improvement of citizen perceptions about the city's services. The abovementioned survey has rated the city's services pretty much the same for the past few years. The realtors' index this year ranked the city even lower than last year. Clearly, more should be done to improve the service quality and citizen satisfaction.

The city manager, Joe Smith, has a theory that links citizens' evaluations with their perceived importance of a service, believing that citizens are happier if they perceive that important city services are improved. For example, public safety is perceived by citizens as being more important than others because its failures often mean the loss of properties or even lives. So budgets should be tilted in favor of these important services. New technologies as well as innovative managerial practices should be adopted in these services first. Nonetheless, it is unclear whether this thinking is correct. Joe is eager to test this theory. His analysis questions include the following: What services may affect citizen satisfaction? Are some services more important than others to influence citizen satisfaction?

Step 2: Understanding the Performance

Joe believes that two sets of variables affect a citizen's satisfaction about a city government: service variables and the citizens' socioeconomic–personal attributes. The service variables include the citizen's assessment on individual services such as policing, local road maintenance and transportation, parks and recreation, and garbage collection. A citizen is happier if he or she perceives a higher quality of services. Another set of variables describes a citizen's socioeconomic and personal characteristics. Joe believes that household income and age should have significant influence over citizen satisfaction. Citizens with greater incomes may be more difficult to please because they tend to pay higher taxes and have higher expectation for services. Older citizens may be more difficult to be satisfied because they use some city services more often and have higher expectations for these services.

To answer his analysis questions, Joe develops a multiple regression model that includes all relevant service variables as well as the house income and the age. The model is shown as follows: A citizen's overall satisfaction on the city government = $\alpha +$

β_1 (the citizen's assessment on the quality of policing services) +
β_2 (the citizen's assessment on the quality of local transportation services) +
β_3 (the citizen's assessment on the quality of parks and recreation services) +
β_4 (the citizens' assessment on garbage collection services) +
β_5 (the citizen's household income) +
β_6 (the citizen's age).

In the model, α and β are the population parameters. Because improvement (increase) in a citizen's assessment on individual services should improve (increase) the citizen's overall satisfaction, β_1, β_2, β_3, and β_4 should be positive (i.e., $\beta_1 > 0$, $\beta_2 > 0$, $\beta_3 > 0$, and $\beta_4 > 0$). Also, as elaborated above, citizens with higher incomes and of older ages are less likely to be satisfied with the city government, so β_5 and β_6 should be negative (i.e., $\beta_5 < 0$, $\beta_6 < 0$).

Step 3: Conducting the Analysis

Measurement

The city conducts a citizen survey every year, and the survey instrument includes the measurements of the variables in the above model. An index is created to measure the citizen overall satisfaction with the city government (the dependent variable in the model). Ten survey items are used in the index with a maximum score of 10 and a minimum score of 0. The items ask a respondent's assessment on the efficiency, effectiveness, and responsiveness of the city government as a whole. There are also items to assess a respondent's perception about the livability of the city. This is an interval variable, and a maximum score of 10 indicates a respondent is positive about all 10 items in the survey. A score of 0 indicates the respondent is not positive about any of the items.

A citizen's assessment on individual services is also measured on a 10-point scale. A maximum score of 10 indicates the highest level of quality perceived by the respondent, and the minimum score 0 indicates the lowest level of quality perceived. Household incomes are the annual household earnings of a respondent's household, and the age is the actual age of a respondent at the time of the survey. All these variables can be treated as interval.

Analysis

For the convenience of calculation in this case study, a sample of 20 surveys this year are selected and presented in Table 10–12. The performance prediction model that includes all of these variables is

$$Overall\ Satisfaction = 0.718 + 0.479\ (Assessment\ on\ Policing) - 0.0452\ (Assessment\ on$$
$$Local\ Transportation) - 0.0318\ (Assessment\ on\ Parks\ and\ Recreation) + 0.600$$
$$(Assessment\ on\ Garbage\ Collection) + 0.000006\ (Household\ Income) - 0.0133\ (Age).$$

The F test ($P = .000447$) shows that the model is statistically significant at the .05 level, with about 81% of variation of citizens' overall satisfaction explained by the regression model ($R^2 = .810$). The test for slopes shows that the citizens' assessment on policing is statistically significant at the .05 level ($P = .0312$), and the citizens' assessment on garbage collection is also statistically significant at the .05 level ($P = .0057$). Nonetheless, none of the other variables in the model are statistically significant at the .05 level.

These findings suggest that policing and garbage collection are the two most important services to affect citizens' overall satisfaction with the city, confirming Joe's theory that some services are more important than others to citizens. It appears that citizens want a safe and clean city more than anything else from the city. The final model that includes these two variables of statistical significance is

$$Overall\ Satisfaction = 0.138 + 0.555\ (Assessment\ on\ Policing) + 0.520\ (Assessment\ on$$
$$Garbage\ Collection).$$

Table 10–12

Citizen Survey Data of 20 Selected Residents in Greenfield

Overall satisfaction	Police	Local transportation	Parks	Garbage collection	Income	Age
8	7	4	5	4	168476	28
4	3	10	9	5	54774	54
6	6	8	9	6	58337	39
7	6	8	6	6	69262	34
7	6	4	4	6	74675	60
6	5	3	2	6	84810	45
1	3	6	2	3	64300	48
9	8	6	4	7	64022	54
4	5	8	0	1	60322	43
5	8	7	2	3	104938	70
7	9	5	5	5	150373	28
5	6	8	9	4	76739	52
3	2	5	2	4	87946	72
3	2	4	3	2	67400	52
5	4	6	7	4	59717	35
8	7	2	5	8	42761	62
8	6	4	6	8	67523	67
2	4	1	6	2	77329	25
5	3	2	3	2	76543	36
9	7	4	2	10	49879	53

The final model is statistically significant (the P for the F test is .000000152) with a R^2 of 79.3%. The test of slopes shows that both independent variables are statistically significant at the .05 level. Examination of the model assumptions shows that the model does not suffer from the violation of any model assumption discussed in this chapter.

Step 4: Making Management Decisions

What does the city learn from this model, and how can the city's image improve? The average overall satisfaction score from this sample is 5.60 on a 10-score scale, fitting the city's image of mediocrity. According to results of the regression model, the strategies to improve the image should focus on improving citizens' assessments on policing and garbage collection.

According to the model, a citizen's overall satisfaction is 0.138 (the intercept) when his or her assessment on policing *and* garbage collection services is completely negative (i.e., both variables = 0). One strategy to improve citizen overall satisfaction should focus on citizens' assessments on policing. An improvement in the assessment on policing by 1 score (e.g., from 1 to 2) will lead to a 0.555 improvement in the overall satisfaction index (i.e., the slope for the policing assessment = 0.555). An improvement in the assessment on policing by 2 scores (e.g., from 1 to 3) will lead to an improvement in the overall satisfaction score by more than 1.00 (i.e., $2 \times 0.555 = 1.11$).

If the city wants to improve citizen overall satisfaction to a level greater than 7.0, it will have to improve the assessment on policing by 3 scores to arrive at an improvement of overall satisfaction score by $3 \times 0.555 = 1.67$, for an improved average score of the overall satisfaction at 7.27 (i.e., the current average overall satisfaction scale of 5.60 + the improved overall satisfaction scale of 1.67).

Another strategy of improvement can center on efforts to improve citizens' assessments on garbage collection. The slope for the assessment on garbage collection (0.520) is similar to that for the assessment on policing (0.555), so both strategies should have similar effects on citizen overall satisfaction. It should be concluded that, if the city wants to improve the overall satisfaction to a level greater than 7.0, it will have to improve the assessment on garbage collection by 3 scores to arrive at an improvement of overall satisfaction score by $3 \times 0.520 = 1.56$, for an improved average score of the overall satisfaction at 7.16 (i.e., the current average overall satisfaction scale of 5.60 + the improved overall satisfaction scale of 1.56). Of course, the city can adopt the above two strategies simultaneously to accelerate their impact on citizen overall satisfaction.

Practices

Key Terms

Exact form of a relationship
Performance modeling
Purposes of performance modeling
Performance predication
Statistical modeling
Simple regression modeling
Basic performance model
Performance prediction model
Simple regression model
Intercept
Slope (regression coefficient)
Method of least square
Sum of squared errors (or residuals)
Prediction error of a regression model
Interpretation of a performance model (focusing on the intercept and the slope)
Coefficient of determination r^2
Standard error of the estimate
F test for the model
Sums of squares (SS)
Mean squares (MS)
t tests for the intercept and the slope
Confidence intervals for the intercept and the slope

Multiple regression modeling
Multivariate analysis
Bivariate analysis
Joint impact of multiple causes
Statistical control
Multivariate performance prediction model (or multiple regression model)
Intercept and slopes in multiple regression
Partial regression coefficient (the slopes in multiple regression)
Interpretation of the multiple regression model
Coefficient of multiple determination R^2
Multiple correlation coefficient
Adjusted R^2
Standard error of the estimates and the inferential statistical measures in multiple regression
Final models and using them in performance predictions
Linearity
Curvilinear relationship
Homoscedasticity
Heteroscedasticity
Multicollinearity
Model specifications
Measurement level for regression models
Excel Data Analysis Regression Procedure

Practice Problem 10–1

A county manager suspects the performance of the county's service departments is a function of their resource input. In other words, resourceful departments perform better. The county has 13 service departments (e.g., sheriff office, fire department, public works department, etc.). Their performance is measured by how well they achieve service objectives. An average percentage measure is used to include all major service goals in creating the measurement. For example, an 80% indicates that a department has achieved 80% of all its stated service goals. The scale of the measure goes from 0 to 100. The resource input is measured by the total expenditure per full-time employee. The data of this year are shown in Table 10–13.

1. Develop a performance prediction model to assess the relationship between the performance and the resource input. Explain the intercept, the slope.
2. Explain the goodness of your model by examining r^2 of the model and the standard error of the estimate.
3. Treat your data as a sample from a specific year. Perform an F test of the model and a t test of the slope. Explain the meaning of these inferential statistics.
4. Conduct proper tests on model assumptions to detect any violation of the assumptions. Try to correct a violation if it is found.
5. Write a conclusion on whether or not your analysis supports the manager's suspicion that resources determine performance. Explain your conclusion to the manager and other county officials who know nothing about regression.

Table 10–13

Departmental Performances and Resource Inputs

Department ID	Performance score	Expenditures per employee ($)
1	90	80440
2	80	118340
3	95	65766
4	100	86368
5	100	70810
6	100	142857
7	71	65393
8	91	85469
9	100	87940
10	82	74280
11	86	97577
12	76	73846
13	75	64833

Practice Problem 10–2

Continue the above problem. Now suppose that the manager wants to add several new variables in the model to predict the performance. One variable is employee performance. Every year, every full-time employee is assessed in a performance appraisal in which a supervisor provides a quantitative assessment of all job responsibilities of the employee. The measure is scaled on a 10-point scale with 10 = the highest performance and 1 = the lowest performance. The average score of all employees in a department is used to represent employee performance for that department.

The operational process may also influence performance. The operation processes of departments vary greatly. Some departments are more labor intensive (e.g., sheriff office) while others use more capital (e.g., fire, public works, transportation). The personal expenditure (i.e., the expenditure on salaries and benefit) per employee is used to measure the labor intensity of the departments and thus the differences of their operational processes.

Finally, the use of technology is believed to influence performance. The percentage of the departments' expenditures on purchasing and maintaining telecommunication and information technology during the past 3 years has been used to measure the use of technology. Data are reported in Table 10–14.

1. Develop a multivariate performance prediction model to assess the relationship between the performance and independent variables in Table 10–14. Explain the intercept, the slopes.
2. Explain the goodness of your model by examining R^2 of the model and the standard error of the estimate.

Table 10–14

Performance of County Departments

Department ID	Performance score	Expenditure per employee ($)	Employee performance	Personal expenditure per employee ($)	Technology expenditure in total expenditure (%)
1	90	80440	5.7	52771	0.19
2	80	118340	6	47475	0.27
3	95	65766	7.3	37381	0.23
4	100	86368	9	44926	0.36
5	100	70810	9.2	43827	0.24
6	100	142857	8	47920	0.3
7	71	65393	6	37413	0.24
8	91	85469	6.6	59515	0.15
9	100	87940	7.6	48642	0.3
10	82	74280	7	52124	0.13
11	86	97577	9	49108	0.17
12	76	73846	8	46622	0.17
13	75	64833	5.1	46700	0.26

3. Treat your data as a sample from a specific year. Perform an F test of the model and t tests of the slopes. Explain the meaning of these inferential statistics.
4. Conduct proper tests on model assumptions to detect any violation of the assumptions. Correct a violation if it is found.
5. Write a brief analysis report to explain your findings to the county manager and other county officials who know nothing about regression analysis. Make recommendations of performance improvement based on your analysis. Also, do you want to collect more data and conduct more analyses? Why or why not?

Practice Problem 10–3

Oftentimes, a smart thing to do first in developing a performance model is to visually examine the shape (linear or curvilinear) and direction (positive or negative) of a possible relationship. Table 10–15 shows reading efforts and reading outcomes of 18 high school classes participating in an experimental intensive reading program. The reading effort is measured by the weekly average class reading hours on the required literature. The reading outcome is measured by a reading test score that has a scale from 50 (poorest reading outcome) to 100 (the best reading outcome).

1. Use Excel to create a scatter chart for these two variables to visualize the relationship. Explain the relationship based on the scatter chart. Does the reading effort improve the reading outcome? Is the reading outcome improved at the same pace for all classes?

Table 10–15

Reading Efforts and Reading Outcome

Class ID	Weekly average class reading hours	Average class reading score
1	1	73
2	1	74
3	2	85
4	2	86
5	2	88
6	3	90
7	3	91
8	3	91
9	4	94
10	4	93
11	4	94
12	5	95
13	5	94
14	5	95
15	5	96
16	0	55
17	0	57
18	0	59

2. Develop a performance prediction model and explain the meaning of the model.
3. Is there any violation of the model assumption on linearity, based on your chart? If so, how do you treat the violation? In examining the violation of the assumption, use r^2 to judge if there is any improvement of a new model. In other words, does the treatment improve the r^2? (Hint: Try the cube root transformation. Use Excel Insert Function POWER command. Set Power = 1/3.)

Practice Problem 10–4

If you successfully complete Problem 10–3, you should conclude that reading effort and reading outcome have a curvilinear relationship. Increase in reading time will improve reading scores. Nonetheless, the improvement rate varies. The improvement is much greater when the reading hours increase from 0 to 1 or 1 to 2, and the improvement slows down when reading hours increase from 2 to 3 or from 3 to 4. There is almost no improvement when reading hours increase from 4 to 5. This form of a curvilinear relationship between efforts and outcomes is popular in management (a decline in marginal return).

Now, let us look at another popular form of a curvilinear performance relationship. Table 10–16 shows math study efforts and math testing outcomes of the same 18 high school classes participating in an experimental intensive math education program.

Table 10–16

Math Efforts and Math Outcome

Class ID	Average weekly hours on math	Average class math score
1	0	52
2	0	50
3	0	53
4	1	55
5	1	54
6	1	53
7	2	58
8	2	57
9	2	56
10	3	64
11	3	69
12	3	65
13	4	78
14	4	80
15	4	78
16	5	93
17	5	88
18	5	89

1. Use Excel to create a scatter chart for the two variables to visualize the relationship. Explain the relationship based on the scatter chart. Does the math study effort improve the math outcome? Is the math outcome improved at the same pace for all classes?
2. Develop a performance prediction model and explain the meaning of the model.
3. Is there any violation of the model assumption on linearity, based on your chart? If so, how do you treat the violation? In examining the violation of the assumption, use r^2 to judge if there is any improvement of a new model. In other words, does the treatment improve the r^2? (Hint: Try the square transformation. Use Excel Insert Function POWER command. Set Power = 2 or 3.)

Section V

Evaluating Performance

CHAPTER 11

Performance Evaluation Basics

Imagine that your city has experienced an abnormally high level of traffic accidents in the tourist district. A performance analysis shows that a new traffic signal system confuses tourists. With a strategy to redesign the system currently underway, you expect traffic accidents to be reduced to the normal level. How will you know if your strategy works? You need a performance evaluation. So far in this book we have learned how to describe and monitor performance (Chapters 3 to 7), and how to discover the causes of underperformance and develop proper strategies to improve performance (Chapters 8 to 10). Some strategies may work and others may not. From this chapter on, we will study how to evaluate the impact of performance improvement strategies.

This chapter introduces performance evaluation basics, as well as the evaluations involving one performance benchmark. Chapter 12 covers evaluations of two performance samples, and Chapter 13 deals with more than two performance samples.

Some Important Concepts

Once causes of underperformance are identified and a performance improvement strategy is implemented (see Chapter 8 for the components of a strategy), a performance evaluation should be conducted to assess the effectiveness of the strategy. Does an increase in budget improve the response time? Does the change in instructional mode improve students' academic performances? Does a better collaboration among law enforcement agencies reduce crimes? Does the intensified nutrition education result in people's healthy eating behaviors? This section defines performance evaluation and describes key concepts in an evaluation.

What Is Performance Evaluation?

Three conditions must exist for an evaluation. First, a performance improvement strategy has been developed and implemented to tackle an issue of underperformance. Second, in the strategy, a performance enhancement initiative has been constituted and implemented. Third, the implementation of the initiative is long enough so that the observation of its impact is possible.

A *performance enhancement initiative* (PEI) consists of specific implementation actions of performance improvement. It is a series of systematic and interventional activities designed to produce a well-defined result in performance improvement; it is *not* the corrective activity of varying degrees of informality such as completing a few reports of impressionistic estimates about how things have been going. Managerial behaviors or actions without a clear goal or implementation actions of performance improvement, such as annual budget increase to cope with the cost of inflation or responses to emergent staff shortage by temporary hiring, are not PEIs.

A PEI can be in the form of a new program(s), a policy change, a process change, or their combined changes. It should be developed from the analytical result of performance understanding discussed in Chapters 8 to 10. That is, the development of a performance improvement strategy, which constitutes a PEI, must be based on the theoretical underpinning and/or empirical evidence showing that the strategy should result in a significant performance improvement.

Realize that a PEI is an interventional activity that targets the causes of underperformance. There are two attributes of a PEI intervention—*intensity* and *length*. A school counseling program may hire more counselors and initiate more program activities to increase the intensity of the program. A police department may keep its community policing program running for multiple years to increase the length of the intervention. The interventional intensity and length should affect the performance.

Performance evaluation is the process that assesses the impact of a PEI on a performance. It is designed to examine, for example, the impact of a health insurance plan on the insurance coverage or the impact of a redesigned traffic control system on traffic accidents. Different from performance monitoring discussed in Chapters 5 to 7, performance evaluation is a comprehensive and thorough assessment of a PEI. The existence of a PEI is a precondition for performance evaluation, but is not required for performance monitoring. Moreover, performance evaluation is often conducted at the beginning or the end of a production or service delivery cycle when assessment data become available, while performance monitoring is an ongoing assessment of the production or service delivery process during a production or service cycle.

Why Performance Evaluation?

Evaluating PEIs provides the feedback for continual performance improvement. An effective PEI should be continued, a less effective PEI should be modified, and an ineffective PEI should be terminated. Continual assessment on PEIs is the key to develop and to sustain a high performance in an organization. Figure 11–1 describes the purpose of performance evaluation in the production process of an organization. It demonstrates the circumstance in which performance evaluation provides a feedback loop for an organization to adjust its inputs (the resource allocations) for continual performance improvement.

Performance evaluation should be conducted at the end of a production cycle to allow enough time for a PEI to influence the production process, and it should also be conducted on a regular basis for continual performance improvement. Realize that the impact of a PEI can vary from time to time. A PEI strategy that significantly improves performance this year may not work next year. A strategy to round up terrorists effectively this time may not work next time, because terrorists adapt. This is why performance evaluation has to be conducted on a continual and regular basis.

Figure 11–1

Cycle of Continual Performance Improvement.

Input ➡ Process ➡ Outputs/Outcome ➡ **Evaluation** ➡ Input ➡ Process ➡
Outputs/Outcome ➡ **Evaluation** ➡ Input ➡ Process ➡ Outputs/Outcome
Evaluation ➡ Input ➡ ...

Why Use Statistics in Performance Evaluation?

In this book, it is assumed that the data in performance evaluation are from samples, not population, so inferential statistics are used in evaluation. This assumption is made for several reasons. First, there are many cases in which data are indeed from samples. Second, the assumption allows the generalization of evaluation results. When data from an agency being evaluated are treated as a sample from a population that includes other similar organizations, the results of the evaluation can be applied to these organizations.

For example, imagine that you collected data to assess the effect of a counseling program in a high school. Your data show that the group counseling is effective in improving participating students' psychosocial behaviors. Does the effect exist if you assess a similar counseling program in other high schools? Can you generalize this evaluation result to other schools? To answer these questions, you need to treat your data as a sample and to apply inferential statistics in evaluation.

Finally, perhaps most important, an evaluation is conducted as part of a continual improvement process described in Figure 11–1. Even if the data are obtained from the population for the evaluation, they only constitute a sample from the longer period of this continual process. For evaluation results to infer the process and the performance improvement, the data should be treated as a sample. For example, imagine that you evaluate the crime rate in a month. Although the crime rate represents all crimes that occur in that month (i.e., the population information of the month), it is a sample of a year or a longer time. To be able to generalize the results for a longer time, you need to treat the information as a sample and to apply inferential statistics in performance evaluation.

The Key Requirement in Performance Evaluation: Performance Comparison

How do you assess the effect of a PEI? Imagine that you perform poorly in a math course, and you develop a study plan to improve it. The plan includes the hiring of a math tutor and intensified efforts in completing math exercises. How do you assess the effect of this study plan? You can take the math course again and compare your performance with the previous one. This section illustrates the key element of performance evaluation—performance comparison.

Once the data of a performance are collected, an empirical observation of the performance can be made. *Performance comparison* is possible when multiple observations of the performance are available, or when the performance can be compared with a benchmark. Performance comparison is the only way to assess a change in performance and therefore the effect of a PEI on the performance. This is why it is impossible to conduct performance evaluation without performance comparison. In the above example, it is impossible to demonstrate the improvement of your math score without comparing it with a comparable score.

There are different methods to create performance comparisons. In our example, you can measure your current math score against a previous one or compare your score with those of your classmates. The methods to create a performance comparison are called *performance evaluation designs*.

Imagine that you are a performance analyst for a city's emergency medical response unit, and your unit had experienced an increase in citizens' complaints about the slow response to their requests. One year ago, four additional emergency response workers (dispatchers and first responders) were hired to increase response capability in order to improve emergency medical response. Now, you are asked to conduct a performance evaluation to assess if the staff growth has worked. How do you conduct your assessment? You can compare response times before and after the staff growth. If response times are shorter after the growth, you have some evidence that the staff growth worked. Realize that you have just developed an evaluation design, a method of comparison, to assess the impact of a PEI (the staff growth).

Several Important Evaluation Designs

This section introduces several basic and popular evaluation designs. Most other designs are various forms of these basic designs.

Comparing with a Performance Benchmark

This comparison applies when you attempt to match up your performance to a benchmark. For example, you can draw a sample of response times of your city's medical emergency response team and compare the average of these response times with a national standard. Similarly, you can compare the crime rate last year with the average in the previous 20 years. As defined in Chapters 3 and 5, the performance benchmark can be any expected or established performance level deemed to be proper by a performance analyst. It can be a national, regional, or local standard, or the average of the past performances. The design diagram is

$$PO.$$

The intervention of a PEI is represented by P, and O is the observation of a performance sample. The design requires completion of a PEI intervention, a performance sample, and a performance benchmark. Because there is only one sample in this design, it is known as the *one-shot design*.

The one-shot design is very easy to develop. There is no need for multiple observations of performance. The single observation of the performance can be made anytime as long as performance data are available. Because of its flexibility, this design is perhaps one of the most popular in performance evaluation in the public and the nonprofit organizations. Nonetheless, the design lacks the ability to draw a valid conclusion on the PEI impact, because the single observation fails to measure performance change. This point will be discussed later in design assessment.

The statistical analysis of the one-shot design is the center of the discussion in the later part of this chapter, where mean comparisons as well as proportion comparisons are discussed. Numerical examples will be given.

Comparing Two Performance Samples

The one-shot design cannot tell whether the performance has improved, deteriorated, or remained unchanged over time. To measure performance change and thus the impact of a PEI, you need to turn to other designs. Let us say that, in the emergency medical response example, you want to compare the response times before and after the staff growth. You draw two samples of the response times—a pretest sample before the staff growth and a posttest sample after the growth.

The design created is known as the *pretest–posttest single group design*. This is one of the most popular designs that compare two performance samples, and it allows analysts to observe the possible effect of a PEI intervention. In our example, we compare the average response times before and after the staff surge, for a design diagram shown as

$$O_1 \; P \; O_2.$$

The observations of pretest and posttest samples are represented by O_1 and O_2, respectively, and P is the PEI intervention. The performance comparison is $O_2 - O_1$. Let us say that the average response times before and after the staff growth are 6.3 minutes and 5.7 minutes, respectively. The comparison, shown in Table 11–1, indicates that the staff increase may improve the average response time by −0.6 minutes (i.e., 5.7 − 6.3; the negative sign indicates shortened, and therefore improved, response times).

Now you have some evidence that the staff growth improves the response times. How confident are you in your evidence to say that it is the staff growth that *causes* the improvement in response times? Suppose, during the staff growth this year, the state also completed a highway construction in your region so the traffic congestion has been improved. You are not really sure if the response time improvement is the result of the traffic improvement or the staff growth or both.

Table 11–1

Response Times Before and After the Staff Growth

Last year		This year
6.3 minutes	Staff growth	5.7 minutes

To specify the exact impact of the staff growth, or in other words, to separate the impact of the staff growth from the traffic improvement, you need something called a *control group*. Here is how a control group works. Assume that the average response times of our response team were 6.3 minutes and 5.7 minutes before and after the staff growth. Let us also say that we find a neighbor city that also has a medical response team. Both cities are located in the same geographical region in which the highway goes through, but the neighbor city did not have a staff growth this year. Suppose that the average response times in this neighbor city were 6.2 minutes last year and 6.0 minutes this year. A comparison of the response times of these 2 response teams is shown in Table 11–2.

The comparison shows that the response time in our city improves by −0.6 minute after the staff growth. However, the response time in the neighbor city without the staff growth also improves by −0.2 minutes (i.e., 6.0 − 6.2). So we can conclude that this 0.2 minute improvement is the result of the traffic improvement. The improvement in response times from the staff growth is only −0.4 minutes, which comes from −0.6 − (−0.2).

This design is known as the *pretest–posttest control group design* in which the performance of a *target group* is measured up against the performance of a *control group*. In our example, the target group is our city's emergency medical unit, and the control group is the team from the other city. The design alignments can be illustrated in the following diagram:

$$\text{Target Group:} \quad \boldsymbol{O_1\, P\, O_2}$$
$$\text{Control Group:} \quad \boldsymbol{O_3 \quad O_4}.$$

Observations of pretest and posttest samples for the target group are represented by O_1, O_2, respectively; $O_2 - O_1$ is the result of performance improvement for the target group. Observations of pretest and posttest samples for the control group are O_3, O_4, respectively; $O_4 - O_3$ is the result of performance improvement for the control group. A comparison of two performance samples can be made between $O_2 - O_1$ and $O_4 - O_3$.

When is a control group needed? It is needed to eliminate the impact of so-called confounding variables on performance. In our example, the traffic improvement is a variable that influences the response time. This influence does not come from the PEI intervention (the staff growth). In performance evaluation, a non-PEI variable that influences the performance is a *confounding variable*. There could be many confounding variables in a performance evaluation. In our example, in addition to the traffic improvement, other possible confounding vari-

Table 11–2

Response Times in a Pretest–Posttest Control Group Design

	Last year		This year
Our city:	6.3 minutes	Staff growth	5.7 minutes
A neighbor city:	6.2 minutes		6.0 minutes

ables include the declined population that reduces the workloads for medical emergency responses, the number of adult residents in the population that tend to need less medical emergency services, and even the number of days of good weather that reduce the number of traffic accidents. A control group is needed when there are apparent impacts of confounding variables on the performance, and the control group is used to eliminate these impacts and to identify the effect of the PEI on performance.

How do you choose a control group? One way is through a *true experimental design*, also known as a *classical experiment*, in which subjects are randomly assigned to either the target group or the control group. The assignment process can be designed so that a subject has an equal chance to be assigned to either the target group or the control group. This assignment process is known as *random assignment* or *randomization*. The random assignment equalizes the study environment for the target and the control groups so there is no substantial difference between these two groups. Because both groups are equal in all aspects of the study except that the target group experiences PEI and the control does not, the experimental design rules out the impact of confounding variables on the target group *alone* so that, if there is any difference in performance between these two groups, the difference should be attributed to the PEI. An experimental design is often considered the best to rule out the impact of confounding variables. However, random assignment is highly unfeasible in most performance evaluations of human organizations. It is very costly or impossible to randomly assign subjects into different groups. For example, it is impossible to randomly assign emergency responses to a city having staff growth or to a city not having staff growth. Because of the high unfeasibility, the use of an experimental design in performance evaluation is often ruled out.

That leaves us a more feasible way of choosing a control group—*matching*. We know the control group should not experience the PEI intervention, and it is used to eliminate the impact of confounding variables. Assume that we can figure out what these confounding variables are before the evaluation, and then we can go out to find a control group that matches the target group so that both groups are equal in all aspects of the impact by the confounding variables —meaning that they are equally affected by these confounding variables.

How? Let us say that, in our example of emergency medical responses, the confounding variables that affect response times include the population size and density of a city, the age composition of the population in the city, the geographic location of the city, and the traffic condition in the city. Suppose we can find an emergency response team in another city whose population size and density, age composition of the population, geographic location, and traffic condition are the same or mostly similar to those in our city (i.e., the city of the target response team). Because the only difference between these two teams is that the target group has increased its staff and the other team has not, we can say any difference in response times between these groups should come from the impact of the staff growth.

Another popular design of two samples involves a control group but without a pretest. Imagine that your city adopts an Internet service that allows citizens to pay their utility bills online. Some citizens use it, while others do not. You want to assess the performance of the utility payment by using a citizen satisfaction survey. You survey both the Internet users and users of traditional payment methods (mail or in person) and compare their satisfaction in the manner demonstrated in Table 11–3.

Table 11–3

User Satisfaction Rating in a Posttest Control Group Design

Target Group:	Internet payment	Satisfaction rating
Control Group:	Traditional payment methods	Satisfaction rating

The users of traditional methods constitute a control group, and their satisfaction is used as a baseline to compare with that of the Internet users. If the satisfaction rating of the Internet group is greater than that from the traditional group, you may have some evidence that the performance of the utility payment is improved by the Internet access. This design, known as a *posttest control group design*, has the following design diagram:

$$\textit{Target Group:} \quad \textbf{\textit{P O}}_1$$
$$\textit{Control Group:} \quad \textbf{\textit{O}}_2.$$

Nonetheless, this design does not have a pretest. If the satisfaction rating of the Internet user group is indeed higher, how do you know that it is from the Internet access? In fact, without knowing the satisfaction rating before the Internet use, it is difficult to know if their satisfaction has changed, and therefore, it is hard to argue that the Internet use has improved satisfaction.

The statistical comparison of two performance samples will be discussed in Chapter 12. Mean as well as proportion comparisons are presented and numerical examples will be provided.

Comparing More Than Two Performance Samples

Let us say you have response time data of several years before and after the staff growth. You can create a *trend comparison design* that allows you to observe the possible impact of the staff surge for a relatively long time. A trend comparison design extends the pretest–posttest single group design by obtaining more performance observations. A case of three performance observations before and after a PEI intervention is shown in the following diagram. This design collects six samples from six observations:

$$O_1 \ O_2 \ O_3 \ P \ O_4 \ O_5 \ O_6.$$

The trend comparison design requires more than two performance samples, so its construction is more difficult than the one-shot design and the pretest–posttest single group design. However, because it does not need a control group, it is easier to construct than the pretest–posttest control group design.

Another popular design in this category involves the creation of two or more control groups. Imagine that you study the impact of a reading program in an elementary school. A group of students volunteer for the program. You use a standardized reading test before and after the program to measure participants' reading improvements. What are some of the possible confounding variables? It is conceivable that older students may improve their reading more quickly because they have larger vocabularies. So a control group can be created to match students' ages by ensuring that the students in the control group, who do not participate in the reading program, are as old as those in the reading group. In addition, it may be true that female students may be better readers than male students or vice versa. Reading may be affected by gender. So a second control group can be constructed to have the gender composition (percentage of females) the same as that of the reading group. This design has three groups—one target and two control groups. It is known as a *pretest–posttest design with multiple control groups*, demonstrated in the following diagram:

> *Target Group (the reading group):* $O_1 \, P \, O_2$
> *Control Group 1 (matched by age):* $O_3 \quad O_4$
> *Control Group 2 (matched by gender):* $O_5 \quad O_6$.

The reading program is P. The reading improvements are $O_2 - O_1$ for the reading group, $O_4 - O_3$ for the first control group, and $O_6 - O_5$ for the second control group. A comparison can be made for these improvements, and there are three samples of reading improvements in this design.

Another design of more than two samples involves the creation of multiple control groups without pretests. Let us use the above example on the Internet payment of utility bills. To discover if the ability to pay utility bills online improves citizens' satisfaction on utility payment methods, you can compare Internet users' satisfaction with users of mail payment (Control Group 1) and users of payment in person (Control Group 2), as shown in Table 11–4. The design diagram is shown as follows:

> *Target Group:* $P \, O_1$
> *Control Group 1:* O_2
> *Control Group 2:* O_3.

If the satisfaction rating of the Internet group is greater than those of the two control groups, you can argue that you have some evidence that the performance of the utility payment is improved by the Internet access. This design is known as a *posttest design with multiple*

Table 11–4

User Satisfaction Rating in a Posttest Design with Multiple Control Groups

Target Group:	Internet payment	Satisfaction rating
Control Group 1:	Mail payment	Satisfaction rating
Control Group 2:	Payment in person	Satisfaction rating

control groups. Because it does not have a pretest, it suffers from the same shortcoming as that in a posttest control group design discussed above. Without a pretest, it is difficult to know the change made by the Internet access, so it is difficult to conclude that the Internet use has improved satisfaction.

Chapter 13 will present tools to compare more than two performance samples. Many examples will be provided in mean and proportional comparisons of more than two samples.

Assessing a Design

Which design should you use? How do you know that the design is good? Because a design is used to discover if a PEI has any impact on a performance, the key criterion to judge a design is to see if it can do that. A design that has greater ability to identify the impact is said to have higher *internal validity*. Internal validity concerns the capability of a design to develop the causality between the PEI intervention and the performance by ruling out the impact of confounding variables on the performance.

A design capable of distinguishing the PEI impact from the impact of the confounding variables has greater internal validity. The one-shot design, the posttest control group design, and the posttest design with multiple control groups lack this capability, so they have weak internal validity. As illustrated in the above medical emergency example, a design that has a control group(s) and a pretest–posttest alignment helps rule out the impact of many confounding variables, so the pretest–posttest control group design and the pretest–posttest design with multiple control groups have high internal validity.

However, designs with high internal validity often are difficult to construct. Compared with other designs, the pretest–posttest control group design and the pretest–posttest design with multiple control groups are costly to create because they require the development of a control group(s), a pretest sample(s), and a posttest sample(s). They are less feasible to construct. *Design feasibility* refers to the design requirements needed to construct a comparison. A design with fewer requirements is said to be more feasible. The one-shot design, which has no pretest samples or control groups, is most feasible than any other design introduced in this book, and the pretest–posttest design with multiple control groups is least feasible (the experimental design excluded).

Because a design with greater internal validity is often weaker in design feasibility, a challenge in performance evaluation is to find a feasible design that meets the requirement of internal validity. That said, when choices have to be made, the priority of consideration should always be given to the principle of internal validity, not design feasibility, in selecting a design. This is because the purpose of a design is to identify the causation between a PEI and its impact on performance, not to satisfy the need of design feasibility.

Note that design feasibility is different from a design's *external validity*, a notion that there is a possibility that the conclusion drawn from a design may not be generalized to the real world due to the significant contextual differences created in a design. External invalidity is a serious concern in a true experimental design, which tends to be conducted in a controlled environment that is not "real." A detailed coverage of external validity is not presented here because the focus of discussion in this chapter is not on experimental designs.

Comparing with a Performance Benchmark: The Mean Comparison

This comparison is created by the one-shot design discussed previously in this chapter. A performance sample is compared against a benchmark. The benchmark can be a mean measure or a proportion (percentage) measure. A mean measure should be used when the performance data are interval; a proportion measure is proper when the data are nominal or ordinal (review Chapter 3 for nominal, ordinal, and interval measures). This section discusses the comparison of a mean measure.

Suppose your performance benchmark for medical emergency response times is a national average of 6.0 minutes. You select a sample of 25 calls for emergency medical responses this year, and the average response time is 5.7 minutes, 0.3 minute less than the national average. The sample data, shown in Table 11–5, indicate that you beat the national average. However,

Table 11–5

Medical Emergency Response Times of 25 Selected Cases

Case ID	Response times
1	5.67
2	5.57
3	6.08
4	5.37
5	5.43
6	5.46
7	5.78
8	5.58
9	5.63
10	5.37
11	5.36
12	6.18
13	6.00
14	6.56
15	5.66
16	6.04
17	5.53
18	6.19
19	6.41
20	5.00
21	4.80
22	5.00
23	5.53
24	6.30
25	6.10

the average of 5.7 minutes comes from a sample of 25 calls. How do you know that the average response time of *all* emergency responses in your agency is still better than the national average? And more importantly, what is the chance that this better-than-average response happens in the future? To answer these questions, you need a hypothesis test. Statisticians call the test with one sample mean the *one-sample hypothesis test for a mean* or the *significance test for a mean*.

Hypotheses

You may want to refresh yourself with hypothesis testing procedures in Chapter 9. The first step in a hypothesis testing is to construct a null hypothesis (*Ho*) and an alternative hypothesis (*Ha*). Recall that the null hypothesis is a statement that the population parameter has the value that shows *no effect*. In this case, we can state that our average response time is not different from (or equal to) the national average 6.0 minutes or, by symbol $\mu = 6.0$ minutes, and μ represents the average response time. It is equivalent to saying that the 0.3 minute difference in the sample does not exist if we count the response times of all medical emergencies.

On the contrary, the alternative hypothesis is that the average response time is different from the national average 6.0 minutes, or $\mu \neq 6.0$ minutes, for a two-tailed test. Realize that "different" means greater or less. You construct a one-tailed test if you state that the average response time is less than 6.0 minutes. Review Chapter 9 on how to set up a one-tailed or two-tailed test.

Test Statistic

Stated in Chapter 9, the test statistic is a value calculated from the sample data to test the null hypothesis. For this test, the test statistic is a t statistic that comes from

$$t = \frac{\bar{X} - \mu}{\sigma_{\bar{x}}}.$$

In the equation, $\bar{X}$ is the sample mean, which is 5.7 minutes in our example, and μ is the population mean. It is the performance benchmark with which the sample is compared. In our example, it is the national average response time of 6.0 minutes. The standard error of the sample, $\sigma_{\bar{x}}$, is calculated from the following equation.

$$\sigma_{\bar{x}} = \frac{\sigma}{\sqrt{n}}.$$

In the equation, σ is the standard deviation of the sample and n is the sample size. In our example, $\sigma = 0.45$, which can be easily calculated from Excel Insert Function (STDEV in fx). So, $\sigma_{\bar{x}} = 0.45/\sqrt{25} = 0.0907$ and $t = (5.7 - 6.0)/0.0907 = -3.306$. This test has $n - 1$ degrees of freedom.

P-value

Remember that *P*-value is the probability that the null hypothesis is rejected, but it is true. To obtain the *P* in this example, we need to use Excel TDIST procedure in the Insert Function (*fx*), shown in Screen 11–1.

You should place the *t* value in the *x* window, as shown in Screen 11–1. Realize that I put 3.306 (not −3.306) because Excel does not take a negative value in this procedure. Because the *t* distribution is symmetric, the *P*-value is the same for either a positive or a negative value of 3.306. Thus, we can use 3.306 to replace −3.306. The two-tailed *P*-value is .002968, with degrees of freedom 25 − 1 = 24. The one-tailed *P* value is .002968/2 = .001484.

The Significance Level α

Recall that α is the level of estimated error *tolerated* by the evaluator (you). You can set the significance level at .05, which means that you allow less than 5% of a chance that the null hypothesis is rejected by error.

Conclusion

Because $P < \alpha$ (i.e., .002968 < .05), we reject the null hypothesis that our average response time is equal to the national average 6.0 minutes and conclude that there is sufficient evidence to indicate that our average response time is not equal to 6.0 minutes. In fact, our

Screen 11–1

P-value for One-Sample *t* Test for a Mean.

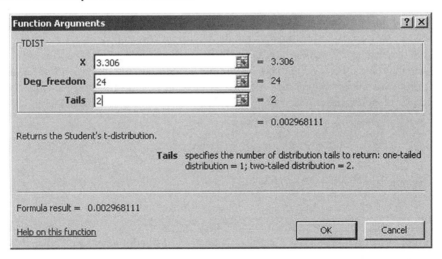

average response time is less than 6.0 minutes, and our performance is indeed better than the national average.

Comparing with a Performance Benchmark: The Proportion Comparison

The above mean comparison of performance is proper for interval variables. A percentage (proportion) measure should be used for nominal or ordinal variables. Suppose you survey 100 residents in your city (population 100,000), and 80 of them (80%) are satisfied with city services. If your performance benchmark is a 75% satisfaction rating, have you achieved your performance target? Because the 100 people constitute a sample, you are really not sure about the answer until you do a hypothesis test that more than 75% of all residents are happy with your services. The hypothesis test that compares a performance sample with a proportional benchmark is known as the *one-sample hypothesis test for a proportion* or the *significance test for a proportion*.

Hypotheses

The null hypothesis is that the population proportion π is 75% or $\pi = \pi_0$ or $\pi = 75\%$ in our example; π_0 is the performance benchmark. The alternative hypothesis is that the population proportion is not 75% or $\pi \neq \pi_0$ or $\pi \neq 75\%$ for a two-tailed test. In this example, however, I would like to conduct a one-tailed test by stating that the population proportion is larger than 75% (i.e., $\pi > 75\%$).

Test Statistic

For a sample size larger than 30, the sampling distribution of the sample proportion $\hat{\pi}$ is approximately normal. So we can use a *t* test for the test statistic. The standard deviation of the sample is $\sigma = \sqrt{\pi_0(1-\pi_0)}$, and the standard error of the sample is $\sigma_{\hat{\pi}} = \sqrt{\pi_0(1-\pi_0)/n}$. Notice that the benchmark proportion (π_0 or 75%), not the sample proportion $\hat{\pi}$ or 80%, is used to calculate the standard error due to the assumption of normal approximation for the sampling distribution of parameter values π (a detailed discussion beyond the scope of this book). In this example, $\sigma_{\hat{\pi}} = \sqrt{\pi_0(1-\pi_0)/n} = \sqrt{(0.75 \times 0.25)/100} = 0.0433$. The *t* statistic is

$$t = \frac{\hat{\pi} - \pi_0}{\sigma_{\hat{\pi}}}.$$

In this example, $t = (0.80 - 0.75)/0.0433 = 1.1547$.

P-value

The one-tailed *P* with 99 (i.e., n − 1 = 100 − 1) degrees of freedom can be calculated from the Excel TDIST procedure as shown in Screen 11–2. The one-tailed *P* is .1255, and the two-tailed *P* is .2510.

Screen 11–2

P-value for One-Sample *t* Test for a Proportion with a Large Sample Size.

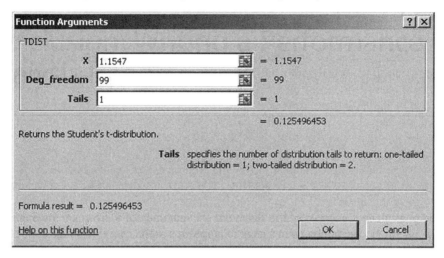

The Significance Level and Conclusion

Let $\alpha = .05$. Because $P > \alpha$, we fail to reject the null hypothesis, and we conclude there is no sufficient evidence to indicate that the satisfaction rate is larger than 75%. This result means that, even if our sample shows an 80% satisfaction rate, we do not have enough evidence from the sample to say that the true satisfaction of all residents is larger than 75%, and if we did say that, the chance is 12.55% that we would be wrong.

One possibility for the failure to reject the null hypothesis is the small sample size. Realize that a smaller sample results in a larger standard error and a smaller *t* value, which makes it more difficult to reject the null hypothesis even if the sample proportion shows a difference. In this case, you may want to survey more residents to obtain more definite results of the hypothesis testing. As an exercise, everything else unchanged, what is the *P*-value if you increase the sample size from 100 to 1000? The one-tailed *P*-value should be .000137, and you obtain sufficient evidence to reject the null hypothesis at the .01 level and conclude that the satisfaction rate is larger than 75%.

A Case Study

The department of public administration at a university located in a suburban city has seen a sluggish enrollment for the past 20 years. The annual enrollment in the Master of Public Administration (MPA) program has been around 90 students with an up-and-down trend. The

MPA program is the department's only degree program, and the enrollment number is used by the university to determine the department's budget.

Step 1: Defining the Issue

The department chair and the coordinator of the MPA program have been in constant discussion about the ways to increase the enrollment. Seven years ago the MPA program received a university grant to boost the enrollment. The MPA coordinator developed a MPA recruitment enhancement plan (REP), based on the findings of a recruitment study, which suggest that the main cause of the lethargic enrollment figure is the potential candidates' lack of awareness about the program. About two-thirds of undergraduate students surveyed in the study never heard of the program. Consequently, the REP mainly includes a marketing effort to increase the awareness about the program.

Since then, the MPA program has mailed the program flyers and the coordinator's recruitment letter every semester to potential students identified through a database that includes local and state governments as well as the university's undergraduate programs in social sciences and management. The Web site of the program has been updated to keep potential applicants informed about the curriculum information, faculty research, and extracurricular activities. Program information workshops are conducted throughout the year. The program also actively participates in the university's job fair. In addition, the program has been advertised in the local newspaper and national conferences. Outstanding students' profiles are posted on the Web site of the profession's national organization.

The MPA coordinator believes that the enrollment performance has improved since the REP program. The enrollment data of the last 7 years since the REP are shown in Table 11–6. An annual enrollment of 90 students has been used by the department chair and faculty, formally in meetings and informally in private conversations, so it has become a norm to gauge the MPA enrollment performance. Data in Table 11–6 show that the 7-year enrollment average is 93.0, better than the benchmark of 90. Still, there were 2 years during which the enrollment dropped below 90. The coordinator decides to conduct a performance evaluation.

Table 11–6

Enrollment of the MPA Program

Year	Annual enrollment
1	93
2	97
3	100
4	95
5	88
6	94
7 (this year)	84

Step 2: Determining the Evaluation Question and the Evaluation Design

The evaluation assesses the impact of REP on the enrollment. The coordinator wants to know if the REP increases the enrollment. So the initial evaluation question proposed by the coordinator was, has REP improved the enrollment?

The coordinator has been collecting enrollment data for the past 7 years since the implementation of REP. Nonetheless, the quality of enrollment data before that was poor when enrollment data were often mixed with other databases, which resulted in lack of uniformity in data collection. Thus, the coordinator could not make any meaningful enrollment comparison with the data before REP. A one-shot design is the only choice of the evaluation, in which the 7-year average enrollment can be compared with the benchmark of 90.

The coordinator understands the weak internal validity of the one-shot comparison. It is clear that such design produces no strong evidence that any enrollment change is the result of the REP. The impact of many non-REP factors on the enrollment cannot be ruled out by this design. Such factors include the university's overall enrollment trend, the university's recruitment efforts, the MPA program quality change, and even the change in the local economy. Causality between the REP and the enrollment change cannot be drawn by such a one-shot comparison. Because of the inability of the design to draw causality between the REP and the enrollment improvement, the coordinator has changed the evaluation question subtly from, has REP improved the MPA enrollment, to, has the MPA enrollment increased since the REP, compared with a benchmark of 90.

The chair is not very happy with the question, believing that the coordinator asked a self-applauding question. Because the average enrollment since the REP is 93.0, the coordinator could claim the program has exceeded its benchmark of 90 right away. But there were 2 years of below-90 enrollment in the past 7 years. And importantly, will the enrollment continue to grow from now? In other words, the chair wants to treat this 7-year period as a time in a longer enrollment period and therefore the 7-year data as a sample of a larger population. The chair wants a hypothesis test to assess the chance of the enrollment growth. So the chair adds a new question: what is the chance of the average enrollment above the benchmark of 90, based on the 7-year enrollment data? She also wants to be 95% sure about the result (i.e., an α-level of .05).

Step 3: Conducting the Analysis

The hypothesis test compares the post-REP enrollment with the performance benchmark of 90. The null hypothesis is the average post-REP enrollment is 90 students. The alternative hypothesis is that the average post-REP enrollment is not 90 students for a two-tailed test, or that the average post-REP enrollment is greater than 90 for a one-tailed test. The coordinator wants the one-tailed test, arguing that the evaluation question indicates the direction of the test by stating the enrollment is greater or has increased. Of course, a one-tailed test makes it easier to reject the null hypothesis, so it is easier for the coordinator to claim the victory of enrollment increase.

The t statistic for the one-tailed test is 1.466, and the P is .0966. So we fail to reject the null hypothesis at the .05 significance level, and we conclude there is no sufficient evidence to indicate that the average post-REP enrollment is greater than 90.

Step 4: Using the Results

The coordinator is very unhappy about this result. He argued that, if the significance level were set at the .10 level, an enrollment increase would be found. Nonetheless, the chair believes that a 9.66% error rate is too high to draw a conclusion of enrollment increase. This result gives the chair no confidence that the enrollment will continue to grow larger than 90 students, particularly in light of the enrollment decline in the very recent year. The chair and coordinator finally settled with the solution that the result of the analysis temporarily will not be published, and the analysis will be performed again with enrollment data of 3 more years.

Practices

Key Terms

Performance enhancement initiative (PEI)
Intensity and length of an intervention
Performance evaluation
Cycle of continual performance improvement
Performance comparison
Performance evaluation designs
Comparing with a performance benchmark
One-shot design
Comparing two performance samples
Pretest–posttest single group design
Pretest–posttest control group design
Target group
Control group
Confounding variables
True experimental design
Random assignment or randomization
Matching in selecting a control group
Posttest control group design
Comparing more than two performance samples
Trend comparison design
Pretest–posttest design with multiple control groups
Posttest design with multiple control groups
Internal validity of a design
Design feasibility
External validity of a design
Mean comparison with a performance benchmark (one-sample hypothesis test for a mean)
Proportion comparison with a performance benchmark (one-sample hypothesis test for a proportion)

Practice Problem 11–1

Psychosocial functional score (PFS) is used to assess school-age children's psychosocial behaviors. A score of 25 points or above is considered normal. A school counseling program has used PFS to assess the participating students' progress in the program. A sample of 15 participating students is tested, and their PFSs are shown in Table 11–7. Conduct a performance evaluation to assess if the participants' average PFS is greater than 25.

Practice Problem 11–2

Return to class (RTC) is used to measure the performance of a school clinic of 4 workers. The RTC in the clinic has been around 85%, indicating that 85% of clinic visitors (students) have been returned to the classes after treatment. Last year, 2 additional workers were hired to improve the performance of the clinic. Recently, a sample of 325 clinic visitors has been included in a study; 285 of them have returned to the classes for an 87.69% RTC. Conduct a hypothesis test for proportion to find out if the RTC increases after the staff increase.

Practice Problem 11–3

PEI efforts have been made to reduce the clerical error rate in processing passports for citizens who travel oversea. A performance benchmark of 10% or less is established. A recent data collection shows that 29 of 250 selected cases of passport processing have errors. Conduct a hypothesis test to assess if the error rate is greater than the performance standard.

Table 11–7

Psychosocial Functional Scores (PFS) of 15 Students

Participant ID	PFS
1	29
2	32
3	18
4	23
5	27
6	19
7	34
8	32
9	27
10	27
11	23
12	26
13	32
14	29
15	34

Table 11–8

Arrest Rate in an Urban City

Month	Number of arrests per 100,000 populations
1	5.30
2	6.10
3	3.40
4	10.30
5	4.30
6	5.00
7	4.90
8	2.90
9	5.20
10	2.90

Table 11–9

Satisfaction Ratings of 25 Selected Residents in an Urban City

Resident ID	Satisfaction about city services*
1	3
2	4
3	4
4	5
5	4
6	5
7	4
8	4
9	3
10	4
11	5
12	4
13	5
14	4
15	4
16	4
17	3
18	5
19	2
20	5
21	5
22	3
23	4
24	5
25	5

*1 = very dissatisfied; 2 = dissatisfied; 3 = neutral; 4 = satisfied; 5 = very satisfied.

Practice Problem 11–4

Table 11–8 shows the monthly arrest rates (the number of arrests per 100,000 populations) in an urban city after a police crackdown on serious crimes. Treat the data as a sample of a population and the police crackdown as a continual effort in a long-term performance improvement cycle. Conduct a hypothesis test to see if the average arrest rate is less than 6.00.

Practice Problem 11–5

A PEI has been developed to improve citizen satisfaction toward city services in an urban city. Table 11–9 shows 25 selected citizens' perceptions about city services. Conduct a hypothesis test that the citizen satisfaction rate is 60% or above.

CHAPTER 12

Comparing Two Performance Samples

I magine that you work for a city's utility department. For the past few weeks, the department has received an increasing number of residents' calls reporting errors in their water
bills. Some errors were in customers' names and billing addresses, while others were
wrong billing categories and amounts. You made several calls and also checked the billing
information in the department's database and realized that the cause of the problems mainly
resulted from an outdated database. The department used to update its utility billing system
frequently, but because of a budget cut, the system has not been updated for the past year. You
decided to request a supplemental funding for an immediate update, and the request has been
approved, and the system has been updated.

How do you know if the update reduces the number of billing errors? You can compare
two samples—the error rates before and after the update, for a declining error rate may indicate
that the update works. In this chapter, we examine the tools to compare two performance
samples.

Creating a Comparison

How do you create a performance comparison for two samples? Thoroughly discussed in
Chapter 11, the pretest–posttest single group design allows the comparison of two samples
before and after a PEI. There are two ways to draw samples though. In the first method, the
same subjects are drawn twice. For example, you can compare the error rates of the same water
users before and after the update. The error rate after the update is matched against that before
the update for every user, producing two *matched samples* (also known as *paired samples*).

The two paired samples are related to each other because they are drawn from the same
subjects, so they are also known as *dependent samples*. Just like students having better scores
in the first test are likely to score higher in the second test on the same topic, the error rates
before and after the update are expected to be associated. Utility accounts with more errors
before the update are more likely to have more errors after the update.

Then what are independent samples? Imagine that you draw a different group of water
users after the system update to create two completely different groups of water users before

and after the update. The error rates of these two groups of users are unrelated to each other. You may have different numbers of accounts in these two groups. These two groups constitute two *independent samples*.

Therefore, the samples drawn from a pretest–posttest single group design, which does not involve a control group, can be either dependent or independent. What are samples for a design that has a control group? Because a control group and a target group are two different groups, the samples drawn from them are two independent samples. This chapter presents the tools to compare two samples. Comparisons of the mean and the proportions are discussed.

Comparing Two Dependent Performance Means

Data in Table 12–1 show the number of errors before and after the system update in 20 residents' water billing accounts. Does the update reduce the error rate? The average number of errors before the update is 1.15; it is 0.55 after the update. It appears that the error rate is reduced after the update. Nonetheless, the data are from a sample of only 20 users. You need a hypothesis test to know if the improvement really occurs for all users.

Table 12–1

Number of Errors in Water Bills

Water bill account ID	Before the system update	After the update
1	0	0
2	1	0
3	2	1
4	0	2
5	2	0
6	1	0
7	2	0
8	1	0
9	1	1
10	1	1
11	0	1
12	0	0
13	1	1
14	1	0
15	1	0
16	2	1
17	2	1
18	3	1
19	1	0
20	1	1

Hypotheses

The null hypothesis is that the average number of reporting errors is the same before and after the system update. The alternative hypothesis is that the average number of reporting errors is different after the update for a two-tailed test. If you prefer a one-tailed test, the alternative hypothesis is that the average number of reporting errors is less after the system update.

The null hypothesis states that the PEI does not have any impact on the performance so the performance mean does not change or the means before and after a PEI are equal. Let μ_1 and μ_2 be the means before and after the PEI, respectively. The null hypothesis is $\mu_1 = \mu_2$ or $\mu_1 - \mu_2 = 0$. The alternative hypothesis is that the means before and after the PEI are not equal or $\mu_1 \neq \mu_2$ for a two-tailed test. To make it one-tailed, you can state that the mean after the PEI is greater (or less) than the mean before the PEI. Clearly, the means in these hypotheses are population parameters.

Test Statistic and *P*-value

The test is a t *test for two dependent samples*. The t statistic can be calculated from Excel Data Analysis ToolPak (review Chapter 3 on its access). Let us use the data in Table 12–1 to illustrate this calculation process. After you input the data:

1. Choose *t*-**Test: Paired Two Sample for Means** in the **Data Analysis** window. You should see a screen shown as that in Screen 12–1. You can use the Variable 1 Range window for the error rate data before the system update and the Variable 2 Range window for the data after the update. The Hypothesized Mean Difference is $\mu_1 - \mu_2 = 0$.
2. Make sure you check the **Labels** box if you include the variable names in the data input ranges. I set the alpha, the significance level α, at .05. Click **OK**.

The testing results are shown in Screen 12–2. The Excel presents the t statistic (2.6975) and *P*-values for one-tailed (.00713) and two-tailed tests (.01427). The t statistic when the P is equal to the significance level .05 is also presented. This value is called the *critical value* or the *critical t* (t Critical in the Excel output), which was introduced in Chapter 7. Both one-tailed and two-tailed critical t values are given by Excel (1.72913 and 2.09302).

An easier way to obtain the *P*-value is to use the Excel Insert Function (*fx*) TTEST procedure, shown in Screen 12–3. In the TTEST Function Arguments window:

1. Input your data (do not include the label rows) in Array 1 and Array 2.
2. Decide on the one- or two-tailed test in the **Tails** window, and type *1* for the two-paired samples comparison in the **Type** window. The screen shows the *P*-value (.01427), as the formula result, for a two-tailed test for two paired samples. The procedure does not provide the t statistic, but the test can proceed without the t as long as the *P*-value is available.

The Significance Level and the Conclusion

Let the significance level α be .05. Because $P < \alpha$, we reject the null hypothesis and conclude there is sufficient evidence to indicate that the average number of reporting errors is different

Screen 12–1

t Test for Two Dependent Samples.

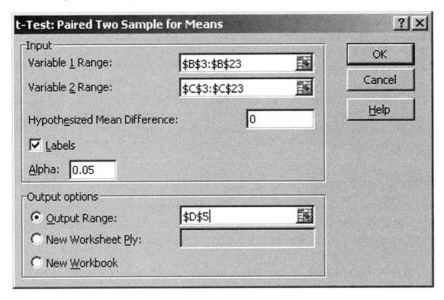

after the system update. The average number of reporting errors is 1.15 before the update and 0.55 after the update. You can conclude that the average number of reporting errors is less after the update.

Statistical Significance and Managerial Significance

It is important to distinguish between *statistical significance* and *managerial significance*. In the above example, the system update might have reduced the error rate. Should the city conduct the system update on a continual basis? Realize that the system update is a managerial decision out of consideration of many factors including the costs and the benefits of the update. The evidence of statistical significance is *not* always sufficient enough for making a managerial decision. For example, the data show the average number of errors has been reduced from 1.15 to 0.55, for a reduction of 0.6 (i.e., 1.15 − 0.55) number of error for each account on average. Suppose that each update would cost the city $1 million. Should the city conduct the update every year? Does the city want to continue to spend $1 million in system updates for an error reduction less than 1.00 per account?

Another Example

A police department initiated a crackdown on crime this year. Crime rate data in Table 12–2 show the monthly crime statistics last year before the crackdown and this year after the

Screen 12–2

Results of the *t* Test for Two Dependent Samples.

Ch12examples.xls [Compatibility Mode] - Microsoft Excel

| | Home | Insert | Page Layout | Formulas | Data | Review | View | Add-Ins |

D5

Number of Errors in A Water Bill Account

	A	B	C	D	E	F
1						
2	Water Bill Account	Before System Update	After System Update			
3						
4	1	0	0			
5	2	1	0	t-Test: Paired Two Sample for Means		
6	3	2	1			
7	4	0	2			
8	5	2	0		Before System Update	After System Update
9	6	1	0	Mean	1.15	0.55
10	7	2	0	Variance	0.660526316	0.365789474
11	8	1	0	Observations	20	20
12	9	1	1	Pearson Correlation	0.037476047	
13	10	1	1	Hypothesized Mean Differen	0	
14	11	0	1	df	19	
15	12	0	0	t Stat	2.697516588	
16	13	1	0	P(T<=t) one-tail	0.007132746	
17	14	1	1	t Critical one-tail	1.729132792	
18	15	1	0	P(T<=t) two-tail	0.014265493	
19	16	2	1	t Critical two-tail	2.09302405	
20	17	2	1			
21	18	3	1			
22	19	1	0			
23	20	1	1			

t-Test: Paired Two Sample for Means

Input

Variable 1 Range: $B$3:$B$23

Variable 2 Range: $C$3:$C$23

Hypothesized Mean Difference: 0

☑ Labels

Alpha: 0.05

Output options

◉ Output Range: $D$5

○ New Worksheet Ply:

○ New Workbook

OK

Cancel

Help

Screen 12–3

The TTEST Procedure for Two Dependent Samples.

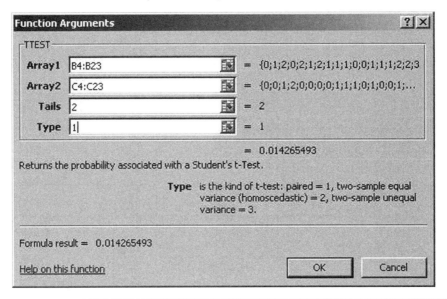

Table 12–2

Monthly Reports of Serious Crimes

Month	Last year before crackdown	This year after crackdown
January	46	44
February	55	42
March	48	49
April	45	57
May	48	46
June	63	54
July	54	57
August	70	64
September	66	65
October	64	65
November	65	59
December	45	45

crackdown. The monthly average is 55.75 last year and 53.92 this year. So the police chief claimed that the crackdown has reduced crimes.

Is the chief correct? Will the reduction continue if the crackdown continues? What is the chance the reduction happens by accident? To answer these questions, the data should be treated as a sample, so a hypothesis test can be performed. This treatment is justifiable because crime data are collected continually over time, and the data in Table 12–2 are only a sample of that larger longitudinal database.

Crime data are paired for each month, so they are two dependent samples. Table 12–3 shows Excel results. The *P* for the one-tailed hypothesis that the monthly average crime rate is lower after the crackdown is .1699, larger than the significance level at .05. So we fail to reject the null hypothesis, and we conclude there is no sufficient evidence to indicate that the average crime is less after the crackdown or that the crackdown reduces the crime. In fact, we have a 16.99% chance of making a wrong prediction if we say that the crime will be less after the crackdown. It is likely that the crime reduction this year happened by chance, and it may not happen again if the crackdown continues.

Comparing Two Dependent Performance Proportions

Mean comparison is proper for the performance measured at the interval level. When the performance is a nominal or an ordinal variable, the proportion (percentage) measures should be used in comparing two samples. Let us say you study a nonprofit health care program that targets children's obesity. The program consists of a series of instructional and physical activities. You drew a sample of 144 school-age students and found that 20 of them were obese and

Table 12–3

t Test Results for Two Dependent Samples of Crime Rate

	Before crackdown	After crackdown
Mean	55.75	53.91666667
Variance	87.65909091	72.62878788
Observations	12	12
Pearson correlation	0.75054211	
Hypothesized mean difference	0	
df	11	
t Stat	0.997753647	
P (T <= *t*) one-tail	.169920688	
t Critical one-tail	1.795883691	
P (T <= *t*) two-tail	.339841377	
t Critical two-tail	2.200986273	

124 had normal weight before the program last year. The normal rate was $124/144 = 86.11\%$. One year after the program, you studied the same sample of the students, and only 5 students were obese and 139 were normal for a normal rate of $139/144 = 96.53\%$. Does the normal rate change after the program?

Hypotheses and Test Statistic

The performance measure is the proportion of children in normal weights—the normal rate. Because two observations of the weight were made for each child, the samples are paired and dependent samples. A proper test for comparing two dependent proportions is the *McNemar test for two dependent proportions*. The null hypothesis of the test is that two population proportions are the same. In our example, the null hypothesis is that the normal rates of weight before and after the program intervention are the same. The alternative hypothesis is that they are different.

The test statistic has the χ^2 (chi-square) distribution with 1 degree of freedom (review Chapter 9 for this distribution). For calculating the χ^2 statistic in our example, it is also known that 2 obese students before the program are still obese after the program, and 18 obese students before the program are normal now. Three normal students before the program become obese after the program, and 121 students are normal before and after the program. These data are used to construct Table 12–4.

For the moment, I would ask you *not* to consider the last row of totals (20 and 124) and the last column of the totals (5 and 139). There are two categories (obese and normal) for the data before the program in two rows, and two categories (obese and normal) for the data after the program in two columns. This table is known as a 2×2 table. The upper left cell (2) in Row 1 and Column 1 can be named as C_{11}. The upper right cell (18) in Row 1 and Column 2 is C_{12}. The cell in the lower left corner (3) is C_{21}, and C_{22} is the cell in the lower right corner (121). Then,

$$\chi^2 = \frac{(C_{12} - C_{21})^2}{C_{12} + C_{21}}.$$

Table 12–4

The Obesity Example

		After the program		
		Obese	**Normal**	**Total**
Before the program	Obese	2	18	20
	Normal	3	121	124
	Total	5	139	144

Screen 12–4

The CHIDIST Procedure for a McNemar Test.

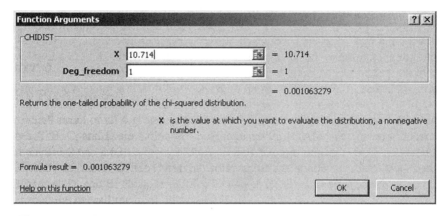

In this example, $\chi^2 = (18 - 3)^2/(18 + 3) = 225/21 = 10.714$. To obtain the *P*-value associated with $\chi^2 = 10.714$ with 1 degree of freedom, you can use the Excel CHIDIST procedure in the Insert Function (f_x), shown in Screen 12–4. The *P* is .001063.

The Significance Level and Conclusion

Let the significance level $\alpha = .05$. Because $P < \alpha$, we reject the null hypothesis that rates of normal weights before and after the program are the same, and we conclude that there is sufficient evidence to indicate that they are different. This result suggests that the program reduces students' obesity.

Comparing Two Independent Performance Means

Imagine that you are a performance analyst for an elementary school whose academic performance is measured by students' standardized testing scores. The scores have not been improved for the past several years. The 5th graders have done particularly poorly in the testing. A program to improve the math testing scores has been experimented on the 5th graders since last year. The program, Marching to High Performance (MATH), adopts a learning theory known as peer learning by using volunteer tutors in an intensive after-class learning workshop twice a week. Two participating 5th graders are paired with a volunteer tutor, often a student of science major from a nearby college.

MATH participants are voluntary. It requires strong commitment. Only 22 of 87 students in the 5th grade have completed the program. The standardized test results, measured on a 0 to 100 scale with 100 being the best, show the average test score improved from 56.47 last year to 59.56 this year. This is a 3-point improvement; however, unless you create a control group of non-MATH students and look at their score change, you are not quite sure if this 3-point improvement is the result of the MATH program. If the score of the non-MATH group also improved by 3 points, there would not be enough evidence to say that MATH improved testing scores.

To match the MATH group with a non-MATH control group, it is conceivable that you want both groups starting at the same math level so that the students in both groups are at the same learning stage with the same learning curve. The MATH group had an average testing score of 56.47 last year. You chose a group of 25 non-MATH 5th graders that had an average test score of about 56.47 last year. The students in this control group also took the test this year. Table 12–5 shows the testing score improvement for the students in both groups.

Students' scores in the MATH group improve 3.09 points on average, and the students' scores in the non-MATH group improve 1.52 on average. Because the data are from samples, a hypothesis test should be conducted to assess if the difference really occurs.

Table 12–5

Math Score Improvement

MATH group	Non-MATH group
5	0
5	3
3	−2
8	7
8	2
9	5
−7	−2
7	1
8	1
4	9
−3	7
6	4
−6	6
4	5
−3	−4
−7	−6
2	2
0	0
1	2
9	−3
6	2
9	−2
	2
	4
	−5

Hypotheses

Because the two groups consist of different students, their testing scores are unrelated. The two samples of test score improvements are two independent samples. The hypothesis test is a *t test of two independent sample means*. The null hypothesis is the average performances of the two samples are the same. In this example, it is the average test score improvements in the MATH group and the non-MATH group are the same. Let μ_1 and μ_2 be the average performances for two groups. The null hypothesis is $\mu_1 = \mu_2$ or $\mu_1 - \mu_2 = 0$.

The alternative hypothesis is that the average performances of the two samples are different for a two-tailed test or $\mu_1 \neq \mu_2$ or $\mu_1 - \mu_2 \neq 0$. In our example, we can state that the average test score improvement in the MATH group is different from that in the non-MATH group for a two-tailed test. For a one-tailed test, the alternative hypothesis is that the average score improvement in the MATH group is greater (or less) than that in the non-MATH group (i.e., $\mu_2 > \mu_1$ or $\mu_2 < \mu_1$).

Test Statistic

The test statistic is a *t* statistic, which can be easily calculated from Excel Data Analysis ToolPak: *t*-Test with Two-Sample Assuming Unequal Variances (we will discuss this assumption on the variances later). In the Data Analysis window of the data sheet:

1. Select *t*-**Test: Two-Sample Assuming Unequal Variances**.
2. Select the scores in the MATH group in the Variable 1 Range and the scores of non-MATH group in the Variable 2 Range, as shown in Screen 12–5. The Hypothesized Mean Difference is $\mu_1 = \mu_2$ or $\mu_1 - \mu_2 = 0$. Make sure you check the **Labels** box if you include variable names in the data ranges.
3. Choose an output range that does not overlap with the data.
4. Click **OK.** You should see the results in Table 12–6.

The *P*-value can also be obtained from the TTEST procedure in Excel Insert Function (f_x). This procedure is shown in Screen 12–6.

1. Input your data in Array 1 and Array 2 in the **TTEST Function Arguments** window.
2. Decide on the one- or two-tailed test, and type *3* in the **Type** window for the two samples assuming unequal variance.

The screen shows the *P*-value (.2614) for the two-tailed test. This TTEST procedure is easier to perform than that in Data Analysis; however, it does not provide the *t* statistic.

The *t* statistic is calculated with a procedure that assumes two unequal population variances for the MATH and the non-MATH groups (review Chapter 5 for the concept of variance). In other words, the population variances of the two groups are assumed to be different. Nonetheless, the result from this *t* test can be misleading if the population variances of these two groups are in fact equal. In that case, we can assume equal variances for these two groups and put their sample variances together to estimate a "pooled" variance in calculating the *t* statistic. In

Screen 12–5

Two-Sample *t* Test Assuming Unequal Variances.

t-Test: Two-Sample Assuming Unequal Variances

Input
Variable 1 Range: $A$2:$A$24
Variable 2 Range: $B$2:$B$27
Hypothesized Mean Difference: 0
☐ Labels
Alpha: 0.05

Output options
⦿ Output Range: $F$19
○ New Worksheet Ply:
○ New Workbook

OK
Cancel
Help

Table 12–6

Results of a Two-Sample *t* Test Assuming Unequal Variances

	MATH group	**Non-MATH group**
Mean	3.090909091	1.52
Variance	28.27705628	15.34333333
Observations	22	25
Hypothesized mean difference	0	
df	38	
t stat	1.139941035	
P (T <= t) one-tail	.130722658	
t critical one-tail	1.685953066	
P (T <= *t*) two-tail	.261445316	
t critical two-tail	2.024394234	

Screen 12–6

The TTEST Procedure for Tests Assuming Unequal Variances.

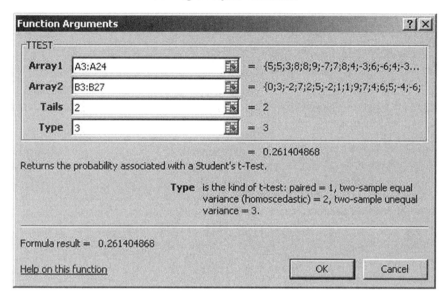

Excel, the *t* statistic with a pooled variance is calculated from Excel Data Analysis: *t*-Test with Two-Sample Assuming Equal Variances. In the Data Analysis window of the data sheet, select ***t*-Test: Two-Sample Assuming Equal Variances**. The rest of the steps in this Excel procedure are the same as those for the above test assuming unequal variances. Table 12–7 shows the results from a test using data in Table 12–5.

Screen 12–7 shows the TTEST procedure Excel Insert Function (f_x) to obtain the same *P*-value. In the TTEST Function Arguments window, make sure that you type 2 for the two samples assuming equal variance in the Type window. The screen shows the *P*-value (.2513) for a two-tailed test.

Here are words of caution. There are many cases where you can assume either equal variances or unequal variances for your samples, so it is easy to choose a *t* test type. However, there are other cases in which you are unsure about whether you should assume equal variances or unequal variances for your samples. For these cases, I recommend that you perform both *t* tests and compare their *P* values. If they are different, choose the test that has a larger *P*. Because a larger *P* makes it less likely to reject the null hypothesis, you are less likely to make a mistake to reject the null hypothesis when you really should not.

The Significance Level (α) and Conclusion

The *P* for a two-tailed test with equal variances assumed is .2513, and the *P* for the one-tailed test is .1256. Let $\alpha = .05$. Because $P > \alpha$, we fail to reject the null hypothesis, and we conclude

Table 12–7

Results of a Two-Sample *t* Test Assuming Equal Variances

	MATH group	Non-MATH group
Mean	3.090909091	1.52
Variance	28.27705628	15.34333333
Observations	22	25
Pooled variance	21.37907071	
Hypothesized mean difference	0	
df	45	
t stat	1.162221906	
P (T <= *t*) one-tail	.12563618	
t critical one-tail	1.679427442	
P (T <= *t*) two-tail	.25127236	
t critical two-tail	2.014103302	

Screen 12–7

The TTEST Procedure for Tests Assuming Equal Variances.

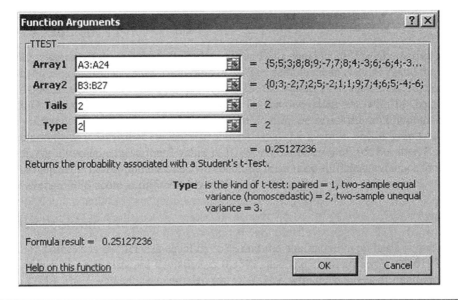

there is no sufficient evidence to indicate that the average test score improvements of the MATH group and the non-MATH group are different for a two-tailed test. For a one-tailed test, we conclude that there is no sufficient evidence to indicate that the average score improvements in the MATH group is greater than that in the non-MATH group.

This finding indicates that, if we conclude that the MATH program improved the test score, the chance that this conclusion is wrong is 12.56% (the *P* for the one-tailed test). It also shows that, although the sample averages of the two groups show a difference of 1.57 points (i.e., 3.09 − 1.52) in improvement, the difference may not exist if the program is extended to all students.

Based on the above conclusion, a recommendation can be made to discontinue the program, to continue the MATH program to gather more data, or to continue the program with more intensified intervention strategies (e.g., more study times or more workshops in the MATH curriculum).

Comparing Two Independent Performance Proportions

After an initiative to improve service quality this year, a county government wants to know if the initiative has any impact on citizens' satisfaction for the county's service. According to a survey, 308 of 350 respondents were satisfied with the service last year before the initiative, and 234 of 260 citizens surveyed were happy with the service this year. The survey is confidential. Names of respondents are not gathered so there is no way to pair the 2 groups of respondents. The 2 samples are independent. The satisfaction rates were 308/350 = 88% last year and 234/260 = 90% this year. These sample satisfaction rates show an increase in citizen satisfaction. However, are the rates really different among all residents? We need a hypothesis test to answer this question.

Hypotheses

The null hypothesis in this example is that the satisfaction rates of these 2 years are the same. The alternative hypothesis is that the satisfaction rates are different for a two-tailed test and that the satisfaction rate this year is greater than that last year for a one-tailed test.

Let π_1 denote the proportion for the first population and π_2 the proportion for the second population. The null hypothesis is that two population proportions are the same or $\pi_1 = \pi_2$ or $\pi_1 - \pi_2 = 0$. The alternate hypothesis is that two population proportions are different or $\pi_1 \neq \pi_2$ or $\pi_1 - \pi_2 \neq 0$ for a two-tailed test or that $\pi_2 > \pi_1$ or $\pi_2 < \pi_1$ for a one-tailed test.

Test Statistic

The test statistic is *t* statistic for two sample proportions, $\hat{\pi}_1$ and $\hat{\pi}_2$, with sample sizes n_1 and n_2, calculated from the following equation:

$$t = \frac{\hat{\pi}_1 - \hat{\pi}_2}{\hat{\sigma}_d}.$$

In the equation, $\hat{\sigma}_d$ is the standard error of the test, estimated from

$$\hat{\sigma}_d = \sqrt{\frac{\hat{\pi}_1(1-\hat{\pi}_1)}{n_1} + \frac{\hat{\pi}_2(1-\hat{\pi}_2)}{n_2}}.$$

In our example, $\hat{\pi}_1 = 0.88$ and $n_1 = 350$; $\hat{\pi}_2 = 0.90$ and $n_2 = 260$. Therefore,

$$\hat{\sigma}_d = \sqrt{\frac{0.88(1-0.88)}{350} + \frac{0.90(1-0.90)}{260}} = 0.02545.$$

Then, the t is

$$t = \frac{\hat{\pi}_1 - \hat{\pi}_2}{\hat{\sigma}_d} = \frac{0.88 - 0.90}{0.02545} = -0.7858.$$

The t is negative in this example because $\hat{\pi}_1 - \hat{\pi}_2$ is negative or $\hat{\pi}_2 > \hat{\pi}_1$ (the satisfaction rate this year is larger than that last year). If we reverse the positions of $\hat{\pi}_1$ and $\hat{\pi}_2$ in the t formula, we then have a positive t value, shown as follows:

$$t = \frac{\hat{\pi}_2 - \hat{\pi}_1}{\hat{\sigma}_d} = \frac{0.90 - 0.88}{0.02545} = 0.7858.$$

Both calculations of the t are correct because they both indicate that $\hat{\pi}_2 > \hat{\pi}_1$ (90% is larger than 88%). You just need to be aware of how the t statistic formula is set up.

P-value, Significance Level, and Conclusion

The P-value is calculated from the Excel Insert Function TDIST procedure shown in Screen 12–8, with $n_1 + n_2 - 2$ degrees of freedom or $350 + 260 - 2 = 608$ in this example. Recall that the TDIST does not take a negative t value, so we place a positive value 0.7858 in the window for the t (again, it is the x window in screen 12–8). The P for both 0.7858 and −0.7858 are same because the t distribution is symmetric. The two-tailed P is .4323, and the one-tailed P is .2162.

Let $\alpha = .05$. Because $P > \alpha$, we fail to reject the null hypothesis. We conclude there is no sufficient evidence to indicate that that the satisfaction rates of these 2 years are different (two-tailed) or that the satisfaction rate improves this year (one-tailed).

A Case Study

Spring Park Health Foundation (SPHF) is a nonprofit organization that offers programs aiming at the mental and the physical health of school-age children. The foundation receives most of its funding from private donations. It serves a suburban area of about 300,000 residents and 16 schools. One SPHF program is Children in Shape (CIS), an educational program designed

Screen 12–8

t Test for Two Independent Proportions.

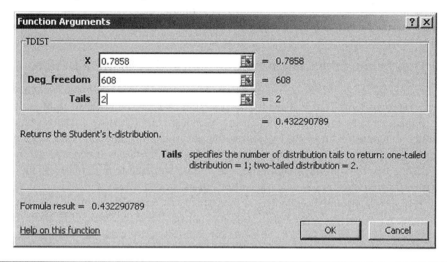

to convey the awareness about healthy eating and the harm of unhealthy foods. The goal of the program is to improve participating students' physical health and fitness.

Step 1: Defining the Issue

The CIS offers the students a healthy eating lecture and a healthy eating school lunch program; it also conducts workshops to provide teachers and parents with the latest knowledge on nutrition. To measure the program's performance, schools have collected data of body mass index (BMI) and data from a nutrition consumption survey. The self-reported survey shows students have eaten healthier. A trend analysis shows that, on average, students consume 7% more vegetables, 10% more fruits, and 6% less foods of fat–oil–sweet over the last 4 years. However, the BMI data show no significant improvement.

One theory that explains the nonexistence of BMI improvement concerns physical activities. According to the theory of the reasoned action, health improvement occurs only when a long-term behavioral pattern is established. To improve the BMI, a student must not only respond immediately to the program by eating better, but also develop a long-term behavior pattern that sustains the improvement. One indicator of such long-term behavioral change is the increase of physical activities.

It has been discussed by SPHF managers to include a new component in the CIS that emphasizes the importance of daily physical activities. The physical activity component (PAC) includes the addition of a physical activity module in the healthy eating lecture. Also, the program adopts a math curriculum in which teachers include physical activity information in their math lecturing and exercises for students.

The addition of the PAC is expensive, and no one is completely sure if it works. Thus, SPHF managers decide to experiment it in one school first. If it works, the concept will then be expanded to other schools. In order for the result to be representative, SPHF selected a middle school whose students mostly come from the middle-class families in the SPHF service area. The experimental school has about 400 students.

Step 2: Determining the Evaluation Question and Evaluation Design

Nancy Grace is the program evaluator for SPHF. She knows that the ultimate outcome of the PAC is to improve BMI. That is a long-term goal that may not be realized right way, so she decides to measure the change of physical activities of the participating students, which is an intermediate outcome for the PAC. She uses the percentage of students who have physical activities at least 1 hour a day for the past month—the activity rate—to measure the impact of PAC, believing that the improvement of the activity rate will lead to the improvement of BMI. Thus, her evaluation question is, has the activity rate changed after the PAC.

The PAC has been implemented for a year since last year. The activity rate of students was obtained in August last year before the PAC and in May this year after the PAC for a pretest–posttest single group design. The data for the design are collected through a student–parent survey. In the survey, a student and the parents are asked to answer questions regarding physical activities of the student. All students in the experimental school participated in the PAC, but only 137 students and their parents completed the surveys twice for two paired samples (dependent samples).

Step 3: Conducting the Analysis

In August last year before PAC, 76 of the 137 surveyed students had physical activities at least 1 hour a day on average for an activity rate of 76/137 = 55.5%, and in May this year after the PAC, 85 of the 137 (62.0%) had that level of physical activities. Table 12–8 shows the data.

Because the 2 samples are dependent proportions, the McNemar test is proper. The test statistic is $\chi^2 = (22 - 13)^2/(22 + 13) = 2.314$. The P is .128 for the statistic with 1 degree of freedom. Let the significance level α be .05. Because $P > \alpha$, we fail to reject the null hypoth-

Table 12–8

Percentage of Students Working Out an Hour or More Daily

		This year		
		No	**Yes**	**Total**
Last year	No	39	22	61
	Yes	13	63	76
	Total	52	85	137

esis, and we conclude there is no sufficient evidence to indicate that the PAC has changed the students' levels of physical activities.

Step 4: Making Recommendations and Actions

Clearly, an activity rate improvement from 55.5% to 62.0% does not provide enough evidence statistically to support the PAC. Some SPHF staff argue that if the significance level α were at the .150 level, the null hypothesis would be rejected, and it would be concluded the PAC might increase the physical activities of students. However, Nancy believes that an error of .150 is too high. She estimates that the PAC is costing the foundation about $100,000 a year. She needs strong evidence to show that the money is well spent, and there is reason to expand the PAC to other schools. Therefore, Nancy recommends that the PAC will be continuously implemented at the current experiment school for 1 more year to generate more data for an analysis to obtain more conclusive results.

Practices

Key Terms

Matched (paired) samples (dependent samples)
Independent samples
Comparing two dependent performance means
t test for two dependent samples (test procedures for the mean)
Statistical significance
Managerial significance
Comparing two dependent performance proportions
McNemar test for two dependent proportions (test procedures)
Comparing two independent performance means
t test for two independent sample means
Comparing two independent performance proportions (test procedures)
Excel Data Analysis for t Test: Paired Two Sample for Means
Excel Insert Function TTEST procedure for paired samples
Excel Data Analysis: t Test with Two-Sample Assuming Unequal Variances
Excel Insert Function TTEST procedure for a two-sample t test assuming unequal variances
Excel Data Analysis: t Test with Two-Sample Assuming Equal Variances
Excel Insert Function TTEST procedure for a two-sample t test assuming equal variances

Practice Problem 12–1

Global Assessment Functioning Score (GAF) has been used to measure the psychological status of students. A high school counseling program funded by a nonprofit health care organization has used GAF to assess the improvement of the participating students. GAF is obtained before and after the program. Table 12–9 shows the GAF of 10 students selected from the program.

Table 12–9

Global Assessment Functioning Scores in a High School Counseling Program

Student ID	Before initiative	After initiative
1	57	53
2	44	42
3	55	65
4	62	65
5	61	68
6	65	75
7	38	46
8	51	60
9	61	64
10	45	49

Table 12–10

Service Satisfactions of 80 Residents

		After the initiative		
		Satisfied	Unsatisfied	Total
Before the	Satisfied	38	12	50
initiative	Unsatisfied	20	10	30
	Total	58	22	80

Conduct a hypothesis test to evaluate if the program improves GAF. Explain your test results to the director of the organization who has no idea what hypothesis testing is.

Practice Problem 12–2

A focus group of 80 citizens has been followed up with 2 surveys of their satisfaction after a city implemented an initiative to improve communication with the residents. Citizen satisfaction data are reported in Table 12–10. Conduct a hypothesis test that the satisfaction rate changes after the initiative.

Practice Problem 12–3

Conduct the following experiments. In the first experiment, choose one of your favorite locations away from your home. It could be a supermarket, a shopping mall, or a playground.

Choose the route you normally use. Record how much time it takes you to get there in minutes. On your way back, take a different route and count the time in minutes. Record your travel times for 10 trips so you have 2 samples with 10 cases of travel times. Conduct a hypothesis test to assess the mean difference of these 2 samples after the route change. In this experiment, make sure you drive the same vehicle and at approximately the same time of a day to rule out the impact of these confounding variables on travel time. The route change can be seen as an everyday life equivalent of a PEI.

In the second experiment, choose the route you often use from home to the favorite location. Start recording your travel times to there up to 10 times (in minutes). Then, choose an alternative route and record your travel times to there up to 10 times (in minutes). Conduct a hypothesis test to assess the mean difference of these 2 samples. In this experiment, make sure you drive the same vehicle and at approximately the same time of day to rule out the impact of these confounding variables on travel time. The change of the route can be seen as an everyday life equivalent of a PEI.

What are the differences between these two experiments? Are the samples from these two experiments different? Do you conduct different types of *t* tests?

Practice Problem 12–4

The human resource department in a large county government has conducted a training program to improve recruitment performance. Table 12–11 shows the number of days to fill open positions before and after the training. A sample of 15 positions before the training and a sample of 20 positions after the training are selected for analysis.

Conduct a hypothesis test(s) to assess if the training improves the recruitment performance of the department. Explain your test results to the director of the department who knows nothing about hypothesis testing.

Practice Problem 12–5

An education campaign had been carried out by a city's parks and recreation department to encourage its residents to conserve water. The campaign includes a series of workshops on gardening and environmental protection. The workshops are open to the public free of charge. Also, a monthly newsletter is sent to citizens to introduce water conservation methods. A survey was mailed out to water users before and after the program to assess the performance of the campaign in increasing residents' willingness to conserve water. A 6-point measure is developed to measure a citizen's willingness to conserve water, with 6 being the most willing and 1 being the least willing. Table 12–12 shows the results from two samples of residents surveyed.

Conduct a proper hypothesis test(s) to assess if the campaign increases residents' willingness to conserve water. Make recommendations based on test results. (Hint: To conduct a test of the mean difference, you need to assume that the willing to conserve water is an interval variable.)

Table 12–11

Number of Days to Fill a Position

Before training	After training
42	43
38	26
41	35
32	29
29	45
36	34
33	34
26	28
20	20
54	20
32	20
41	23
32	22
32	32
38	28
	17
	35
	37
	28
	48

Table 12–12

Residents' Willingness to Conserve Water

Before campaign	After campaign
2	4
3	2
5	4
2	3
4	5
3	2
3	3
4	4
2	4
3	6
5	4
4	4
3	2
2	4
3	4
3	5
2	5
2	5
3	5
4	5
	3
	3
	3
	3
	5

Practice Problem 12–6

A university administration has implemented a strategy to improve the graduation rate, defined as the percentage of enrolled students who graduate after a period considered as the standard length of study. The strategy includes increasing courses offered, offering online courses, and increasing penalties for prolonged stay in the program.

Of 1232 students surveyed before the strategy was implemented, 665 graduated within the standard length of study. Of 1064 students surveyed after the strategy was implemented, 638 met the standard. Conduct a hypothesis test to see if the graduation rate improves. Explain your test results to the university president who knows little about hypothesis testing.

CHAPTER 13

Comparing More Than Two Performance Samples

R ecall that, in an example in Chapter 12, we learned how to compare 2 independent performance samples in a math training program (MATH) designed to improve students' math performances. In that example, a group of students participating in the MATH training program were tested before and after the program, and their math score improvements were compared with those of non-MATH students in a control group. Both the MATH and non-MATH groups were matched on their pretest math scores to ensure both groups were at the same learning stage. Both groups have the same average math score of 56.47 in the pretest.

There are 22 students in the MATH group and 25 in the non-MATH group. Suppose that there are 11 girls and 11 boys in the MATH group, and 10 girls and 15 boys in the non-MATH group. There are fewer girls and more boys in the non-MATH group. This gender discrepancy in the control group could become a confounding variable. How? Assume that girls generally perform better in the posttest than boys (or vice versa). Then a greater score improvement in the MATH group may be caused by the discrepancy in the gender composition of the 2 groups, not by the math training.

To eliminate the impact of the gender composition as a confounding variable, you construct a second control group with a similar gender composition of the MATH group. Now, you have three samples in comparison: the MATH group and two control groups. This chapter discusses tools of comparing more than two performance samples.

Creating a Comparison

The evaluation designs to construct more than two performance samples are discussed in Chapter 11. They include trend comparison designs, pretest–posttest designs with multiple control groups, and posttest designs with multiple control groups. In a trend comparison design, multiple samples can be drawn from the same group over time. For example, to assess the impact of a budget increase on crimes, you can measure crime rates multiple times before and after the budget increase to observe crime rate changes. The trend comparison design does not involve a control group though. If you have multiple control groups, such as those in the MATH example above, you have either a pretest–posttest design with multiple control groups or a posttest design with multiple control groups.

There are two obvious benefits of collecting more than just two samples. First, you will have more choices in comparison. Take the case of three samples. There are four possible comparisons as shown in Table 13–1. Multiple comparisons allow you to gain more performance improvement information than a single two-sample comparison.

Second, a trend comparison design with multiple observations over time can help you assess the *long-term impact of a PEI* on performance. Imagine that you conduct a training program to improve workers' skills in your organization, and it takes a long time for the trainees to master these skills. You will not see the immediate improvement in workers' productivity. However, if you can measure their productivity over time, you may be able to detect the long-term impact of the training.

The samples in comparison can be independent or dependent. You can observe the performance of a same group multiple times to create dependent samples, or you can draw the independent samples from different groups. This chapter first discusses the tools for dependent samples, followed by those for independent samples.

Comparing Dependent Performance Samples (Repeated Measurements)

In Chapter 12, we used an example of water billing errors to conduct a two-sample comparison in which we compared the number of water billing errors before and after a billing system update for the same 20 customers, creating a comparison of two dependent samples. Now, let us say that, a few months later after the previous two samples, we want to check on the reporting errors again just to make sure everything is going well. We collect the data of the errors for the same 20 water billing accounts. The data of this second inspection after the system update are reflected in Table 13–2 along with the data of the previous two samples.

In statistics, the design that extracts more than two matched samples is known as a design of *repeated measurements*. Now we have three matched (dependent) samples. Let μ_1, μ_2, and μ_3 be population average numbers of errors before the update, the first inspection after the update, and the second inspection after the update, respectively. There are two different ways to compare these three averages. You can pair μ_1 against μ_2, μ_1 against μ_3, and μ_2 against μ_3, respectively, in which you create three separate two-sample t tests on the null hypotheses that

Table 13–1

Possible Comparisons of Three Samples

Sample 1 vs. Sample 2
Sample 1 vs. Sample 3
Sample 2 vs. Sample 3
Sample 1 vs. Sample 2 vs. Sample 3

Table 13–2

Number of Errors in Water Bills (Repeated Measurements)

Water bill account	Inspection before system update	First inspection after update	Second inspection after update
1	0	0	0
2	1	0	0
3	2	1	1
4	0	2	0
5	2	0	1
6	1	0	1
7	2	0	1
8	1	0	1
9	1	1	2
10	1	1	0
11	0	1	0
12	0	0	0
13	1	1	0
14	1	0	1
15	1	0	0
16	2	1	0
17	2	1	0
18	3	1	1
19	1	0	0
20	1	1	0

$\mu_1 = \mu_2$, or $\mu_1 = \mu_3$, or $\mu_2 = \mu_3$. We saw this type of comparison in Chapter 12. The other way is that you compare all μ_s simultaneously to test a null hypothesis that $\mu_1 = \mu_2 = \mu_3$, which is that the average numbers of errors are the same all three times. This section discusses this type of comparison.

Intuitively, rejecting $\mu_1 = \mu_2 = \mu_3$ is more difficult than rejecting any one of $\mu_1 = \mu_2$, $\mu_1 = \mu_3$, or $\mu_2 = \mu_3$, though the math derivation process of this proof is beyond this book. In other words, proving μ_1 is different from μ_2 *and* μ_3 is more difficult than proving μ_1 is different from either μ_2 *or* μ_3.

Hypotheses, Test Statistic, and *P*-value

In the billing error example, the null hypothesis is that the average billing errors are the same for all the three inspections. The alternative null hypothesis is at least one average is different. The test statistic comes from an *F* test of repeated measurements. The *F* statistic can be calculated from Excel Data Analysis ANOVA: Two-Factor Without Replication. In the **Data Analysis Window**, select **ANOVA: Two-Factor Without Replication**. It is very important that the Input Range includes the first column of the data that represent the billing account ID and the variable names (labels) in the first row, shown in Screen 13–1.

The Excel output should include an ANOVA table, as shown in Table 13–3. To understand where the F value comes from, you may want to review the concept of variance in Chapter 5 first. The calculation of the F value involves a comparison of variances of rows, columns, and errors. The row variance represents the variance of individual cases (i.e., each billing account in our example), while the column variance is the variance of the 3 samples (20 billing accounts in each sample).

Realize that, in our hypothesis, we test that average billing errors are the same for all three times of inspections whose samples are the three columns of the data. So the hypothesis concerns the comparison of the columns. In other words, we need to obtain the F value for the columns, which involves a comparison of the averaged variances of columns and errors in the following fashion:

$$F = \frac{\text{MS}_{\text{columns}}}{\text{MS}_{\text{error}}}.$$

$\text{MS}_{\text{columns}}$ is the mean square of columns and MS_{error} is the mean square of errors. To obtain the mean square of the columns, you need first to calculate the sum of squares for the columns ($\text{SS}_{\text{columns}}$), defined as $\text{SS}_{\text{columns}} = \sum_i n_i (\bar{Y}_i - \bar{Y})^2$. In this equation, n_i is the number of cases in column i (i = 1, 2, 3 in this example), and $\bar{Y}_i$ is the mean of the column. $\bar{Y}$ is the mean of all cases, known as the grand mean; Σ is the summation sign. In our example, we have 20 cases in each column, so n_i = 20. The grand mean is 0.717. The mean for column 1 ($\bar{Y}_1$) is 1.15. The means for column 2 ($\bar{Y}_2$) and column 3 ($\bar{Y}_3$) are 0.55 and 0.45, respectively, so $\text{SS}_{\text{columns}}$ is $20(1.15 - 0.717)^2 + 20(0.55 - 0.717)^2 + 20(0.45 - 0.717)^2 = 5.73$. You then divide it by the degrees of freedom of the column (df_{columns} = the number of columns − 1) to obtain the mean square of the columns ($\text{MS}_{\text{columns}}$). Because there are 3 columns in this example, the degrees of freedom are 3 − 1 = 2; therefore, $\text{MS}_{\text{columns}}$ is 5.7333/2 = 2.8667.

Billing accounts also supply variance. Each account's overall mean, the average of the three cases for each account, varies from the grand mean. These data are in rows so their

Table 13–3

Calculating the F in Repeated Measurement

			ANOVA			
Source of Variation	**SS**	**df**	**MS**	**F**	**P-value**	**F crit**
Rows	10.85	19	0.571053	1.391026	.189189	1.867331
Columns	5.733333	2	2.866667	6.982906	.002614	3.244821
Error	15.6	38	0.410526			
Total	32.18333	59				

Screen 13–1

The Excel Procedure for Repeated Measurement.

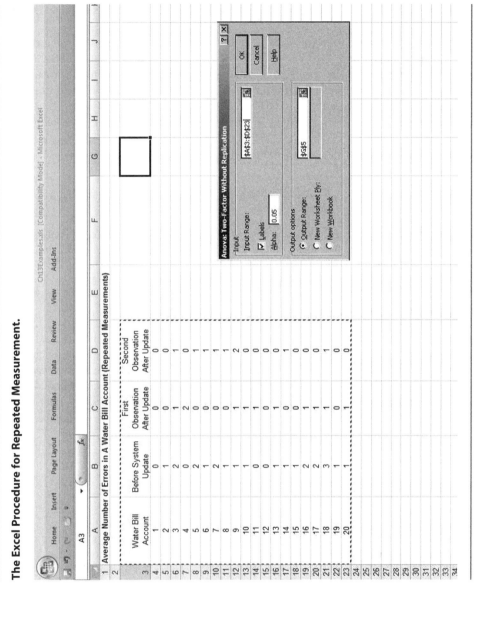

Average Number of Errors in A Water Bill Account (Repeated Measurements)

Water Bill Account	Before System Update	First Observation After Update	Second Observation After Update
1	0	0	0
2	1	0	0
3	2	1	1
4	0	2	0
5	2	0	1
6	1	0	0
7	2	0	1
8	1	1	1
9	1	0	2
10	0	1	0
11	0	0	0
12	1	1	0
13	1	0	1
14	1	0	0
15	2	1	1
16	2	1	0
17	3	1	1
18	1	0	0
19	1	1	1
20	1	1	0

Anova: Two-Factor Without Replication

Input
Input Range: $A$3:$D$23
☑ Labels
Alpha: 0.05

Output options
◉ Output Range: $G$5
○ New Worksheet Ply:
○ New Workbook

OK
Cancel
Help

variance is called the *sum of squares for the rows* or SS_{rows}. It is 10.85 (see Table 13–3 for this statistic).

The sum of squares for errors (SS_{error}) is the variance left over after you subtract variances in columns and rows from the total variance (i.e., $SS_{error} = SS_{total} - SS_{columns} - SS_{rows}$). The total variance is measured by the total sum of squares (SS_{total}), which is the total variance in all 60 cases from the grand mean in this example. SS_{total} is 32.18 (see Table 13–3 for this statistic). We know $SS_{columns}$ is 5.73 and SS_{rows} is 10.85, so SS_{error} is $32.18 - 5.73 - 10.85 = 15.60$.

The mean square of errors (MS_{error}) is the SS_{error} divided by the degrees of freedom for errors (df_{error}), which is $df_{total} - df_{rows} - df_{columns}$ and $59 - 19 - 2 = 38$. So, MS_{error} is $15.60/38 = .4105$. The F for columns in our example therefore is

$$F = \frac{MS_{columns}}{MS_{error}} = \frac{2.8667}{0.4105} = 6.9829.$$

The P-value associated with the F statistic is .002614. The Excel printout gives the F for a P-value equal to .05, which is also known as the critical F value or F crit in the Excel output in Table 13–3.

The Significance Level and Conclusion

Let the significance level $\alpha = .05$. Because $P < \alpha$, we reject the null hypothesis that the average billing errors for all 3 inspections are the same. We conclude that there is sufficient evidence to indicate that, of the 3 inspections, at least 1 has a different billing error average. Because the sample billing error averages are 1.15 before the system update and .55 and .45 after the system update, we have some evidence that the billing error average is less after the system update. This finding suggests that the system update changes the average number of billing errors.

Comparing Independent Performance Samples (One-Way ANOVA)

Recall that, at the beginning this chapter, we constructed a second control group to evaluate the impact of a math training program, MATH, on students' math performances. This second non-MATH group is designed to match the gender composition of the MATH group in order to eliminate the possible impact of gender discrepancy on math scores. Assume that this second control group consists of 23 non-MATH students. Now we have 2 control groups—one matching the MATH group by the pretest score, and another matching it by the gender composition. With these 2 control groups, we can eliminate the confounding impact of the learning stage and gender composition on math performance. Table 13–4 shows the math score improvements of these 3 groups. Does the MATH program improve math scores after controlling for these 2 factors?

Table 13–4

Math Score Improvement (Posttest Score – Pretest Score)

MATH Group	Non-MATH Group 1 (matched by pretest score)	Non-MATH Group 2 (matched by gender composition)
5	0	−3
5	3	0
3	−2	1
8	7	2
8	2	0
9	5	6
−7	−2	2
7	1	−2
8	1	5
4	9	−4
−3	7	5
6	4	2
−6	6	−3
4	5	5
−3	−4	4
−7	−6	0
2	2	−1
0	0	7
1	2	−1
9	−3	0
6	2	1
9	−2	3
	2	1
	4	
	−5	
Average 3.09	Average 1.52	Average 1.30

Hypotheses

The three groups contain different students, constituting three independent samples. Let μ_1, μ_2, and μ_3 be population average score improvements for the MATH Group, the non-MATH Group 1 (matched by pretest scores), and the non-MATH Group 2 (matched by gender composition), respectively. Realize that we can conduct two different types of comparisons to find out if the MATH program improves test scores. In the first type of comparisons, we can conduct two separate t tests that compare μ_1 with μ_2 or μ_1 with μ_3, testing a null hypothesis that $\mu_1 = \mu_2$ or $\mu_1 = \mu_3$. This type of two-sample comparison is discussed in Chapter 12.

The second type involves a comparison of all μ_s simultaneously to test a null hypothesis that $\mu_1 = \mu_2 = \mu_3$. That is, the population means are the same for all groups. This section presents this test. The null hypothesis in our example is that the average score improvements are the same for all three groups. The alternative null hypothesis is at least one average improvement is different. As mentioned above in testing dependent samples, rejecting $\mu_1 = \mu_2 = \mu_3$ is more difficult than rejecting any one of $\mu_1 = \mu_2$ or $\mu_1 = \mu_3$. Proving μ_1 is different from μ_2 *and* μ_3 is more difficult than proving μ_1 is different from μ_2 *or* μ_3.

Test Statistic

The test static, the F value from an F test with independent samples, can be calculated from Excel Data Analysis ANOVA: Single Factor. Statisticians also call this hypothesis test *one-way ANOVA*. In the Excel Data Analysis Window, select **ANOVA: Single Factor.** Screen 13–2 shows the Excel procedure. It is important that you include all the data when selecting the Input Range.

The Excel output should include a printout of the ANOVA table, as shown in Table 13–5. The first part of the table presents descriptive statistics of the three groups. The derivation of the F value, shown in the bottom part of the table, involves calculating several differences in the samples. These differences are measured by variances in a manner similar to that discussed above in comparing dependent samples.

The first concept you need to know is the *within-groups difference*. This is the difference between individual scores in each group and the mean of each group, measured by the variance

Table 13–5

Excel Output Tables of ANOVA Single Factor

SUMMARY				
Groups	**Count**	**Sum**	**Average**	**Variance**
MATH Group	22	68	3.090909	28.27706
Non-MATH Group 1 (matched by pretest score)	25	38	1.52	15.34333
Non-MATH Group 2 (matched by gender)	23	30	1.304348	9.130435

ANOVA						
Source of Variation	**SS**	**df**	**MS**	**F**	**P-value**	**F crit**
Between groups	42.84368154	2	21.42184	1.234181	.297604451	3.133763471
Within groups	1162.927747	67	17.35713			
Total	1205.771429	69				

Screen 13–2

The Excel Procedure for One-Way ANOVA.

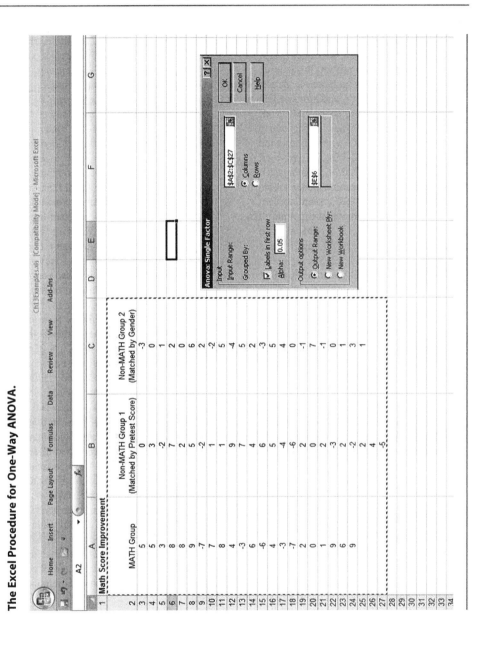

of the group. In our example, the average score of the MATH group is 3.09, the within-groups difference of this group is the variance from $(5 - 3.09)^2 + (5 - 3.09)^2 + (3 - 3.09)^2 \ldots (9 - 3.09)^2 = 593.82$. This difference, along with the with-groups differences of the 2 control groups (368.24 and 200.87), are added up to 1162.93 (i.e., $593.82 + 368.24 + 200.87$), which is known as the *within-groups sum of squares* or SS_w; and SS_w is used to define the *within-groups mean squares* or MS_w in the following manner:

$$MS_w = \frac{SS_w}{N - g}.$$

The number of cases in all 3 samples is N, and g is the number of groups. $N - g$ is the degrees of freedom for within-groups differences. It is $22 + 25 + 23 - 3 = 67$ in our example. So,

$$MS_w = \frac{1162.93}{67} = 17.3571.$$

Another important concept is the *between-groups difference*. This is the difference between the group means and the overall mean of all individual scores (the grand mean). It is estimated from a statistic called the *between-groups sum of squares* or SS_b, defined as $SS_b = \sum_i n_i (\bar{Y}_i - \bar{Y})^2$.
In this equation, n_i is the number of cases for group i ($i = 1, 2, 3$ in this example), and $\bar{Y}_i$ is the mean of the group. The grand mean of all cases is $\bar{Y}$, and Σ is the summation sign. In our example, we know that the mean scores are 3.09 for the MATH Group, 1.52 for non-MATH Group 1, and 1.30 for non-MATH Group 2. The grand mean of all 70 scores is 1.9429. So SS_b is $22(3.09 - 1.9429)^2 + 25(1.52 - 1.9429)^2 + 23(1.30 - 1.9429)^2 = 42.8437$. The measure of the between-groups difference, the *between-groups mean squares* or MS_b, is defined as

$$MS_b = \frac{SS_b}{g - 1} = \frac{42.8437}{3 - 1} = 21.4218.$$

In the equation, $g - 1$ is the degree of freedom for this measure. Therefore, the F value is

$$F = \frac{MS_b}{MS_w} = \frac{21.4218}{17.3571} = 1.2342.$$

Let us see why the use of the F value makes sense in this test. The essence of one-way ANOVA is to compare the between-groups difference measured by MS_b with the within-groups difference measured by MS_w. Everything else being equal, a larger between-groups difference leads to a larger F and a smaller P, making it more likely to reject the null hypothesis and to conclude a difference exists among groups. In our example, to expect that the MATH improves math scores, the score difference between MATH and non-MATH groups (i.e., the between-groups difference) should be large in relation to the difference within each group.

P-value, the Significance Level, and Conclusion

The *P*-value for the *F* (1.2342) is .2976 in this example. Let $\alpha = .05$. Because $P > \alpha$, we fail to reject the null hypothesis, and we conclude that there is no sufficient evidence to indicate that at least one group has a different score improvements average. This conclusion indicates that, though the sample averages show greater improvements of MATH students from the first control group (3.09 − 1.52 = 1.57) and the second group (3.09 − 1.30 = 1.79), there is not enough evidence in these samples to indicate that a difference exists in population. If we conclude that a difference exists in population, we have a 29.76% chance of being wrong.

A Case Study

The information and technology department (ITD) in a large urban county is responsible for purchasing, installing, and maintaining the county government's communication and networking equipment and infrastructures, for developing and updating the county's Web site, and for providing a repository of the county's electronic databases. ITD serves 11 departments in the county government and has 10 employees including the director, the assistant director, 7 computer technicians, and a receptionist.

Step 1: Defining the Issue

ITD uses several performance measures to assess the achievement of its mission to provide reliable and relevant technology, training, and support for the county's departments and employees. One measure is the rate of repeated repair requests, known as the *triple-R rate* (RRR). When a user encounters a technology-related problem, he or she sends an electronic message to ITD. An ITD technician is assigned to fix the problem within 24 hours. The problems range from software application issues to network hardware malfunction. A repeated repair request occurs when the problem is not addressed to the satisfaction of the user, and a request to correct the same problem is made to the ITD within a week upon the completion of the technician's first visit. The RRR rate is the proportion of the number of repeated repair requests in total initial requests. For example, a 10% RRR rate indicates that, of 100 initial requests, 10 receive repeated requests from users for the same repairs. A higher RRR indicates a worse performance of ITD.

Because of strong competition from the private sector for the skillful computer workers, the technicians in ITD have a high turnover rate. Oftentimes, new employees are hired in a rush to fill the positions left by technicians who left the organization. Newly hired technicians sometimes lack the knowledge on the network and technologies used by the county government. Many believe that the high turnover is the reason for a high RRR rate at ITD. To address this underperformance, ITD decided to implement a training program 4 years ago for its technicians. The training covers the latest technologies and their applications adopted by the county government. The vendors and the ITD directors serve as instructors or mediators in these training sessions conducted once a month or upon request. ITD technicians are required to participate in the training. Other county employees are also encouraged to attend.

Step 2: Determining the Evaluation Question and the Evaluation Design

The ITD director, Mr. Jerry Tewd, wants to know if the training has improved the RRR rate. He collects the data of the past 4 years, shown in Table 13–6, which are broken down by each department.

The average RRR rate for all 11 departments before the training was 12%. The average RRR rate improved to 7% in the 1st and the 2nd year, but declined a little to 8% in the 3rd year after the training. This data pattern suggests that the department's performance, measured by the RRR rate, has improved after the training; however, the data also cause a concern that ITD may not sustain a same rate of improvement over time. Does the performance improvement happen by chance? Can the department sustain this improvement for long? What is the chance that the performance decline in the 3rd year reoccurs in the future?

To answer these questions, Jerry needs to treat the data as sample RRR rates from a longer time and conduct a hypothesis test. He can conduct two-sample comparisons between the rate before the training and that of each year after the training. However, the training is conducted continually for 3 years, so it is more interesting to compare the rates simultaneously and over time to assess the continuous and long-term improvement. Jerry's evaluation question is: Has the rate changed over time for the past 3 years? The RRR rate is observed 4 times over time to constitute a trend comparison design with 4 samples. Because the rate is measured on the same subjects (departments) to create 4 matched (dependent) samples, the statistical tool for repeated measurements is proper.

Step 3: Conducting the Analysis

Table 13–7 shows the results from an F test of the 4 dependent samples. The P for a null hypothesis that the average RRR rates are equal all 4 times is .0058. Let the significance level

Table 13–6

Annual Rates of Repeated Repair Requests

Department	Year before training	1st year after training	2nd year after training	3rd year after training
1	0.23	0.12	0.18	0.18
2	0.16	0.01	0.03	0.11
3	0.18	0.00	0.09	0.07
4	0.14	0.03	0.06	0.07
5	0.08	0.14	0.09	0.07
6	0.09	0.05	0.05	0.06
7	0.02	0.03	0.03	0.05
8	0.14	0.12	0.07	0.04
9	0.09	0.08	0.08	0.01
10	0.08	0.05	0.00	0.09
11	0.12	0.10	0.04	0.10
Average	0.12	0.07	0.07	0.08

Table 13–7

Results of the Test of Repeated Measurements for the RRR Rate

			ANOVA			
Source of variation	**SS**	**df**	**MS**	**F**	**P-value**	**F crit**
Rows	0.05355	10	0.005355	3.611219	.00304975	2.16458
Columns	0.022589	3	0.00753	5.077654	.00581368	2.922278
Error	0.044486	30	0.001483			
Total	0.120625	43				

$\alpha = .05$. Because $P < \alpha$, Jerry rejects the null hypothesis that the average RRR rates in these 4 years are the same. He concludes that there is sufficient evidence to indicate that at least 1 average rate is different. From the data, it is clear that the rate has improved after the training. A same result is drawn from t tests that compare the RRR rate before the training with rates in the 1st year after the training (P for one-tailed test = .016441), in the 2nd year after the training (P for one-tailed test = .000995), and in the 3rd year after the training (P for one-tailed test = .004375). Jerry concludes that the rate has changed over time.

Recall that the average RRR rate was 8% in the 3rd year after the training; it is a 1% decline from the 7% in the previous year. Jerry conducted a t test that compares the RRR rates of these 2 years. The result shows that there is no sufficient evidence to indicate that the rate declined (P for one-tailed test = .2200) at the .05 significance level. This 1% decline may not occur in the future.

Step 4: Drawing Conclusion and Recommendation

Jerry concludes that the training has indeed improved the performance of ITD. He recommends a continuation of the training and asks the county manager to include permanently a line item of the training cost in the county administration's budget proposal. He also recommends that the RRR rate be closely monitored and that this same analysis be performed every year.

Practices

Key Terms

Long-term impact of a PEI
Comparing dependent performance samples (hypothesis testing procedures)
Repeated measurements
Excel Data Analysis ANOVA: Two-Factor without Replication
Comparing independent performance samples (hypothesis testing procedures)

One-way ANOVA
Within-groups difference
Within-groups sum of squares
Within-groups mean squares
Between-groups difference
Between-groups sum of squares
Between-groups mean squares
Excel Data Analysis ANOVA: Single Factor

Practice Problem 13–1

A city's park and recreation department uses the number of unsafe or hazardous spots to measure its performance in maintaining playground safety in its 5 parks. Two years ago, after a widely publicized safety incident in a city's park, the department implemented a set of new rules in maintenance to ensure playground safety. Table 13–8 shows the number of unsafe or hazardous spots found in each inspection in the past 3 years.

Treat the data as random samples and conduct a hypothesis test to assess if the new rules change the performance of the department in maintaining playground safety.

Practice Problem 13–2

A major traffic control system was installed 2 years ago in a major traffic intersection to improve the traffic. The monthly number of major traffic accidents has been reported. Table 13–9 reports the data for the past 3 years.

Table 13–8

Number of Unsafe or Hazardous Spots Found in Each Inspection in City's Parks

Two years ago	Last year	This year
24	15	21
32	23	29
21	27	21
26	21	22
32	33	15
21	21	22
14	19	12
34	21	
	12	
Mean = 25.50	Mean = 21.33	Mean = 20.29

Table 13–9

Monthly Number of Major Traffic Accidents in a Major Intersection

	Before new system	1 year after new system	2 years after new system
January	2	3	1
February	4	5	3
March	5	4	2
April	1	0	1
May	2	1	1
June	2	1	1
July	5	2	2
August	4	4	5
September	2	1	2
October	4	3	5
November	2	1	1
December	4	2	5
Average	3.08	2.25	2.42

Table 13–10

Daily Number of Accidents Per 1000 Students

School 1	School 2	School 3
3.82	6.58	9.47
1.01	0.59	4.86
5.96	7.00	8.65
8.99	7.17	5.54
8.85	7.83	6.45
5.54	8.68	2.71
0.14	1.17	8.63
4.07	5.50	9.30
7.65	6.84	7.37
1.39	4.09	7.09

Let μ_1, μ_2, and μ_3 be the monthly averages before the new system, 1 year after the system, and 2 years after the system, respectively. Treat the data as samples. Conduct 2 separate hypothesis tests of $\mu_1 = \mu_2$ and $\mu_1 = \mu_3$ to discover any difference in the accident rates since the system installation. Does the system reduce the accident rate? Conduct a hypothesis test of $\mu_1 = \mu_2 = \mu_3$ to assess if the system changes the traffic accidents. Are your conclusions from these 2 types of hypothesis testing different? If they are different, could you explain why?

Practice Problem 13–3

Table 13–10 shows the daily number of clinic accidents per 1000 students in 3 high schools. The data were collected in 10 randomly selected days in each school. These days are not the same for the 3 schools. The measure is used to assess the performance of a school health care program in School 1, which is funded by a nonprofit foundation as an experiment to reduce clinic accidents among school-age children. The employees in the health care program conduct regular health care education workshop to students and teachers. Conduct a proper hypothesis test(s) to assess if the program in School 1 changes or reduces the number of accidents in the school.

Section VI

Conclusion

CHAPTER 14

Conclusion: Writing a Performance Analysis Report

There are many ways to communicate the result of a performance analysis to people: a conversation, a presentation, a meeting, or even a news conference. However, a written report is a primary means. A well-prepared report not only shows the seriousness of the analysis and allows the reader sufficient time to digest the result, it also leaves a trace of records for possible follow-up studies.

Reports differ in purposes and scopes. A report aimed at discovering causes of underperformance requires more technical or statistical analyses than a weekly monitoring exercise that tracks the routine of daily operations. Besides, the author of a report may have his or her own points of emphasis in analysis and writing. In spite of these differences, there are commonly accepted guidelines in report writing that should make the delivery of the information effective. This chapter presents these guidelines.

Report writing is a process of generating or refining ideas that benefit the decision making in management. The stakeholders of an organization (e.g., managers, elected officials, nonprofit board members, or concerned citizens or customers) must be kept involved from the start of the writing. It is important to inform stakeholders about the progress of the writing, to establish their expectations for the delivery time, and to urge them into allocating enough time for reading and digesting. It is also important to deliver at least one round of a draft before the final report to obtain the stakeholders' feedback. A draft report gathers stakeholders' feedback that should benefit the writing of the final report, and it also allows the stakeholders additional time to think over and to digest the results of the analysis.

A report may have multiple reader groups of managers, legislators, citizens, auditors, business owners, or nonprofit board members. Their knowledge about an organization varies greatly. An assumption should be made that readers have interests in an organization's operations and performance but no working knowledge of statistics, performance management theories, performance measurement, and performance analysis designs. The statistical and mathematical calculations of a report should be kept minimal to allow the reader an easy access to the findings of the report. In general, a completed performance analysis report should constitute the following components:

- an executive summary
- an introduction
- a discussion of the theory and/or the design
- a discussion of data collection
- a section on results
- a section of conclusions and recommendations

This chapter presents important principles in writing these components by discussing what should be done (do's) and what should be avoided (don'ts) in the report. An example of a performance evaluation is presented to illustrate the use of these principles.

Writing the Executive Summary

This is a summary of the report's purpose, key findings, conclusions, and recommendations. It gives the reader a quick overview of the report. It also illuminates the value of the report, helping the reader develop an interest in reading the whole report.

Do's

- Name the organization, the program, the initiative, the process, or the activity whose performance is being analyzed.
- State the purpose and the importance of the analysis.
- State the key analysis question(s).
- Present the key findings and conclusions.
- Present key recommendations.

Don'ts

- Do not exceed one page. Be concise.
- Do not elaborate the theory in the analysis.
- Do not discuss data collection method(s).
- Do not include tables or graphs unless necessary.

Example

The Healthy-Eating Awareness Development (HEAD) program is designed to improve school-age children's health through healthy consumption of foods. The program is funded by the nonprofit Summerfield Foundation. This analysis examines the impact of HEAD on participating students' consumption of fruits and vegetables in Summerfield Elementary School in 2005, 2006, 2007, and 2008. The analysis attempts to find out if HEAD has increased students' consumption of fruits and vegetables.

The result shows an increased consumption of fruits and vegetables during the study period, although the improvement eroded after 2007. The finding suggests that HEAD results in students' healthier consumption, although efforts should be made to sustain the impact over time.

The analysis team recommends that the foundation continue to provide funding for the HEAD program. The team also recommends an intensified intervention in later years of HEAD by actively involving parents and teachers in the program. In addition, the team recommends that the foundation develop a database that allows the analysis team to examine the potential impact of food consumption on body mass index (BMI) and academic performance of students.

Writing the Introduction

This section allows the reader to understand what the analysis is and why the analysis is needed.

Do's

- Introduce the reason(s) for the analysis.
- Introduce the organization, the program, the initiative, the process, or the activity whose performance is being analyzed.
- State the purpose of the analysis.
- State the analysis question(s).
- Specify the analytical objective of the analysis—whether this analysis is performance description, performance monitoring, performance understanding, or performance evaluation.
- Discuss the importance (the need) of the analysis.

Don'ts

- Do not exceed more than two pages. Be concise.
- Do not discuss the theory, the design, and the data collection method.
- Do not present analysis results.
- Do not include tables or graphs unless necessary.

Example

Obesity among school-age children has become prevalent in the United States. The latest research links child obesity with high consumption of foods in fats, oils, and sweets and low consumption of fruits and vegetables. The Healthy-Eating Awareness Development (HEAD) program is designed to influence students' food consuming behaviors by implementing program activities based on the latest research on the brain and nutrition. The program is funded by Summerfield Foundation and targets students in Summerfield Elementary School.

Based on the latest research, the program designs a series of curriculum and extracurricular activities that promote healthy eating among the students in Summerfield Elementary School.

This performance analysis examines the impact of these activities on participating students' food consumption. HEAD program data were analyzed to answer the following question: has HEAD increased participants' consumption of fruits and vegetables.

This is a performance evaluation that assesses the outcome of a performance enhancement initiative in HEAD. The result of this performance evaluation can be used to develop effective strategies in health care education to improve school-age children's physical health and possibly academic performances.

Writing the Theory and/or the Design

You may want to review Chapter 2 on what a performance theory is, why it is needed, and how to develop it. A theory is particularly important for a performance analysis that focuses on performance understanding (Chapters 8 to 10) or performance evaluation (Chapters 11 to 13). In a performance evaluation like the example in this chapter, a theory helps explain why a performance enhancement initiative (the HEAD program in this case) may impact the performance.

Do's

■ Discuss the theory of performance analysis. Clearly specify the relationship between the performance and the causes in an analysis that emphasizes performance understanding. In a performance evaluation, specify how the performance enhancement initiative affects the performance.
■ Thoroughly present the organization, the program, the initiative, the process, or the activity whose performance is being analyzed. Provide the information about the organizational structure, the human resources, and the financial resources of the organization or program being analyzed.
■ Discuss the design used in performance evaluation.

Don'ts

■ Avoid the use of technical jargon. Remember you are writing for a layperson whose knowledge on performance analysis is limited. If you have to use a term unfamiliar or abstract to the reader, define and explain it.
■ Avoid lengthy discussions. If the complexity of the theory or the design requires a lengthy discussion, consider placing part of it in an appendix.
■ Do not get involved in detailed discussion on data collection methods.
■ Do not discuss findings.

Example

The development of HEAD activities is based on the latest research that links nutrition intake, particularly fruits and vegetables, with the physical health and academic performance of school-age students. The Behavior-Action theory suggests that the nutrition consumption of school-age children affects their brain and physical development. Consistent and sufficient healthy food intake from vitamin-rich fruits and vegetables may improve children's physical health and brain functions. The research also suggests that healthy students may be less likely to miss classes and more likely to improve their academic performance at school.

Based on this theory, HEAD has developed a series of activities aiming at promoting consumption of healthy foods among students at Summerfield Elementary. Consultants are used to train teachers and students about current research regarding nutrition and exercises as well as the effects of healthy eating habits on a child's capacity to learn and to perform at school. Healthy nutrition advisement is used in developing and revising the menu at the school cafeteria, which provides more choices of fruits and vegetables. The foundation also funds the menu revisions to include more vegetable-rich snacks at the cafeteria. Moreover, the program provides a Health Math curriculum that incorporates healthy eating examples and cases in teaching mathematical principles. Finally, the program funds a program director position to administer the program, to coordinate the efforts, and to conduct program evaluation and assessment.

In addition to the program director position, the program also hires 3 part-time nutrition consultants. HEAD has been in place in Summerfield Elementary since 2005. The program has been operated on an annual budget of $100,000. Due to the increasing popularity of this program, the Summerfield Foundation is interested in expanding HEAD into other schools in its service region. Nonetheless, before making the financial commitment of expansion, the foundation wants to know the impact of HEAD in Summerfield Elementary.

We, a team of analysts, are tasked to conduct this analysis. This is a performance evaluation that assesses the impact of a performance enhancement initiative (i.e., HEAD). The analysis tests the Behavior-Action theory in a local setting at Summerfield Elementary. To observe the possible impact of HEAD, we adopt a trend comparison design to gather the consumption data for fruits and vegetables 4 times—once before HEAD was implemented in August 2005 and 3 times after HEAD was implemented in August of 2006, 2007, and 2008. The same students' consumptions are measured, constituting the data for repeated measurements. This design allows us to compare the consumption over time to observe the impact of HEAD for a relatively long time.

Writing the Data Collection

This section of the report should discuss how the measures are developed, what data collection methods are used, and how data are collected.

Do's

- Describe what measures are used to assess the performance and causes of the performance (underperformance). If necessary, use a table to list all measures used. If there is a long list of measures and the development of these measures is complex, use an appendix for the listing and the method of development.

- Describe the data collection method. For example, if a survey is conducted, describe who is surveyed, how many people are surveyed, and how many of them respond to the survey. If archival data are used, describe who collects the data, how the data are collected, and how often the data are collected.
- Attach the data collection instrument at the end of the study. If a survey, an interview protocol, or a protocol for archive search is developed, include it in an appendix.

Don'ts

- Do not include the study instrument in the text.
- Avoid lengthy discussion on the measurement development and the data collection method. Keep the descriptions of the data collection methods concise.
- Avoid the use of technical jargon.

Example

The period of data collection effort spans 3 years, from August 2005 to August 2008. Sixty Summerfield Elementary School students reported their nutrition consumption all 4 times in August 2005, 2006, 2007, and 2008. Consequently, these students were included in the analysis. This sample excludes new students admitted into Summerfield during the study period to ensure the elimination of possible bias as the result of changes in the sampling frame.

During data collection, participants were asked to select their food intake for breakfast, lunch, dinner, and snacks. An instrument that includes 96 food pictures helped them make selections. This instrument is attached to this study in an appendix. The selections were then classified into food pyramid categories of fruits or vegetables, as well as fats–oils–sweets, milk, meat, and bread–cereal–rice–pasta. A combination category was also used.

One selection of a food item from the food pyramid pictures is defined as one serving of the food intake. A participating student's food intake of fruits and vegetables at breakfast, lunch, dinner, and snacks is aggregated to arrive at the daily number of servings in fruits and vegetables, which is the primary measure of the performance for the HEAD program.

Writing the Results

This section presents the results of a performance analysis. It often constitutes the major part of a report.

Do's

- Present analytical results.
- Present the results in a sequential order of descriptive statistics of each variable (also known as univariate analysis), bivariate analysis, and multivariate analysis. For example, say that you examine how students' academic performances are affected by study efforts and study methods. There are three variables in the study: academic performance, study efforts, and

study methods. In presenting the results, you should first present descriptive statistics (i.e., the mean, the median, the mode, and the standard deviation) of each of these three variables separately (Chapters 3 to 5). Then, you analyze the bivariate relationship between study efforts and academic performance and the bivariate relationship between study methods and academic performance (Chapter 9). Finally, you develop a multivariate analysis to examine how both study efforts and study methods affect academic performance simultaneously (Chapters 10).

Don'ts

- Avoid jargon. Try to write as if talking to a layperson who has no knowledge about performance analysis and statistical tools.
- Do not discuss managerial–policy implications or recommendations. The Result section presents findings from the analysis. The managerial–policy implications or recommendations should be included in the Conclusion section.
- Avoid inaccurate or misleading results. Be precise and accurate in the presentation. Statistical significance is not managerial significance, and statistical evidence is not enough for changes of policies or managerial practices. Failing to reject the null hypothesis does not mean the acceptance of the null hypothesis. Failing to reject the null hypothesis can be as informative for performance improvement as rejecting it.
- Do not manipulate results. Let the data speak. Do not go on a mission to prove something. Do not write results to please a specific stakeholder (e.g., the sponsor of the analysis).
- Do not present unnecessary analyses. If the purpose of the analysis is to simply track the performance, there is no need to examine the causes of the performance. Use the right analytical or statistical tool. Avoid the tendency to use more advanced tools. Remember, a simpler tool is always better than the advanced one if both are sufficient to answer the analysis question.

Example

This analysis examines the number of daily servings of fruits and vegetables of 60 Summerfield students from 2005 to 2008. Of the 60 students in the sample, 27 are male (45%) and 33 (55%) are female. The gender distribution is shown in Figure 14–1. Of the students in the sample, 18 were in the 1st grade (30%) and 42 in the 2nd grade (70%) in August 2005 when the data collection of this analysis started.

Table 14–1 shows the average daily servings of fruits and vegetables for all students in the sample in August 2005, 2006, 2007, and 2008. The results show that students consumed an average of 2.54 servings of fruits in August 2005 before HEAD was implemented. The consumption increased to 3.75 servings in August 2006 during the 1st year of HEAD implementation, resulting in an average increase of 1.21 (i.e., 3.75 − 2.54) in servings. This is a 1.21/2.54 = 47.6% increase (improvement). Nonetheless, the consumption has declined since August 2006, by 2.7% in August 2007 and by an alarming 17.0% in August 2008.

The data also show that students consumed more vegetables during the study period. Students on average consumed 1.53 servings of vegetables a day before HEAD in August 2005,

Figure 14–1

Gender Distribution of the Students.

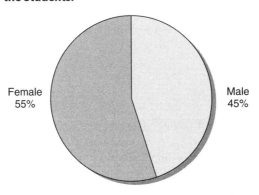

Female
55%

Male
45%

Table 14–1

Average Daily Servings for Fruits and Vegetables of 60 Summerfield Students in the HEAD Program

	August 2005	August 2006	August 2007	August 2008
Fruits	2.54	3.75 (47.6%)	3.65 (−2.7%)	3.03 (−17.0%)
Vegetables	1.53	2.05 (34.0%)	2.43 (18.5%)	2.48 (2.1%)

The growth rates are in parentheses. For example, the average daily fruit servings were 2.54 in August 2005 and 3.75 in August 2006. This is an improvement of 1.21 (i.e., 3.75 − 2.54) servings. The fruit consumption increased by 1.21/2.54 = 47.6% from 2005 to 2006 by that measure.

while their consumption increased to 2.48 servings per day 3 years after HEAD was implemented in August 2008. However, the rate of improvement has slowed from 34.0% during the 1st year of HEAD in August 2006 to 18.5% in August 2007 and only 2.1% in August 2008.

Hypothesis tests are conducted to compare the consumption differences over time, as the data are treated as a sample. The result from a *t* test of 2 dependent samples shows that the difference in fruit consumptions between 2005 and 2006 is statistically significant at the .05 level, indicating that HEAD may have increased students' fruit consumptions in the 1st year of implementation. Nonetheless, the result from a *t* test that compares the fruit consumption between 2005 and 2008 shows that the difference is not statistically significant at the .05 level, indicating the HEAD has difficulty sustaining students' fruit consumptions surge in the long term.

Vegetable consumption increased from 1.53 servings in 2005 before HEAD to 2.48 servings 3 years after HEAD in 2008, and this difference is statistically significant at the .05 level, based on a t test of 2 dependent samples. The average daily consumption difference between 2005 and 2006 as well as that between 2006 and 2007 are also statistically significant at the .05 level. These results suggest that HEAD increases participating students' vegetable consumptions.

Moreover, an F test of repeated measurements shows that students' average consumptions in fruits and vegetables have changed during the study period, and the change is statistically significant at the .01 level, providing further evidence that HEAD may improve participating students' consumptions in fruits and vegetables.

Writing the Conclusions and Recommendations

This section summarizes the key findings and draws conclusions of the analysis. It also discusses the managerial implications and recommendations based on the findings.

Do's

- Summarize the key findings.
- Discuss the managerial implications of each finding.
- Present managerial recommendations of each finding.
- Discuss methodological limitations of the study.

Don'ts

- Do not discuss the theory, the design, the measurement, and the data collection method. Be concise in writing. Think more, write less.
- Do not misinterpret or overstretch a finding while discussing its implications and recommendations. A relationship does not mean causation. Statistical significance does not necessarily guarantee managerial merit.

Example

This analysis examines the impact of HEAD on the nutrition intake of 60 students attending Summerfield Elementary School. It analyzes students' reported consumptions of fruits and vegetables in August 2005, 2006, 2007, and 2008. The results show that students eat more fruits and vegetables since HEAD was implemented in August 2005. Nonetheless, the increase in consumption for vegetables has slowed, and the consumption for fruits has even declined since 2006. These results suggest that HEAD increases school-age students' consumption of healthy foods, but the improvement is short term.

These findings have several managerial implications for HEAD. First, the Summerfield Foundation should consider the continuation of the funding for HEAD because it may have significant positive impact on students' health. Second, managerial strategies should be developed to sustain the positive impact of the HEAD program over the long run. The results indicate that the healthy eating message delivered by HEAD may fade away over time among some students who may go back to their old dietary habits of eating unhealthy foods. Therefore, HEAD should intensify its current efforts to stress the need of long-term healthy eating. HEAD consultants should emphasize the long-term benefit of a healthy diet. One possible strategy of intensification is to actively involve parents and teachers in HEAD activities in order to create a culture of healthy eating among students and their families.

Finally, new HEAD activities should be developed to sustain the benefit of a healthy diet and to keep students interested in such a diet. HEAD consultants may want to frequently change and update the healthy food menu in school cafeterias, introducing new healthy food items to generate students' interests. HEAD consultants should update their knowledge of nutrition on a regular basis and learn how to deliver that knowledge effectively to teachers and students.

This analysis has a few methodological limitations. First, it has a relatively small sample of 60 students. Future analyses should consider a larger sample. Second, the sample is collected in a single school. The result may not apply to the programs in other schools that are demographically different from Summerfield Elementary. Third, the evaluation uses a single group. Future evaluations should consider the creation of a control group to rule out the impact of some confounding variables (e.g., the national trend of healthy diet, peer impact) on consumption. Finally, this analysis uses students' self-reported measures of food consumption, which could be subjective and unreliable. Future analyses should consider more objective measures such as BMI as the performance measure of HEAD. Data of student academic measures should also be collected in the future to test any possible link between healthy eating behaviors and academic achievements.

Appendix A
Statistical Topics, Coverage, and Excel Procedures

Statistical Topic	Chapter of Coverage	Excel Procedure
Mean	3	Insert Function (f_x): AVERAGE or Data Analysis Descriptive Statistics
Median	3	Insert Function (f_x): MEDIAN or Data Analysis Descriptive Statistics
Mode	3	Insert Function (f_x): MODE or Data Analysis Descriptive Statistics
Frequency	3	Data Analysis Histogram
Percentage	3	Data Analysis Histogram
Cumulative percentage	3	Data Analysis Histogram
Variance	5	Insert Function (f_x): VAR and VARP or Data Analysis Descriptive Statistics
Standard deviation	5	Insert Function (f_x): STDEV and STDEVP or Data Analysis Descriptive Statistics
z-score	5	Insert Function (fx): STANDARDIZE
Empirical rule	6	Insert Function (f_x): AVERAGE and STDEV
z-score for confidence interval	7	Insert Function (f_x): NORMSINV
t-score for confidence interval	7	Insert Function (f_x): TINV
Probability and probability distributions	7	Insert Function (f_x): NORMSINV or TINV
Sampling	7	Data Analysis Sampling or Data Analysis Random Number Generation
Data sorting	9	Sort and Filter group on the Data tab
Data selection	9	Insert Function (f_x): COUNTIF
Contingency table creation	9	Insert Function (f_x): COUNTIF

(continued)

Statistical Topic	Chapter of Coverage	Excel Procedure
Correlation analysis	9	Insert Function (f_x): CORREL, or PEARSON, or Data Analysis Correlation
Hypothesis testing procedures and the t test	9	Insert Function (f_x): TDIST
Chi-square (χ^2) test	9	Insert Function (f_x): CHIDIST or CHITEST
Simple regression	10	Data Analysis Regression
Multiple regression	10	Data Analysis Regression
One-sample testing	11	Insert Function (f_x): TDIST
Two-sample tests for two dependent samples	12	Insert Function (f_x): TTEST or Data Analysis t-Test: Paired Two Sample for Mean. Insert Function (f_x): CHIDIST
Two-sample tests for two independent samples	12	Insert Function (f_x): TTEST or Data Analysis t-Test: Assuming Equal Variance (or Unequal Variance). Insert Function (f_x): TDIST
Test of more than two dependent samples (repeated measurements)	13	Data Analysis ANOVA: Two-Factor without Replication
Test of more than two independent samples (One-Way ANOVA)	13	Data Analysis ANOVA: Single Factor

Appendix B
Answers to Practice Problems

Chapter 2

Practice Problem 2–4

1. Interval
2. Interval
3. Interval
4. Interval
5. Ordinal
6. Interval
7. Ordinal
8. Interval
9. Ordinal
10. Interval
11. Nominal
12. Interval

Chapter 3

Practice Problem 3–1

1. The majority of units (60%) collected less than 40,000 tons of trash a year. Most of the units (90%) picked up less than 50,000 tons annually. The units with a collection between 30,001 and 40,000 tons are more than any other collection range (40%).
2. The average of trash collected by a unit was 38,200 tons annually. The median was 38,000 tons annually, where half of the units collected more, and the other half had less. The mode is not available because no 2 units collected the same amount of trash.

Practice Problem 3–2

1. The park had an average of about 17 visitors daily, but the average is largely skewed by 2 extreme values, 100 and 150. The park might have held some special events in these 2 days that attracted many visitors. In half of the days, the park had 4 or fewer visitors (median = 4). In a typical day, there were 3 visitors in the park. Clearly, the use of average is biased to represent the performance of the park.
2. I choose performance ranges of 0 to 3 visitors, 4 to 5, 6 to 10, and more than 10. I choose 3 and 5 as the boundaries because 3 is the mode and the data show that the park had 5 or fewer visitors in many days. The results of the Excel Histogram process show that the park saw 5 or fewer visitors in the majority of the days (64%). In 80% of the days, the park had 10 visitors or fewer. The park had 3 or fewer visitors in 36% of the days.
3. These results support the city manager's suspicion about the low attendance rate of the park, so the budgetary reduction may be considered if the current park budget request exceeds its service need. Nonetheless, because there are days when there are a large number of visitors for special events, the city may want to consider hiring temporary workers on these days. Also, if the park's budget is reduced, the city needs to show willingness to allocate supplemental funds in the case of the special events in the park that will attract more visitors.

Practice Problem 3–3

1. The average daily number of clinic visitors is about 8 people (7.59). The median number of daily number of visitors is 8, so is the mode (in 20 of the 90 days the clinic saw 8 visitors).
2. I choose 6 and 9 as boundaries because, according to the condition given in this problem, they were used in reporting last year's data. So I use the performance ranges of 5 and below, 6 to 9, and more than 9.
3. The clinic saw 6 to 9 visitors for 58.89% of the days. In 80% of the days, it saw 9 or fewer visitors. In 20% of the days (18 of the 90 days), it had 10 or more visitors. This result supports the nurse's observation that there has been an increase in the number of clinic visitors, and the nurses have been seeing more visitors more frequently this year.

Practice Problem 3–4

If you have nonnumerical measures in your database, the first thing you do in Excel analysis is convert them into numeric measures. I use a numeric scale 1 to 5 for student satisfaction ratings, and 1 for males and 2 for females. After the conversion, I use Excel to obtain the descriptive information about the student satisfaction and gender. The analysis results indicate that 60% (i.e., 35% + 25%) of students surveyed are either satisfied or very satisfied with the services. But still, 25% of students are either dissatisfied or very dissatisfied with the service. On average, student satisfaction rating (3.5) is between satisfied (4) and neutral (3). The median satisfaction rating is 4.0. More students (7 or 35% of the students surveyed) are satisfied with the service than any other rating categories (the mode = 4). The results also show that 45% (9 of 20) of students surveyed are male and 55% are female students. Because gender is a nominal variable, it does not make sense to interpret the mean and the median, although Excel calculates them. The mode of the gender is 2 (the female students).

Chapter 4

Practice Problem 4–1

1. The response time in this question is an average measure. So the growth rate is a proper measure. Realize that the response time is a measure of negative performance, with a greater value indicating a performance decline. The calculation for the growth rates should be easy with Excel. For example, the growth rate for the most urgent incidents is 3.79% [i.e., (5.48 − 5.28)/5.28] for the 2nd year, suggesting a performance decline in that year.
2. You may want to make two graphs, one for the average response times and one for the growth rates. In making the growth rate graph, you may want to set zeros for the growth rates at Year 1 to have an equal start for different response times, which allows proper graphical presentation effects.
3. The response time average for the most urgent incidents has improved for the past 4 years after a performance decline in Year 2, constituting a positive performance trend. On average, the response time for the most urgent incidents has shortened (improved) at an average annual rate of 3.51% for the past 5 years, with the largest improvement occurring this year for 10.26% improvement or an average response time shortening of 0.52 (i.e., 5.07 − 4.55) minutes. The response average of every year in the past 5 years has been better than the city's performance goal of 6.00 minutes.

   The average response for the urgent incidents was stable around 7.15 minutes for the first 3 years, but deteriorated rapidly at Year 4 to 8.69 minutes (22.39% deterioration). Although there is an improvement of 5.06% this year (Year 5), the average response for the urgent incidents is still worse than the performance benchmark of 8.0 minutes. This analysis indicates that the response to urgent incidents is an area for further performance improvement.

   The presentation of response data for nonurgent incidents does not show a clear trend, although there was a significant performance improvement in Year 4 when the average response was shortened by 11.53% or 1.5 (i.e., 13.01 − 11.51) minutes. The average response this year (Year 5) worsened slightly but was still better than the responses of the first 3 years. The data appear to support 2 conclusions. First, because all responses are longer than the performance goal of 11.00 minutes, there is room for continual performance improvement. Second, the fact that there was a large improvement in Year 4 and the performance did not worsen largely in Year 5 indicates that the response is on track to improve, so a close monitoring for more data is needed.

Practice Problem 4–2

1. The only measure of performance in this question is the treatment success rate. The other two measures, the number of staff and the program budget, are input measures. Input mea-

sures are not performance measures. Because the success rate is a percentage measure, both the percentage ratio and the percentage difference are applicable.

2. You should be able to present the percentage differences and the percentage ratios of the last 5 years.

3. The results should demonstrate the performance change of the program for the past 5 years. The success rate improved from 42% to 55% from Year 2 to Year 3, and the rate seems to be stabilized around 50% since then, which is a significant improvement. A participant's chance to succeed has improved from 40% 5 years ago to 54% this year, for a 35% (i.e., 54%/40% − 100%) improvement over 5 years. In other words, a program participant's chance of success is 35% greater today than it was 5 years ago. The largest improvement occurred in Year 3, when the percentage ratio increased to 130.95%, indicating that a program participant's chance of success increased by 30.95% from the previous year. Although both percentage ratios and percentage differences show some fluctuation of performance after that (particularly during Year 4 when a decline of performance is observed over the previous year), it appears that the success rate stabilizes above 50%.

Practice Problem 4–3

3. The PCI condition change can be measured by the growth rate, which should show that there was a whopping 45.1% PCI improvement in Year 2, and the improvement has been slow but continual since then. Effort should be made to explore the reason of the drastic improvement in Year 2 for possible future performance enhancements.

   The continual improvement of the PCI index does not reflect in citizen satisfaction rating, which actually has declined for the past 3 years from 63% to 55%, constituting a negative performance trend during the period. This clearly points out an area for further improvement.

Practice Problem 4–4

3. The percentage of responses less than 4 minutes in total responses has declined for the past 7 months from 26% in January to 18% in July, for a negative performance trend. Note that this is a measure of positive performance so a downward trend indicates a performance decline. There is an 8% performance decline from January to July (the percentage difference = 26% − 18% = 8%). In addition, the city's performance after March falls behind the city's performance benchmark that 25% of the responses are within 4 minutes. These results indicate room for performance improvement.

   We also saw a decline in the percentage of responses between 4 and 6 minutes for the past 7 months except in the month of April. The responses less than 6 minutes (48% in July) fall far behind the city's benchmark of 60%. Combined with the findings about responses less than 4 minutes, we can conclude that the city's performance in medical responses has deteriorated for the past 7 months. The rate of deterioration measured by the percentage difference is 8% for the responses less than 4 minutes and 12% for responses less than 6 minutes.

   The sign of the performance decline is further manifested by the increase in responses of more than 6 minutes. The responses between 6 and 8 minutes have gradually increased from 24% (i.e, 84% − 60%) in total responses in January to 26% (i.e., 74% − 48%) in July. More importantly, the responses of more than 8 minutes have increased sharply from 16% (i.e.,100% − 84%) in total responses in January to 26% (i.e.,100% − 74%) in July. Clearly, the city needs to reduce the number of responses of more than 8 minutes to improve its overall performance of medical responses.

Chapter 5

Practice Problem 5–1

1. The overall mean of all 4 groups is 5.15, and the standard deviation is 2.84. The means for Offices A, B, C, and D are 5.42, 4.17, 5.67, and 5.33, respectively. The standard deviations for them are 2.64, 2.62, 2.74, and 3.42. The variances are 6.99, 6.88, 7.52, and 11.70. Assessed by the mean, Office C has the worst record and should be retrained first, followed by Offices A, D, and B. However, Office D's mean (5.33) and standard deviation (3.42) are larger than the overall mean of all groups (5.15) and the overall standard deviation (2.84), indicating a substandard and unreliable performance. So there should be consideration to retrain workers in Office D first.
2. Use the STANDARDIZE in Excel Insert Function for the calculation. The largest z-score is 1.71, which occurred 3 times when the number of errors was 10. The smallest z is −1.46, which also happened 3 times when there was only 1 error.

Practice Problem 5–2

1. Follow the police response example in the text of this chapter to complete this question. The possible comparisons in the monitoring include the monthly comparison with the same month last year, the mean so far this year, the mean last year, the variance, the standard deviation, or the range so far this year.
2. The month-to-month comparison shows significant increases in calls in January (503), April (454), and August (577), while the comparison also indicates significant declines in calls in March (429) and September (327). The close monitoring of the changes is needed in the future to identify any change of call patterns in these months. The number of calls peaked during the summer months from May to August, increasing the workload for the dispatchers during this time. There were little month-to-month changes in May and June, the 2 months that had the highest numbers of calls for the past 2 years.

Chapter 6

Practice Problem 6–1

Even if your math skill does not change at all, it is still hard to get two exact same scores for the same test. The one-point difference is likely a random variation that may result from common causes such as the change of testing environment (how quiet the testing room is for example), the change of testing time of the day, or even typos.

Practice Problem 6–2

Make sure the organizational performance you choose is a repeated activity that is measured frequently so that the performance variation can be observed and the causes of the variation can be speculated.

Practice Problem 6–3

With 2 standard deviations used to create the chart, the UPL for the total response time (call-taking time + dispatch time) is 665.09 seconds, and the LPL is 246.71 seconds. Call no.6 has a response time close to the UPL (661 seconds). The delay was apparently caused by an unusual long dispatch time (563 seconds), which is very close to the UPL for the dispatch time (568.15 seconds). A close examination is needed to find the cause of the delay in dispatch for this call. The UPL for the call-taking time is 121.93 seconds, and the LPL is 16.67 seconds. Call no.18 has a call-taking time longer than the UPL (148 seconds). An investigation should be launched to discover the cause of the holdup for this call.

Practice Problem 6–4

The numbers of cases on the 9th day (10 cases) and the 10th day (12 cases) reached to an unusual high for 2 consecutive days. The number of cases on the 10th day is higher than the UPL of a PMC created with the mean and 2 standard deviations (11.85 cases). I would consider issuing warnings in these 2 days. Moreover, the number of cases on the 14th day (14 cases) is also higher than the UPL, and an issuance of warning should be considered on this day too.

Chapter 7

Practice Problem 7–1

The sample mean is 11.90, and the sample standard deviation is 3.90. With a sample size of 250, the stand error is 0.2467. The *t* for a 95% confidence interval is about 1.970 from the TINV function (249 degrees of freedom). The lower bound of the 95% confidence interval is 11.41, and the upper bound is 12.39. We are 95% confident that the true absence rate for all students falls in the interval. Similarly, the *t* for a 99% confidence interval is 2.596. The lower bound for the interval is 11.260, and the upper bound is 12.540. We are 99% confident that the true absence rate is in the interval.

Realize that the lower bound of the 95% confidence interval (11.41) is still higher than the state average (11.30), and the lower bound of the 99% interval (11.26) is very close to the average, which supports the newspaper's allegation that the district has a higher absence rate.

Practice Problem 7–2

The sample mean is 0.4628 (i.e., 895/1934), and the standard error is 0.01134. The *t* for a 95% confidence interval is 1.961 (use TINV for this calculation). The lower bound of the 95%

confidence interval is 0.4405 (or 44.05%), and the upper bound is 0.4850 (or 48.50%). So we are 95% confident that the satisfaction rate is between 44.05% and 48.50%. By a similar calculation process, you should be able to say that we are 99% confident that the rate is between 43.35% and 49.20%.

Practice Problem 7–3

The sample mean is 1.600, and the sample standard deviation is 1.3139. With a sample size of 20, the standard error is 0.2938. The *t* with the degrees of freedom of 19 is 2.0930. We are 95% confident that the accident rate is between 0.9850 and 2.2149. The department should mobilize the system because the upper bound of the interval is higher than the performance standard of 2.00.

Chapter 9

Practice Problem 9–1

The average length of the face-to-face interviews is 3.9 days, and the average length is 4.2 days for the phone interviews. The result shows no evidence that phone interviews speed up the hiring process. An Excel column chart can be used to demonstrate the visual.

Practice Problem 9–2

The contingency table has 3 rows (dissatisfied, somewhat satisfied, satisfied) and 4 columns (less than 3 years, 3 to 6 years, 7 to 10 years, and more than 10 years). Of the customers surveyed, 66.7% (4 of 6) with less than 3 years of experience with the department are unhappy, while 84.62% (i.e., 53.85% + 30.77%) of customers with 7 to 10 years of experience are either somewhat happy or happy. Also, all customers with more than 10 years of experience are either somewhat happy or happy. Therefore, customers' satisfaction appears related to their length with the department.

Practice Problem 9–3

A strong positive relationship between weekly study hour and the score is found ($r = .668$). There appears to be very little relationship between the age and the score ($r = -.003$), and the relationship between the score and the number of classes taken in the program is weak ($r = .138$).

Practice Problem 9–4

A hypothesis test of the correlation coefficient between the weekly study hour and the class score should be conducted. The null hypothesis is that the 2 variables are not associated, and the alternative hypothesis is that they are associated. The *t* statistic is 3.238, and the *P*-value is .00648. At the α-level of .05, because $P < \alpha$, we reject the null hypothesis and conclude that there is sufficient evidence to indicate that the class score is associated with the weekly study hour.

The P-value for the t test of the correlation coefficient between age and the class score is .9923 ($t = -0.0098$), and the P-value for the t test of the correlation coefficient between the number of classes taken and the class score is .6246 ($t = 0.5012$). In both cases, we fail to reject the null hypothesis at the α-level of .05, and we conclude there is no sufficient evidence to indicate that either age or the number of classes taken is associated with the class score.

Practice Problem 9–5

A chi-square test should be conducted. The null hypothesis is that customer satisfaction is not associated with the length of time with the department, and the alternative hypothesis is that they are associated. I use Excel Insert Function CHITEST process to obtain the P-value (.0548). At the α-level of .05, because $P > \alpha$, we fail to reject the null hypothesis, and we conclude there is no sufficient evidence to indicate that a customer's length with the department is associated with his or her satisfaction level with the service. In fact, if you state that there is a relationship between these 2 variables, your chance to make a wrong conclusion is 5.48%. Realize that this conclusion is very different from that in Problem 9–2 when the information is treated as the population information.

Chapter 10

Practice Problem 10–1

1. The model is the performance score = 75.34 + 0.0001495 (expenditure per capita). The performance score is 75.34 once the expenditure per capita is zero. For every $10,000 increase in expenditure per capita, the performance score increases by 1.495 (i.e., .0001495 × 10,000).
2. The r^2 is .1039, indicating that about 10% of variation of the performance score is explained by expenditure per capita. The model's standard error of estimate is 10.46.
3. P-value for the F test is .2827. We fail to reject the null hypothesis at the .05 significance level, and we conclude there is no sufficient evidence to indicate that expenditure per capita is related to the performance score at the .05 significance level (i.e., $\alpha = .05$). P-value for the t test of the slope of expenditure per capita is .2827. Again, we fail to reject the null hypothesis that these 2 variables are associated at the .05 level. It should be concluded that there is no sufficient evidence to say that expenditures per capita affects performance.
4. The examinations of linearity and homoscedasticity are conducted, and no violation of these model assumptions is found.
5. The result of the performance model indicates that resource may not affect performance at the departmental level. A department's performance is affected by factors rather than its level of financial resource. If a conclusion that resource and performance are related is drawn, there is a 28.27% chance that the conclusion is wrong. Even if such a conclusion is drawn, the regression model indicates that an increase in expenditure per capita by $10,000

may only improve performance by 1.495 points. This improvement may be too small to warrant any significant attention for the management.

Practice Problem 10–2

1. The model is performance score = 3.583 − .00000315 (expenditure per capita) + 4.444 (employee performance) + .000757 (personal expenditure per employee) + 82.837 (technical expenditure in total expenditure). The intercept is 3.583, which is the performance score when the values of all independent variables in the model are zeros. You also want to explain the meanings of the slopes. For example, the slope of employee performance is 4.44, indicating that the performance score increases by 4.44 points for each point of increase in employee performance, while the values of all other independent variables are held constant (controlled).

2. The r^2 is .580, indicating that 58% of variation of the performance score is explained by the regression model. Because there are 4 independent variables in the model and also because the number of cases (13) is relatively small, you may consider using the adjusted r^2 (.370), which shows that 37% of variation of the performance score is explained by the regression model. Both the r^2 and the adjusted r^2 in this multiple regression model are larger than the r^2 in the simple regression model in Problem 10–1, indicating that the multiple regression is a better model. The same conclusion should be drawn from the analysis of the standard error of estimate, which is 8.398, smaller than that in the simple regression (10.46).

3. *P*-value is .1032 for the *F* test. At the .05 significance level, we fail to reject the null hypothesis, and we conclude there is no sufficient evidence to show a relationship between the performance score and any of the independent variables in the model. If we draw a conclusion that there is a relationship, we have a 10.32% of the chance to be wrong. Interestingly, contrary to the above finding, *P*-value for the *t* test of the slope of employee performance is .044, smaller than the significance level of .05, and we thus conclude that there is sufficient evidence to indicate that employee performance is related to the performance score. Nonetheless, no other independent variables are found to be related to the performance score at the .05 level. These findings seem to suggest that, among all independent variables in the model, employees' performances may have the largest impact on the performance score; however, more data are needed to draw a more definite conclusion.

4. The residual plots for each independent variable do not show signs of violation of the model's homoscedasticity. A correlation analysis that involves all independent variables does not show signs of multicollinearity. The values of all correlation coefficients are in an acceptable range, while the largest is −.429 between employee performance and technology expenditure.

5. The results of the analysis suggest that employees' performances may affect an organization's performance, but more data are needed to confirm or disallow this conclusion. The model only explains about 37% of the performance variation, indicating that the model misses variables that may affect performance. Efforts should be made to include more variables relevant to the performance score in the model.

Practice Problem 10–3

A scatter plot shows that the relationship appears curvilinear. Reading score improvement slows down after the number of weekly reading hours reaches 2. So a linear model, reading score = 64.58 + 7.09 (reading hours), violates the model assumption of linearity. With an Excel cube root transformation (set power = 1/3 in the Insert Function f_x) of the reading hours, a transformed model, reading score = 56.03 + 23.10 (transformed reading hours), is developed. A scatter plot shows that the relation between the transformed reading hours and the reading scores is linear. The r^2 for the transformed model is .985, better than the r^2 of the untransformed model (.916), which indicates that the transformed model is a better performance prediction model.

Practice Problem 10–4

The analysis should be similar to that in Problem 10–3. You should observe a curvilinear relationship between math study hours and math scores, though the shape of the relationship is different from that in Problem 10–3. The improvement in math scores is slower when the study hours are less than 2 hours a week; the improvement accelerates when the study hours are more than 2 hours. An Excel power transformation (set power = 2 or 3 in the Insert Function f_x) should be used to transform the study hours, making the relationship more linear. The analysis of r^2 should prove that the transformed performance prediction model is a better performance prediction model.

Chapter 11

Practice Problem 11–1

The null hypothesis is that the participants' average PFS is equal to 25. The alternative hypothesis is that it is greater than 25 for a one-tailed test. The sample mean is 27.467, and the sample standard deviation is 5.041. With a sample size of 25, the standard error is 1.302. So the t value is 1.895. From Excel TDIST, the P-value is .0395 for the one-tailed test, with 14 (i.e., 15 – 1) degrees of freedom. At the α-level of .05, because $P < \alpha$, we reject the null hypothesis, and we conclude there is sufficient evidence to indicate that the average PFS is greater than 25. However, for a two-tailed test, the P-value is .0789. At the α-level of .05, because $P > \alpha$, we will fail to reject the null hypothesis, and we conclude there is no sufficient evidence to indicate that the average PFS score is different from 25.

Practice Problem 11–2

The null hypothesis is that RTC is equal to 85%, and the alternative hypothesis is that RTC is greater than 85%. The standard deviation is 0.3571, and the standard error is 0.0198. The t value is 1.358. The P-value for a one-tailed test is .08769, with the degrees of freedom of 324. If $\alpha = .05$, because $P > \alpha$, we fail to reject the null hypothesis, and we conclude there is no sufficient evidence to indicate that RTC is greater than 85%. In other words, you would have an 8.769% chance of being wrong if you concluded that RTC is greater than 85%. Apparently, a sample improvement of 2.69% (i.e., 87.69% − 85%) in RTC is not sufficient to indicate an improvement in population.

Practice Problem 11–3

The null hypothesis is that the error rate is equal to 10%, and the alternative hypothesis is that it is greater than 10% for a one-tailed test. The sample error rate is 11.6% (i.e., 29/250). The t with the information given is 0.843. The P-value for a one-tailed test is .1999, with the degrees of freedom of 249. If $\alpha = .05$, because $P > \alpha$, we fail to reject the null hypothesis, and we conclude there is no sufficient evidence to indicate that the error rate is greater than 10%.

Practice Problem 11–4

The null hypothesis is that the arrest rate is 6.00, and the alternative hypothesis is that it is less than 6.00 for a one-tailed test. The sample mean is 5.03, and the standard deviation is 2.14. With a standard error of .6742 and a sample size of 10, the t is −1.43. The P is .0930 for the one-tailed test (note that Excel TDIST does not take a negative t value so you have to use a positive t of 1.43), with 9 degrees of freedom. At the α-level of .05, because $P > \alpha$, we fail to reject the null hypothesis, and we conclude there is no sufficient evidence to indicate that the arrest rate is less than 6.00.

Practice Problem 11–5

The null hypothesis is that the satisfaction rate is equal to 60%, and the alternative hypothesis is that it is greater than 60% for a one-tailed test. The sample satisfaction rate is 80% (20/25; you need to convert the satisfaction raw scores to percentage). The standard deviation is .490, and the standard error is .098. The t with the information given is 2.041. The P-value for a one-tailed test is .026, with the degrees of freedom of 24. If $\alpha = .05$, because $P < \alpha$, we reject the null hypothesis and conclude that there is sufficient evidence to indicate that the satisfaction rate is greater than 60%.

Chapter 12

Practice Problem 12–1

This is a test to compare 2 paired (dependent) sample means with a null hypothesis that average GAF scores are the same before and after the program. The P-values are .00650 for a one-tailed test and .0130 for a two-tailed test. At the significance level (α) of .05, because $P < \alpha$, we reject the null hypothesis and conclude there is sufficient evidence to indicate that the average GAF score is greater after the counseling program. You can tell the director that the program may improve the average GAF score.

Practice Problem 12–2

The null hypothesis for this test of 2 dependent sample proportions is that the satisfaction rates are the same before and after the city's initiative to improve communication. The McNemar test should be used. The P is .157. At the significance level of .05, because $P > \alpha$, we fail to reject the null hypothesis, and we conclude there is no sufficient evidence to indicate that the satisfaction rate changes.

Practice Problem 12–3

In the first experiment, you match 2 observations of time for each trip for a total of 10 trips so you construct 2 dependent samples. In the second experiment, because the trips are independent in 2 routes, the 2 samples of trip times are independent.

Practice Problem 12–4

This is a test to compare 2 independent sample means with a null hypothesis that average numbers of days to fill a position are the same before and after the training. The P-values are .050 for a one-tailed test and .100 for a two-tailed test with equal variances assumed. With unequal variances assumed, the P-values are .048 for a one-tailed test and .0960 for a two-tailed test. To take a more conservative approach in testing, I choose to use the result from the test with the assumption of equal variance. At the significance level (α) of .05, because P (one-tailed) $= \alpha$, we fail to reject the null hypothesis, and we conclude there is no sufficient evidence to indicate that the average number of days is shortened by the training. You tell the director that, though the comparison of the sample means shows a reduction in the number of days of hiring ($30.20 - 35.06 =$ about 5 days), the difference is not large enough for you to conclude that the reduction really occurs for all recruitment cases. Larger samples may provide more conclusive results.

Practice Problem 12–5

The null hypothesis for this test of 2 independent sample means is that the average willingness scores are the same before and after the program. The P-value is .00812 for a one-tailed alternative hypothesis that the average willingness score is higher after the program. The test assumes equal variances (you should reach the same conclusion from a test assuming unequal variances). At the significance level of .05, because $P < \alpha$, we reject the null hypothesis and conclude there is sufficient evidence to indicate that the average willingness score is higher after the program. The program may improve citizens' willingness to conserve water, and a recommendation to continue the program should be made.

Practice Problem 12–6

This is a test to compare 2 independent proportions with a null hypothesis that graduation rates are the same before and after the strategy. The P-values are .00191 for a one-tailed test and .00382 for a two-tailed test. At the significance level (α) of .05, because $P < \alpha$, we reject the null hypothesis and conclude there is sufficient evidence to indicate that the graduation rate is greater after the strategy. The school should be encouraged to continue the strategy.

Chapter 13

Practice Problem 13–1

The inspections are conducted independently in different years so these 3 samples constitute 3 independent samples. The null hypothesis is that the unsafe or hazardous spot averages are the same for the 3 years, and the alternative hypothesis is that at least 1 average is different. The results of Excel Data Analysis ANOVA: Single Factor show a P-value of .2408. At the significance level (α) .05, because $P > \alpha$, we fail to reject the null hypothesis, and we conclude there is no sufficient evidence to indicate that at least 1 average of the unsafe and hazardous spots is different. The new rules may not change the average number of unsafe and hazardous spots.

Practice Problem 13–2

The samples are dependent samples. The P-value for a t test with a null hypothesis $\mu_1 = \mu_2$ is .0126 for a one-tailed test. At the significance level .05, because $P < \alpha$, we reject the null hypothesis and conclude that there is sufficient evidence to indicate that the accident monthly average 1 year after the new system is lower than that before the new system.

The P-value for a t test with a null hypothesis $\mu_1 = \mu_3$ is .0601 for a one-tailed test. At the significance level .05, because $P > \alpha$, we fail to reject the null hypothesis, and we conclude there is no sufficient evidence to indicate that the monthly accident average 2 years after the system is lower than that before the new system. But, if α is set at the .10 level, we reject the null hypothesis and conclude there is sufficient evidence to indicate that the monthly accident average 2 years after the system is lower than that before the new system. These above results provide evidence that the new system at least works for a period of time.

Interestingly, the result of the test of $\mu_1 = \mu_2 = \mu_3$ shows that the P-value is .1065. Because it is greater than the significance level .05, we fail to reject the null hypothesis that monthly accident averages are equal all 3 times. We further conclude there is no sufficient evidence to indicate that at least 1 monthly accident average is different.

The above two types of hypothesis testing give different conclusions. As stated in the text, the test on $\mu_1 = \mu_2 = \mu_3$ is a more rigorous test in that it makes it harder to reject the null hypothesis (to find the difference) than two-sample t tests do. Despite my inclination to use the more rigorous test in hypothesis testing, I do find it important to be flexible in choosing the test. One obvious advantage of the two-sample t test is that it allows you to specify the direction of the test for one-tailed testing, which is not possible for the F test in repeated measurements.

Practice Problem 13–3

The P-value for a t test using 2 independent samples of Schools 1 and 2 with unequal variances assumed is .2782 for a one-tailed test. At the significance level .05, because $P > \alpha$, we fail to reject the null hypothesis, and we conclude there is no sufficient evidence to indicate that the accident average in School 1 is lower than that in School 2. However, the P-value of a t test using 2 independent samples of Schools 1 and 3 with unequal variance assumed is .0419 for a one-tailed test. At the significance level .05, because $P < \alpha$, we reject the null hypothesis and conclude there is sufficient evidence to indicate that the accident average in School 1 is lower than that in School 3.

As expected from a more rigorous one-way ANOVA test for the difference of average accidents in all 3 schools, the P-value of the F test is .1935. At the significance level .05, because $P > \alpha$, we fail to reject the null hypothesis, and we conclude there is no sufficient evidence to indicate that at least 1 school's accident average is different, which suggests that the program does not change the accident level.

This is another example that two types of tests with the same samples but different hypotheses give different conclusions. You may want to refer to my answer in Practice Problem 13–2 to choose a test of your preference.

Appendix C
Useful Web Sites

M any governments and nonprofits have used performance information in management and decision making. The information in the following Web sites should help you see how this information is used. Many of these addresses were provided by Mr. Mark D. Abrahams of the Abrahams Group (http://www.theabrahamsgroup.com) who shared this information with the members of American Society for Public Administration (ASPA) section on Public Performance and Management (SPPM). Addresses have been updated recently.

Resources

Alfred P. Sloan Foundation, Performance Assessment of Municipal Governments Program
   http://www.sloan.org/programs/govt_projects.shtml
Association of Government Accountants, Certificate of Excellence in Service Efforts and Accomplishments Program
   http://www.agacgfm.org/performance/sea/
Association for Budgeting & Financial Management, Data Sources and Links in States and Local Governments
   http://www.abfm.org/
Association of Local Government Auditors, Service Efforts and Accomplishments
   http://www.governmentauditors.org/content/view/32/41/
Balance Scorecard Institute, Strategic Planning and Management System
   www.balancedscorecard.org
Government Accounting Office, Managing for Results, Enhancing Agency Use of Performance Information for Management Decision Making
   http://www.gao.gov/new.items/d05927.pdf
GASB Special Report: Suggested Criteria for Effective Communication of Performance Information
   http://www.seagov.org/sea_gasb_project/suggested_criteria.shtml
GFOA Recommended Practice on Performance Management: Using Performance Measurement for Decision Making and Updated Performance Measures
   http://www.gfoa.org/services/rp/budget/budget-performance-management.pdf

GFOA Best Practices in Public Budgeting
    http://www.gfoa.org/services/nacslb/
ICMA Center for Performance Measurement
    http://www.icma.org/main/bc.asp?bcid=107&hsid=1&ssid1=50&ssid2=220&ssid3=297
Information Resource Center, Managing for Results
    http://www.financeproject.org/irc_pubs.cfm?p=24&id=24
Municipal Research and Services Center of Washington
    http://www.mrsc.org/Subjects/Management/performancemeasurement.aspx
National Center for Public Productivity at Rutgers University
    http://www.ncpp.us/
National Performance Management Advisory Commission
    http://www.pmcommission.org/
Public Performance Measurement and Reporting Network
    http://ppmrn.rutgers.edu/
The Performance Institute, Transferring Knowledge to Transform Government
    http://www.performanceweb.org/

Cities and Counties

City of Albuquerque Progress Report
    http://www.cabq.gov/progress/index.html
City of Anchorage, Investing for Results
    http://results.muni.org/programs.php
City of Ankeny, IA, Performance Measurements
    http://www.ci.ankeny.ia.us/Index.aspx?page=711
City of Austin, Performance Auditing
    http://www.ci.austin.tx.us/auditor/performance.htm
City of Baltimore, CityStat
    http://www.baltimorecity.gov/news/citistat/index.html
City of Charlotte, Performance Management & Strategic Planning and Performance Reports
    http://www.charmeck.org/Departments/Budget+-+City/Performance+Measures.htm
    http://www.charmeck.org/home.htm
City of Chattanooga, Community Research Council of Chattanooga
    http://www.researchcouncil.net
Clark County, Nevada, Annual Performance Reports
    http://www.accessclarkcounty.com/depts/site_map/Pages/index.aspx
City of Des Moines, Performance Measurement System
    http://www.ci.des-moines.ia.us/performance.htm
Fairfax County, Virginia, Performance Management Initiative
    http://www.fairfaxcounty.gov/dmb/perf_measure.htm
City of Kansas City (MO), Annual Auditor Reports (including performance audits)
    http://www.kcmo.org/auditor.nsf/web/annualreports?opendocument
King County, Washington, KingStat
    http://www.metrokc.gov/dnrp/measures/default.aspx

King County, Washington Department of Natural Resources and Parks
  http://dnr.metrokc.gov/dnrp/performance/index.htm
Maricopa County, Arizona, Managing for Results
  http://www.maricopa.gov/mfr/
  http://www.maricopa.gov/mfr/AboutIndicators.aspx
Multnomah County, Performance Audits
  http://www.co.multnomah.or.us/auditor/
City of New York, Mayor's Management Report
  http://www.nyc.gov/html/ops/html/mmr/mmr.shtml
City of Palo Alto CA, Service Efforts and Accomplishments Report
  http://www.cityofpaloalto.org/depts/aud/service_efforts_and_accomplishments.asp
City of Philadelphia, City Reports online
  http://www.phila.gov/reports/archive.html
City of Phoenix, City Manager's Executive Report
  http://www.ci.phoenix.az.us/MGRREPT/index.html
City of Portland (OR), Performance Audit Reports
  http://www.portlandonline.com/auditor/index.cfm?c=27096&
Prince William County (VA) Service Efforts and Accomplishments Report
  http://www.pwcgov.org/default.aspx?topic=04005900070
County of San Mateo, California, Indicators for a Sustainable San Mateo County
  http://www.sustainablesanmateo.org/
City of Seattle, Performance Perspective Newsletters
  http://www.ci.seattle.wa.us/audit/otherpubs.htm
Washington DC, NeighborhoodInfo DC
  http://www.neighborhoodinfodc.org/
City of Worcester, The Research Bureau
  http://www.wrrb.org/

States

Arizona, Managing for Results
  http://www.ospb.state.az.us/handbook.asp
Connecticut, Connecticut Economic and Policy Council
  http://www.cpec.org/content/view/12/41
  http://www.civicradar.com
Florida Government Accountability Report
  http://www.oppaga.state.fl.us/government/
Illinois Public Accountability Reporting
  http://www.ioc.state.il.us/Office/PAP/reports.cfm
Illinois, Performance Audits
  http://www.auditor.illinois.gov/
Iowa, Managing for Results
  http://www.resultsiowa.org/

Louisiana Performance Accountability System
  http://doa.louisiana.gov/opb/lapas/lapas.html
Maine Marks
  http://www.mainemarks.org/indicators/indi_main.htm
Minnesota Milestones
  http://www.lmic.state.mn.us/datanetweb/chi.html
Oregon Benchmarks
  http://egov.oregon.gov/DAS/OPB/obm.shtml
Oregon Commission on Children and Families, Outcomes and Accountability
  http://www.oregon.gov/OCCF/Mission/Outcomes/miout.shtml
Rhode Island, Department of Health, Performance Measurement & Reporting
  http://www.health.ri.gov/chic/performance/index.php
Texas Education Agency, Accountability Rating System
  http://www.tea.state.tx.us/perfreport/account/
Utah, Summary of Goals and Key Performance Measures
  http://governor.utah.gov/PLANNING/UtahTomorrow/StrategicPlan2000.htm
Virginia, Performance Measures Review
  http://www.apa.virginia.gov/reports.cfm?departmentID=535&method=reports
Washington, Government Management, Accountability, and Performance (GMAP)
  http://www.accountability.wa.gov/
Washington, Governor's Priorities of Government
  http://www.ofm.wa.gov/budget/pog/default.htm

The Federal Government

Reports on the Government Performance and Results Act
  http://www.gao.gov/new.items/gpra/gpra.htm
Performance Management, U.S. Office of Personnel Management
  http://www.opm.gov/perform/

Nonprofits

Accenture, Identifying Enablers of Nonprofit High Performance
  http://www.volunteermatch.org/corporations/resources/docs/Accenture.pdf
Center for Nonprofit Management, Performance Evaluation
  http://www.cnm.org/content.aspx?page=PMRC
The Center for What Works, Benchmarking for Nonprofits, Performance Measurement Toolkit for Nonprofits and Funders
  http://www.whatworks.org/displaycommon.cfm?an=1&subarticlenbr=13
Corporation for National and Community Service Performance Reports
  http://www.cns.gov/about/role_impact/performance.asp
Council for Nonprofit Innovation, Performance Management
  http://www.cniweb.org/Centers/PM.html

Foundation Center, Learn about Nonprofit Management
  http://foundationcenter.org/getstarted/learnabout/npomanagement.html
Harvard Business School, Social Enterprise Initiative, Resources for Nonprofit Strategy, Management, and Performance
  http://www.hbs.edu/socialenterprise/resources/management.html
Nonprofit Good Practice Guide
  http://www.npgoodpractice.org/Default.aspx
Non-Profit Organizations Knowledge Initiative (NPOKI), Performance Management for Nonprofit Organizations
  http://www.npoki.org/start/index.htm
Outcome Management in Nonprofit Organizations, an Urban Institute Publication
  www.urban.org/Uploadedpdf/310348_ActionAgenda.pdf
Performance Improvement for Charities, Altruvest Charitable Services Links and Tools
  http://www.altruvest.org/altruvest_resources.html
Resources for Professional Interest, American Society of Association Executive (ASAE)
  http://www.asaecenter.org/

Index

Page numbers followed by f, t, or s denote figures, tables, or screen shots, respectively